After Misogyny

After Misogyny

HOW THE LAW FAILS WOMEN AND
WHAT TO DO ABOUT IT

Julie C. Suk

UNIVERSITY OF CALIFORNIA PRESS

University of California Press
Oakland, California

© 2023 by Julie C. Suk

First Paperback Printing 2024

Library of Congress Cataloging-in-Publication Data

Names: Suk, Julie Chi-hye, 1975- author.
Title: After misogyny : how the law fails women and what to do about it /
    Julie C. Suk.
Description: Oakland, California : University of California Press, [2023] |
    Includes bibliographical references and index.
Identifiers: LCCN 2022032720 (print) | LCCN 2022032721 (ebook) |
    ISBN 9780520381957 (cloth) | 9780520402973 (paper)
    9780520381964 (ebook)
Subjects: LCSH: Women—Legal status, laws, etc.—Social aspects |
    Women—Legal status, laws, etc.—Social aspects—United States.
Classification: LCC K644 .S85 2023 (print) | LCC K644 (ebook) |
    DDC 342.08/78—dc23/eng/20221201
LC record available at https://lccn.loc.gov/2022032720
LC ebook record available at https://lccn.loc.gov/2022032721

32 31 30 29 28 27 26 25 24
10 9 8 7 6 5 4 3 2 1

For all the women of the world who struggle invisibly to make it better for us all.

Contents

Introduction: Legal Patriarchy and Its Aftermath   1

PART I   HOW THE LAW FAILS WOMEN: MISOGYNY
BEYOND MISOGYNISTS

1. The Equal Protection of Feminists and Misogynists   29

2. Overentitlement and Overempowerment   60

3. Misogyny and Maternity: Abortion Bans
as Overentitlement   87

PART II   WHAT TO DO ABOUT IT: REMAKING
CONSTITUTIONS AND DEMOCRACY

4. From Patriarchy to Prohibition: Resetting
Entitlements through Constitutional Change   123

5. Rebalancing Power through Parity Democracy   152

6. Building Feminist Infrastructures: The
Constitutionalism of Care   180

Conclusion: Toward a Feminist Remaking of
Constitutional Democracy   211

Acknowledgments   235

Notes   241

Selected Bibliography   293

Index   313

Introduction

LEGAL PATRIARCHY AND ITS AFTERMATH

> Patriarchy is our judge
> That imprisons us at birth
> And our punishment
> Is the violence you DON'T see.

Women chanted this anthem at protests throughout the world, beginning in Santiago, Chile, in the autumn of 2019. Pointing to the persistence of sexual violence and reproductive injustice, women around the world have been marching to end the violence that is often unseen, namely, the law's active neglect of women's full personhood. American women brought this anthem to New York outside the courthouse where the culminating event of the #MeToo movement was unfolding: the rape trial of Hollywood power broker Harvey Weinstein. From the #MeToo movement to demands for equal pay, abortion rights, childcare, and even brand-new constitutions, women in constitutional democracies throughout the world are remaking the law after patriarchy. Feminist protesters performed this anthem in Chile, Argentina, Colombia, Mexico, the United States, Ireland, South Korea, India, and points in between. They sought state responsibility for realities that they could only marginally control.

Patriarchy is our judge
That imprisons us at birth,
And our punishment
Is the violence you CAN see.
It's femicide.
Impunity for my killer.
It's our disappearances.
It's rape.

Titled "A Rapist in Your Path," it was chanted by a self-proclaimed "feminist flash mob" outside the Chilean Supreme Court during a wave of popular protests that culminated in the drafting of a new constitution for the nation.[1] Femicide, impunity, disappearance, and rape are some of the manifestations of misogyny that raise the central questions of this book: Why does the law remain indifferent to women's deaths, disappearances, and rape a generation after most constitutional democracies officially ended legal patriarchy and guaranteed women equal protection of the laws? Why does misogyny remain palpable within legal orders that have proclaimed gender equality? And what can feminists do to overcome these failures of law? This book examines the strategies, successes, failures, and challenges of feminist lawmaking after the laws of patriarchy have been repealed.

It's the cops.
It's the judges.
It's the state.
It's the president.
The oppressive state is a macho rapist.
The rapist is you.

Misogyny, this book proposes, endures after patriarchy because patriarchy loses its force as law. People who embrace patriarchal gender relations maintain them through other legal means. Misogyny is conventionally understood as woman-hatred, but it is much more, and much worse for women, than hatred. Misogyny is the set of practices that keep women down in order to keep everyone and everything else up. Misogyny entails plenty of violence, much of it hateful, as unsavory men beat, rape, and kill women because they are women. But something about women's disappearances points to what is often missing when we approach misogyny as synonymous with woman-hatred. In Latin America, women disappeared under military dictatorships like the one in Chile, and were subject to torture, often of a sexual nature, hidden from public view. But the defining feature of disappearance was not violence; it was violence for which the state held nobody accountable. Disappearances were not unique to women in authoritarian regimes—men disappeared too. Yet the state's failure to prevent or respond to violence against women was not unique to military dictatorships or authoritarian government. Even in liberal constitutional democracies that celebrate the rule of law, enforce legal gender equality, criminalize violence against women, and prohibit sex discrimination in the workplace and schools, the state fails persistently to investigate, punish, eradicate, and prevent violence against women, from rape to femicide to workplace sexual harassment to campus sexual assault. The law enables men, and the society designed to fulfill their vision, to benefit from keeping women down, albeit in ways that are hidden from view.

It is this failure of law to which women in all corners of the world are saying "No more." The law's failure goes far beyond disappearances in distant lands. In the United States, a society controlled by men benefits enormously from women's invisible reproductive work, which it extracts from women by failing to support mothers while increasingly restricting access to abortion.

Patriarchy was a set of legal rules that lost their validity when constitutional democracies committed to gender equality throughout the twentieth century. Yet after patriarchy, the harms women endure are still escaping legal notice or accountability, and women's needs and contributions to society often remain invisible to the law. A range of expectations and entitlements maintain patriarchal gender relations, even after the laws that structured patriarchy as a legal system have fallen away. Misogyny, this book argues, is this aftermath of patriarchy. In a legal and social order that officially embraces gender equality rather than patriarchy, men's sense of entitlement to women's sacrifices is misplaced; it rests upon an illegitimate undervaluation of women's worth and contributions to the common good. At the same time, women's unpaid work remains essential to men's continued survival and to the survival of their offspring. Men, and the society founded and framed to meet their needs, derive irreplaceable benefits from women when women bear the enormous burdens of biological and social reproduction. This book argues that continued enjoyment of these reproductive benefits is a form of unjust enrichment and that continued extraction of these benefits is an abuse of power. Misogyny is this engine of overentitlement and overempowerment that continues even after it is no longer driven by patriarchal legal rules. With this fuller definition and analysis of misogyny, this book examines how the law fails women after patriarchy, even under laws of gender equality, and what to do to remake the law after misogyny.

THE LAWS OF PATRIARCHY

There is no more thorough account of patriarchy as a legal system than Simone de Beauvoir's founding text of twentieth-century feminism, *The Second Sex*, the French book that sparked an intellectual epiphany in American legal icon Ruth Bader Ginsburg.[2] The late justice Ginsburg, now recognized as a founding mother of modern American legal feminism, pioneered legal strategies that were shaped by feminist thinkers and legal developments around the world.

"This world has always belonged to males, and none of the reasons given for this have ever seemed sufficient,"[3] de Beauvoir wrote in 1949. Patriarchy's triumph was "neither an accident nor the result of a violent revolution."[4] Rather, patriarchy emerged as a reaction against primitive practices regarding kinship, property, and matrilineal descent.[5] Because the mother was necessary for the birth of a child, whereas the father's role in procreation was more difficult for early peoples to establish, communities produced children recognized as belonging to them through their association with the mother.[6] This account drew on Friedrich Engels, who in turn deployed the work of anthropologists Lewis Morgan and Johann Jakob Bachofen to depict a transition from matrilineal to patrilineal kinship orders that was driven by the rise of private property ownership and its protection by law.[7] Men could not accumulate property and increase wealth across generations by bequeathing their private property to their own children without some means of identifying children as their own offspring.

The legal protection of marriage fulfilled this function, insofar as marriage required the wife to limit her procreative activities, that is, sexual relations, to her husband. Hence, the legal protection of marriage enabled the legal recognition of paternity.[8] The legal inequality of the husband and the wife, achieved by the legal authority of the husband over the wife, and the economic dependence of the wife on the husband, enabled legal protection of private property and its intergenerational growth. Whereas in matrilineal communities child-rearing and the management of the household could be seen as public services with a public character, once the family became a legally protected social unit that maintained private property across generations, the wife became the head servant to the man who headed the household.[9]

As Gerda Lerner has noted, Engels showed how men's political and economic dominance was enabled by their control over female sexuality.[10] The German socialist thinker August Bebel built on Engels's and Bachofen's accounts of the transition to patriarchy in *Woman under Socialism*, an important intellectual source for women constitution makers on the left at Weimar in 1919 and Bonn in 1949. Bebel explicitly linked the rise of patriarchy to reproductive control: "The mother-right vanished; the father-right stepped into its shoes. Man now became a private property-holder: he had an interest in children, whom he could look upon as legitimate and whom he made the heirs of his property: hence *he forced upon woman the command of abstinence from intercourse with other men*."[11]

Patriarchy became a core feature of Western legal systems that defined families and protected private property. Patriarchy was established and enforced in Roman law, which shaped the Western legal tradition in the civil law systems of continental Europe and many bodies of law in the common law of England and America. Roman law established rights, obligations, and authority within the family—the most important social unit in Roman society. The family was the group of persons subject to the power of the male head of the household, the *paterfamilias*.[12] The law was patriarchal in the sense that it legitimized the nearly absolute power of the *paterfamilias* over his children. *Patria potestas* included the right of life and death (*ius vitae necisque*) over the children, which appeared to allow the father to kill his own children at will, without facing legal punishment.[13] The law gave the *paterfamilias* a similar power—*manus*—over his wife.[14] Through various periods of Roman legal history, the status of women varied—from no legal personhood under the law to some legal rights independent of their husbands or fathers. Roman women, married or not, were generally subject to some limitation on their capacity for independent legal action; their authority to act was almost always derived from a man, such as a husband, father, or guardian.[15] Roman law criminalized adultery asymmetrically. A married woman was guilty of adultery if she had sexual relations with a man other than her husband, but a man was guilty of adultery only if he had sexual relations with a married woman, whether he was married or not.[16]

The modern legal orders established in the eighteenth and nineteenth centuries in Europe and the United States adopted some of the legal features of Roman law that empowered men and disempowered women. Blackstone's *Commentaries* famously articulated the doctrine of coverture: "By marriage, the husband and wife are one person in law: that is, the very being or legal existence of the woman is suspended during the marriage, or at least is incorporated and consolidated into her husband."[17] In other words, marriage made the woman disappear from legal personhood. Exclusive male entitlement to the control of marital property and undivided male legal authority over children of a marriage were features of the common law in most states throughout the nineteenth century.[18] Patriarchal law set this supreme male entitlement and empowerment as the natural and legitimate baseline distribution of entitlements. In the United States, before the law began to recognize the political and legal equality of women, patriarchy was enforced through various bodies of law, including common-law doctrines of coverture.[19] Married women had no legal personhood independent of their husbands; they were deprived of all civil and political rights on the assumption that every man represented his wife and children in the exercise of his own legal rights.[20] In many states, any property that a woman owned prior to marriage came within her husband's control. Women could not enter into contracts, sue, or be sued independently of their husbands. Even if a married woman engaged independently in market work, her earnings belonged to her husband, who exerted exclusive control over how they were spent.[21] From the eighteenth century or earlier, the common law, as described in Lord Matthew Hale's treatise, entitled husbands to sexual intercourse with their wives at will by making marriage an exception to the criminalization of rape.[22]

In 1873, the US Supreme Court upheld a state's decision to exclude women from the legal profession on the grounds that a person who was unable to enter into contracts on her own could not represent clients as a lawyer.[23] In *Bradwell v. Illinois*, Justice Bradley famously justified the exclusion of women from independent rights to property, contract, and work in his concurring opinion, emphasizing that "man is, or should be, woman's protector and defender" and that "the paramount destiny and mission of woman are to fulfil the noble and benign offices of wife and mother."[24] Women bore and raised children, worked within the home to maintain the household to meet men's and children's survival needs, and cared for the family to enable it to be the fundamental unit of social reproduction. Men in power—including the justices of the Supreme Court— justified women's exclusion from the public economic sphere by enforcing women's role in the private nonmarket sphere of the home.

By subsuming married women under the legal personhood of their husbands, the laws of patriarchy enforced men's expectation that women provide sexual and reproductive services according to men's will. The law entitled every husband to sexual intercourse, the bearing and care of his children, and household work from his wife on demand. It also entitled the husband, as master of the household, to secure his wife's obedience by subjecting her to corporal punishment or chastisement should she defy his commands.[25] In exchange, the law obligated husbands to support their wives and to represent them in the legal system, and married women remained economically and legally dependent on their husbands. While the law imposed duties on men to represent their wives' and children's interests, it respected men's significant, nearly unlimited discretion in carrying out these responsibilities.

FROM PATRIARCHY TO GENDER EQUALITY UNDER LAW

From the mid-nineteenth century, the movement for women's rights fought to eradicate each of these common-law rules. The 1848 Declaration of Sentiments, authored by Elizabeth Cady Stanton and presented at the first Woman's Rights Convention at Seneca Falls, characterized these male prerogatives as "tyranny," noting specifically men's legal ability to deprive wives of the wages that they earned and the law's empowering of husbands to "administer chastisement."[26] But the demand for which Cady Stanton and the nineteenth-century women's movement is most known is suffrage for women. To exemplify the "absolute tyranny" of "man toward woman," the Declaration of Sentiments included "He has never permitted her to exercise her inalienable right to the elective franchise."[27] After decades of effort across generations, the Nineteenth Amendment became part of the US Constitution in 1920, proclaiming that "the right of citizens of the United States to vote shall not be denied or abridged by the United States or by any State on account of sex."[28]

By then, some, but not all, of the legal rules of coverture had been repealed or reformed one by one, state by state. To abolish all of the legal rules that enforced men's tyranny over women in one fell swoop, some suffragists proposed another constitutional amendment, the Equal Rights Amendment (ERA), in 1923.[29] By the time Congress finally adopted the ERA nearly fifty years later in 1972 and sent it to the states for ratification, the US Supreme Court had begun to rely on the Equal Protection Clause of the Fourteenth Amendment to strike down the legal rules that enforced patriarchy. For example, *Reed v. Reed* invalidated a state law that automatically preferred a father over a mother as the administrator of their deceased son's estate.[30] The Supreme Court concluded that the law's preference for males over females was arbitrary[31]—it empowered men without a rational basis, contrary to the constitutional guarantee of equal protection of the laws. Put another way, we can see how gender equality under the law transforms a power authorized by patriarchal law into an overempowerment. Additional cases litigated by Ruth Bader Ginsburg throughout the 1970s consolidated constitutional law against any patriarchal legal rules that presumed or enforced the dependent status of married women or the family caregiving obligations of women.[32] These Supreme Court decisions invalidated patriarchy as a legal system, citing *Bradwell v. Illinois* with unequivocal disapproval and repudiation.[33] But the court could not end patriarchy as a set of social norms.

Thus the legal system still enabled and tolerated various social practices that produced benefits for men—and the society they still controlled—at women's expense. From unwanted sexual relations to the lion's share of the risks and burdens involved in reproducing the next generation, women continued to be expected to sacrifice their own well-being for the benefit of husbands, children, and other family members. This collective overentitlement to women's forbearance results from laws that effectively concentrate decision-making power in men, locking in their power to control collective institutions. The powers of these institutions can be abused to extract disproportionate work from the less powerful to serve the public good, resulting in the unjust enrichment of those who hold power and the society they control. These dynamics of overentitlement and overempowerment are the core engines of misogyny. Hateful violence against women in the form of rape, femicide, and disappearance are only misogyny's most visible manifestations. Other, less visible manifestations are no less pernicious.

American legal feminists pursued reforms toward gender equality that focused on "the violence you CAN see," to quote the protest anthem, namely male perpetrators' wrongful and injurious acts harming female victims—from outright exclusion of women from full citizenship status, to sexual violence. Ruth Bader Ginsburg's trailblazing work to eradicate patriarchal law through constitutional litigation (discussed in more detail in chapter 1) took down laws that excluded women from the opportunities that marked men's status as full citizens. Decades later, the #MeToo movement has also gone after "the violence you CAN see," namely women's experiences of sexual assault and harassment at the hands of powerful, often famous men. The #MeToo movement has focused on identifying rapists and predators to hold them accountable under the law, criminally or otherwise.

But much more attention must be given to the violence you don't see, namely the underlying economic and legal conditions that set the terms of interaction between empowered men and the females they feel entitled to dominate. This book broadens the lens by putting American legal feminism in conversation with a century of feminist legal theory and constitution making outside the United States. Legal remedies for sexual violence and gender-based discrimination redress some harms to women, but they do not address the undeserved benefits that accrue to men (including to men who have never committed any sex crimes) and to a society corrupted by such injustices. De Beauvoir's account of patriarchy reveals it to be a legal system aimed at aggrandizing men's property and power. Logically, then, restitution of the unjust enrichment of men and reduction of men's abuse of power should be the starting points for patriarchy's abolition. Discrimination on account of sex, the inequality of legal rights, and violent attacks on women's bodies are merely symptoms of the overentitlement and overempowerment that constitute misogyny.

THE TRANSITION TO MISOGYNY AFTER PATRIARCHY

Dubbed the philosopher of the #MeToo movement,[34] Kate Manne has insightfully argued that the conventional account of misogyny as woman-hatred is incomplete and misguided. Rather, twenty-first-century episodes of violence against women are misogynist not primarily because they reveal woman-hatred but because they are efforts to control women after the law has stopped embracing male supremacy. Manne depicts misogyny as the social, not legal, punishment of women who depart from their role in the patriarchal script. Women who do not play the "giver" role that men could expect the law to enforce under patriarchy are thus subject to vigilante enforcement of patriarchy.[35] These enforcers—the rapists, the woman-killers—accord with our conventional image of misogynists. While this social punishment is no longer authorized by the laws of a constitutional democracy committed to gender equality, it is enabled by the law insofar as the legal system fails, perhaps willfully, to investigate, punish, remedy, or prevent violence against women. Even while the law enforces gender equality and nondiscrimination, some men continue to feel entitled to women contributing willingly what they were coerced by law to contribute under patriarchy: sex, pregnancy, motherhood, and housework.

This sense of entitlement does not necessarily stem from hatred; it stems from a comfort with the social arrangements enforced by patriarchal law that enabled the flourishing of men and their communities, as well as the transmission of that flourishing across generations through biological and social reproduction. Without women willing to give freely what law extracted from them under patriarchy, the comforts of human flourishing as men defined it begin to unravel.[36] Misogyny is the vigilante punishment of women who challenge male power and endeavor to reset the presumed entitlements of a patriarchal society. Even when law stops enforcing these entitlements, it can enable the vigilante enforcement of patriarchal norms. There is a legal dimension to the postpatriarchal engine of misogyny.

In a legal and social order fully committed to the equal legal personhood of women and men, indeed, of all persons of all genders, it would be unjust to entitle men to women's acquiescence to unwanted sex, pregnancy, motherhood, and household work. We might refer to any such expectation as an overentitlement, one that depends on a gross underestimation of the burdens that these expectations impose and an inequitable undervaluing of women's essential contributions to the survival of men, children, and the community. This overentitlement is not eradicated as long as empowered men who benefit from women's forbearance continue to regard it as their natural set of baseline entitlements. In a legal order thoroughly implementing the equal legal personhood of all persons of all genders, anyone who used their decision-making power to enjoy these unfair benefits instead of compensating or redistributing them could be described as abusing their power. We might refer to any such abuse as overempowerment. Whereas philosophers like Manne focus on overentitled men trying to control women directly, any strategy for overcoming misogyny must take on an equally pernicious and perhaps more widespread manifestation: the collective overentitlement of a society designed and controlled by overempowered men to the benefits and enrichments that flow from women's losses and sacrifices. That collective overentitlement is enabled by legal rules that appear on their face compatible with legal gender equality. Men's overempowerment is perpetuated by legal rules that are distinct from the staples of patriarchy. As a project of law, moving the legal order past patriarchy, past the transition of misogyny, toward feminism and real equality requires attention to this manifestation of law's misogyny.

AFTER MISOGYNY: TOWARD FEMINIST LAWS AND DEMOCRACY

The persistence of patriarchal gender relations after the advent of legal gender equality has been a theme of feminist legal theory and scholarship over the last fifty years, including significant work by Black feminists seeking to unlock the intersecting race and gender hierarchy of white male supremacy. *After Misogyny* builds on this work by putting American legal feminisms in conversation with the recent and ongoing work of feminist constitutional movements outside the United States. In the United States, feminist legal theory since the 1980s pointed to the persistence of male supremacy, evidenced by the survival of patriarchal norms in liberal equality law. Catharine MacKinnon, for instance, wrote: "The liberal state coercively and authoritatively constitutes the social order in the interest of men as a gender, through its legitimizing norms, relation to society, and substantive policies. It achieves this through embodying and ensuring male control over women's sexuality at every level, occasionally cushioning, qualifying or de jure prohibiting its excesses when necessary to its normalization."[37]

For MacKinnon, the laws of rape and sexual assault in a liberal regime of gender equality exemplified how male power still continued to define state power. The law nominally respected women's personhood by treating them as capable of consenting. The line between rape and intercourse came down to whether a woman consented. Criminal law has long defined rape as intercourse with force or coercion, and without consent.[38] This definition hides the persistence of patriarchal control of women's sexual activity: "When sex is violent, women may have lost control over what is done to us, but absence of force does not ensure the presence of that control."[39]

Women endure sexual violations that would not be recognized under the criminal law as rape, because "the level of acceptable force is adjudicated starting just above the level set by what is seen as normal male sexual behavior, including the normal level of force, rather than at the victim's, or women's, point of violation."[40] The male perspective and experience define the baseline expectations from which rape is adjudicated. By contrast, a feminist distinction between rape and intercourse, MacKinnon proposed, would arrive at the meaning of the sexual act in question from the woman's point of view. It is not lack of consent that should define the violation, or the degree of force utilized in coercing sex, but whether the act is one of female subordination under male control. From Roman law to common law, patriarchal law protected men's control over women's sexual activities, whether by criminalizing adulterous acts by a married woman or by decriminalizing the husband's rape of his wife. In late twentieth-century legal regimes after patriarchy, "When a rape prosecution is lost on a consent defense, the woman has not only failed to prove lack of consent, she is not considered to have been injured at all. . . . Because he did not perceive she did not want him, she was not violated. She had sex. Sex itself cannot be an injury. Women consent to sex every day. Sex makes a woman a woman. Sex is what women are *for*."[41]

Extending this logic, MacKinnon urged lawyers and jurists to challenge sexual harassment in the workplace as sex discrimination. Because "the exchange of sex for survival has historically assured women's economic dependence and inferiority as well as sexual availability to men," so that "women's sexuality largely defines women as women in this society," it should follow in a legal regime prohibiting discrimination because of sex that "violations of [women's sexuality] are abuses of women as women."[42] Nonetheless, even when a legal order repudiates patriarchy by prohibiting discrimination and requiring the equal treatment of women as independent legal persons, MacKinnon's account suggests a dynamic that Reva Siegel has termed "preservation through transformation."[43] The rules and rhetoric of rape law after patriarchy has been repudiated look entirely different from the Roman law of *patria potestas* and the common law of coverture, but the legal system still plays a significant role in maintaining male control over female sexual activity. It deploys legal standards that appear to vindicate the free and equal status of all persons regardless of gender, namely consent.

The dynamics of preservation through transformation come into sharper focus if we expand the frame of misogyny beyond woman-hatred, so as to define the overentitlement and overempowerment of men as the core function of patriarchal legal rules. With this reframing, the prescriptions for overcoming patriarchy are different from nondiscrimination and legal equality. After misogyny, the new dynamics of overentitlement and overempowerment must be identified, often beyond the areas of law that currently proscribe antiwoman bias and violence. Other bodies of law regulate gender relations, directly or indirectly, by assuming or enforcing overentitlement and overempowerment.

MacKinnon's groundbreaking work proposed that the law of sexual assault and sexual harassment recognize the gendered concentration of power as discrimination, rather than normal sexual relations,[44] as they were under patriarchal law. Similarly, feminist legal theorists developed the female perspective on other dimensions of patriarchal power over women's bodies also stemming from patriarchal control of procreation. Robin West observed that "many women and no men experience pregnancy. Many women and no men give birth, menstruate, and lactate. Many women and fewer men perform the bulk of childcare and elder care around the world for either no or very low wages."[45] The formal equality achieved by the Supreme Court's invalidation of laws that treat women and men differently, on equal protection grounds, is inadequate because it does not address the "invisible harms women sustain, . . . harms that, by virtue of past and present practice, have not registered as worthy of regulation or eradication or deterrence or compensation by traditional patriarchal regimes."[46]

These "invisible harms" include, as MacKinnon detailed, forced sexual intercourse, but West also emphasized unwanted pregnancy, sometimes forced and sometimes consensual.[47] Both sex and pregnancy can be consensual and unwanted at the same time. Women consent to unwanted sex out of a sense of duty, or out of a need for material support if they are economically dependent upon the relationship for their own or their children's survival. Sometimes, women consent to unwanted sex out of fear of future violence; this sex is patriarchal but not "rape" even in a liberal legal order that no longer enforces patriarchal law. Should law or public policy intervene to change the power dynamics that shape unwanted but consensual sex, pregnancy, motherhood, or other gendered situations? Women have sex, get pregnant, give birth, breastfeed, and care for children, all of which can be a "source of meaning as well as a source of oppression."[48] Patriarchal laws made these functions obligatory for women. But even after patriarchy, under liberal gender equality, pregnancy and motherhood can remain oppressive because they often involve relationships of economic dependence on others, and/or because the state strenuously neglects mothers' needs. Overcoming patriarchy may require reducing the negative effects of caregiving on other important dimensions of an autonomous person's life. Legal feminism of the 1970s enlarged women's opportunities within the workplace; at the same time, West notes, "We need to take care not to negate . . . the vision, the moral perspective and the political sensibility that accompany immersion in a world of caregiving, of relationality, and of kinship."[49] Women's immersion in the world of social reproduction is undervalued when caregiving is valued far less than market work, in ways that negatively affect the subsistence and flourishing of those who need care and those—often women—who provide it.

Proposing a "reconstructive feminism" to direct the reform of law, Joan Williams embraced this proposition at the dawn of the twenty-first century in a game-changing book, *Unbending Gender: How Family and Work Conflict and What to Do about It*.[50] Williams shifted the focus of legal feminism from sexual violence and harassment to "the design of (market and family) work and the entitlements that flow from it."[51] Without diminishing the significance of MacKinnon's work on sexual violence, Williams pointed out that "if we woke up tomorrow and found a society where dominance was not eroticized, people still would be thwarted in the dreams they hold for their children and for themselves."[52] Discrimination against workers —often working mothers— because of their caregiving responsibilities perpetuated gender stereotypes and expectations. These expectations diminished women's ability to enjoy the autonomy in life pursuits that our liberal constitutional commitment to liberty and equality purports to guarantee.

The undervaluing of women's disproportionate contributions to reproduction, both biological and social, has animated feminist legal thinking outside the United States about the law's protection of motherhood. Indeed, the duty of the state to protect mothers was a common feature of European constitutions adopted in the twentieth century, along with explicit constitutional provisions guaranteeing the equal rights of women and men and the equality of the spouses in marriage. The notion that mothers should be protected by the community and by its political and legal institutions was developed in the writings of Swedish, German, and Russian feminists in the late nineteenth and early twentieth centuries.

In an essay entitled "Motherliness" that was translated into English and published in the *Atlantic Monthly* in 1912, the Swedish feminist Ellen Key acknowledged that the women's movement enabled women to assert their full humanity, "all the attributes, independent of sex, which she shares with man," and applauded women's participation in trades to earn their livelihoods if they did not have children, or when their children were older. "But for most women it ought still to be the dream of happiness, some time in their lives, to have fulfilled the mission of motherhood, and during that time to have been freed from outside work in which they, only in exceptional cases, would be likely to find the same full outlet for their creative desire, for feeling, thought, imagination, as is to be found in the educative activity in the home."[53] The law had a role to play. Key demanded, on behalf of "Motherliness," "all the legal rights without which woman cannot, in the fullest sense of the word, be either child-mother or community-mother."[54] She called on women to demand "the state-given *mother-stipend* without which she cannot be at the same time child-bearing, child-rearing, and self-supporting."[55]

Ellen Key's provocative work on motherhood influenced some German feminists to form a league for the protection of motherhood. The Mutterschutz League, led by Helene Stöcker, demanded the legal equality of man and woman in marriage (and, by implication, reform of the German Civil Code) and support for women's "will to motherhood" through measures that would make it possible for women to bear and rear children while still keeping their jobs or finding work.[56] Claiming that motherhood was women's highest individual fulfillment, with the mother-child bond being near-sacred, they embraced Ellen Key's proposals of publicly financed payments for mothers raising children, including Key's radical idea that the "right to motherhood"—a mother's right to be supported by society during a child's earlier years for the socially valuable and fulfilling work she did—should include unmarried women. Mothers should not need to depend on marriage and husbands in order to mother.[57]

The Mutterschutz League similarly advocated for state policies to make motherhood the fulfilling experience that it ought to be. At the center of their demands was financial support for mothers in the form of maternity insurance or maternity benefits. But they also advocated for the decriminalization of abortion. They advanced a "New Morality" based on free love, women's sexual emancipation, and the rights of unmarried mothers. Women created new life, and affirming it meant protecting the health and well-being of all children, including those born outside of marriage. An important project of the Mutterschutz League was to expose the contempt for motherhood expressed through the public ostracizing of unmarried mothers and illegitimate children. Motherhood—whether within marriage or without—could not be "immoral." The shame foisted on unmarried pregnant women, the very idea that any women could "fall from virtue" because of motherhood, was itself morally suspect under the "New Morality."

Many left-wing intellectuals of the early 1900s, including Max Weber and Werner Sombart, were associated with the Mutterschutz League.[58] Women participated in political parties across the ideological spectrum that participated in the making of the Weimar Constitution, which was among the first constitutions in the world to include a provision explicitly entitling mothers to the protection and care of the community. Laws protecting working mothers in particular spread throughout Europe, supported by coalitions across political ideologies and parties. Alexandra Kollontai, a Russian feminist leader during the Russian Revolution of 1917, noted that "children are dying" "like flies"[59] as factories were becoming a "grave of maternity."[60] Kollontai pointed to the trend in every country toward laws that defended the working mother, noting the eight weeks of paid maternity leave in France, Germany, and Switzerland, as of 1914, to call for sixteen weeks in the new Soviet regime.[61] The trajectory of feminist legal change in Europe, unlike that in the United States, included support for mothers as a necessary condition of women's emancipation. Chapter 6, "Building Feminist Infrastructures: The Constitutionalism of Care," provides a historical and contemporary account of the nexus between motherhood protection and gender equality in European constitutions.

Proposals to value and protect motherhood have been the source of conflict rather than coalition in the United States. Disagreements ensued after women won the vote regarding whether the Constitution could embrace equal rights for women by way of an Equal Rights Amendment, while also defending mothers with special protections from the heightened threats of the industrial workplace to maternal health. That conflict prevented the necessary coalition to pass the ERA for nearly fifty years.[62] As a justice, Ruth Bader Ginsburg warned against special protections for women based on maternity, fearing that such protections could be distorted to justify women's exclusion from economic opportunities and perpetuate gender-unequal arrangements for sharing domestic work.[63] At the same time, some American feminist legal theorists have recognized the significant downsides of the law's refusal to recognize the special burdens of maternity. Martha Fineman, for instance, sees reformers' focus on the "lack of equal sharing between women and men of domestic burdens in the family" as a strategic "dead end." Instead, "Arguments for reform must now acknowledge that the societally constructed role of mother continues to exact unique costs for women. This is true in spite of decades of attempts to equalize family responsibility and to draft gender-neutral, equality-enhancing rules."[64] For Fineman, the main problem with motherhood is not gender-role stereotyping but dependency, for which the market makes no allowances and for which the state offers only scant (and highly stigmatized) support. Children are dependent on the parent (overwhelmingly the mother), and the parent responsible for caregiving is dependent on someone for economic sustenance—a breadwinning partner or the state. Whereas feminists working toward equality in the public sphere assumed that women's increased activity in the workplace would correspond to men's increased involvement in family life, gendered divisions of family labor have persisted. "Someone is going to suffer in the workplace if there is caretaking to be done in the home," Fineman points out.[65] Legal feminism's focus on equality, domination, agency, and special treatment has failed to solve the "inherently unequal and dependent relationship that children have with mothers and others who care for them."[66]

What might a reckoning with this set of problems look like? In observing the childcare disruptions wrought by the COVID-19 pandemic, one sociologist said, "Other countries have social safety nets. The U.S. has women."[67] Women are the "shock absorbers" of society's primary dependencies, absorbing the nonmarket costs of meeting the needs of nonautonomous minor children and health-impaired elderly parents.[68] When the law authorizes no support or compensation to the people who personally absorb the costs of promoting the welfare of others, it enforces society's overentitlement to women's forbearance and sacrifices. It enforces patriarchal norms without deploying patriarchy's core legal elements.

American feminist theorists working at the intersection of race, class, and gender have identified additional problems—which can be described as reproductive injustice—that exemplify the overentitlements and overempowerments of misogyny following patriarchy. Where MacKinnon highlighted the need to approach sexual violence from the perspective of women's experiences, Black feminists have shown how injustices related to motherhood come into sharper focus when Black women's experiences are the starting point. Pauli Murray, the pioneering civil rights attorney, introduced the idea of "Jane Crow" in the law in 1965. Murray's briefs challenging the exclusion of both Black jurors and female jurors shaped Ginsburg's arguments in the cases that shaped constitutional sex equality law. How might we understand equal protection of the law for women, Murray asked, if we took into account the fact that nonwhite families were more than twice as likely to be headed by women? Or that the vast majority of nonwhite families headed by women—three-fourths of them at the time—lived in poverty?[69]

Murray further argued that Black women had the most to gain from the equalization of power promised by the Equal Rights Amendment, having submitted written hearing testimony to Congress on the subject. Black women were "doubly victimized by the twin immoralities of racial and sexual bias," she wrote. White feminists' critique of forced sex and compulsory motherhood takes on new complexity when one considers that the rape of Black women to produce slaves deprived Black women of the opportunity to mother their own children.[70] After slavery, Black women enjoyed none of "advantages of the idealizations of 'womanhood' and 'motherhood' which are part of the American mythology."[71] Indeed, as Angela Davis later noted, the slave economy depended upon Black women's fertility as a "coveted treasure" and source of wealth, without valuing Black mothers or Black motherhood. Enslaved Black women did not enjoy the respected status or ideological exaltation of motherhood; they were not regarded as legal mothers of their children but as breeders.[72] *After Misogyny* identifies common themes across the insights of Black feminist theorists' leading work on reproductive justice toward the end of the twentieth century and the European motherhood radicals at the century's beginning. While American legal scholars often assume that those white European feminists were the opposite of intersectional, this book considers the connections between their calls to center motherhood as a social project and the reproductive justice visions of feminists of color in the United States to be worth exploring.

In the 1990s, critical race feminist theorist Kimberlé Crenshaw suggested that, once understood, the convergence of race, gender, and class domination with regard to violence experienced by poor women of color would lead to different priorities of resource allocation than those that emerge from responses to violence against white privileged women. For instance, domestic violence support services for poor women of color or immigrant women would likely need to address housing issues and to provide basic information about available resources as much as they would need to deal with the assault itself.[73] Furthermore, Dorothy Roberts has identified the laws and policies that have subjected Black women's bodies to reproductive control. Government doctors forcibly sterilized thousands of Black women in the 1960s and 1970s. Black women have been targeted in campaigns for long-acting contraceptives as legislators and policy makers have sought to control population growth.

Welfare reforms in the 1990s were designed to discourage women receiving public assistance from bearing more children by putting caps on the number of children that could be supported by welfare benefits.[74] Black women were prosecuted for smoking crack while pregnant and had their children placed in foster care because of racially disparate charges of child neglect due to poverty. These attacks on Black women's reproductive autonomy prevented African Americans from bearing and raising children to enlarge their communities, Roberts argues. Black women's experience as the objects of reproductive control by the state led to a movement focused on reproductive autonomy beyond the right to be free from state intrusion when seeking an abortion. The term *reproductive justice* itself was coined by Black women and their health organizations to broaden the lens of reproductive freedom. Because Black women have experienced forced sterilization and skepticism about their ability to mother their own children, the assertion of reproductive freedom requires not only the ability to choose an abortion but also the freedom to bear and raise children in a healthy, safe, and supportive environment.[75]

Khiara Bridges has noted that the constitutional protection of privacy in the body and family life, while a useful concept for all women, has seldom helped poor women and women of color. "For the marginalized, indigent women who must turn to the state for assistance if they are to achieve healthy pregnancies and infants, privacy is a concept of great significance; indeed, the devastating absence of privacy may be that which distinguishes their experiences with the state from their monied counterparts."[76] Bridges draws on the insights of Martha Fineman, who exposed the dynamic by which families become "public" rather than "private" in the American legal order when the father becomes absent; any family headed by an unmarried mother becomes a "public family" subject to the state's intervention.[77] The concept of reproductive justice, responsive to the experiences of the most vulnerable women and women of color, is a central one for overcoming misogyny. Society often benefits from coercing motherhood from Black women, as exemplified by the laws of property and rape that defined female enslavement before slavery's abolition and by more modern efforts to police Black women's pregnancies.

Furthermore, in the United States, the Black Lives Matter movement has amplified the structural nature of racism. It was Black Lives Matter that identified the system—*the cops, the judges, the state, the president* wielding the power of institutions—as the destroyer of Black lives. Hateful bigots are part of the problem, but the oppressive state is the core. The #MeToo movement, combined with subsequent mobilizations around reproductive rights, has brought feminist movements closer to a parallel reckoning with misogyny. This book provides the conceptual frames and articulates the legal narratives of that twenty-first-century structural reckoning.

Part I, "How the Law Fails Women: Misogyny without Misogynists," consists of three chapters that illustrate misogyny's persistence with the help of the law. Misogyny can persist independently of misogynists, or men who hate women. I explain the concepts of overentitlement and overempowerment to account for the misogyny that persists in the law. These concepts are then applied to laws banning or restricting abortion in several countries. Contrasting the transformations in abortion law in the United States and those of several other countries illustrates how abortion restrictions perpetuate overentitlement and overempowerment, an effect with implications for the future of abortion law after the fall of *Roe v. Wade.*

Part II, "What to Do about It: Remaking Constitutions and Democracy," explores selected examples of feminist lawmaking from the late nineteenth century to the present. The complex story of the Prohibition Amendment and its repeal in the United States provides a surprising illustration. Women were active in the quest for a constitutional amendment prohibiting the manufacture and sale of alcohol in the United States, and their movement functioned, in intent and operation, to reset legal entitlements that overempowered men and left women vulnerable to violent domestic abuse and destitution. Twentieth- and twenty-first-century legal feminism in constitutional democracies outside the United States has focused more on institutions than on individuals, resetting baseline entitlements and restructuring decision-making power. In Europe and Latin America, constitutional amendments recognized mothers' contributions to the public good and enabled women to share decision-making power in governing institutions. From gender parity quotas to policies that ease or compensate the burdens of motherhood, many democratic constitutional institutions have developed new paradigms that go beyond American nondiscrimination and privacy norms to overcome misogyny.

Ultimately, the book contributes two major insights, one conceptual and the other procedural/institutional. First, misogyny is best understood through the paradigm of overentitlement rather than through the paradigm of animus. And second, combating misogyny, thus understood, requires the transformation of a society's foundational norms and baseline entitlements, which is why women in countries around the world have pursued constitutional change. Women have been empowered beyond the enforcement of rights by courts, through inclusive lawmaking processes in which women have voice and share real power.

Chapter 1, "The Equal Protection of Feminists and Misogynists," articulates the limits of the most significant tool of twentieth-century legal feminism in the United States, the Equal Protection Clause. In the twenty-first century, the gender equality jurisprudence spawned by the late justice Ruth Bader Ginsburg's strategy as an advocate has become a weapon of misogyny as well as feminism. Ginsburg borrowed a key feminist insight from Sweden, namely that ending patriarchy required the emancipation of men from traditional gender roles, not only women. But transplanting that idea in the United States through litigation under the Equal Protection Clause had its limits. Emancipation from traditional gender roles was woefully incomplete without a fuller governmental infrastructure, beyond judge-made doctrine, to support the emancipation of both women and men from traditional gender roles. American legal feminism both ignored and enabled many features of the existing social, political, and legal infrastructure that burdened and disempowered women. Institutions that hindered gender emancipation endured, as long as they did not directly enforce sex classifications or outmoded stereotypes about gender roles. The American story of equal protection shows how hard it is to borrow good ideas from other countries to remake American law.

But it doesn't mean feminists should stop trying. Chapter 2, "Overentitlement and Overempowerment," maps out the new definition of misogyny that forms this book's central theoretical contribution, developing ideas found in the legal doctrines of unjust enrichment and abuse of right, which have been most robustly elaborated in European civil law countries. I propose that misogyny is men's overentitlement to women's forbearance, and men's overempowerment causing detriment to women. The concepts of overentitlement and overempowerment offer an alternative to the commonly held view that misogyny must involve hatred of women, or the conscious desire to control them. Misogyny is in fact most pervasive when it involves no hatred or physical violence against women. Its control is quotidian. The laws of misogyny underestimate and belittle women's contributions, while allowing men and the society they control to benefit from and depend upon women's sacrifices. The misogynist is more parasite than predator. Unjust enrichment and abuse of right cases provide accounts of distributive injustice and the corruption of power that illuminate this new understanding of misogyny. In a range of cases involving property and contract, French and German courts developed the logic of unjust enrichment and abuse of right to illuminate why overentitlement and overempowerment are wrong. These ideas helped women in cases involving divorce and indebtedness, bringing the gendered dynamics of overentitlement and overempowerment into sharper focus. Once reframed as overentitlement and overempowerment, misogyny requires different legal strategies to overcome it, beyond criminal punishment of sexual assault and tort-analogous antidiscrimination remedies. Combating misogyny entails resetting expectations and entitlements, and rebalancing power.

Chapter 3, "Misogyny and Maternity: Abortion Bans as Overentitlement," applies the overentitlement and overempowerment frames to show what's really wrong with laws banning abortion. For nearly fifty years, *Roe v. Wade* protected a woman's right to choose an abortion, holding that abortion bans violated the constitutional right to privacy in the body and in procreation. *Roe* perpetuated a vision of human reproduction as a personal and private matter, which kept the state out of women's reproductive lives. Chapter 3 provides a somewhat different account of the misogyny of banning abortion. It draws on Black feminist visions of reproductive justice as well as the twenty-first-century abortion law that has emerged in pro-life countries to show how pregnancy must be treated as a public, rather than private, problem. These developments underscore the unjust enrichment of society by the disproportionate and uncompensated burdens and risks shouldered by women who become pregnant, stay pregnant, give birth, and raise their children as primary caregivers. Banning abortion perpetuates society's overentitlement to women's sacrifices, as does failure to compensate the burdens and reduce the risks of maternity. This framing emerged in the German Constitutional Court's abortion decisions and the evolution of Irish abortion law through judicial dialogue with the legislature and the people in the constitutional amendment process. After the Supreme Court overruled *Roe v. Wade's* privacy right to abortion, there is a need to understand alternative ways of protecting abortion access pioneered in pro-life countries.

Chapter 4, "From Patriarchy to Prohibition: Resetting Entitlements through Constitutional Change," proposes that the law can disrupt overentitlement and overempowerment by resetting baseline entitlements. It exposes an unsung American example of this feminist strategy: the women's temperance movement that culminated in the Prohibition Amendment to the US Constitution. Often dismissed as a constitutional mistake, the Prohibition Amendment left a remarkable but forgotten legacy of women taking action against the hardships they endured at the hands of drunken men. Women organized politically and eventually demanded a constitutional amendment to disarm the wealthy liquor industry and the powerful institutions that enabled male drunkenness and the harms it caused to wives and children. Asserting constitutional property rights, liquor businesses fought to keep saloons and other spaces of toxic masculinity thriving. While historians have documented the decades-long movement by women for temperance and prohibition, the legacy of Prohibition for feminist constitutionalism beyond booze has been underappreciated. Addressing misogyny—men's overempowerment—meant amending the

Constitution to reset the legal entitlements of a powerful liquor industry. Prohibition did not last, but the quest for it enabled women's empowerment through organizations that achieved other reforms that improved women's political, legal, and economic status.

Chapter 5, "Rebalancing Power through Parity Democracy," builds on a key insight from the reframing of Prohibition: combating misogyny means tempering the power of overpowerful institutions, rather than going after bad men. One important goal of constitutional sex discrimination litigation in the United States was the gender integration of some male institutions, beginning with saloons. From the bar to bars, the Supreme Court had blessed the exclusion of women from many professions, including lawyering (*Bradwell v. Illinois* in 1873) and bartending (*Goesaert v. Cleary*, 1948). But since the 1970s, the court opened up bastions of male power to women, most notably the Virginia Military Institute, in the 1996 decision authored by the late justice Ruth Bader Ginsburg. Yet opening these institutions to women's participation did not end men's overempowerment in them.

By contrast, many advanced democracies comparable to the United States have progressed from women's token participation toward women's equal share of control in these institutions. Constitutional amendments of the late twentieth century paved the path for gender quotas requiring equal shares of power between women and men. Many countries now require gender balance by law with regard to positions of political and economic power. Chapter 5 explores the evolution of gender quotas through constitutional amendments in several European countries. Now a global constitutional norm, gender parity was a requirement for the Chilean election of the constituent assembly that drafted a new constitution for the nation in 2021 and 2022. Although the constitution it proposed was not adopted by Chilean voters in September 2022, it reset the terms of debate about constitutional reform and inclusion, in Chile and around the world. Equal power, rather than nondiscrimination, is becoming the organizing principle of legal feminism outside the United States.

Chapter 6, "Building Feminist Infrastructures: The Constitutionalism of Care," argues that the transition from patriarchy to democracy requires a new infrastructure for reproduction, biological and social. The COVID-19 crisis made visible the extent to which American society depends on women's undervalued essential contributions as workers and their unpaid work as mothers. In the early twentieth century, many postwar European constitutions recognized the contributions of mothers, which formed the foundation of care infrastructures. Their legal histories reveal both the potential and the dangers of protecting motherhood by law as a strategy to advance gender justice. Meanwhile, the Irish Citizens' Assembly process has revisited the Irish Constitution's protection of mothers to develop a twenty-first-century constitutionalism of care, compatible with a policy infrastructure for gender equality. Chapter 6 explores the inclusive constitutional processes that have, over time, built infrastructures of care.

Having begun with the problem of men controlling women through law, *After Misogyny* concludes by proposing some strategies of democratic constitutionalism, short and long term, for women to fully share justly in the life of law and society in the United States. Throughout the world, misogyny's engine of overempowerment has been slowed by democratic constitutionalism, with women empowering themselves to make constitutions change. These efforts—though not without resistance and struggle— are establishing new foundations of equality and inclusion for twenty-first-century democracies. Instead of seeking individual justice against misogynists, new movements are focused on establishing comprehensive legal orders that reset entitlement and power to remake constitutional democracy.

PART I How the Law Fails Women

MISOGYNY BEYOND MISOGYNISTS

1 The Equal Protection of Feminists and Misogynists

The late justice Ruth Bader Ginsburg became the "founding mother" of constitutional equality law in the United States because of her ground-breaking work invalidating the laws of patriarchy. Armed with the constitutional guarantee of equal protection of the laws, she litigated landmark Supreme Court cases that struck down laws authorizing men's control over women's lives. A distinctive feature of Ginsburg's widely celebrated litigation strategy was the selection of male plaintiffs to challenge these laws. Ginsburg believed that patriarchal laws and the gender roles they imposed were oppressive to men as well as women. This legal strategy was designed to attack patriarchy as a legal system. Yet the jurisprudence that she spawned became a weapon of misogynists defending patriarchy in the twenty-first century.

How?

WOMEN'S LIBERATION AND GENDER EMANCIPATION

Ginsburg's belief that traditional gender roles oppressed men as well as women was largely shaped by the public policy debates that occurred in the 1960s in Sweden, where Ginsburg began her career as a legal scholar. Ginsburg's intellectual engagement with Swedish law occurred by happenstance, when discrimination against women by American law firms led her legal career into an academic research job in comparative law. At Columbia University, where she had graduated at the top of her class, she was hired by the Project in Comparative Procedure, with an assignment to research and write a book about Swedish civil procedure with a Swedish law professor.[1] Ginsburg had no special knowledge or interest in Sweden prior to this assignment; she learned Swedish in New York to prepare for a months-long stay in Sweden to complete the research with her assigned coauthor.[2]

Ginsburg arrived in Sweden in 1962, in the midst of a national debate about the need for public policy to overcome the traditional sex roles of men and women. As she recalled many years later, she was struck by the writings of feminist public intellectual Eva Moberg.[3] Women, traditionally mothers and homemakers, were increasingly moving into the labor market and the public sphere. Earlier work by sociologist and politician Alva Myrdal had shed light on women's two roles at home and at work,[4] giving rise to public policy debates about how these two roles could be accommodated. In 1961, Moberg's essay "The Conditional Emancipation of Woman" asked, in Ginsburg's paraphrase, "Why should the woman have two jobs and the man only one?"[5] Ginsburg was struck by Moberg's insistence that both men and women should have two roles. Women's emancipation thus depended on men taking on a greater role in the home, particularly in the care of children as fathers.

That insight was the subject of a June 1970 speech given by Swedish Social Democratic prime minister Olof Palme to the Women's National Democratic Club in Washington, D.C., titled "The Emancipation of Man."[6] Not only was men's increased participation in parenting and household work necessary to allow women's increased participation in the workplace; it would also emancipate men from the confining role and oppressive pressure of traditional masculinity. "Is not the role of the father as important as the role of the mother? Should not the household work and the care of the children be shared by the parents whilst the society simultaneously makes greater efforts for the children?"[7] In raising these questions, Palme noted, "It is not only the traditional female role which has disadvantages." Citing sociologists, he pointed out that "men have a higher criminal record, more stress and illnesses due to strenuous work, higher suicide rates and, as a rule, they die at an earlier age than women. In the school it is the boys that have the greatest adaption problems. . . . The social pressure on the man to assert himself, fight his way in life, to be aggressive and not to show any feelings create[s] contact difficulties and adaption difficulties."[8] The feminine role of mother and homemaker constrained women's economic opportunities and potential outside of the home, and the masculine role as providers constrained men's social, emotional, and physical well-being. The solution was not only for both sexes to branch out into the positive dimensions of the role assigned to the other sex but for the state to reduce the negative aspects of each gender role through collective democratic action and responsibility.

"The Emancipation of Man" relied heavily on sociological studies that were included in Edmund Dahlström's 1961 Swedish edited volume, which was translated in 1967 to English as *The Changing Roles of Men and Women*. Dahlström's work, along with Eva Moberg's essay, articulated what came to be known as the "sex role debate," which was in full force at the moment that Ginsburg arrived in Sweden to study civil procedure. Dahlström's analysis noted that the first step in overcoming these sex roles was political and legal equality for women, such as "the right to equal education; equal inheritance rights; legal equality in marriage; equal rights in working life; access to public positions and equal political rights."[9] However, this "formal legal equality" did not result in "real social, vocational, or even political equality."[10] In the present system, Dahlström observed, "motherhood and woman's love of her child are exploited to restrict her freedom as an individual."[11] What was needed was "man's participation and co-responsibility within the family," because "both men and women have one main role, that of a human being. For both sexes, this role would include child care."[12]

Dahlström's analysis ended with explicit proposals for changes in law and public policy, which then made their way into Sweden's report to the United Nations, included in the English translation of the volume.[13] These proposals went far beyond formal legal equality and the prohibition of discrimination. They included a transformation of the educational curriculum to socialize boys and girls similarly; the Swedish government report suggested that both boys and girls should learn home economics, including childcare, as well as woodworking.[14] Another important proposal was to transfer at least some childcare to the state, so that it would no longer be a full-time occupation for any person. State provision of day care facilities was crucial, as was state coverage of childbirth costs so that these costs would be "shared by all employees and not be borne by working women alone."[15] In these proposals, there is a recognition that the raising of children is to the society's benefit, rather than a purely private project. Finally, "Conditions on the labour market should be so arranged as to make it easier to combine gainful employment with care of the home."[16] From educational curricula to funding and building an infrastructure of childcare and health care, to regulating and restructuring the labor market, overcoming the oppressive operation of sex roles required proactive and prospective governmental intervention at the level of policy, rather than legal remedies in the event that the sexes were treated unequally.

Ginsburg cited both Dahlström's *Changing Roles of Men and Women* and Prime Minister Palme's "Emancipation of Man" in her landmark brief for the ACLU in *Reed v. Reed*, the first US Supreme Court case to strike down a sex-discriminatory law on the basis of the constitutional guarantee of equal protection of the laws in the Fourteenth Amendment.[17] Citing Palme in a larger discussion of advances in women's rights outside the United States, specifically the UN Charter and decisions of the West German Federal Constitutional Court, Ginsburg remarked in that footnote, "The public opinion is nowadays so well informed that if a politician should declare that the woman ought to have a different role than the man and that it is natural that she devotes more time to the children he would be regarded to be of the Stone Age."[18]

In *Reed v. Reed*, Ginsburg represented Sally Reed, the mother of a deceased son. Idaho law gave a preference to males over females in the appointment of administrators of a deceased person's estate and thereby appointed her estranged husband, the boy's father, as the administrator. The brief argued that "the distance to equal opportunity for women in the United States remains considerable in the face of the pervasive social, cultural, and legal roots of sex-based discrimination" and proceeded to excavate those roots.[19] "The traditional division within the home—father decides, mother nurtures—is reinforced by diverse provisions of state law."[20] Existing law, including Idaho's, enforced these traditional sex roles, Ginsburg claimed, when doing so was arbitrary and bore no rational relationship to a legitimate governmental interest.

The Supreme Court agreed and held in *Reed v. Reed* that the Idaho law's mandatory preference for men was an arbitrary legislative choice that violated the Equal Protection Clause.[21] Ginsburg's litigation strategy to challenge arbitrary sex distinctions in the law emerged in the years that followed. Influenced by the Swedish debate on sex roles, Ginsburg believed that arbitrary sex classifications harmed men as well as women and became interested in representing male plaintiffs to challenge laws that treated men and women unequally. But her male-plaintiff cases, which grew out of a feminist pursuit of women's emancipation, would become the legal progenitors of the men's rights movement litigation that continued without her.

Before writing the *Reed v. Reed* brief, Ginsburg had already begun work litigating on behalf of a male plaintiff, Charles Moritz.[22] Her work on that case is now dramatized in the movie *On the Basis of Sex*.[23] Charles Moritz was an unmarried man who lived with his aging and ailing mother. The tax code allowed a deduction for expenses for the care of dependents, but only for women, widowers, or husbands of women who were incapacitated or institutionalized. Because Moritz had never married, he was not eligible to deduct the expenses for the services of a caregiver he hired to care for his mother while he traveled and worked. Teaming up with her tax lawyer husband Martin Ginsburg, Ruth Bader Ginsburg authored a brief urging the Tenth Circuit to scrutinize the statute's unequal treatment of similarly situated men and women.[24] The court invalidated the statute over a year later, citing the Supreme Court's decision in *Reed v. Reed*.[25]

The courts' opinions in *Reed v. Reed* and *Moritz v. Commissioner of Internal Revenue* simply declared the sex-based classifications arbitrary, worthy of scrutiny, and invalid,[26] without explicitly engaging the argument that sex roles oppressed women and men. Ginsburg brought the Swedish sex role debate—what American legal scholar Cary Franklin has called the "anti-stereotyping principle"[27]—to her first Supreme Court oral argument in *Frontiero v. Richardson*.[28] The Supreme Court invalidated a military benefits scheme that treated males and females employed in the service differently for the purposes of dependent coverage. Spouses of servicemen were automatically covered, whereas the spouses of servicewomen were covered only upon evidence that they were actually financially dependent. Borrowing copiously from Ginsburg's brief, the court repudiated as "romantic paternalism" its earlier decisions enforcing traditional sex roles, including man as "woman's protector and defender," and woman as "wife and mother."[29] These "gross, stereotyped distinctions between the sexes" had the effect of "relegating the entire class of females to inferior legal status without regard to the actual capabilities of its individual members."[30]

After *Frontiero* scrutinized stereotyped distinctions between the sexes—albeit without judicial agreement on the appropriate level of scrutiny—Ginsburg's subsequent cases challenging gender stereotypes in the law proceeded with male plaintiffs resisting the law's prescription of the roles of male provider and female caregiver. At issue in *Kahn v. Shevin* was a Florida statute that gave widows, but not widowers, a property tax exemption. The court upheld the property tax exemption for widows only, reasoning that widows were generally materially worse off than widowers: "There can be no dispute that the financial difficulties confronting the lone woman in Florida or in any other State exceed those facing the man. Whether from overt discrimination or from the socialization process of a male-dominated culture, the job market is inhospitable to the woman seeking any but the lowest paid jobs."[31] In so stating, a majority of the court suggested that the law could treat men and women differently in order to compensate for the financial difficulties and discrimination that women could face.

Weinberger v. Wiesenfeld, which Ginsburg litigated the following year, challenged the unequal treatment of widows and widowers for benefits eligibility under the Social Security Act. At the time, the Social Security Act authorized benefits to be paid to a widow and dependent children upon the death of her husband if he had worked and contributed to Social Security.[32] Stephen Wiesenfeld's wife had worked as a schoolteacher for a number of years and contributed to Social Security before she died in childbirth. Mr. Wiesenfeld had hoped to depend on Social Security survivors' benefits so that he could care for their infant son. After he was denied, Ginsburg represented him in litigation challenging the unequal treatment of men and women who survived their deceased spouses. The Supreme Court, affirming the judgment for Wiesenfeld, reasoned that the denial of benefits to him was in fact a discrimination against his deceased wife: "In this case social security taxes were deducted from Paula's salary during the years in which she worked. Thus, she not only failed to receive for her family the same protection which a similarly situated male worker would have received, but she was deprived of a portion of her own earnings in order to contribute to the fund out of which benefits would be paid to others."[33] In concluding that the unequal treatment of widows and widowers was irrational, the court explained:

> Even in the typical family hypothesized by the Act, in which the husband is supporting the family and the mother is caring for the children, this result makes no sense. The fact that a man is working while there is a wife at home does not mean that he would, or should be required to, continue to work if his wife dies. It is no less important for a child to be cared for by its sole surviving parent when that parent is male rather than female. And a father, no less than a mother, has a conditionally protected right to the "companionship, care, custody, and management" of the children he has sired and raised.[34]

Through her arguments in the *Wiesenfeld* case more than any other, Ginsburg attempted to transplant the Swedish agenda of overcoming the entrenchment of sex roles in law and society. Echoing Palme's "Emancipation of Man," the *Wiesenfeld* decision established that laws that presumed and encouraged fathers to be less likely than mothers to care for their own children were contrary to the constitutional commitment to equal protection of the laws.

In another victory for male plaintiffs, *Califano v. Goldfarb* invalidated a different provision of the Social Security Act that treated widows and widowers differently with regard to survivors' benefits.[35] If a husband died, his widow could automatically receive survivors' benefits. But if a wife died, her widower could receive survivors' benefits only upon showing that he had been receiving half of his support from his wife. Following the logic of *Wiesenfeld*, the Supreme Court held that creating these hurdles for widowers constituted a discrimination against female wage earners, affording them less protection for their surviving spouses than was provided to male wage earners.[36] Leon Goldfarb, the litigant in that case, was a retired federal employee and could not show that he had received half his support from his wife prior to her death. The court's majority opinion pointed to the statute's coverage of all widows, even those who were not dependent. The "differential treatment of nondependent widows and widowers" was premised on the "presumption that wives are usually dependent," which reflected an "archaic and overbroad generalization" about sex roles.[37]

But Leon Goldfarb, unlike Stephen Wiesenfeld, was not a man who was defying traditional sex roles by forgoing a career to engage in the traditionally female role of caregiver. Goldfarb had worked and could not show that he had been dependent on his wage-earning wife. When constitutional sex equality required him to be included in survivors' benefits, such a solution did not necessarily combat traditional sex roles. The court's holding did not require nondependent widowers who defied traditional gender roles to be included in survivors' benefits; it only required nondependent widowers *to be treated the same as* nondependent widows. To do otherwise would be to presume women to be dependent regardless of individual factual circumstances.

Four justices dissented in *Califano v. Goldfarb,* on the grounds that the "nature of the legislative problem" that Congress had addressed through the distributive scheme for social welfare benefits permitted Congress to make different assumptions about the economic neediness of men and women "if reasonably supported by the underlying facts."[38] Congress could make a legislative judgment that "elderly wives and widows of Social Security recipients were needy groups, and that of the two, the plight of widows was especially severe." The justices acknowledged that some widows were not needy, and therefore that including all widows was overinclusive, but argued that being overinclusive could be efficient if it prevented the need to create a "procedural leviathan" to determine which widows were needy and which weren't, when most widows in the existing political economy had in fact depended on their husbands' incomes.[39]

"Whatever his actual needs," Justice Rehnquist noted, "Goldfarb would, of course, have no complaint if Congress had chosen to require proof of dependency by widows as well as widowers, or if it had simply refrained from making any provision whatever for benefits to surviving spouses."[40] If Congress had refrained from providing benefits to widows at all— thereby treating widows and widowers the same by giving nothing to both—the equal protection problem would not arise. Yet if Congress had refrained from providing benefits to spouses of the deceased altogether, the spouses who had been dependent on a wage-earning spouse would be left destitute—as a factual matter, many more wives than husbands. The dissent flagged a perverse dynamic that could be unleashed through anti-discrimination litigation to strike down social welfare policy: avoiding the equal protection problem through a gender-neutral rule could cause greater harm and disadvantage to women than to men.

In subsequent decisions, the Supreme Court struck down gender-conscious state action primarily when it was likely to perpetuate traditional gender roles. In *Mississippi University for Women v. Hogan,* a male plaintiff persuaded the court to invalidate a public university admission policy that admitted only women, not men, to a nursing program.[41] The court could not identify any "exceedingly persuasive justification" for treating the sexes differently under these circumstances.[42] It acknowledged that such a justification could be present if the gender classification functioned to overcome the disadvantages sustained by women due to the operation of traditional gender roles. But limiting a nursing program to women only could not be understood as a form of compensation for past discrimination against women. Gender classifications had to be "free of fixed notions concerning the roles and abilities of males and females," the court reasoned. Indeed, having a nursing program that was for women only appeared to perpetuate these fixed notions of men's and women's abilities, given that "women earned 94 percent of the nursing baccalaureate degrees conferred in Mississippi" in the year before the school first opened its doors.[43]

EQUAL PROTECTION OF MALE INTOXICATION

Yet the Supreme Court enabled some other instances of government treating men and women differently as compatible with the constitutional ban on sex discrimination, interpreted into the Fifth and Fourteenth Amendments' guarantee of equal protection. In additional cases brought by male plaintiffs challenging laws that allegedly treated them worse than similarly situated females, the Supreme Court devised the approach known as "intermediate" scrutiny. As a doctrinal matter, a court must scrutinize a law when it is challenged for classifying on the basis of sex and/or treating males and females differently. As all the cases from *Frontiero v. Richardson* to *Mississippi University for Women v. Hogan* reflect, sex-unequal treatment by government is unconstitutional if it perpetuates overbroad generalizations about women's and men's abilities, also known as gender stereotypes. Sex-unequal treatment by government is illegitimate absent an "exceedingly persuasive justification." *Craig v. Boren* was the case that consolidated this "intermediate" level of scrutiny, as distinct from the "strict" scrutiny applied to the "suspect" classification of race.[44] In that case, a male plaintiff challenged an Oklahoma law that burdened males more than females in their quest to purchase alcohol.

The Oklahoma law prohibited the sale of "nonintoxicating 3.2% beer" to males under the age of twenty-one and to females under the age of eighteen. Craig, a male between eighteen and twenty-one years of age, challenged the law in litigation, joined by a female plaintiff who was a licensed vendor of "near-beer." The female beer seller (occupying a legitimate role for women a generation after *Goesaert v. Cleary*) invoked the threat of punishment were she to sell to eighteen-year-old males and challenged the economic injury she sustained because of her inability to sell to this population.[45] With Justice Brennan delivering the majority opinion, the court concluded that the law's unequal treatment of males and females violated equal protection. The "weak congruence" between gender and the "characteristic or trait that gender purported to represent" required the legislature to "choose either to realign their laws in a gender-neutral fashion, or to adopt procedures for identifying those instances where the sex-centered generalizations actually comported with fact."[46]

The three-judge district court had upheld the different near-beer drinking ages for males and females, on the basis of the State of Oklahoma's argument that they were justified by concerns of traffic safety.[47] Statistical evidence had been presented, suggesting higher rates of arrests for drunk driving for males between ages eighteen to twenty than for females of the same age range. But the Supreme Court did not find this data persuasive, even if true, because only 2 percent of males and 0.18 percent of females in the relevant age group were arrested for drunk driving. "While such a disparity is not trivial in a statistical sense, it hardly can form the basis for employment of a gender line as a classifying device."[48]

The court also called into question the appropriateness of using socio-logical and statistical data about the different behavior of demographic groups as a basis for law's different treatment of these groups for purposes of public health policy:

> Indeed, prior cases have consistently rejected the use of sex as a decision-making factor even though the statutes in question rested on far more pre-dictive empirical relationships than this. . . .
>
> It is unrealistic to expect either members of the judiciary or state officials to be well versed in the rigors of experimental or statistical technique. But this merely illustrates that proving broad sociological propositions by statis-tics is a dubious business, and one that is inevitably in tension with the nor-mative philosophy that underlies the Equal Protection Clause.[49]

The "normative philosophy that underlies the Equal Protection Clause" is not spelled out here, but it appears to be a rejection of statistical gener-alizations about groups as a premise for the law's different treatment of individuals belonging to those groups. Justice Brennan suggests that it is incumbent on legislatures to devise ways of sorting those individuals who need to be burdened more by the law than others, rather than relying on the gender of each individual person as a "proxy."[50]

The holding of the case is that the Oklahoma statute is an "invidious discrimination" against males age eighteen to twenty. In reversing the dis-trict court, the Supreme Court left it to the Oklahoma legislature "to rede-fine any cutoff age for the purchase and sale of 3.2% beer that it may choose, provided that the redefinition operates in a gender-neutral fash-ion."[51] In the aftermath of the Supreme Court's decision, the Oklahoma legislature redefined the cutoff age at eighteen for all persons to purchase 3.2 percent beer, ensuring that Craig and his younger fraternity brothers could buy beer for themselves as early as freshman year, without relying on their female classmates to buy it for them.

The male plaintiffs associated with *Craig v. Boren* were members of a fraternity on the campus of Oklahoma State University. The case was initi-ated by Mark Walker, who celebrated his twenty-first birthday as the liti-gation was pending and thus lost standing as a plaintiff.[52] He then recruited his junior fraternity brother Curtis Craig, who also aged out of standing before the case went to the Supreme Court.[53] Ultimately, the only litigant who still had standing was Carolyn Whitener, the owner of the Honk-and-Holler that sold near-beer to college students.[54] Having alleged that she suffered economic injury as a result of Oklahoma's sex-differentiated law, it was clear that only lowering the age for males to purchase beer to eighteen—rather than raising females' age for beer purchase to twenty-one—would remedy her injury. Following the Supreme Court's decision in 1976, the near-beer age in Oklahoma was eighteen for both males and females until 1983, when a federal statute required all states receiving federal highway funds to adopt a drinking age of twenty-one.[55]

Having filed an ACLU amicus brief in *Craig v. Boren*, and having served as an adviser and consultant to the Oklahoma attorneys who brought and argued the case, Ruth Bader Ginsburg saw the case as a perfect vehicle by which to persuade the nine men on the Supreme Court to develop a doctrine of scrutiny for gender classifications in the law, largely because it involved a formal distinction that did not have serious institutional and economic consequences for the government.[56] If judges ruled against gender classifications in her Social Security cases, the court's decision could require other branches of government to spend millions of dollars in paying benefits to men. *Craig v. Boren*, by contrast, would just let eighteen-year-old fraternity boys buy nonintoxicating beer. (Indeed, the idiosyncrasy of Oklahoma law, dating back to the Prohibition era, was that all persons regardless of sex had to be twenty-one to purchase intoxicating liquors, including "high-point" beer of the intoxicating variety.)[57] The outcome in *Craig v. Boren* increased profits for liquor sellers without requiring a costly overhaul of government programs like Social Security, so the case made constitutional gender equality easier for unelected judges to quaff.

Nonetheless, no attention has been given to the potential effects of facilitating adolescent males' access to beer on toxic masculinity and campus gender relations—and the implications for campus cultures of sexual assault. Although the *Craig v. Boren* litigation at the trial court level focused exclusively on the effect of allowing eighteen- to twenty-year-old boys to buy beer on drunk driving and road safety, the causal connection between drunkenness and violence against women has a long history dating back to the women's movement for Prohibition in the nineteenth century.[58] The twenty-first-century #MeToo movement has brought the connection between alcohol and sexual violence, particularly among young people on or near college campuses, into sharper focus.[59] Indeed, now-justice Brett Kavanaugh's remark "I like beer" persists in the nation's collective memory of his judicial confirmation hearings, in which credible claims that he committed sexual assaults while underage and under the influence of beer were made.[60]

Nonetheless, the Equal Protection Clause gave males—including fraternity brothers—the equal constitutional right to buy beer in *Craig v. Boren*, without regard for the potential to nourish spaces of toxic masculinity. Coincidentally, Mark Walker, the original fraternity brother who initiated the lawsuit that became *Craig v. Boren*, died tragically in a fatal traffic accident before the Supreme Court decided the case. It is unclear from available sources as to whether drunk driving had any role in that particular accident, but it is noteworthy that the law he challenged—and the eventual national legislation raising the drinking age to twenty-one—was an effort to reduce traffic accidents.

In the twenty-first century, studies link alcohol to sexual assault, especially on college campuses.[61] Many campus sexual assault allegations involve alcohol consumption on the part of both victim and perpetrator, raising questions about both the validity of the victim's consent and the likelihood of judgement-impaired aggression. Ninety-nine percent of college sexual assault allegations involve male perpetrators and female victims.[62] The equal protection analysis and outcome in *Craig v. Boren* would make it difficult for policies to rely on such data to take gender-differentiated problem-solving approaches to the purchase and consumption of alcohol. *Craig v. Boren* includes a long discussion of the Twenty-First Amendment to the Constitution, which repealed Prohibition and reserved plenary power to the states to prohibit and regulate alcoholic beverages, including, for instance, the power to regulate spaces of toxic masculinity. *Craig v. Boren* made clear that this plenary power is limited by the constitutional principle of sex equality, which legal feminists of the 1970s envisioned as sameness of treatment for males and females in most circumstances.[63] But what if treating men and women the same enables toxic masculinity? I will return to that discussion in chapter 4 in examining the feminist legacy of the Prohibition Amendment and its repeal, and in chapter 5 on integrating masculine spaces and empowering women.

EQUAL PROTECTION AND UNWANTED SEX

The successful male-plaintiff equal protection cases throughout the 1970s, and the intermediate scrutiny standard established by *Craig v. Boren*, provided tools by which men could challenge another gender differentiation in the law: the age of consent to sexual intercourse, as expressed in statutory rape laws. Traditionally, all rape laws, including statutory rape laws, were framed in such a way that only females could be victims and only males could be perpetrators. In California, the statutory rape law prohibited "an act of sexual intercourse accomplished with a female not the wife of the perpetrator, where the female is under the age of 18 years."[64] In 1978, a 17 1/2-year old boy was prosecuted for sexual intercourse with a sixteen-year-old girl, under circumstances that rendered her consent ambiguous. The facts would fail the "affirmative consent" standard that California law later imposed to draw the line between legitimate consensual sex and rape on college campuses.[65] Nonetheless, in 1978, sex with any female under the age of eighteen was statutory rape under California law, whether she consented to it or not. The criminal defendant, Michael M., challenged his statutory rape conviction, arguing that the statute violated the Equal Protection Clause in criminalizing sex with a female under eighteen but not sex with a male under eighteen. In *Michael M. v. Superior Court*, the Supreme Court applied the intermediate scrutiny standard articulated in *Craig v. Boren* but upheld the different treatment of males and females in California's statutory rape law. Nonetheless, in the years that followed, the California legislature rewrote the statutory rape law with gender-neutral language.[66]

In *Michael M.*, Justice Rehnquist, who had dissented in *Califano v. Goldfarb*, justified a gender-differentiated statutory rape law, persuaded by the justification proffered by the state of California: that such gender differentiation was substantially related to the important governmental purpose of preventing unwanted teen pregnancy. The court noted that only females could get pregnant. Thus sexual intercourse producing an illegitimate pregnancy would have "significant social, medical, and economic consequences for both the mother and her child," which would not be borne by the father.[67] "Young men and women are not similarly situated with respect to the problems and risks of sexual intercourse. Only women may become pregnant, and they suffer disproportionately the profound physical, emotional and psychological consequences of sexual activity."[68] The disproportionate burdens of unwanted teen pregnancy and unwed parenthood on females, as compared to males, justified a criminal law that imposed greater burdens on and incentives for males to avoid the act that would produce the pregnancy: "Because virtually all of the significant harmful and inescapably identifiable consequences of teenage pregnancy fall on the young female, a legislature acts well within its authority when it elects to punish only the participant who, by nature, suffers few of the consequences of his conduct. It is hardly unreasonable for a legislature acting to protect minor females to exclude them from punishment."[69]

When the biological difference between females and males—namely the ability to become pregnant—imposes, as a matter of biology, a greater responsibility on the female resulting from sexual intercourse, Justice Rehnquist suggests that the law's imposition of a greater responsibility on the male to avoid the pregnancy is reasonable and fair. His account characterizes the law as an exemption from criminal prosecution for the person who would, because of female biology, suffer the biological consequences of sexual intercourse—a justifiable sex-based privilege for girls.

The actual facts of the *Michael M.* case, detailed by Justice Blackmun in a long footnote of his concurring opinion, suggest the functional role played by statutory rape laws in circumstances where sexual intercourse between minors seems less than fully consensual but when evidence is lacking beyond a reasonable doubt to establish the coercive elements of criminal rape.[70] Describing the sixteen-year-old girl with whom Michael M. had the sexual encounter giving rise to this case, Justice Blackmun wrote, "His partner, Sharon, appears not to have been an unwilling participant in at least the initial stages of the intimacies that took place."[71] Yet in the long starred footnote accompanying that sentence, Blackmun quotes at length from Sharon's testimony in court, which suggests she was "not unwilling" at the beginning of the encounter but seriously calls into question her consent to intercourse, which occurred while Michael M. perpetrated other forms of violence on her:

> "The Witness: Yea. We was lying there and we were kissing each other, and then he asked me if I wanted to walk him over to the park; so we walked

over to the park and we sat down on a bench and then he started kissing me again and we were laying on the bench. And he told me to take my pants off.

I said "No," and I was trying to get up and he hit me back down on the bench and then I just said to myself, "Forget it," and I let him do what he wanted to do and he took my pants off and he was telling me to put my legs around him and stuff.[72]

Her testimony makes clear that, after she says "No," his hitting her back down is what causes her to "forget" her will to say "no." And it is he, not she, who pulls her pants off and penetrates her. Justice Blackmun's long quotation of the record continues:

Q: Did you have sexual intercourse with the defendant?
A: Yeah.

Q: He did put his penis into your vagina?
A: Yes.

Q: You said that he hit you?
A: Yeah.

Q: How did he hit you?
A: He slugged me in the face.

Q: With what did he slug you?
A: His fist.

Q: Where abouts in the face?
A: On my chin.

Q: As a result of that, did you have any bruises or any kind of an injury?
A: Yeah.

Q: What happened?
A: I had bruises.

The Court: Did he hit you one time or did he hit you more than once?
The Witness: He hit me about two or three times.[73]

Justice Blackmun, the judicial author of *Roe v. Wade,* noted "the State's adamant and rigid refusal to face, or even recognize, the 'significant consequences'—to the woman—of a forced or unwanted conception."[74] He also noted that the two teenagers were drinking—expressing his personal view that the case was an "unattractive one to prosecute at all,"[75] while deferring to legislative and prosecutorial discretion in upholding the statute and its application here.

Viewing these facts through the lenses of feminist legal theory, both Catharine MacKinnon and Robin West would see rape law's consent line as obfuscating the persistence of patriarchal power relations and the unwantedness of the sex that occurred, even if legally consensual.[76] Statutory rape, unlike ordinary rape, does not turn on consent and therefore might provide a path, albeit imperfect, by which the law can presume the existence of power dynamics that are awkward to prove. By twenty-first-century standards that are more informed by feminist legal theory, the violent hitting and slugging that accompanied the sexual encounter and Sharon's saying "No" and never "Yes" would make the encounter seem less than consensual and perhaps more likely to be prosecuted as sexual abuse or rape even in the absence of the statutory rape provision.[77] It would not be controversial to characterize Michael M.'s violent behavior as an aggressive manifestation of toxic masculinity.

Yet, it was Michael M., not Sharon, who deployed Ginsburg's prior achievements in constitutional sex discrimination law to pursue his liberation. And while he did not prevail before the Supreme Court in 1981, he did persuade Justice Brennan, a liberal champion of civil rights who dissented in *Michael M.* Justice Brennan wrote, "Applying the analytical framework provided by our precedents, I am convinced that there is only one proper resolution of this issue: the classification must be declared unconstitutional."[78] For Justice Brennan, it was not even a difficult or close question. Gender classifications must be scrutinized, "whether the classification discriminates against males or against females," and therefore, the state had the burden of showing that a "gender-neutral statute would be a less effective means of achieving" its goal of deterring unwanted pregnancy.[79] Brennan rejected the argument that a gender-neutral statute would deter girls from reporting violations since they would be as criminally liable as their perpetrators, arguing that the evidence of this dynamic was insufficient. From this, he concluded that the real purpose of California's statutory rape law was to further "outmoded sexual stereotypes, rather than to reduce the incidence of teenage pregnancies."[80]

Although a five-justice majority of the court permitted the gendered statutory rape law to stand, supported by Rehnquist's plurality opinion, a few years later in 1993, Justice Brennan's perspective and the commitment to gender neutrality prevailed. The legislature amended California's statutory rape law to discard gender-specific language.[81] The provision upheld in *Michael M.* has been rewritten to criminalize "an act of sexual intercourse accomplished with a person who is not the spouse of the perpetrator, if the person is a minor. For the purposes of this section, a 'minor' is a person under the age of 18 years and an 'adult' is a person who is at least 18 years of age."[82]

Under this gender-neutral version of the statutory rape law, both Sharon and Michael M. would have been guilty of a misdemeanor (as well as victims of each other's crimes). Similarly situated teenage girls could expose themselves to criminal liability by reporting such borderline-consensual encounters, which creates significant incentives not to report. In a separate dissenting opinion in *Michael M.*, Justice Stevens acknowledged this argument, made by the State of California in view of the facts of this specific case. The state suggested that, on the ground, "prosecutors will commonly invoke this statute only in cases that actually involve a forcible rape, but one that cannot be established by proof beyond a reasonable doubt."[83] But he then rejected it, saying, "The assumption implies that a State has a legitimate interest in convicting a defendant on evidence that is constitutionally insufficient."[84] Yet there remains no solution to the problem of under-reporting incentivized by the revised gender-neutral statute, as young women might be unlikely to report coercive sexual encounters that fall short of criminal rape beyond a reasonable doubt, for fear of exposing themselves to criminal liability. Furthermore, the gender neutrality of statutory rape law in effect makes proof of forcible rape beyond a reasonable doubt the only viable avenue for holding male sexual aggressors accountable for factual scenarios similar to the facts of *Michael M.*

Since it is a subject of much concern and discussion in the *Michael M.* case, imagine the hypothetical but wholly plausible scenario in which sixteen-year-old Sharon is impregnated by her sexual encounter with Michael. If the pregnancy as a legal matter is deemed the result of rape, federal law would make it possible to receive public funding for an abortion. But in the absence of a rape reported promptly to a law enforcement agency or public health service, the Hyde Amendment prohibits the use of federal funds.[85] These dynamics raise the question of whether the equal protection arguments that brought about gender neutrality in statutory rape law make it less likely for teenage girls impregnated by unwanted but ambiguously consensual sex to be able to access a funded abortion. If equal protection law makes it more difficult for government to act on the gender-asymmetric risks and burdens of unwanted sex and pregnancy, might this body of law enable toxic masculinity more than it enables the conditions by which girls and women control their own lives?

EQUAL PROTECTION AND "PATERNITY FRAUD"

Litigants and social movements with a range of purposes distinct from feminism tried to develop and extend constitutional sex discrimination doctrine. Among these were men who continued to press claims, invoking Ginsburg's past litigation, to attack laws that worked to the detriment of men, especially fathers. Their equal protection victories may have strengthened, rather than undermined, patriarchal social norms. In several new legal contexts where Ginsburg had not ventured, men's rights activists formed organizations that attacked laws treating men less favorably than women as unconstitutional. In the 1990s and early 2000s, the National Coalition for Men (NCFM) alleged that fathers were subject to gender-based discrimination in family court regarding custody and other rights in the context of divorce. Men's rights organizations also litigated to seek remedies for a new harm that they called "paternity fraud" and lobbied legislatures to recognize and alleviate the problem.[86]

Paternity fraud allegedly occurs when the mother of a child misidentifies a man as a child's legal father, when in fact the biological father of that child is someone else. This typically gives rise to financial and other legally enforceable obligations imposed on the man whom a mother has identified to be the father of her child, including, most significantly, child support. Before paternity fraud became a core cause for the organized men's rights' movement, one of the Supreme Court's major sex discrimination decisions, *J.E.B. v. Alabama*, grew out of a man's allegations of paternity fraud.[87] *J.E.B.* held it unconstitutional for the state as litigant to deploy peremptory strikes in civil litigation on the basis of gender, affirming an Equal Protection Clause that rejects "invidious, archaic, and overbroad stereotypes about the relative abilities of men and women."[88] The liberal justices in the majority justified the decision by characterizing it as overcoming the long and unfortunate history of sex-based discrimination "during most of our country's existence" against women in jury participation, including the exclusion of women altogether from the jury pool.[89]

Does it mean anything that the lower-court verdict that was reversed as unconstitutional in *J.E.B.* was actually delivered by an all-female jury rejecting a man's claims of paternity fraud?[90] The civil proceeding, brought by the State of Alabama on behalf of a single mother, sought to obtain child support from the putative father of a minor child. At trial, the state used peremptory challenges to strike men from the jury, resulting in the empaneling of an all-female jury. Although the defendant claimed at trial that he was not the child's father, the jury returned a verdict that included a finding of his paternity, and the court entered an order directing him to pay child support. At trial, the state had introduced blood test results as evidence of J.E.B.'s paternity, which J.E.B. tried to have excluded, alleging that the state had failed to establish a proper chain of custody. The female supervisor of the lab that handled the blood samples in question testified that the blood samples had been checked for signs of tampering and that there was no sign of tampering. J.E.B. questioned the sufficiency of her expert testimony to establish the validity of claims, invoking an Alabama precedent that suggested the insufficiency of expert testimony to establish the validity of DNA tests.

In effect, J.E.B., in asserting that the evidence of his paternity was false, that he was not the father of the child, and that he should not be legally obligated to support the child, was arguing that neither the mother of the child nor the female scientific expert should be believed. The suggestion here was that the allegation of his paternity was either sincerely mistaken or a deliberate falsification. Such claims constitute what the men's rights movement now calls "paternity fraud." Having been permitted to take both the blood samples and the lab supervisor's testimony into account, the all-female jury concluded that J.E.B. was the father of the child, leading to the court's child support order. In short, the jury believed the women in the courtroom: the mother of the child and the expert witness. In the context of sexual assault, feminist scholar Deborah Tuerkheimer documents a long-standing "credibility complex" by which women are seldom believed in courts of law.[91] But in this case, the jury—all females—believed women, for once. Yet in concluding that using peremptory strikes to remove men from a jury was unconstitutional sex discrimination, the Supreme Court set aside the judgment on the (female) jury's verdict. The state, on behalf of the single mother, would thus have to expend additional resources to prove paternity in yet another proceeding, one before a jury with fewer women on it. Or it could choose not to pursue the case any further, leaving the mother with no child support contributions.

Since then, the NCFM has made "paternity fraud" one of its signature issues in lobbying and litigation.[92] As in the *J.E.B.* case, an assertion of "paternity fraud" often arises when the state attempts to collect child support on behalf of single mothers, as most states require women receiving welfare benefits to name the father of the child. Once a father is identified, the state proceeds to establish paternity and collect child support payments. Yet the term *paternity fraud* does not accurately describe situations of allegedly misidentified paternity. It portrays the mother as sexually promiscuous and intending to lie, trick, and deceive the alleged father or the state (or both) with the mercenary motive of collecting money in the form of child support to which she is not entitled. The "duped dad" is a victim of a conniving, hypersexualized woman. Recall that through the laws of patriarchy, as recounted by Simone de Beauvoir and Friedrich Engels, men achieved control over women's sexual activity and reproduction in order to ascertain their paternity of the children who inherited their private property.[93] A man who alleges "paternity fraud" reveals an anxiety about his lack of control over women's sexual activity and reproduction, that is, the absence of patriarchal laws. When women can have sex with whomever they wish, and decide whether to bear a child, a man can end up giving away his private property to the child of another. When the courts are receptive to claims of "paternity fraud," they nourish a nostalgia for patriarchal law and enable men's backlash against their loss of control over women's sexual activity and reproduction. The decision of a female jury to believe women and to reject a "paternity fraud" claim was nullified by a Supreme Court purporting to enforce gender equality, effectively strengthening future prospects for "paternity fraud" litigation.

EQUAL PROTECTION IN THE MILITARY

In 1996, the Supreme Court decided *United States v. Virginia,* the land-mark decision on constitutional sex equality authored by Ruth Bader Ginsburg shortly after she became Justice Ginsburg. The Supreme Court required the Virginia Military Institute, the state's premier military acad-emy, to open its doors to females.[94] Virginia's long-standing policy of excluding women was premised on the rationale that likely lies behind the long-standing exclusion of women in many roles in the military, including combat missions: fundamental differences between women and men made men, and not women, suited for the "adversative" training for mili-tary combat. VMI required it of its students.[95] The "adversative" method was characterized by "physical rigor, mental stress, absolute equality of treatment, absence of privacy, minute regulation of behavior and indoctri-nation in desirable values."[96] The method was designed to be "comparable in intensity to Marine Corps boot camp."[97] The Supreme Court, in a 7–1 opinion authored by Ruth Bader Ginsburg, now as a justice, held that Virginia had no "exceedingly persuasive justification" for excluding all women from the "citizen-solider training afforded by VMI."[98]

At the heart of the equal protection violation were "generalizations about 'the way women are.'"[99] Even if such generalizations held true for "most women," such a fact could "no longer justify denying opportunity to women whose talent and capacity place them outside the average descrip-tion."[100] Justice Scalia, the lone dissenter in the VMI decision, noted that "the tradition of having government-funded military schools for men is as well rooted in the traditions of this country as the tradition of sending only men into military combat."[101] Indeed, if the logic of the Supreme Court majority is that it's inappropriate to generalize about the suitability of adversative pedagogy for all women or for all men, it follows that gen-eralizations about the suitability of military combat roles for all men to the exclusion of all women would be similarly illegitimate.

Nonetheless, Justice Ginsburg crafted the decision carefully to allow gender-differentiated policies premised on generalizations about women's experience of subordination and disadvantage, which she assumed to be different from generalizations about the "the way women are." "Through a century plus three decades and more of that history, women did not count among voters composing 'We the People,'" Justice Ginsburg wrote.[102] "Sex classifications may be used to compensate women 'for particular economic disabilities [they have] suffered,'" she declared, or "to advance full development of the talent and capacities of our Nation's people"; and she cited, among other cases, the *Cal Fed* case of 1987, which validated a gender-differentiated maternity leave policy.[103] But equal protection prohibited the use of gender lines to "create or perpetuate the legal, social, and economic inferiority of women."[104]

The exemption of women from the military draft has raised questions for decades about how equality can be ensured to both women and men. Congress ended the military draft in 1973, but a statute continued to require all men, but no women, to register in case of any future urgent need for a draft. The male-only military draft registration requirement was challenged in *Rostker v. Goldberg*,[105] but the Supreme Court upheld it in 1981. The Supreme Court reasoned that, in the event of a military draft, the military primarily needed persons eligible for combat roles. Because women were not included in combat roles at the time, treating men and women the same for the purposes of registration for the military draft would fail to meet military needs.[106] Therefore, the Supreme Court did not regard the male-only registration rule as premised on "a traditional way of thinking about females,"[107] but rather as premised on combat preparation, the presumed purpose of any future draft. However, in 2015, the Defense Department announced that women were eligible for all combat roles in the military, two years after most combat roles were opened up to women.[108] Once women were combat-eligible, the reasoning justifying *Rostker* appeared to be obsolete.

Recent years have seen renewed litigation attempting to eradicate the male-only draft registration scheme. The lens of gender discrimination in the military draft raises questions of framing: Does a men-only military draft discriminate against women by excluding them from an important marker of their status as citizens? Or does it discriminate against men by forcing them to risk their lives for the country, while women are privileged to be exempted? Depending on one's answer to the question, the way to remedy the discrimination changes. If being eligible for the draft is an indicator of superior status, the solution is to draft both men and women. If being exempt from the draft is the privilege that must be equalized, the solution is to abolish the draft as well as its registration scheme. Each solution poses vastly different outcomes with regard to gender relations.

A federal district court struck down the male-only draft-registration rule by applying *United States v. Virginia*,[109] but the Fifth Circuit reversed, noting that it could not, as an appellate court, overrule *Rostker v. Goldberg*, the controlling Supreme Court precedent.[110] Only the Supreme Court could. But the Supreme Court declined to hear that case in 2021, with Justice Sotomayor, joined by Justices Breyer and Kavanaugh, writing a short memorandum opinion explaining that Congress, not the court, should take the first stab at rewriting the draft registration statute.[111]

EQUAL PROTECTION CHALLENGES TO WOMEN'S ADVANCEMENT AND SAFE SPACES

Ruth Bader Ginsburg was not the only lawyer who pursued equal protection cases on behalf of male plaintiffs, especially after she became a federal judge in 1981. Her victories emboldened some men to embrace the idea of men's rights to gender-equal treatment in a manner that reinforced, rather than challenged, the laws of patriarchy. While Ginsburg carefully selected her male plaintiffs and crafted their argumentation as part of a feminist strategy to eradicate patriarchal laws, the jurisprudence written by a mostly male Supreme Court left openings by which patriarchy could also be strengthened by this line of litigation. Activists for men's rights formed organizations with litigation strategies of their own, including the NCFM, the organization of men's rights activists that litigated against the male-only military draft.[112] Although the NCFM was joined by the ACLU Women's Rights Project—an organization founded by Ginsburg—in the military draft case, the NCFM has independently litigated many other cases in the past two decades to attack laws that promote women's economic opportunities or create safe spaces for women victims of domestic and sexual violence, claiming that such laws discriminate against men.

In one such case, *Woods v. Horton*, a California appellate court invalidated state funding for domestic violence shelters for women victims of domestic violence and their minor children (of any gender).[113] The NCFM represented several men who alleged that their wives or girlfriends had abused them. After being turned away from female-only domestic violence shelters, they brought a lawsuit invoking the provision of the California constitution guaranteeing equal protection and nondiscrimination.[114] Men's rights activists have attacked a California statute that granted an exception to the prohibition against discrimination on the basis of sex for the state funding of "lawful programs which benefit members of protected bases," including women.[115] The statute permitted the state to provide grants to battered women's shelters that provided emergency shelter to women and their children, and transitional housing programs that assisted women in finding housing, jobs, and legal representation and provided other support services.[116]

That litigation also challenged state programs for inmate mothers. The state funded an alternative sentencing program for women prisoners who were pregnant or parents of one or more children under the age of six, who had been sentenced to less than thirty-six months, allowing at least one eligible child of such women to reside with the mother at the prison.[117] The NCFM argued that gender-specific statutes, in allocating taxpayer funding for programs for "women and their children" or inmate mothers, discriminated against men. The court agreed, but only with regard to the domestic violence shelters.[118] There is ample evidence that women suffer higher rates of domestic violence than men,[119] but the constitutional prohibition of sex discrimination in California has made it illegal for the government to fund domestic violence shelters that are for women only, thereby leaving the most vulnerable victims less likely to seek out and receive the support and safe space that they need.

The NCFM has also relied on state civil rights laws that prohibit sex discrimination to challenge a whole range of private-sector initiatives designed to empower women and girls, particularly in arenas where they have been underrepresented. The NCFM's members and lawyers have brought over one hundred lawsuits targeting organizational programs that support women in overcoming unequal pay and underrepresentation.[120] Invoking the California Unruh Civil Rights Act, which prohibits businesses in the state from discriminating on the basis of sex, the NCFM's complaints frequently allege that programs limited to women only are discriminating against men in violation of the state's civil rights law.[121] The NCFM has sued, inter alia, the Financial Services Information Sharing and Analysis Center, a nonprofit that helps the financial services industry with physical security and cybersecurity, for awarding a "diversity scholarship" to women attending industry conferences.[122] That organization established a scholarship for women because 90 percent of the professionals working in the national security and cybersecurity field are male. The NCFM has also sued Sony Electronics to invalidate their Alpha Female Creator in Residence Program, which was offered at the height of the #MeToo movement and was open only to women working in photography, videography, and filmmaking, an opportunity that would result in a mentorship with Sony and exhibits showcasing the female creators' work.[123] The NCFM's legal position is that opportunities for women only are illegal sex discrimination, even when they seek to overcome women's underrepresentation in a male-dominated field.

The NCFM also sued Ladies Get Paid, a company that provides seminars and coaching for women's career development.[124] Founded in 2016, Ladies Get Paid hosted meetings and events for women only to speak in a "safe space" about money and issues contributing to women's unequal pay and uncomfortable gender dynamics at work.[125] The NCFM claimed that Ladies Get Paid discriminated against men, again in violation of the Unruh Civil Rights Act, by excluding men from buying tickets to these events. Because Ladies Get Paid was a small woman-owned start-up suddenly beset with legal fees to defend the litigation, its lawyers advised the company to settle the case rather than risk having to pay damages and attorneys' fees, which could have destroyed the company.[126] Ladies Get Paid decided to open its events to men to avoid being bankrupted by litigation, but it would not have done so if a well-funded men's rights organization had not sued them in pursuit of this questionable legal theory in the first place.

Sony has answered the NCFM's complaint;[127] it presumably has the resources to continue litigating. However, many small start-up businesses devoted to helping women overcome their disadvantage and underrepresentation in a field do not. They are often run by women entrepreneurs, who are on the whole less likely than their male counterparts to attract funding. The NCFM brought multiple lawsuits against Ladies Get Paid, which led Ladies Get Paid to start a crowdfunding page to pay some of its legal fees before deciding to settle rather than pay for continued litigation, such as answering the complaint.[128] The NCFM has sued or threatened to sue a whole host of similar women's organizations, including Chic CEO, Geek Girl, and Girl Tech,[129] the latter two being organizations that run programs to encourage women and girls to pursue STEM fields. Deployed by men's rights organizations, laws prohibiting sex discrimination—both constitutional and statutory, state and federal—are effectively shutting down efforts in both the public and private sectors to overcome the disempowerment of women that can be traced back to patriarchal gender relations. In short, the primary legal tools of gender equality are becoming significant legal tools to strengthen patriarchy.

THE TROUBLE WITH TRANSPLANTS: GENDER EQUALITY'S MIGRATION FROM SWEDISH LEGISLATION TO AMERICAN LITIGATION

In Sweden, by contrast, where Ginsburg discovered a feminist vision of the "emancipation of man," men's rights expanded to overcome patriarchy, not to reclaim it. To understand how, legal feminism must focus on law-making institutions and processes, which are as important as the substantive vision of emancipation. Scholars of comparative law have long debated the wisdom and mechanics of "legal transplants," the dissemination of legal ideas across legal systems and borders.[130] While the migration of legal ideas is inevitable, transplants are never perfect.[131] The Swedish vision of gender equality summarized in the 1970 speech of Prime Minister Palme during his visit to the United States—emerging from sociological and feminist movement work of the 1960s—led to the adoption of systematic legislative agendas throughout the 1970s that comprehensively supported women's increased participation in the labor market and in politics. New policies also encouraged men's participation in parenting and household work.

One policy proposal, elaborated at length in "The Status of Women in Sweden," the 1968 report by the Swedish government for the UN, was individualized income taxation of husbands and wives.[132] The Riksdag adopted that proposal in 1971.[133] It provided an incentive for women to work, and their income was no longer treated by tax law as part of the husband's income. Public childcare was greatly expanded through legislation in 1974 to support families with two working parents.[134] As women increasingly entered the labor market in the decades prior to the 1970s, families had relied on unpaid and underpaid work by relatives, friends, and nannies. A series of reforms in the 1970s shifted this care to state institutions for childcare and education, which began to assume that dual-earner/dual-carer households were the norm.[135] In addition, another legislative reform made Sweden the first country in the world to introduce a gender-neutral paid parental leave in 1974.[136] Although working women had had access to state-based paid maternity leave in the past, making paid leave available to fathers encouraged fathers to stay home from work to care for children and enabled women to return to work after giving birth.[137] In short, an infrastructure of gender equality was established in Sweden by ambitious legislation and policy making. By contrast, in the United States, litigation attacking gender stereotypes in the law did not lead government to provide high-quality childcare for all children (so as to emancipate men and women to work), nor did it produce paid parental leave for both genders.

In Sweden, the infrastructure supporting egalitarian rather than patriarchal gender relations became possible starting in 1971 not only because of changes in the cultural attitudes toward gender roles but also, quite significantly, because of major constitutional reform of policy-making institutions. After debates about institutional design that took place concurrently with the sex role debate of the 1960s, Sweden's elected bicameral legislature, the Riksdag, transformed itself from a bicameral legislature to a unicameral body, streamlining the path to adopting major legislation.[138] The electoral system was also revamped to institute a proportional representation system.[139] These changes facilitated the increased proportion of women elected to the legislature.[140] The normative vision of gender emancipation was implemented by expanding the role of government in social and economic life. The basic structure of governmental institutions—namely the legislature—was altered to enable an acceleration of policy making by which the leftward shift in popular culture converged with a new tax base and programs to enlarge the scope of Swedish governance.[141] Eventually, the constitution's text was amended to consolidate the new institutional framework.[142]

Ginsburg attempted to transplant the ambitious normative vision of gender emancipation that she encountered in Sweden through litigation within the available American constitutional framework of equal protection. This meant attacking governmental action and weakening the reach of government in social and economic life. Existing laws that enforced traditional sex roles were struck down by courts, but this mode of intervention, by design, invalidated patriarchal state action without replacing it with more robust gender-egalitarian state action.[143] The primary legal tools of gender equality were laws prohibiting discrimination, which proved limited in their ability to advance the emancipation of men and women. In Sweden, the Riksdag did not even adopt a general antidiscrimination law until 1980,[144] after it had first implemented a range of well-funded policy regimes to encourage men and women to change the organization of their work and family lives. Although the Swedish Constitution explicitly prohibits sex discrimination,[145] and directs courts not to apply any laws that they deem to be unconstitutional, antidiscrimination litigation and judicial review have not been deployed as major vehicles for the pursuit of gender emancipation in Sweden.

One of Justice Ginsburg's last judicial opinions for a court majority on gender equality indicated an understanding that courts, as compared to legislatures, are constrained in their ability to deliver full equality. In the 2017 case of *Sessions v. Morales-Santana*, the Supreme Court invalidated, on Fifth Amendment equal protection grounds, the different treatment of men and women under the Immigration and Nationality Act's provisions on the acquisition of US citizenship for a child born abroad.[146] If the child was born to unmarried parents and the mother was a US citizen, the statute required the mother to live continuously in the United States for one year prior to the child's birth in order for the child to obtain citizenship.[147] If the father was the US citizen, he had to have lived in the United States for at least ten years prior to the child's birth, at least five of which had to be after the age of fourteen, in order to pass on his citizenship to the child. The case grew out of a deportation proceeding against a criminal defendant who claimed that he was a US citizen, despite being born abroad, because his father, though not married to his mother, was a US citizen. Because the father of the defendant had not met the statute's residency requirement, whether Morales-Santana was a US citizen was in question, with direct implications for his deportability.

Justice Ginsburg, writing for the Supreme Court majority, held that government failed to accord all persons "equal protection of the laws" in enforcing this gender line drawn by Congress. The court concluded that gender-differentiated treatment in the statute was based on "overbroad generalizations about the way men and women are" and therefore could no longer survive the constitutional scrutiny required under *United States v. Virginia*.[148] At the same time, the court refrained from thus concluding that Morales-Santana was a US citizen, as he would have been under the statute if the parent with US citizenship had been his mother, rather than his father. Justice Ginsburg explained: "While the equal protection infirmity in retaining a longer physical-presence requirement for unwed fathers than for unwed mothers is clear, this Court is not equipped to grant the relief Morales-Santana seeks, i.e., extending to his father (and derivatively to him), the benefit of the one-year physical-presence term that § 1409(c) reserves for unwed mothers."[149]

The court could only mandate equal treatment; and equal treatment could mean requiring the longer physical presence requirement for unwed mothers to make them equal to unwed fathers, or shortening the physical presence requirement for unwed fathers to make them equal to unwed mothers. Quoting a precedent and citing several other cases, Justice Ginsburg wrote, "How equality is accomplished . . . is a matter on which the Constitution is silent."[150] Furthermore, how equality would be accomplished was a matter for Congress—the democratically elected lawmaking branch—rather than the court.

Similarly, the constitutional prohibition of sex discrimination is silent on how equality should be accomplished with regard to military service. If a rule requiring males, but not females, to register for the military draft is premised on the exclusion of all females, an exclusion that is based on stereotypes and generalizations about the traditional roles and capacities of women and men, it follows that such a rule must be changed. But how? One option is to require females as well as males to register for the draft. Constitutional sex equality can also be achieved by abolishing the draft registration altogether, or by replacing the draft registration with an all-gender registration for national service beyond military service.[151] Within the logic of legal bans on sex discrimination—the primary legal tool to combat misogyny—making women register for the military draft is more easily understood as a requirement of legal equality than, say, the whole host of reforms that would actually reduce the unequal status of women currently serving in the institution. With the increased presence of women in the military, and now their eligibility for combat roles, the military has seen a rising epidemic of sexual assault and violence against women. Furthermore, gender stereotypes and subordination manifested in women's exclusion from military conscription might be better overcome by recognizing and properly compensating the crucial work that is largely performed by women and equally, if not more, essential to the safety and survival of the nation than military service—childbearing and child-rearing. I will develop this idea more fully in later chapters.

But it should be clear that US sex equality law has evolved, through the idea of nondiscrimination, to protect misogyny as well as feminism. Without a strong state and an effective legislature—like the institutions that emerged in Sweden in the 1970s—the feminist infrastructure of gender-equal relations at home and in institutions of power could not materialize from litigation alone. Meanwhile, men deployed gender equality litigation to enforce their entitlements to drink on campus, to avoid prosecution for nonconsensual sex, and to challenge juries that believed women. The nostalgia for patriarchy unleashed the dynamics of misogyny.

2 Overentitlement and Overempowerment

If misogyny is not the hatred of women, what is it?

Misogyny must include the injuries and injustices women suffer because they are women. Sometimes those injuries are violent, and the injustices are accompanied by hatred. But neither violence nor hatred is a necessary feature of misogyny. This chapter introduces the concepts of overentitlement and overempowerment as core elements of misogyny reconceptualized as gender-based injustice imposed upon women. It draws on two concepts that have long been part of the Western legal tradition, unjust enrichment and the abuse of right, to illuminate the unjust distributions of property and power that the law maintains even after it stops enforcing the laws of patriarchy. The logic of cases remedying unjustified enrichments and curbing abuses of legal rights in France and Germany in particular sheds light on what's wrong with the overentitlement of society at women's expense and the overempowerment of men to society's detriment.

WHEN WOMEN DISAPPEAR

Vanessa Guillén disappeared in April 2020. She was a twenty-year-old Mexican American army officer stationed at Fort Hood, Texas. An even-

tual investigation revealed that she had died at the hands of a fellow sol-
dier.[1] Prior to her disappearance, Guillén had complained for months
about sexual assault and sexual harassment on the military base, but these
complaints had fallen on deaf ears.[2]

Almost a year later in Atlanta, a young white man shot and killed eight
people in several massage spas, seven of them women, six of whom were
Asian American.[3] The gunman explained that he had a "sex addiction"
and had sought to eliminate the sources of temptation by shooting Asian
women who worked at these massage establishments.[4] In an announce-
ment about the suspect, the sheriff's office remarked that the gunman was
having "a really bad day."[5] The Atlanta shootings drew attention to the
oversexualization of Asian women, which fueled violence against them,
resulting in their deaths. That day of carnage was then characterized by a
man with law enforcement power as someone having "a bad day." Following
an initial investigation of the shootings, FBI director Christopher Wray
announced that the attacks were not linked to race, citing local police
officers who distinguished between sexual addiction and racial animus.[6]

While addiction to sex with Asian women may appear wildly different
from hatred of Asian women, the lens of overentitlement brings the two
closer together. The Atlanta shootings, American literature professor
Anne Anlin Cheng wrote in *The Atlantic*, cast light on "American male
fantasies of entitlement to Asian female bodies."[7] While these fantasies of
entitlement did not register to the FBI as animus, Cheng characterized
this entitlement as "both quotidian and dangerous":

> For many women of color, the idea that misogyny and racism often go hand
> in hand is a fact of life. Almost every woman of Asian descent I know who
> grew up in America has experienced some version of strange men cooing at
> her, "Me love you a long time," or has endured the unctuous hailings of ni
> hao ma and konichiwa or the intrusive come-ons that mix flattery with a
> vague sense of threat. As a young woman on the receiving end of such
> unwanted attention, I never said anything about it, because I suspected that
> most people would consider such incidents minor inconveniences, even
> though these kinds of encounters always produced a sickening sensation in
> the pit of my stomach.[8]

Violent intrusions by which men act on their sense of entitlement to
women's bodies are too often treated—by law and society—as minor

inconveniences that women are expected to endure. Those who complain about such minor feelings are ostracized for being "out of line."[9] Asian women like the spa shooting victims and immigrant women of color like Vanessa Guillén lived daily among men who simply expected to use women's bodies at their pleasure. This was all unremarkable until these women were dead. Men—and the society that they largely control and shape—have long taken what they want, sexually or otherwise, from women's bodies, for their pleasure and enrichment. Patriarchy authorized this male entitlement by law, but after patriarchy this unjust enrichment of men at women's expense continues, even though it is no longer an entitlement officially protected by law.

The sexual violence called out by the #MeToo movement exposed another significant dynamic of patriarchy that remains in society today: the abuse of power by men who hold it. What's wrong with the sexual behavior of men like Harvey Weinstein is not merely that he forced his unwanted body on unwilling individuals but that he abused his power, acting as though the will of these women did not matter. He wielded his economic and social power in Hollywood to extract sex from women who lacked the power to refuse. When their careers and livelihoods are on the line, women know that refusal will be punished. The concepts underlying the legal doctrines of unjust enrichment and abuse of right, underdeveloped in US law but robustly theorized in several leading civil law systems, can illuminate these core dynamics of modern misogyny. Modern misogyny attempts to enforce the overentitlement and overempowerment after patriarchal law has stopped doing so.

The collective overentitlement by society to women's forbearance flows from men's overempowerment. Misogyny operates even without flagrant woman-haters because of overentitlement and overempowerment. Animus, hatred, and violence are products and consequences of overentitlement and overempowerment, not the other way around. Thus laws that target animus, hatred, and violence rather than their sources are inadequate to overcome misogyny. As the evolution of American sex equality law illustrates, they can leave the core of misogyny intact.

Legal rules that enable patriarchal social relations between genders can survive in modern legal regimes that purport to embrace the equal legal status of women. After the laws of patriarchy have been invalidated, these laws of misogyny can persist. Under liberal legal regimes, women are kept subordinate, as they were under patriarchal law, when men and organized society take too much from them—sometimes through violence and rape, but often through myriad other means. Parasites, more than predators, are most responsible for women's losses. Thus construed, the core problem of misogyny is taking too much from women, beyond the entitlements required by a nonpatriarchal account of justice. Violence and discrimination against women are neither the necessary nor the core dynamics by which patriarchy is enforced.

The accounts of injustice and abuse of power in the legal doctrines of unjust enrichment and abuse of right can shed light on these dynamics of overentitlement and overempowerment. While the legal doctrines of unjust enrichment and abuse of right have been marginal in US law, they were robustly developed, justified, and theorized in the European civil law tradition. Yet these ideas are not absent from US law. Scholars have debated whether unjust enrichment should form the basis of slavery reparations litigation in the United States.[10] And more recently the COVID-19 pandemic triggered many lawsuits by students against universities that shifted to virtual teaching, demanding partial tuition refunds and alleging unjust enrichment as one legal theory.[11] This chapter reads the foundational unjust enrichment cases, as well as abuse of right cases in continental Europe, to underscore the conceptual similarities to the overentitlement and overempowerment that form the core of modern misogyny. The conceptions of justice underlying these doctrines can illuminate what overentitlement is, why it is unjust, and how it operates as a gendered phenomenon in some legal institutions and legal practices. When misogyny is understood as overentitlement, the legal strategies needed to overcome it come into sharper focus: criminal punishment of sexual assault and tort-analogous antidiscrimination remedies gravely miss the mark. Once we understand misogyny as a society's unjust enrichment through its overentitlement to women's sacrifices, and a society's diminishment through abuses of rights by overempowered men, what's needed is a fundamental reordering of baseline entitlements, rights, and powers in the legal order.

UNJUST ENRICHMENT

Most legal systems around the world, in varying degrees and forms, have a concept of restitution for unjustified enrichments. In the United States, restitution is a marginal claim,[12] often parasitic on the tort cause of action. The tort cause of action permits a victim injured by a wrongful act to recover damages from the wrongdoer upon a showing of a causal link between the wrongful act and the injury.[13] The wrongful act and wrong-doer are as necessary to tort recovery as the loss or injury that the plaintiff seeks to redress. In most American jurisdictions, the plaintiff may seek restitution for those losses only as an alternative to tort damages, when the damages authorized by tort law appear inadequate to recognize the breadth of the loss sustained. Nonetheless, many legal systems have recognized a cause of action for unjust enrichment, wherein the loss by the plaintiff is causally linked, not to a wrongful act by an alleged wrongdoer, but to an identifiable benefit that is causally linked to the loss.[14] When the enrichment of one person occurs at the loss of another, the law authorizes restitution when such enrichment can be deemed unjust or unjustified.

John P. Dawson, the Harvard law professor who shaped the study of comparative law in the United States in the mid-twentieth century, traced the American Law Institute's Restatement of Restitution to Roman law origins. The Restatement's central principle, that "a person who has been unjustly enriched at the expense of another is required to make restitution to that other," embodied the simple intuition of justice, attributed to Pomponius in the second century AD, that "no one be made richer through another's loss."[15] Dawson also recognized Karl Marx's development of a related idea—that "gains received by economic groups other than labor—particularly by owners of land and other capital assets—were unjustified by their contribution to the economic product and in the long run were taken from labor." Nonetheless, this idea made its way into the private law regimes of legal orders beyond Marxist ones, because "the ideal of preventing enrichment through another's loss has a strong appeal to the sense of equal justice" underlying any commitment to the rule of law.[16]

The concept of unjust enrichment can be traced to a legal claim in Roman law to recover the value of a transfer made to fulfill an obligation that did not exist but had previously been believed mistakenly to exist.

Under the rubric of *condictiones,* a person could claim restitution of whatever was obtained without legal ground;[17] the *condictio sine causa* addressed situations where another person was retaining something that he had received without legal ground. Pomponius's statement, with which Professor Dawson began his comparative study of unjust enrichment in modern US and European law, was a statement of a general principle rather than a specific cause of action or a well-theorized doctrine. The principle was manifested in a number of types of legal claims under the Roman law.

The principle was modernized by the nineteenth-century German legal thinker Carl von Savigny, who led the nineteenth-century German "Historical School" that reclaimed Roman law as the foundation for the German Civil Code that was in development.[18] Savigny parsed the *condictiones* in Roman law, including in the *ius commune* that developed in medieval and early modern legal systems. What they all had in common was that (1) one person's estate was increased, (2) another person's estate was decreased, (3) the increase and decrease were causally linked, and (4) a situation of unjustified retention resulted.[19] A retention was "unjustified" if there was no legal ground for it, meaning that the shift in wealth could be legally valid only if it was agreed to by the person at whose expense it had occurred. Savigny's analysis of the *condictiones* in Roman law was highly influential to the development of law in the nineteenth century, shaping the unjust enrichment action that was codified in the German Civil Code that went into effect in 1900.[20]

German Civil Code § 812(1) provides that "a person who obtains something as a result of the performance of another person or otherwise at his expense without legal grounds for doing so is under a duty to make restitution to him."[21] In addition, the German Civil Code's provisions on unjustified enrichment create an obligation of restitution in the event of gains at another's expense that are "contrary to good morals," the closest translation into US legal language being "contrary to public policy."[22] Section 817 specifies, however, that a claim for restitution may be barred in circumstances where the person who rendered performance (i.e., the plaintiff in an unjust enrichment claim) "was likewise guilty" of a breach of public policy.[23]

Even before Savigny's reconstruction of the Roman law origins of unjust enrichment, the English case of *Moses v. Macferlan* in 1760 recognized the possibility of a legal remedy for money mistakenly had and received.[24] Lord Mansfield invoked other Roman law terms rather than *condictiones*— namely *quasi ex contractu,* found in Justinian's Institutes. *Quasi ex contractu,* the intellectual ancestor of quasi-contract, was simply a miscellaneous umbrella for, in Dawson's words, "a heterogeneous group of unclassifiable obligations."[25]

Moses v. Macferlan began with a debt of twenty-six pounds by Moses to Macferlan. Moses did not pay. In arbitration, the parties agreed that Moses would pay Macferlan only twenty pounds and endorse and transfer four promissory notes that he had received from a third party over to Macferlan. A term of this settlement agreed to by the parties was that Macferlan would not bring further legal action to recover this debt. But then Macferlan sued Moses to compel him to pay the value of the four promissory notes, and won.[26]

Moses then sued Macferlan to recover six pounds. A central issue was whether such a claim fit the debt or assumpsit causes of action at law, leading to the emergence of an equitable principle to address questions of injustice that these legal writs did not reach. Lord Mansfield articulated the simple intuition that the law must provide a path to the payment of "money paid by mistake; or upon a consideration which happens to fail; or for money got through imposition, (express or implied) or extortion; or oppression; or an undue advantage taken of the plaintiff's situation, contrary to laws made for the protection of persons under those circumstances. In one word, the gist of this kind of action is, that the defendant, upon the circumstances of the case, is obliged by the ties of natural justice and equity, to refund the money."[27]

In nineteenth-century English law, claims for restitution in the event of unjust enrichment were brought and recognized in courts of equity. The typical claim was for the recovery of a payment that was made accidentally. In England, the 1841 case of *Kelly v. Solari* involved a claim against a widow who had received life insurance payments under her late husband's policy.[28] The insurer discovered, after paying her, that the husband, Mr. Solari, had not paid a premium prior to his death and therefore that the life insurance policy had lapsed. The insurer had paid the widow without ascertaining that she was, in fact, entitled to the payments. She had received a benefit as a result of the insurer's mistake. The insurer claimed that the widow was, upon discovery of the mistake, legally obligated to repay the amount.[29]

The widow was "innocent"—her receipt of the payment was not the result of any wrongdoing or fault on her part. Indeed, that is what her lawyers argued. Yet the absence of wrongdoing had no bearing on whether she was legally obligated to pay. The relevant fact was that the receiver was not entitled to the payment. Furthermore, the lack of entitlement created a situation by which nonrepayment by the widow to the insurer would render the retention unconscientious. Maintaining the state of affairs would amount to an excess entitlement that the law ought to reverse.[30] In other words, overentitlement is unjustified under familiar norms and principles that operate across the legal order and therefore must be remedied by the law.[31]

In French law, the route to restitution for unjust enrichment was paved through another body of Roman law. Roman law included the quasi-contract category *negotiorum gestio,* or the management of affairs.[32] Damages resulting from one person managing the affairs of another without proper legal authority could give rise to obligations of repair. The Roman law action of *in rem verso* has also been an intellectual ancestor of unjust enrichment in French law. The Roman *actio de in rem verso* was actually part of the Roman law of patriarchy. Whereas the *paterfamilias* had near-absolute authority over his children and slaves, the *actio in rem* was a doctrine that limited that power. If another person entered into a transaction with a child or a slave, that is, with any person within the patriarch's power (*potestas* or *manus*), that third party could recover from the *paterfamilias* or master any enrichment that accrued to him as a result of the transaction.[33] The possibility of such recovery reveals the intuition that, notwithstanding the clearly established legal authority of the patriarch, there can still be injustice in some situations where value created by the slave or the child flows to him. Even within the legal order of patriarchy, the precursors of unjust enrichment doctrine made it possible to imagine the injustice of patriarchal power in some circumstances, which could trigger legal intervention. The notion that some legal empowerments are legitimate and unjustly excessive at the same time provides a helpful vocabulary for unpacking the gendered relationships of power that continue to be the target of legal feminism in the twenty-first century.

The French Civil Code of 1804 authorized restitution in the context of "quasi-contracts,"[34] and by the end of the nineteenth century, legal scholars and courts permitted the action *in rem verso* where value created by a transaction between two parties accrued to the benefit of a third party. An 1892 case involving manure established this principle.[35] A lease between a farm property owner and the tenant was terminated because of the tenant's failure to pay rent. As part of the settlement, the tenant relinquished to the landlord the standing crop in partial reduction of his liability for unpaid rent. After the property owner took repossession of the farmland, Boudier, the purveyor of manure, sought to recover from the property owner the value of manure that he had delivered to the tenant, without having been paid for said manure.

In addition to viewing the case solely through the lens of privity of contract, that is, whether the landowner inherited the contractual obligations of his tenant upon termination of the lease, the Cour de cassation (the highest French court for judicial matters) invoked the action *in rem verso*. Here, the manure seller was entitled to a remedy from the landowner, having contracted with the tenant, because of "the principle of equity which forbids one to enrich oneself at the expense of another." Therefore, restitution was possible when "the plaintiff alleges and offers to establish the existence of an advantage which, by a sacrifice or an act, he has conferred on the other party."[36] The idea that a person who has made sacrifices for the good of others can be legally entitled to the value of those sacrifices, if taken to its logical conclusion, has obvious implications for women's unpaid labor within the home as housewives and mothers, which inure not only to the benefit of their husbands and family members but also to the growth of the larger society.

In US law, the doctrine of unjust enrichment was articulated in the first Restatement of Restitution in 1937. To recover on a claim of unjust enrichment, a plaintiff had to prove the following elements: (1) an enrichment; (2) a loss, detriment, or impoverishment; (3) a causal connection between the enrichment and the loss; and (4) the absence of justification for the enrichment and the loss.[37] Prior to 1938, when the Federal Rules of Civil Procedure merged law and equity into one form of civil action, restitution for unjust enrichment was an equitable claim.[38] Courts thus required the plaintiff to prove an additional fifth element in unjust enrichment claims—that there was an absence of a remedy provided at law, whether through tort, contract, or property doctrines. However, the Third Restatement of Restitution and Unjust Enrichment, completed in 2008, explicitly provides that the absence of a remedy at law need not be shown for an unjust enrichment remedy to be appropriate.[39] Nonetheless, some courts continue to reserve unjust enrichment only for situations where no other remedies are available at law.[40] The elements of unjust enrichment under the Restatement track Savigny's nineteenth-century crystallization of Roman law's *condictiones*.

The Restatement (Third) of Restitution makes clear that "unjust enrich-ment" really refers to legally unjustified enrichment and not to the broad universe of enrichments at another's expense that could be regarded as morally unjust, no matter how compelling such an account of injustice might be.[41] To say that an enrichment that occurred at another's expense is unjustified is to note the lack of any basis for the enrichment. Voluntary gifts have therefore long been excluded from obligations of restitution. In addition, an "officious benefit" conferred by one party on another cannot give rise to restitution. If a benefit is not requested, and not welcome, even if the recipient of the benefit has been enriched by it, it is regarded as a forced transfer, and there is no obligation on the part of the recipient to pay the conferror.[42] Courts have taken the approach, related to the fifth element upon which jurisdictions disagree, that, in the absence of a contract that could have and should have been negotiated if the recipient of the benefit had truly desired the enrichment, courts should refrain from authorizing an unjust enrichment remedy.[43] This approach effectively imposes a duty on all persons to make contracts for the benefits that they would welcome or value; such contracts would correctly price the benefit and loss.

Restitution scholar Douglas Laycock notes, however, that an important and understandable exception to the duty to make contracts was carved by courts for unmarried cohabitants.[44] On the one hand, while it is pos-sible for unmarried cohabiting partners to enter into formal legally enforceable contracts for the household division of labor and property, Laycock notes that "it is contrary to all human experience to expect them to do so."[45] Thus, when unmarried cohabiting partners decide to go their separate ways, unjust enrichment claims are often filed on the theory that one party, often the man, has been enriched by the household labor of the other party, often the woman. Sometimes the unjust enrichment claims are about the costs borne by one party to improve the property of the other, resulting in the property's increased value. While there is nothing in law preventing people from contracting in advance to allocate these benefits and burdens, individuals in romantic partnerships contemplating marriage (sometimes unilaterally) may seek to avoid contractual negotiations that commit to particular domestic arrangements and obligations. Accordingly, the Restatement (Third) of Restitution and Unjust Enrichment § 28 endorses the "modern view" that a person in a "marriage-like" relationship could recover in unjust enrichment from a former partner who left the relationship with jointly created assets.[46]

In the context of marital relationships that ended in divorce, the French Cour de cassation allowed former wives to recover on the unjust enrichment theory from their ex-husbands even when they were married under a regime of separate property. In the 1979 ruling of *D.R. v. J.L.*, the court allowed an unjust enrichment claim by a woman who had cohabited with her husband for thirteen years prior to their nine years of marriage. She claimed that, during their twenty years together, her activities had contributed to the prosperity of a business enterprise that belonged solely to the husband. The lower court had rejected her unjust enrichment theory, reasoning that the Civil Code obligated both spouses to contribute to the expenses of the marriage. However, the Cour de cassation noted that, through her activities during the time of cohabitation prior to marriage, she had contributed valuable work, without compensation, independently of any obligations required by marriage. The court recognized that the "unpaid work" that caused her impoverishment contributed to her husband's corresponding enrichment and could thus form a basis for restitution.[47]

In another divorce ruling of the French Cour de cassation in 1982, an unjust enrichment claim by a woman against her ex-husband, a surgeon, was affirmed. During ten years of their marriage, the wife, a nurse, had worked without remuneration in her husband's medical practice as a nurse-anesthesiologist. The ex-wife successfully utilized the action *in rem verso*. While the ex-husband argued that the action *in rem verso* could proceed only on the basis of the enrichment that existed on the date of the plaintiff's claim, and not at the moment of plaintiff's alleged impoverishment, the court disagreed. The court further elaborated that "it is the work supplied without remuneration which is the engine, at that time, of the impoverishment, by the lack of Mrs. C.'s earnings, and the enrichment of Mr. P., who did not have to pay for the services of a nurse-anesthesiologist."[48]

Contemporaneously in the United States, the California Supreme Court permitted a woman to state a cause of action for the equitable remedy of *quantum meruit* against her former cohabiting nonmarital partner in 1976. In *Marvin v. Marvin*, a woman attempted to recover the value of property she shared with her former cohabitant, as well as financial support, arguing that they had made an oral agreement to that effect.[49] She claimed that she had given up a lucrative career to live with him, acting as his companion and unpaid homemaker, housekeeper, and cook. He compelled her to leave his household and continued to support her for one year.

The Supreme Court of California held that the plaintiff had stated a cause of action for breach of contract and additionally permitted her to amend her pleadings to assert equitable claims beyond contract, express or implied. The court noted, "A nonmarital partner may recover in quantum meruit for the reasonable value of household services rendered less the reasonable value of support received if he can show that he rendered services with the expectation of monetary reward."[50] That decision opened a door to unjust enrichment claims by cohabitants when the partner is enriched by the life in common, whether through the increased value of property in the one cohabitant's name due to the contributions of the other cohabitant, or through the earnings and earning power of one cohabitant enabled by the unpaid household labor of the other cohabitant. Nonetheless, commentators have noted that the case itself did not ultimately result in a successful unjust enrichment remedy for the woman.[51]

Courts are reluctant to regard an enrichment as "unjust" if it appears that the sacrifice was voluntary on the part of the plaintiff, as in the case of a gift or forced transfer. When *Marvin v. Marvin* returned to the lower courts, a trial court ultimately concluded that the cohabiting man was not unjustly enriched by the cohabiting woman's unpaid labor in the household because it was voluntary and because, in the court's view, she benefited from it herself during the duration of their cohabitation: "Plaintiff actually benefited economically and socially from the cohabitation of the parties," the trial judge observed.[52] A baseline assumption that a woman's housekeeping is pleasurable to her, a willing gift to the man, or of lower value than the man's financial contributions may be at work in a court's failure to find the enrichment unjustified.

Even though the Restatement of Restitution and Unjust Enrichment § 28 now recognizes the possibility of unjust enrichment in the context of cohabitation, comment (d) notes that "claims to restitution based purely on domestic services are less likely to succeed, because services of this character tend to be classified among the reciprocal contributions normally exchanged between cohabitants whether married or not. If the services in question cannot be so characterized, a claim in restitution is available to recover their uncompensated value."[53] Thus the claims of unjust enrichment most likely to succeed in US courts involve the benefits of financial contributions to the purchase and improvement of real property, such as a shared home.

In *Salzman v. Bachrach*, an unmarried couple purchased a lot together, on which they planned to build and share a house.[54] Bachrach, a designer and draftsman who had designed homes for fifty years, designed that house, paid one-third of the cost of constructing it, and oversaw the project. The two moved into the house together, but Bachrach quitclaimed his interest in the property to Salzman. Doing so helped Salzman obtain a more favorable mortgage and tax benefits and also allowed her to avoid complications in inquiries made by Salzman's ex-husband, who sought to discontinue his legal obligation to support her, alleging that she was remarried and that her husband jointly owned her new home. Then the relationship between Salzman and Bachrach soured, leading Salzman to ask Bachrach to move out. She changed the locks when he refused. Bachrach sued Salzman, in an effort to reclaim or partition the property, and the Colorado Supreme Court authorized restitution to Bachrach for his contributions to the house. The court held that Salzman had benefited at Bachrach's expense and that it would be unjust to allow Salzman to retain the benefit without paying him.

My purpose here is not to urge courts to be more receptive to unjust enrichment claims by women against men when men are enriched by women's sacrifices in the traditionally female activities of homemaking, child-rearing, caregiving, and having unwanted sex. Although more empathy by judges to women's perspectives in these lawsuits would be a welcome development, my purpose is broader. Law and public policy need to develop a restitutive approach to the benefits conferred on men and on society as a whole by women's sacrifices in order to achieve gender justice. Gender justice is limited by starting with women's injuries and looking for a man to blame because of the serious injustice in windfall gains that are caused by the losses women endure. Women's subordination is not only the result of men's plots to injure women; it stems also, and perhaps more frequently, from organizing society around men's entitlement to the value created by women, especially women's unique and disproportionate contributions to human reproduction—both biological and social. Men enjoy benefits that result from women's sacrifices in the acts of childbearing, child-rearing, and homemaking. The economy and the nation benefit from these sacrifices too. Patriarchal laws, including coverture and the husband's right to chastise his wife, gave these entitlements the force of law. A thorough transition from patriarchal law to the law of gender equality in a democracy should render the entitlements and powers of patriarchy to be excessive and therefore unjust.

When grappling with an enrichment that is alleged to be unjustified, courts do not deem it unjustified when they see the alleged loss, expense, or sacrifice as in fact a benefit to the cost-bearer. If that benefit to the cost-bearer is equal to, or exceeds, the costs borne, there can be no injustice in the causal dynamic between benefit and loss. By this logic, patriarchy was not regarded by its framers as a regime of unjust enrichment, because they believed that women got something of equal value in exchange for their sacrifices. The "separate spheres" tradition defended by Justice Bradley in *Bradwell v. Illinois* posited that women received economic support and legal protection from their husbands in exchange for their household and caregiving labor.[55] Relatedly, courts refuse to deem an enrichment unjust if they see the enrichment as a voluntary gift by the cost-bearer. But it is not sufficient that the cost-bearer consented to or willed a loss or sacrifice to oneself in order to regard the act as a voluntary gift. The cost-bearer must intend to give the benefit to the beneficiary without compensation or other exchange of benefits. In patriarchal legal orders and the societies they sustain, the costs borne by women are assumed to be either equally beneficial to them or otherwise intended as gifts willfully and happily bestowed by women on men, children, and the communities they inhabit. The transition from patriarchy to gender-equal democracy requires resetting the baseline entitlements of the legal regime.

ABUSE OF RIGHT

The legal empowerment of men over women and children, considered normal and legitimate in a patriarchal legal order, must thus be reframed as an abnormal and excessive power that is easily abused. This insight is particularly important as we reason about the deployments of male power that the #MeToo movement has challenged. The #MeToo movement reframed the unwanted sexual encounters that may have been considered normal and banal a generation ago. Even if these were not fully consensual, women were expected to tolerate them in silence as a minor inconvenient condition of remaining employed and safe. The #MeToo movement led women to recast sexual harassment and unwanted sex as violence to which the law must respond.

But how? Alleged perpetrators of these sexual aggressions often interpret these same encounters as consensual acts—often suggesting that they are mutually enjoyable and beneficial exchanges—that the law permits. Some alleged perpetrators go even further and claim that they have rights—whether in personal privacy, sexual autonomy, or due process—to engage in these purportedly consensual acts without intervention or judgment by the law.

Many of the allegedly consensual sexual encounters that the #MeToo movement exposed were initiated by a wealthy man who exerted power over a woman's economic well-being. Whether the woman refused, resisted, or complied, the power imbalance calls into question whether the encounter, even in the absence of coercive physical force, could be described as consensual or freely chosen by both parties. It is the abuse of power, rather than the sexual nature of the dynamics that #MeToo seeks to end, that is at the heart of misogyny. When men have the power to make and destroy women's livelihoods, economic security, and other prospects for a decent life, women lack the power to refuse or prevent men's sexual advances. Sexual advances under these circumstances are abuses of power. And it is this excessive exertion of power—overempowerment—that makes a sexual encounter misogynous. It can, but need not, coincide with physical violence or force.

The doctrine of abuse of right, well developed in many legal systems outside the United States,[56] illuminates what overempowerment is. Jurists in the civil law tradition invented and developed ways to curb it. While the doctrine is largely absent from US law, American judges have dealt with the concrete problems to which abuse of right doctrine applies in civil law regimes by using other legal tools, particularly in disputes relating to property rights.[57] However, a close look at the logic of abuse of right, especially in cases involving the abuse of rights that were features of patriarchal legal orders, reveals how the doctrine set and reset baseline entitlements through judicial accounts of the purposes and proper exercises of the contested rights. Through the abuse of right doctrine, courts enforced norms of behavior between members of a community, without which legal rights and powers would be corrupted.

Three well-known cases of *abus de droit* arising in French property disputes illustrate assumptions about how people should behave fairly toward others. Even when the law appears to authorize certain acts, often by recognizing a right of one individual to do or not do something, courts have judged some exercises of the right to be abusive and therefore unworthy of the legal system's approval, even while acknowledging that the act contravenes no law. The first example is an appeals court judgment against a property owner who built a dummy chimney on the roof of his house obstructing the light in some of the rooms of the neighboring house. French Civil Code Article 552 states that the owner of land can plant or build on it whatever he thinks proper, subject to any statutory limitations or prohibitions.[58] At the time, there were no laws—zoning or otherwise—that barred the property owner from building the dummy chimney on his own roof.

However, the neighboring landowner sued, arguing that, in building the dummy chimney, his neighbor had abused the right granted to him by Civil Code Section 552. Assuming that he built the dummy chimney in order to obstruct his neighbor's light and diminish the neighbor's enjoyment of his property thereby, the Court of Appeal of Colmar concluded that the dummy chimney builder had abused his right.[59] The court reasoned that the homeowner had acted with a spiteful intention, and therefore had no serious or legitimate interest in building the dummy chimney. It awarded damages to the neighbor whose light had been obstructed.

This conclusion reflects an understanding that the intent, not only the effect, of a person's exercise of his legal rights matters to the legitimacy of each exercise. The implication is that, if the homeowner had built something in which he did have a serious or legitimate interest—such as a functioning chimney over a fireplace that kept his home heated in winter—the neighbor could not recover for abuse of right, even if it obstructed the light in his own home as much as (or more than) the dummy chimney did. The underlying logic here is that the property right protected in Civil Code 552 has a legitimate purpose, and any exercises that stray beyond that purpose in a manner that diminishes the interests of others are subject to legal intervention.

The next leading French case, decided by the Court of Appeal of Lyon in 1859, found an abuse of right in the wasteful behavior of a property owner.[60] There were several springs that yielded the famous "Badoit" mineral water. The owner of one of these springs installed a powerful pump, and this diminished the yield of a neighboring spring, belonging to another property owner, by two-thirds. Again, the powerful pump was not contrary to any specific law, and a provision of the French Civil Code defined property ownership as the right to enjoy and dispose of a thing in an unlimited manner as long as it was not done in a manner prohibited by law. There was no evidence that the property owner who installed the powerful pump did so with the intent of depriving his neighbor of water, unlike the dummy chimney builder whose purpose was to diminish his neighbor's enjoyment of his property. Nonetheless, the court inferred a desire to inflict harm from the installation of the powerful pump because of the obvious wastefulness involved.[61]

But it is difficult to say in this case, unlike the dummy chimney case, that the right was exercised in a manner alien to the purpose of the right. If one owns a spring that yields famous and highly coveted mineral water, enjoying it to the fullest possible extent—even excessively—does not seem to depart from the purpose of ownership in that thing. The right is abused, not because the exercise goes beyond the legitimate interest in the right, but because the owner seems insufficiently respectful of his neighbor's interest in the water. If, for instance, the neighbor could use the water more efficiently or for a more valuable purpose, it appears wrong to extract much more than one really needs by installing a very powerful pump. Taking more than one needs, or more than one can put to efficient or valuable use, is an abuse of right when it detracts from others' enjoyment of their rights. As Louis Josserand, the author of a leading French treatise on abuse of right, put it in 1905, "The notion of abuse of rights is invoked to ensure the triumph of the spirit of the law over its text, to protect the right from the selfishness and meanness which would be tempted to get the better of it; the most reliable of all weapons; ultimately a social notion, because it tends to ensure the realization of rights for the highest well-being of the collectivity, loyally, appropriately, unassumingly."[62]

This norm against selfish and mean behavior was then enforced in the third seminal French case, decided by the Cour de cassation in 1915, which involved adjacent property owners yet again. The parties owned adjacent hangars, and one of them, the Clément-Bayard company, housed airships it was building on contract with the French government.[63] The company had been in negotiations with the adjacent hangar owner to purchase that site. While negotiations were ongoing, the adjacent hangar owner built wooden scaffolds with spikes on his own property, which he had every right to do under the French Civil Code's provisions. These scaffolds-spikes made it difficult or impossible for Clément-Bayard to launch their airships, risking serious damage if the company attempted to do so, even from its own hangar. The adjacent hangar owner intended, in building the spikes, to pressure Clément-Bayard to pay a higher price to purchase the property than that initially offered in negotiations. Clément-Bayard sued the adjacent hangar owner, alleging an abuse of right and demanding damages as well as the removal of the obstructions.[64]

The Cour de cassation concluded that the adjacent hangar owner had abused his right. In acting in such a manner as to persuade or induce the neighboring corporation to buy him out, the adjacent hangar owner was acting as a rational profit-maximizer, not out of spite. But the court found that the dominant motive was to inflict harm; he was willing to cause injury to his neighbor's property and threatened to do so just to maximize his own gain. In this situation, in the absence of spite and waste, what is abusive is a pursuit of self-maximization at one's neighbor's expense. A right is abused when its exercise departs from norms of fair play and good faith—even in precontractual negotiations. Even when a person clearly has a right to do something, the abuse of right doctrine enables the judge, speaking for the legal community, to conclude that he is out of line in doing so.

A parallel development with the abuse of right doctrine in property disputes was the idea of abuse of power in public and administrative law.[65] In Germany, the Federal Constitutional Court read the norm against selfishness and meanness into both the German Civil Code and the constitutional right to autonomy enshrined in the German Basic Law. The German Civil Code explicitly authorizes a remedy when a person exercises a right with the intent of causing injury to another.[66] But even in the absence of intent to injure another in exercising one's rights, courts also curb the abuse of legal rights, invoking the Civil Code's provisions invalidating legal transactions that are contrary to "good morals" (*gute Sitten*) and imposing a general duty of good faith (*Treu und Glauben*).[67] It is through the concepts of "good morals" and "good faith" that courts question the legitimacy of exercises of rights that depart from the purpose of the right, curb legally authorized behaviors that are insufficiently mindful of the interests of other members of one's community, and impose a duty of good faith and fair dealing in negotiations,[68] so as to stop efforts by a powerful party to take advantage of a vulnerable party, as the French courts do. In both France and Germany, identifying the abuse of right, like identifying the injustice of any enrichment, necessarily requires courts to draw on ethical and moral conceptions of justice that distinguish between purposive and abusive exercises of legal rights.

In 1993, the German Constitutional Court conceptualized a related constitutional problem of overempowerment for the situation where an economically powerful actor entered into a contract that resulted in excessive debt for an economically vulnerable woman. It determined that a bank had acted contrary to good morals when it asked an underemployed single mother to sign as a surety for the past and future debts of her father, a real estate broker.[69] The German Supreme Court had enforced the surety agreement, but the Constitutional Court permitted the twenty-one-year-old single mother to challenge the constitutionality of that judgment, arguing that the bank had failed to act in good faith and had completed a transaction contrary to good morals. The Constitutional Court began by recognizing that "the Constitution thus obligates the civil courts to use the basic rights as guidelines when interpreting the general clauses" of the Civil Code,[70] specifically the clauses that impose a duty of good faith (§ 242) and invalidate transactions that are contrary to good morals (§ 138).

Although it was clear that both the bank and the woman had signed the contract, the Constitutional Court noted that the woman "would not be able, until the end of her life, to free herself" from the burden of the debt.[71] Thus the contract undermined her constitutional right to autonomy. Whereas freedom of contract entails the autonomy of all parties, including the bank, the Constitutional Court concluded, "If one of the parties has such a preponderant power that, practically speaking, that party alone is able to determine the contents of the agreement, then this means for the other party the imposition of another's will."[72] The Constitutional Court engaged in an analysis of power, recognizing that the right to freedom of contract can be abused in situations where one party is in a "significantly weaker position" and the consequences of the contract would be particularly burdensome for the weaker party.

Furthermore, the weakness of one party relative to another was grounded in social realities; the court noted that women in particular faced weaknesses in the market due to their *Familienhaftung* (family liabilities/responsibilities).[73] The constitutional problem was that overpowerful (*übermachtige*) companies "systematically use contractual freedom in a way that leads to a fundamental endangerment of the institution of marriage and the family and violates the principle of equal rights," the Constitutional Court explained.[74] This situation of a party's overempowerment relative to the other led to the abuse of a right to the detriment of a weaker party, the Constitutional Court found, and this in turn undermined the weaker party's right to autonomy that was part of the constitutional right to free development of personality.[75] Protecting one party's autonomy in a manner that would burden the weaker' party's ability to enter into other contracts for a lifetime was not in keeping with the right to autonomy in the sphere of private law that is at the center of the German Civil Code. Furthermore, the court noted that the Constitution article 20 (I) committed Germany to being a "social state," which also placed limits on the legitimacy of overempowered parties' abuse of their rights.[76]

In Germany, courts have determined that an exercise of rights is abusive if it is grossly inequitable under the circumstances. Even if it falls short of causing injury to another within the meaning of Civil Code Section 226, an exercise of a right can be invalidated as abusive if it is carried out with no regard for the legitimate interests of others. In one illustrative case, the Federal Supreme Court determined that a man abused his right to divorce his wife in circumstances where he deceived her in order to get his marriage dissolved so that he could legally marry another woman.[77]

Similarly, in France, the doctrine of abuse of right has evolved since the 1980s to temper the conduct of overempowered men in the context of divorce. In 1982, the Cour de cassation authorized damages for a woman who claimed that her ex-husband had abused his right to exercise religious freedom in the context of their divorce.[78] Both the claimant and her ex-husband were Jewish. They had obtained a divorce under French civil law. Under Jewish law, the divorce is not complete—meaning that the wife is not free to marry another man in the future in a marriage recognized by Jewish law—unless the husband delivers the *guet* to her as the final step. The *guet*—or "get," as it is known in English—is the legal instrument by which the husband formally emancipates the wife from the marriage, so that she is "permit[ted] to all men." The court determined that a refusal to deliver the *guet*, if motivated by the intention to harm, was an abuse of right.

In the cases regarding the failure to deliver the *guet*, French courts acknowledge that a divorcing husband has a right, under Jewish law, to withhold the *guet*—it is a matter over which he alone has power. The Cour de cassation recognized that delivering or withholding the *guet* was clearly an exercise of his freedom of conscience. Indeed, the right to liberty of conscience (including religion) is enshrined at Article 10 of the French Constitution's Declaration of Rights of Man and is legally protected in a 1905 statute. In the 1982 case, the court determined that, because the civil marriage had been definitively dissolved, the ex-husband's reason for withholding the *guet* could not possibly be a wish for reconciliation. Rather, the court recognized that the husband's motive was to prevent his ex-wife from entering into a new marriage with an Israeli citizen as she intended so as to deprive her of her freedom of marriage, a purpose that the court determined to be "malicious."[79] The ex-husband claimed that he was withholding the *guet* because, under Jewish law, delivering the *guet* would preclude him from remarrying his ex-wife in the future. But the court found that he presented no evidence of a "spirit of reconciliation" that would support the possibility of reconciliation as his legitimate motive for withholding the *guet*. A malicious exercise of a right, however, was abusive and could give rise to the divorcing wife's cause of action for damages under the "abuse of right" doctrine.

In another decision in 1990, the Cour de cassation again recognized that the husband could withhold the *guet* in the course of exercising his "liberty of conscience," but that refusing to deliver it after going through a civil divorce gave rise to liability for damages for abuse of right.[80] Consistent with the grounding of abuse of right as a tort under Section 1382 of the Civil Code, the court further concluded that an order requiring the delivery of the *guet* under penalty of fines was inappropriate; only a damages remedy was appropriate.

In other cases, a divorcing husband has refused to deliver the *guet,* not out of a malicious intent to deprive a woman of her future happiness in remarriage or to cause other harm to her, but as a bargaining chip to negotiate a property distribution or other terms of divorce more favorable to himself. Although the woman would be free to marry another man after a civil divorce under French law, even without receiving the *guet* from her former husband, the inability to enter into a marriage that would be legitimate under religious law and in the eyes of the Jewish community could suffice to pressure a woman of faith to relinquish property interests she might not otherwise give up.[81]

In 2013, the Cour de cassation decided a case in which the evidence revealed that the divorcing husband had refused to deliver the *guet* to his ex-wife because he objected to the proposed terms of the civil divorce regarding the liquidation of their joint assets. He had written in an email, "Due to the failure of a favorable agreement regarding the liquidation of our joint property, nothing and nobody will obligate me to see to it that your personal status change on the religious plane to what you will need, for the rest of your days." The court acknowledged that even in the absence of a legal obligation under the Civil Code to deliver the *guet* to his ex-wife, a husband could be liable for abuse of right where he lacked a legitimate reason for his refusal to do so.[82]

One commentator has suggested that courts have applied the abuse of right doctrine in the context of *guet* delivery because they are bothered by the inequality of power between the husband and wife under religious law, which remains patriarchal. This provision of Jewish law enables men to control their wives' social and economic circumstances even after the marriage ends.[83] Whereas neither the divorcing husband nor wife can remarry until after the husband delivers the *guet*, the consequences of not receiving the *guet* are worse for the woman. If a man remarries without delivering the *guet* to the first wife, Jewish law does not regard the new relationship as adulterous; nor is the legitimacy of the children of his next marriage compromised.[84] By contrast, Jewish law regards the woman who remarries without the *guet* as an adulterer and does not recognize the children of her new marriage as legitimate. Thus the term *agunah*—"chained woman"—describes a woman who is divorced without receiving the *guet*.[85] By framing the husband's refusal to deliver the *guet* as an "abuse of right," judges are effectively reframing these patriarchal legal rules. From the perspective of the postpatriarchal regime of family law, patriarchal expectations amount to one person's illegitimate overempowerment that postpatriarchal law can remedy.[86]

In these cases, the husband's right to deliver or withhold the *guet*, treated as an incident of his right to religious liberty, is presumed to have a legitimate purpose. As suggested by the 1982 case, that purpose could be to salvage the marriage. In the 2013 case, the court suggests a possible legitimate purpose in adhering to a procedural sequencing of civil and religious dissolution of marriage. Nonetheless, if the man exercises the right to pursue a "malicious" or "harmful" purpose of depriving his ex-wife of her freedom to remarry, or to undermine her bargaining position in the divorce settlement of property, the exercise of the right has exceeded the purpose of the right. In the 2013 case, the Cour de cassation also mentions in passing that, on remand, the court should consider that the ex-wife wrote in an email that "the religious divorce was not that important" to her.[87] Whether an abuse of right occurred therefore depends, in part, on whether the right was exercised with due regard for the interests of the other party. As in the nineteenth- and early twentieth-century abuse of right cases in the context of property disputes, the concept of abuse of rights entails a judgment about how people should value one another and deal fairly with each other, regardless of what their legal rights permit them to do.

The concept of abuse of rights, and the related idea of abuse of power, can be traced to Roman law. Roman law was a patriarchal legal regime that gave a male head of household—the *paterfamilias*—extraordinary legal power over his wife, his children, and their children. *Patria potestas*, we have noted, included *vitae necisque potestas*—the power of life and death. It gave the *paterfamilias* the lawful right to kill a person subject to his authority at will, with impunity. Yet there are few recorded instances of this right actually being exercised. Doctrinal writings, legislation, and decrees during the Roman Empire developed to deter men who were over-empowered by the law from actually exercising this particular right abusively, which resulted in very few uses at all. In nine centuries of Roman legal history, there are fewer than fifteen examples of the alleged use of the power, and none after the Augustan Empire.[88]

In practice, known instances of fathers killing sons occurred only in circumstances where the son committed an offense for which he would otherwise have been tried and executed by public authorities.[89] Several scholars who have examined the fewer than fifteen instances of fathers killing their sons have concluded that the right was more a public social responsibility of officeholding rather than an individual freedom to be violent.[90] Men who held public office had to carry out their duties and protect the public interest, even if it caused personal sorrow. When the father's power to kill was actually exercised over a son in circumstances where the son had committed a public offense, it would demonstrate the virtue of a man capable of putting the interest of the country above that of his nearest and dearest.[91] Viewed through this lens, the father's right to kill his son is properly understood as a delegation of the sovereign's political authority. The purpose of the *paterfamilias*'s right to kill those subject to his *patria potestas* is to protect the public good. Exercises at will—maliciously or for no reason—generally did not occur. It is clear that arbitrary violence by fathers against their children would contravene jurists' understanding of the purpose of the right of life and death. Ulpian, the renowned Roman jurist of the classical period, wrote that fathers could not kill their sons without giving them a hearing.[92]

Among the few examples of violence in which the right of life and death was invoked, there is at least one in which Quintus Fabius Maximus put his son to death for a sexual offense, presumably a homosexual act. Yet the father was sent into exile for this.[93] It is unknown why and how the father's killing of his son was subject to legal punishment despite *ius vitae necisque*. It could have been that the son's offense was insufficiently serious, or that the father had a malicious motive, or that the father departed from the recommendation of a family council. All these possibilities, and the simple fact that the killing led to the father's exile, clearly support the Roman understanding that a legal right to kill one' s own child, a core feature of *patria potestas*, could be exercised abusively, in which case the legal system would further intervene.

Even in the context of tremendous discretionary power like *patria potestas*, Romans expected that any significant right or power, including that of magistrates and even the emperor, be exercised in consultation with peers, known as *consilium*.[94] The *consilium* could consist of those whose judgment the empowered person—*paterfamilias* or magistrate or emperor—trusted. Although there was no legal obligation to follow the advice of the *consilium*, or attain its approval before acting, failing to seek such advice would diminish the dignity of the empowered person. In these norms surrounding actual practice of the right of life and death inherent to *patria potestas*, we can find insights about the problem of overempowerment. The law may empower certain actors excessively, but exercising that power arbitrarily or excessively is subject to moral judgment, which sometimes leads to legal limitations.

There are very few known instances of fathers killing their daughters pursuant to their power of life and death, all occurring in situations in which the daughter's chastity was at stake.[95] In one dramatic account by Livy, a father killed his daughter to save her from being raped by the tyrant Appius Claudius. Interestingly, Augustus's *lex Julia de adulteriis* in 18 BC specifically allowed the father to kill his daughter caught in the act of adultery in his own home or in his son-in-law's house.[96] The specificity of this law, framed as an authorization, actually limited the power of the father to kill his daughter, making clear that the power did not extend to at-will killings. Rather, the law authorized the father to kill the adulterous daughter when she was caught in the act in one of two specified places—which came to be understood as *only when* these circumstances were met. Both the intent and effect of the law were to discourage and reduce the practice—already infrequent—of killing one's daughter for unchastity by legitimizing it only in the highly unlikely event that the daughter was caught in the act at home.[97] Similarly, although owners of slaves also had the right to kill their slaves, Justinian limited the master to reasonable chastisement.[98] Such limitations emanated from the principle that persons should not misuse their rights.[99] Mistreatment of slaves by their owners was an excessive use of a right.

Through the notion that rights could be abused—albeit legally—the legal traditions that descended from Roman law defined and limited excessive or abusive exercises of legal rights and powers. As jurists observed, enforcing this doctrine necessarily required moral judgments about social norms. Those making and enforcing the law began to articulate when some exercises of clearly authorized power actually subverted the purpose or values of that power or right, and this evolved into a protection of the dignity and respect of persons adversely affected by the exercise of the right. While certain actors—including male heads of families—held seemingly absolute power under the law, the law developed mechanisms to prevent them from overempowering themselves.

REDEFINING MISOGYNY

In the modern liberal political economy and legal order, some men, often by virtue of wealth or leadership positions in the economy or in politics, possess tremendous power over those who depend on them for their livelihood or future advancement. The law may authorize all persons, including powerful men, to hire or fire whom they please and to engage in consensual sexual relations. Even in the absence of physical violence, empowered men can abuse these rights through aggressive sexual conduct toward persons who are subject to their power. When men wield their power to maximize their gain without due regard for the vulnerable person on the other side of the transaction, they abuse their rights. They corrupt social relations and the economic and political institutions with which the law entrusts them. Understanding misogyny as overentitlement and overempowerment captures this important insight that lies beneath twenty-first-century demands for gender justice.

Remedies for discrimination and the punishment of violence address the symptoms, not the causes, of misogyny thus understood. The principle of unjust enrichment—particularly as it developed in cases involving women's undervalued contributions to the households and livelihoods of men—shows why overentitlement is a problem that the law tries to correct. Within patriarchal legal orders, the abuse of rights and powers was curbed by state intervention. Abuse of right doctrine recognized, enforced, and even transformed the social relations between the powerful and the vulnerable. These doctrines provide conceptual resources for considering how to reset baseline entitlements and the law's delegation of power— necessary processes to overcome misogyny.

3 Misogyny and Maternity

ABORTION BANS AS OVERENTITLEMENT

The United States Supreme Court decided in June 2022 that the right to terminate a pregnancy was no longer protected by the US Constitution. *Dobbs v. Jackson Women's Health* ended nearly fifty years of abortion rights under *Roe v. Wade*, the 1973 case that had become a global symbol of feminist triumph over patriarchy.[1]

Roe had struck down laws banning abortion before viability and had established that the Constitution protected a woman's right to control her own body and to decide for herself whether to bear a child. *Roe* ended a legal regime of patriarchy that had deprived women of autonomy over their sexual and reproductive lives. But opponents of abortion spent fifty years unraveling this legal victory, successfully persuading the Supreme Court to allow abortion bans anew in *Dobbs v. Jackson Women's Health*.[2] In anticipation, Texas passed Senate Bill 8 (SB 8) in May 2021, banning abortions at six weeks of pregnancy under threat of citizen enforcement. One headline read, "The Texas Abortion Ban Is a Performance of Misogyny"[3] Abortion bans have gone into effect in an increasing number of states since the Supreme Court's ruling in *Dobbs*. One pro-choice politician denounced her state's abortion ban as "simple misogyny" and as "the worst kind of government overreach."[4]

In a world without *Roe,* will the United States live under a new legal regime of misogyny?

This chapter shows that, to overcome the misogyny of abortion bans, we need to get a better handle on the real misogyny of banning abortion: It is government underreach, not government overreach. *Roe v. Wade* described abortion bans as a problem of government overreach into the private sphere of childbearing, but other constitutional democracies around the world liberalized abortion access by empowering the government to reduce the reproductive injustices women endured. Abortion bans enforce society's entitlement to women's sacrifices as childbearers for the public benefit of reproducing the community, without sufficient governmental restitution for this unjust enrichment. Reframing the misogyny of banning abortion through the lens of overentitlement opens up new legal paths for defending abortion access without the limiting privacy logic of *Roe v. Wade.*

In the moment that law has constrained access to abortion in the United States, other constitutional democracies have moved in the opposite direction, expanding access to safe, legal, and free abortions. They have done so without reasoning from *Roe*'s vision of the private nature of unwanted pregnancy. Remarkably, countries with histories of Catholic constitutionalism are becoming more receptive to abortion access than many American states.[5] Instead of the *privacy* rationale for abortion rights that the Supreme Court rejected in *Dobbs,* the jurisprudence and legislation of abortion in many other countries focus on the state's *public* responsibility for unwanted pregnancy. They characterize the state as a beneficiary of the burdens and sacrifices women make for collective posterity by continuing a pregnancy and birthing a child. By forcing these sacrifices, laws banning abortion enforce society's overentitlement to women's losses. Abortion law in many other jurisdictions develops this account of the misogyny of banning abortion, which is a departure from finding misogyny in the privacy violation. A future for abortion in America without *Roe* depends on understanding this public, rather than private, dimension of women's reproductive lives.

THE PRIVACY-POVERTY ABORTION COMPROMISE

Roe v. Wade was never a robust protection for actual access to abortion in the United States. It invalidated a Texas law that banned and criminalized abortion in most circumstances, with the Supreme Court reasoning that the pregnant woman's right to terminate a pregnancy without governmental interference was part of every individual's constitutional right to privacy. "A right of personal privacy, or a guarantee of certain areas or zones of privacy, does exist under the Constitution," it noted.[6] Therefore, prior to the viability of the fetus, the state could not constitutionally regulate the determination, made by the woman and her doctor, to terminate a pregnancy.[7] Acknowledging that the Constitution makes no textual mention of privacy as such, the court located the right to privacy in prior cases involving compelled medical exams in the course of civil litigation, involuntary sterilization, child-rearing, the home, marriage, and birth control.[8] These privacy cases protected the individual's right to be left alone by the government, not the right to be supported in making reproductive or other choices of great meaning in a person's life.

In *Eisenstadt v. Baird*, striking down a statute prohibiting unmarried people from obtaining contraceptives on equal protection grounds, the Supreme Court acknowledged that "if the right to privacy means anything, it is the right of the individual, married or single, to be free from unwarranted governmental intrusion into matters so fundamentally affecting a person as the decision whether to bear or beget a child."[9] In *Roe*, Justice Stewart's concurring opinion more explicitly tied the "personal intimacy" of the abortion right to "the right to send a child to private school" and "the right to teach a foreign language" to one's child.[10] Parents' decisions about how to raise a child were, under constitutional precedents, protected from state intrusion. Therefore, *Roe* shielded the individual's decision to have a child at all (or not) from state intrusion as well. In 1974, the Supreme Court deployed this reasoning to strike down a school board policy that required teachers to go on maternity leave for the last five months of pregnancy, recognizing "a right 'to be free from unwarranted governmental intrusion into matters so fundamentally affecting a person as the decision whether to bear or beget a child.'"[11]

But the idea that bearing or begetting a child was none of the government's business had a dark side that implicitly justified governmental blindness to severe reproductive injustices. The right to abortion established in *Roe*, based on a right of personal privacy, was a negative right to be free from state intrusion. *Roe* kept the government out of the womb, and legislatures responded with laws that stopped the government from funding abortions, even those that were medically necessary. Less than a decade after *Roe*, *Harris v. McRae* upheld laws denying public funding for abortions. Litigants in that case challenged congressional appropriations legislation, known as the Hyde Amendment, which made federal funds unavailable to reimburse abortions provided to Medicaid recipients, even when they were medically necessary. Women who were too poor to afford abortions were therefore denied meaningful access to abortion, as the Hyde Amendment denied federal funding even for abortions that were medically necessary to prevent long-lasting physical injury to the pregnant woman.

But the Supreme Court insisted that this outcome was perfectly compatible with *Roe v. Wade*: "Although government may not place obstacles in the path of a woman's exercise of her freedom of choice, it need not remove those not of its own creation," it explained. "Indigency falls in the latter category."[12] Therefore, the court held that "although the liberty protected by the Due Process Clause affords protection against unwarranted government interference with freedom of choice in the context of certain personal decisions, it does not confer an entitlement to such funds as may be necessary to realize all the advantages of that freedom."[13] By protecting a right to be free from governmental intrusion, *Roe* protected abortion access only for those who could afford it, and not for indigent women who depended on the state for health care. Given the logical partnership of *Roe v. Wade* and *Harris v. McRae*, the actual law of abortion in the United States under *Roe* is more aptly described as the *Roe v. Wade–Harris v. McRae* compromise. That compromise made abortion access dependent on personal privacy, which was unavailable to women in poverty.

For this reason, some feminist scholars have been ambivalent about the full effects of *Roe* on the feminist legal landscape. Robin West suggested that *Roe*'s negative right to abortion promoted an antigovernmental stance in matters of childbearing and child-rearing.[14] Critical race feminists, most notably Dorothy Roberts, argued that the pro-choice focus on the negative right to abortion eclipsed the broader principles of reproductive justice in which Black women have more at stake: "Reproductive justice includes the right to have a child, under conditions desired by the one giving birth, the right not to have a child and the right to parent any children one has in a healthy, safe, and supportive environment."[15] Poor Black women's choices are "limited not only by the denial of access to safe abortions, but also by the lack of resources necessary for a healthy pregnancy and parenting relationship."[16] Khiara Bridges argued that courts have rarely relied on the constitutional right to privacy to protect the interests of poor women and women of color who must turn to government for assistance.[17] By keeping government out of pregnancy and parenthood, *Roe* also erected a barrier to government support for the reproductive lives of poor women, whether they chose to bear children or not.

The *Roe v. Wade–Harris v. McRae* compromise that defined pro-choice law in the United States protected the broadest negative right to abortion by comparison to peer liberal constitutional democracies, and the narrowest positive right to abortion as compared to those peer nations. *Harris v. McRae* held that the state had no duty to help pregnant women implement their choice about procreation, whether they wanted to terminate their pregnancies or continue them. Likewise, the right to choose to bear a child championed by the Supreme Court in *Cleveland Board of Education v. LaFleur* in no way entails a constitutional right to state support for childbirth or maternity. The solution to the unconstitutionality of mandatory unpaid maternity leave was to enjoin the policy, which would permit pregnant teachers to work longer. A constitutional right by pregnant teachers to be paid their full salaries while on mandatory maternity leave was not demanded or contemplated as a remedy in those proceedings.

Shortly thereafter, the Supreme Court rejected other efforts by pregnant women to establish a right to paid maternity leave in public law. In *Geduldig v. Aiello*, litigants who had been pregnant and/or had recently given birth challenged a state disability benefits scheme that authorized paid leave for every work-disabling condition except for normal pregnancy and childbirth. The Supreme Court upheld the policy over a constitutional challenge alleging that the denial of these paid statutory benefits in the event of a normal pregnancy and childbirth violated the Equal

Protection Clause.[18] The decision was authored by Justice Stewart,[19] whose *Roe* concurrence and *LaFleur* majority opinion treated childbearing and child-rearing as so intimate and personal as to render state involvement improper.

This dark side of *Roe*—namely *Harris v. McRae*'s validation of the government's abandonment of the reproductive health needs of the poorest pregnant Americans—is consistent with the Supreme Court's overall understanding of the life, liberty, and property protected by the Due Process Clause. In *DeShaney v. Winnebago County Department of Social Services*, the US Supreme Court said that the state did not violate the Constitution when it failed to protect a young boy from severe, violent physical abuse at the hands of his own father, resulting over time in the boy's permanent brain damage. The Fourteenth Amendment guarantee of life, liberty, and property forbids *the state* from itself attacking any person's life, liberty, or property, but it does not "impose an affirmative obligation on the State to ensure that those interests do not come to harm through other means."[20]

The overwhelming burdens of pregnancy, particularly for poor or unmarried women, have not escaped the Supreme Court's notice in the abortion cases. Justice Blackmun's opinion for the court in *Roe* justified the privacy right as an extension of medical privacy particularly when the pregnancy threatens to cause economic ruin or social stigma: "Maternity, or additional offspring, may force upon the woman a distressful life and future. Psychological harm may be imminent. Mental and physical health may be taxed by child care. . . . All these are factors the woman and her responsible physician necessarily will consider in consultation."[21]

Twenty years later, when the Supreme Court reaffirmed *Roe*'s right to terminate a pregnancy before viability in *Planned Parenthood v. Casey*, it acknowledged a stronger state interest in reproduction than it had in *Roe*.[22] Instead of saying, as *Roe* appeared to, that all state involvement in the first trimester was unconstitutional, *Casey* permitted the state to attempt to persuade the pregnant woman to continue the pregnancy, in recognition of the state's interest in protecting unborn life. But regulations that were efforts to persuade could not impose an undue burden on the woman's choice to terminate a pregnancy.

The joint opinion for the court by Justices O'Connor, Kennedy, and Souter concluded that women would be unduly burdened by a law requir-

ing spousal notification before an abortion.[23] It recognized the disproportionate sacrifices women sustain in pregnancy, which affect women's prospects for a decent life: "The mother who carries the child to full term is
subject to anxieties, to physical constraints, to pain that only she must
bear."[24] The court further acknowledged an evolution in attitudes about
whether the sacrifices women make when they become mothers can be
reasonably imposed by the state: "That these sacrifices have from the
beginning of the human race been endured by woman with a pride that
ennobles her in the eyes of others and gives to the infant a bond of love
cannot alone be grounds for the State to insist she make the sacrifice."[25]
Without moving the analysis into the Equal Protection Clause, the court
gestured at the impermissibility of stereotyped visions of the woman's
natural role: "Her suffering is too intimate and personal for the State to
insist, without more, upon its own vision for the woman's role, however
dominant that vision has been in the course of our history and our
culture."[26]

The court suggested that, by its very nature, pregnancy involves enough
risk, forbearance, pain, sacrifice, and suffering that the state cannot force
a woman to continue it. Justice Blackmun, reprising his remarks in *Roe*
about the distressful life that motherhood or additional children may
force upon a woman, explicitly pointed out that women were uncompensated for their conscription into unwanted motherhood: "By restricting
the right to terminate pregnancies, the State *conscripts* women's bodies
into its service, forcing women to continue their pregnancies, suffer the
pains of childbirth, and in most instances, provide years of maternal care.
*The State does not compensate women for their services; instead, it assumes
that they owe this duty as a matter of course.*"[27]

In other words, the state occupies the woman's body for its own benefit—without paying for it. But what if the state did compensate women for
their conscripted services, in the same way that the state pays people for
jury duty and military service? Would that make legally compelled motherhood (with pay) the moral equivalent of compulsory (but compensated)
military conscription? Justice Blackmun wrote, "The assumption—that
women can simply be forced to accept the 'natural' status and incidents of
motherhood—appears to rest upon a conception of women's role that has
triggered the protection of the Equal Protection Clause."[28]

When there is an extensive and humane governmental infrastructure of compensation and support for mothers and children, analogous to what veterans and military draftees receive, the government's regulation of abortion need not produce a dystopia any worse than the one produced in America by the *Roe v. Wade–Harris v. McRae* compromise. A society that supports mothers—while also endeavoring to protect unborn life and reduce the demand for abortion—may be an improvement over a society in which the government stays out of childbearing and child-rearing altogether, doing little to reduce high maternal mortality rates, especially among Black women, and tolerating high levels of economic insecurity for mothers. How would a hypothetical world of compelled-but-compensated motherhood compare to a world where the state does not interfere with abortion on demand but does not pay for permitted abortions and also refuses to provide or compel the provision of health insurance to cover contraceptives, maternity care, paid maternity leave, paid parental leave for men to relieve women of caregiving, state-funded childcare before children reach school age, pregnancy accommodations for safety on the job, or tuition- and debt-free higher education? Is it obvious that the latter option is superior to the first? And are any of these other policies that affect the attractiveness of bearing and raising children relevant to the law of abortion?

Of course, no two societies correspond precisely to either of these two extremes. Under *Roe*, most of the United States came close to option 2. Then, in *Dobbs v. Jackson Women's Health Organization*, the Supreme Court thoroughly rejected *Roe*'s privacy-based right to abortion, because neither abortion nor privacy were in the Constitution's text. The *Dobbs* majority insisted that the Constitution protected only liberties that were firmly rooted in the history and tradition of the nation, and it found the privacy right protected by *Roe* to be incoherent and insufficient to support the right to abortion.[29] After *Dobbs*, many women in America live under a third legal regime that is obviously worse than the first two: motherhood that is both compelled *and* uncompensated. With *Roe* no longer the law of the land, and with a Supreme Court that is thoroughly skeptical of *Roe*'s idea of privacy, advocates for women and girls must confront the serious, if awkward question: Could compelled and *compensated* motherhood also be an improvement over the *Roe v. Wade–Harris v. McRae* compromise, namely uncompelled motherhood that is uncompensated, severely unsupported, and neglected by public policy? This question puts the spotlight on what's really wrong with restricting abortion, beyond its intrusion on personal privacy. Abortion bans misapprehend the state's role in setting the conditions under which women choose whether and how to bear and raise children, and the state's duty, after the repeal of patriarchal law, to secure women's equal status as persons and citizens. Reva Siegel has questioned whether governments that purport to be pro-life deserve the label when they restrict abortion while doing nothing to help women bring a wanted pregnancy to term.[30] After the demise of *Roe*, the battle against misogyny should not resurrect privacy rights in pregnancy but rather pursue laws that fully recognize the public value of the sacrifices pregnant women endure for the benefit of others.

There is much to learn from the growing list of countries around the world, beginning with Germany and Ireland, that now provide public funding for most abortions, essentially on demand in the first trimester, after committing to protecting unborn life in the era of *Roe v. Wade*. Contemporaneous with *Roe*, the German Constitutional Court vehemently rejected abortion on demand in the first trimester, citing the state's positive duty to protect life. The Irish Parliament and voters adopted a constitutional amendment in 1983 protecting unborn life. But both of these legal orders moved gradually toward protecting women's choice to terminate pregnancies, while also easing the burdens of motherhood to protect life, unborn and born. How did pro-choice legal frameworks grow out of pro-life constitutional foundations?

THE EXACTABLE BURDENS OF MOTHERHOOD IN GERMANY

Both German and Irish constitutional law enforced a positive state duty to protect unborn life when the US Supreme Court decided *Roe v. Wade*. Initially, the German Constitutional Court rejected first-trimester abortion on demand as an affront to the state's duty to protect life. Yet in so doing, the German Constitutional Court articulated a robust conception of the state's positive duties, not only to the unborn fetus, but to women facing unwanted pregnancies. That reasoning—in the dicta of the court's abortion decisions—was central to the statutory frameworks that opened up abortion access, adopted by the legislature in dialogue with the Constitutional Court.

The Constitutional Duty to Protect Unborn Life

In 1974, the West German legislature adopted a new law to permit abortions. The law made it legal for women to obtain abortions, essentially on demand, in the first trimester. The Federal Constitutional Court of West Germany struck down this law, declaring it insufficiently respectful of human life.[31] In its 1975 decision, the court rejected the new law liberalizing abortion access, pointing to the state's constitutional duty to protect human life under Articles 2.2 and 1.1 of the Basic Law. Article 2.2 guarantees the right to life and physical integrity; Article 1.1 declares "human dignity" to be inviolable and imposes a duty of the state to protect it. By allowing *all* abortions up until the thirteenth week of pregnancy, as though all of them were purely private decisions immune from state intervention, the Constitutional Court found that the state had neglected its constitutional duty to protect life and dignity. The court acknowledged, however, that the legislature adopting abortion laws had the duty to protect the unborn life while simultaneously respecting the pregnant woman's constitutional rights. Every person has "the right to free development of their personality insofar as he does not violate the rights of others or offend against the constitutional order or the moral law." Therefore, there would be situations where the "right to life of the unborn can lead to a burdening of the woman which essentially goes beyond that normally associated with pregnancy."[32]

The Constitutional Court acknowledged that abortion should be permitted when the burden of a pregnancy on the woman would be too great. But which burdens are "normally" associated with pregnancy and which go beyond? Abortions necessary to save a pregnant woman's life were clearly permitted.[33] Going further, the court framed the question through the concept of "exactability":[34] How much can a state burden an individual woman to fulfill its own constitutional duty to protect unborn life? Even when there was no risk to the woman's life, the court acknowledged that "the general social situation of the pregnant woman and her family can produce conflicts of such difficulty that, beyond a definite measure, a sacrifice by the pregnant woman in favor of the unborn life cannot be compelled with the means of the penal law."[35] While recognizing the possibility that such abortions should not be criminally punishable, the court rejected the 1974 statute because it was overinclusive. By allowing abortion simply at the woman's choice, it theoretically authorized additional abortions beyond these situations of "non-exactable" pregnancies. But the law could only legitimize abortions that were justified by a "reason worthy of esteem within the value order of the German Constitution."[36] A woman suffering from "material distress" or "a grave situation of emotional conflict" could be excused from criminal liability, for instance.[37] Furthermore, the state was obligated, "especially in cases of social need—to support her through practical measures of assistance."[38]

After the 1975 decision, the West German legislature drew up a new statute. Taking the Constitutional Court's concerns seriously, the new law in 1976 recriminalized abortion, except when a doctor separate from the one performing the abortion issued a nonbinding opinion certifying that the pregnancy posed a serious danger to the life or physical or mental health of the pregnant woman, which could not be averted by other means that the woman could reasonably be expected to bear.[39] The statute directed the doctor to consider the "present and future living conditions" of the woman in making this judgment.[40] The law required counseling specifically about the social services available to the woman should she decide to continue the pregnancy.

Although the new law was more restrictive on paper than the law that the Constitutional Court had struck down, it was, in practice, not a far cry from abortion on demand. The new law permitted abortions in most of the circumstances that led pregnant women to demand abortions and created a procedural framework for obtaining legal abortion.[41] While abortions were still criminalized, the law defined several defenses or exceptions to criminal liability and authorized doctors, rather than courts, to use medical judgment to determine whether an abortion came within one of the exceptions. The new statute was similar to *Roe v. Wade* in its legal protection of doctors' judgments about whether an abortion was indicated. It identified the following situations under which doctors could legally authorize abortions:

1. there are strong reasons to suggest that, as a result of a genetic trait or harmful influence prior to birth, the child would suffer from an incurable injury to its health which is so serious that the pregnant woman cannot be required to continue the pregnancy;

2. an unlawful act under Articles 176 to 179 [criminal rape statutes] has been committed on the pregnant woman and there are strong reasons to suggest that the pregnancy is a result of that offence; or

3. the termination of the pregnancy is otherwise advisable in order to avert the danger of a distress which

  (a) is so serious that the pregnant woman cannot be required to continue the pregnancy, and

  (b) cannot be averted in any other way she can reasonably be expected to bear.[42]

These three categories operated in addition to the statute's authorization of legal abortion to avert a serious danger to the woman's mental or physical health in light of her present and future living conditions.

As long as two doctors certified one of the indications following the specific procedural steps prescribed, neither the doctors nor abortion patients were subject to criminal punishment. The law required one doctor to recommend the abortion, and another doctor could then perform the procedure. In practice, this new law greatly expanded access to abortion, while remaining consistent with the 1975 Constitutional Court decision clarifying the state's duty to protect unborn life. Doctors certified abortions upon determining that the physical, psychological, social, or economic burdens of pregnancy and motherhood would be unreasonably excessive for the woman in individual cases. The situations of anxiety, risk to life, economic stress, and stigma explicitly contemplated by Justice Blackmun in *Roe* and the joint opinion in *Casey* could easily give rise to legal abortions under the German statute. Studying the data on medical certifications for abortions, one German commentator observed that "almost every pregnant woman could obtain an indication if she did so with determination."[43] In short, an abortion law that was much more restrictive than *Roe* on paper provided comparably liberal access to abortion on the ground.

Even under a constitutional jurisprudence that emphatically rejected abortion on demand in the first trimester, the regime implemented by the legislature (and not reviewed or struck down by the court) resulted in 146 abortions for every 1,000 live births in 1982.[44] In the United States in

2019, there were 225 abortions per 1,000 live births,[45] under a constitutional jurisprudence that recognizes a negative right to abortion on demand before viability. A democratically elected legislature produced a pro-choice abortion law while respecting rather than defying the pro-life principles enforced by the countermajoritarian Constitutional Court. A synthesis of pro-choice and pro-life emerged from a dialogical process of democratic constitutionalism, where both institutions tried to pursue the state's legitimate interest and duties with regard to human reproduction.

Protecting Life by Supporting Mothers and Gender Equality

After the fall of the Berlin Wall in 1989, German reunification posed a new challenge for the law of abortion. During communism, East Germany had permitted abortions on demand in the first trimester, whereas West Germany from 1976 onward had permitted only those indicated by doctors for the reasons specified in the criminal code. In 1992, the reunified German legislature adopted a new law, the Pregnancy and Family Assistance Act,[46] that permitted abortions in the first trimester as long as the pregnant woman self-certified that the pregnancy caused distress to her. In 1993, a year after *Casey*, the Constitutional Court of the unified Germany struck the new law down,[47] viewing it as essentially abortion on demand. The Constitutional Court reiterated the reasoning from the 1975 West German Constitutional Court decision. This time, though, the Constitutional Court explicitly held that even if unjustified first-trimester abortions had to remain "unlawful," the German Basic Law did not require the legislature to *criminalize* unlawful abortions. It specified that any counseling requirement had to go beyond providing information to the pregnant woman; it had to encourage her to continue the pregnancy, by emphasizing the availability of state support for pregnant women and mothers.

But this time, the German Constitutional Court gave new meaning to the state's duty to protect life by linking it to both Article 6.4 of the Basic Law—the constitutional entitlement of mothers to the special protection and care of the community—and Article 3.2 of the Basic Law—the constitutional guarantee of "equal rights between men and women." The Constitutional Court wrote, "The state does not satisfy its obligation to protect unborn human life simply by hindering life-threatening attacks by third parties. It must also confront the dangers attached to the existing and foreseeable living conditions of the woman and family which could destroy the woman's willingness to carry the child to term."[48] The state had a duty under Article 6.4 to "attend to the problems and difficulties, which the mother could encounter during the pregnancy."[49] The government could fulfill its constitutional duty to care for mothers by "viewing motherhood and childcare as work, which lies in the interests of community and is deserving of its recognition."[50] The court continued:

> The care owed to the mother by the community includes an obligation on the part of the state to ensure that a pregnancy is not terminated because of existing material hardship or material hardship expected to occur after the birth. Similarly, if at all possible, disadvantages for the woman in her vocational training or work resulting from a pregnancy ought to be removed. In fulfillment of its obligation to protect unborn human life, the state must attend to problems likely to cause a pregnant woman or mother difficulty, and try, to the extent legally and realistically possible and justifiable, to alleviate or solve those problems.[51]

It is noteworthy that the court here referred to "parents," not only "mothers," recognizing that "parents who raise children are performing tasks whose fulfillment lies in the interests of the community as a whole."[52] Therefore, the duty to protect life meant that "the state is bound to promote a child-friendly society" in all areas of law and public policy, including housing, work and vocational training for mothers, labor law, and other areas of private law.[53] The court specifically mentioned a law prohibiting landlords from terminating a lease because of the birth of a child. The duty to protect unborn life also entailed laws "which make it possible or easier for parents to meet their financial obligations following the birth of a child."[54] This might involve, for instance, paid parental leave, as well as access to consumer loans.

The Constitutional Court explicitly pointed to the relevance of Article 3.2 of the Basic Law, guaranteeing equal rights between men and women:

> The obligations to protect unborn life, marriage and the family and to ensure equal rights for men and women in the workplace compel the state and especially the legislature to lay the right foundations so that family life

and work can be made compatible and so that childraising does not lead to disadvantages in the workplace. To achieve this it is necessary for the legislature to invoke legal and practical measures which allow both parents to combine childraising and work as well as to return to work and progress at work after taking a break from work for childraising purposes.[55]

The Constitutional Court recognized that the state could protect the unborn by equalizing the burdens between mothers and fathers and by providing child-raising benefits and paid child-raising breaks. Put slightly differently, there are many ways that a state can be pro-life, including by investing in a "child-friendly society." The court recognized the value of childcare and suggested that the state must compensate it: "Furthermore, the state must ensure that a parent, who gives up work to devote herself or himself to raising a child, be adequately compensated for any resulting financial disadvantages."[56] It is fascinating to see how a judicial opinion hostile to abortion (like *Dobbs*) ends up essentially requiring the state to provide paid parental leave for both fathers and mothers, as part of the "right foundations" to make work and family compatible (very unlike *Dobbs*).

This progression is the logical conclusion after a thorough grappling with effective and ineffective ways of protecting unborn life, confronting ample historical evidence of the counterproductiveness of criminalizing abortion: "However, the further third persons intrude into a woman's personal sphere, the greater the danger that she will seek to avoid this by inventing reasons for wishing to terminate or by resorting to the illegal. If this happens, any chance of using understanding and professional counseling to explore her conflict and to help her decide in favor of the child is lost straightaway."[57] Understanding the dilemma from the woman's perspective, the court determined that "effective protection of unborn human life is only possible *with* the support of the mother."[58] The threat of criminal sanctions was futile as a means of persuading the woman to keep the baby. "A threat of criminal sanctions is of little effect at this point so that it is obvious that the law must use preventative means to help her overcome her conflict and meet her responsibility to the unborn."[59]

The court recognized the costs that women bear for the socially valuable process of reproduction. The court's 1975 discussion of "exactability" had initiated this framing. By 1993, there was a clearer acknowledgment of a limit to how much of one's own life and freedom the state could reasonably expect a woman to give to others, particularly when a woman's circumstances left her with very little to give. While the court assumed in 1975 that it was reasonable to expect pregnant women to bear the "normal" burdens of motherhood, by 1993 it acknowledged that even normal motherhood exacts heavy burdens unless the state intervenes to promote a "child-friendly society."

For all the rhetoric of abortion "on demand" in the political arena, most women who seek abortion in the United States are not making an ordinary choice; they are making a difficult choice that can be tragic. They are trying to avoid the real and often life-altering (if not life-ruining or life-threatening) personal costs of continuing a pregnancy, when their life circumstances make those costs too much for them to bear. Many cannot afford to stay pregnant as a financial matter. American women may lack health insurance to cover the costs of prenatal care and childbirth. Because pregnancy often interferes with a woman's education, work, or ability to care for dependents, staying pregnant also imposes long-term financial costs that women absorb.[60] Even in the course of rejecting a pro-choice statute that permitted abortion on demand, the German Constitutional Court articulated two important arguments for supporting women's choice to terminate in most actual circumstances that motivate women to choose abortion: first, that pregnancy and motherhood are burdens that women sustain to the benefit of society; and second, that if the woman carries a fetus to term, the state has a duty to minimize or compensate women's losses in absorbing these publicly beneficial costs. The court recognized the benefits to the community when women sacrifice their careers to raise children—what the 1975 court might have called "normal" motherhood. In 1993, the court recognized the state's duty to ease even these "normal" burdens of motherhood when it exacted a pregnancy from a woman. To persuade women to stay pregnant, the state, at the very least, had to make sure they got paid. To protect fetuses as well as born children, common sense points to protecting women's job security and/or compensating those whose childbearing and child-rearing prevent them from working to subsist economically.

What the German Constitutional Court embraced, which US courts have shunned, is the public dimension of pregnancy and parenthood.

Childbearing and child-rearing involve other people, the society, and the state. Whether the state provides maternity health care, paid leave, day care, quality education, and after-school programs is as relevant as whether the state allows abortions or funds abortions to any person's decision about whether to bear or beget a child. The decision is shaped by the relationship of a person to the community and the state, and whether the state is fulfilling its responsibilities to the persons who do necessary work to perpetuate the community and to empower the state to further its goals. Therefore, criminalizing abortion is not the only—or best—indicator of whether a legal order is "pro-life." Maternity health care, paid leave, day care, pregnancy accommodations on the job, education, and after-school programs are stronger indicators of a pro-life legal order that supports the likelihood of transforming unborn life into born life as well as the life of the born.

While both the 1975 and 1993 decisions rejected abortion on demand, the reasoning made clear that even a pro-life state must permit some abortions, not because childbearing is a private act (as *Roe* maintains) but because childbearing is a public act. Continuing a pregnancy is the burdensome work necessary to transform the unborn fetus into a born child, and only the pregnant person can do it. If the state proclaims an interest in transforming unborn lives into born children, the state has duties to the person who makes that process possible and carries it out. The state must ensure that mothers' lives are not diminished by that process, namely pregnancy and parenthood. In some situations, permitting abortion may be the only way for the state to fulfill its duty. But the state's duty to allow abortions is only one of many duties that the state has in this bundle of duties related to human reproduction, and perhaps not the most significant one.

After the German court articulated anew in 1993 what the constitution required of the state, the legislature responded. In the following years, the legislature took actions, not only to comply with the court's ruling with regard to abortion law, but to realize the constitutional values expounded in the court's decision in other areas of law. First, the legislature adopted a constitutional amendment building on Article 3.2. on the equal rights of men and women, referenced by the court in its abortion discussion. In 1994, a constitutional amendment to that provision added a sentence establishing the state's positive duties with regard to gender equality. Whereas Article 3.2 had previously only guaranteed "equal rights between men and women," and Article 3.3 had prohibited discrimination on grounds of sex, the 1994 amendment added, "The state shall promote the actual implementation of equal rights between women and men and eradicate disadvantages that now exist."[61]

When the German legislature rewrote the abortion law to comply with the Constitutional Court's 1993 ruling, it provided that abortions performed in the first twelve weeks, though "unlawful" in the Criminal Code, would not be criminally punishable. Health insurance would pay only for abortions whose lawfulness could be established. "Lawful" abortions would include those performed for medical reasons, including a serious risk to the pregnant woman's life or health (including mental health and suicide risks), or for embryopathic or criminal reasons.[62] Because the law since 1976 directed doctors to consider the woman's present and future living conditions in certifying legal abortions, social insurance continued to pay for all poor women's abortions, even if their "lawfulness" could not be established.[63] But for those with means, health insurance would cover only "lawful" abortions, namely those performed for medical reasons or for pregnancies resulting from rape. The statute adopted in 1995 requires pregnant women to talk to a counselor and give reasons for having the abortion before it can be performed.[64] The practical reality, as was the case under the 1976 law, is that women can get certifications for "lawful" abortions, paid for by public health insurance, as long as they are willing to tell the state why they are getting the abortion, and most women who seek abortions can plausibly invoke one of the reasons indicated by the law. Otherwise, women have the option of an "unlawful" but not punishable abortion on demand after counseling in the first trimester, albeit unfunded. In reality, over 80 percent of the abortions that take place in Germany are publicly funded.[65]

Furthermore, subsequent legislation expanded paid parental leave for both mothers and fathers, with an eye to policy features designed to encourage fathers to take more leave than they had taken in the past.[66] Both the legislature and the Constitutional Court acknowledged that the take-up of parental leave by fathers directly affects mothers' ability to pursue employment opportunities.[67] The development of German abortion law illustrates (1) that the regulation of abortion is deeply intertwined with the state's orientation toward the full range of reproductive activities, from begetting and bearing a child to birthing and raising one; (2) the state is responsible for the way socially beneficial reproduction affects the mother's prospects for leading a decent life; and (3) how the state implements these constitutional values is a matter for democratically elected lawmaking branches, guided by the judicial elaboration of constitutional principles.

FATAL PREGNANCIES AND CONSTITUTIONAL CHANGE IN IRELAND

The evolution of Irish abortion law showcases an additional path to constitutional change, one involving dialogue between courts (both supranational and national), the legislature, and the people themselves. In Ireland, the emergence of pro-choice policy in a predominantly Catholic pro-life nation occurred through a democratic, public, and transparent process of constitutional amendment. Popular mobilization around the public specter of women facing life-threatening pregnancies facilitated agreement between pro-life and pro-choice perspectives. These processes led to significant changes in constitutional abortion law, including constitutional amendments.

The Eighth Amendment and the Death of a Cancer Patient

A constitutional duty to protect unborn life was added to the Irish Constitution in 1983, largely because pro-life groups sought to stop the spread of *Roe v. Wade* and similar protections for abortion rights in Europe into Irish law.[68] Fear of *Roe* led to the proposal of a constitutional amendment that would have clarified and protected the power of legislatures to prohibit abortion.[69] As it was introduced, a woman named Sheila Hodgers died of breast cancer, shortly after giving birth to a baby.[70] During her pregnancy, she was denied cancer medications because of their potential harmful effects on the fetus. Doctors refused to deliver the fetus early to allow her to be treated for cancer because such a premature delivery could result in the death of the fetus and thus amount to a criminally punishable abortion. Three days after delivering a baby in March 1983, Hodgers died. Hodgers's tragic death shaped the parliamentary debate about the wording of a proposed abortion amendment the following month.

When the Dáil Éireann debated the proposed Eighth Amendment, there was a split on whether its wording should simply stop courts from invalidating abortion laws, should explicitly protect the rights to life of the unborn and of the mother, or should speak explicitly to the legality of abortion when the life of the mother was endangered. One wording read, "Nothing in this Constitution shall be invoked to invalidate, or to deprive of force or effect, any provision of a law on the ground that it prohibits abortion." But the wording that prevailed and was ultimately added to the Constitution was "The State acknowledges the right to life of the unborn and, with due regard to the equal right to life of the mother, guarantees in its laws to respect, and, as far as practicable, by its laws to defend and vindicate that right."[71] The justice minister noted, "Deputies are, of course, by now well aware of what has been in the public press" and expressed concern that the "equal" right to life of the mother would not make clear enough the long-standing legality of abortion to save a pregnant woman's life.[72] But supporters of the "right to life of the unborn" and "equal right to life of the mother" language cited the West German Constitutional Court's 1975 decision and provided the following reassurance: "The Constitution supports the concept that a mother in a life-threatening position must be given the medical treatment required. A mother will continue to have a constitutional right to life and if her life is threatened by illness she is constitutionally entitled to appropriate medical treatment, even if such treatment would result in the termination of her pregnancy."[73]

The Irish people approved the Eighth Amendment of the Irish Constitution by 67 percent of the vote in September 1983. In light of Hodgers's highly publicized death in March, it is doubtful as to whether the Eighth Amendment would been adopted by Parliament or approved by the people if the language protecting "the equal right to life of the mother" was understood to prohibit life-saving abortions. While the proposition that the mother's right to life should be "equal" to that of an unborn fetus raised doubts about whether pregnant women's lives would be prioritized in real situations of conflict, courts used that language to crack open the path to abortion legalization in Ireland, including the eventual repeal of the Eighth Amendment itself.

Legalizing Abortions to Avert Suicide Risks

In 1992, the Irish Supreme Court interpreted the constitutional protection of the "equal right to life of the mother" to legalize abortion for a pregnant girl facing the risk of suicide. A fourteen-year-old girl had been raped by an older man, and her parents intended to travel with her to Britain, where legal abortions were available. Irish law enforcement attempted to stop them, citing the constitutional ban on abortion and insisting that European law did not entitle Irish citizens to travel to other member-states of the European Community for abortions. But the Irish Supreme Court decided the case solely on the basis of Irish constitutional law, taking no position on European law. In *Attorney General v. X*, the Irish Supreme Court concluded that the pregnancy of the fourteen-year-old rape victim posed a danger to her life because the evidence established a credible threat of suicide.[74] The Eighth Amendment, namely Article 40.3.3 of the Irish Constitution, required "due regard for the equal rights of the life of the mother" and therefore authorized legal abortion in Ireland in the circumstances presented.[75]

Faced in the *X* case with a fourteen-year-old girl who had been raped, public sentiment shifted to support a relaxation of the Constitution's rigid ban on abortions. Shortly after the Supreme Court's decision, Parliament sent three proposed constitutional amendments to the people in a referendum.[76] In December 1992, the people chose to amend Article 40.3.3. with two of these three provisions, moving toward liberalization of abortion access. The Thirteenth Amendment provided that the right to life of the unborn would not prevent travel from Ireland to another state to obtain an abortion. The Fourteenth Amendment provided that the right to life of the unborn would not prevent the dissemination of information about abortion. These amendments made clear that Irish citizens would suffer no legal sanctions for traveling to obtain abortions, for whatever reason, and that the law would protect their access to information about their abortion care abroad. A third amendment seeking to roll back abortion access was proposed, but it failed. The failed amendment sought to limit abortions only to situations where the pregnant woman's life, rather than health, was at risk, with language explicitly excluding suicide risks from this exception. Sixty-five percent of the voters rejected the suicide amendment, whereas similar percentages approved the travel and information amendments.[77] In 2002, another referendum was held to revisit the question of whether suicide risk should be excluded from the risks to life justifying legal abortions.[78] The Irish voters rejected that proposed amendment yet again, making it clear that they supported the lawfulness of abortion when pregnancy posed serious mental health risks.

In 2010, the life-threatening situation of a pregnant cancer patient again nudged Ireland to reform its abortion law in the direction of establishing the legality of abortions in an expanding range of circumstances. In *A, B, and C v. Ireland,* the European Court of Human Rights upheld the Irish Eighth Amendment, as well as the provisions protecting travel and information,[79] declining to recognize a privacy-based human right to abortion. At the same time, the European Court weakened the Irish Constitution's abortion ban by ruling that Ireland had failed to adopt a clear legal framework to protect the right to life of the mother when it was threatened by a pregnancy. The cancer patient, Claimant C, had become pregnant while undergoing cancer treatment and had sought an abortion because of the potentially life-threatening risks of continuing a pregnancy during chemotherapy. *A, B, & C v. Ireland* held that Ireland violated the European Convention on Human Rights by not providing a legal framework for determining when a risk to the mother's life warranted a lawful abortion. Claimant C and her doctors were entitled to a procedure by which they could be immunized from prosecution upon concluding that the abortion was necessary to save her life, which Irish law did not then provide.

Savita Halappanavar and the Deadliness of Legal Ambiguity

The absence of such a procedure proved deadly shortly thereafter. A woman died under circumstances where an abortion might have saved her life, because doctors were too afraid to proceed. Savita Halappanavar was seventeen weeks pregnant, carrying a baby she wanted to have, when she went to a hospital in Galway with back pain. She was having a miscarriage, and although her water broke, her body did not expel or deliver the fetus. After doctors detected fetal cardiac activity, they feared that removing the fetus would expose them to criminal prosecution and therefore decided not to accelerate the miscarriage or abort the fetus. Meanwhile, Halappanavar developed sepsis, an infection of tissue that her body did not expel quickly enough during the miscarriage. The infection caused her to have a heart attack, which killed her at the age of thirty-one.[80]

Halappanavar's death exposed the stark practical reality of banning abortions. Even with a constitutionally articulated exception for risks to the mother's life, the Irish abortion ban caused the deaths of pregnant women by chilling doctors from acting in real situations. In real life, seemingly unserious health risks escalate quickly to become life-threatening in a very short time span. Savita's story illustrated how murky the line often was between risks to the mother's life and risks to the mother's physical and mental health. Doctors often make predictions and judgments in rapidly changing medical circumstances. A law that simply allowed abortions to avert life-threatening risks caused doctors to fear prosecution for performing life-saving abortions. If an abortion had prevented Halappanavar from developing sepsis, enabling her survival, for instance, a prosecutor could argue in retrospect that she'd had no life-threatening condition justifying the abortion.

Within less than a year of Halappanavar's death, the Irish Oireachtas (parliament) enacted the Protection of Life During Pregnancy Act of 2013,[81] which finally implemented the European Court of Human Rights' ruling in the *A, B, & C* case. It created a legal framework that made it clear when an abortion to save the life of the pregnant woman would be legal. Abortions would not be prosecuted if two doctors agreed that there was a risk of death from physical illness, but in emergency situations one doctor was authorized to make the decision. In cases of risk to life by suicide, three doctors' assent was required, including a psychiatrist specializing in maternity and a psychiatrist treating the pregnant woman requesting the abortion.

Furthermore, Halappanavar's death occurred in the midst of a pivotal moment of innovation in Irish constitutionalism. In July 2012, the Oireachtas had established the Convention on the Constitution,[82] a body consisting of thirty-three members of the Oireachtas and sixty-six randomly selected citizens from electoral lists, representing a spread of age, gender, socioeconomic status, working status, and region.[83] The Convention was charged with deliberating on eight topics that were ripe for constitutional reform to make recommendations to the Oireachtas. Several of these topics were issues directly bearing on gender equality: same-sex marriage, the constitutional clause recognizing the role of women in the home, the participation of women in public life, and increasing the participation of women in politics.[84] The Convention produced reports making recommendations to the Oireachtas, which then used them as the basis for constitutional amendment proposals that went to referendum by the people. Through this process, a constitutional amendment recognizing marriage equality for same-sex couples was proposed,[85] and was ultimately approved in a 2015 referendum.

The Citizens' Assembly on the Eighth Amendment

With the success of the Convention on the Constitution, the Oireachtas next voted to establish a Citizens' Assembly in 2016 to 2018 to deliberate on additional constitutional reform proposals, including reform of the Eighth Amendment and climate change.[86] Composed similarly to the previous Convention on the Constitution, and chaired by Justice Mary Laffoy, a former justice of the Irish Supreme Court, the Citizens' Assembly met over five weekends throughout 2017 to discuss constitutional reform on abortion.[87] There was an expert committee of law professors, political scientists, doctors, and social workers who distributed papers written by themselves and other experts throughout the nation.[88] Experts were invited to speak on panels to the assembly. Small-group discussions centered on whether the Eighth Amendment should simply be repealed or whether it should be replaced. If the latter, one option would be to simply authorize the Oireachtas to legislate to protect unborn life and the conditions and procedures under which pregnancies could be terminated. Another option would be to establish a constitutional right to abortion, as Roe did in the United States.

The Citizens' Assembly spent many weekends considering the circumstances under which abortions should be legalized, with debates around whether to distinguish between risks to life and risks to health, serious risks versus ordinary risks, physical health versus mental health, and whether it was meaningful to distinguish between abortions for socioeconomic reasons and abortions without regard to reasons. The assembly worked on draft ballots for the constitutional amendment referendum. Ultimately 87 percent of the Citizens' Assembly voted that the Eighth Amendment should not be retained in full, and 57 percent favored replacing it with a provision authorizing the legislature to address termination of pregnancy, including any rights of the unborn and any rights of the pregnant woman.[89]

The Citizens' Assembly heard recordings of interviews with six women whose lives had been affected by the Irish abortion ban, including women who had abortions abroad and women who continued their pregnancies. Two had wanted pregnancies but discovered in the course of the pregnancy that the fetus had abnormalities that would be fatal either in utero or shortly after birth. But the other four had unplanned pregnancies, and the stories illustrated socioeconomic effects that such situations could involve, often lasting a lifetime. Papers presented by the National Women's Council of Ireland, Parents for Choice, and the Coalition to Repeal the Eighth Amendment also included statistics and data about effects of pregnancy on low-income women and families and about the inadequacy of state support for parenthood.[90] Citing recent cuts to the lone parents' allowance in Ireland, data from the Organisation for Economic Co-operation and Development on childcare costs, inadequate supports for families with special-needs children, and maternal mortality in Ireland, the Parents for Choice paper argued, "This country forces us into parenthood and then not only lends no support but actively penalizes us when we're there."[91]

The assembly also deliberated on what should be included in abortion legislation. Strong majorities favored permitting abortion because of risks to the physical or mental health of the woman (79 and 78 percent respectively), as distinct from "real and substantial" or "serious" risks to life only. A strong majority (72 percent) also favored lawful abortions for "socioeconomic reasons."[92] And almost half (48 percent) recommended lawful termination of pregnancy without restriction as to reasons up to twelve weeks of gestation age.[93] These recommendations shaped the abortion bill that was publicized during the referendum campaign on the amendment to repeal the Eighth Amendment. The referendum succeeded by a vote of 66 percent.

Protecting Choice and Motherhood

Following the referendum on the constitutional amendment, the Oireachtas adopted a new abortion statute in 2018. It permits abortions, upon the choice of the pregnant woman, within the first twelve weeks, as long as a three-day waiting period is observed. Essentially, this is abortion on demand in the first trimester, without restriction as to reasons, with the procedural constraint of a waiting period. Legal abortions are fully covered and free of charge for medical card holders in Ireland's public health insurance scheme. Beyond the twelfth week of pregnancy, the law now permits abortions to save the woman's life or to avert serious health risks, mental and physical, following doctor decision-making procedures similar to those established by the 2013 law.

Within a generation, the constitutional law of abortion in Ireland changed dramatically through the dialogue of courts, both national and supranational, the legislature, citizens' assemblies, and the people through the constitutional amendment process. Pivotal steps from pro-life to pro-choice occurred at moments when the public was confronted with a pregnant woman or girl who was likely to die without an abortion, and some who actually did. Privacy—bodily, familial, or medical—was not what saved abortion access. Growing public concern and sympathy for what happened to these women and girls in private did.

In Ireland, the democratic and participatory process of constitutional change played an important role in bringing about the constitutional amendment that opened up access to abortion. In July 2019, the Oireachtas authorized a new Citizens' Assembly on gender equality. The Citizens' Assembly was asked to make proposals that might include policy, legislative, or constitutional change to challenge remaining barriers to gender equality; dismantling economic and salary norms that resulted in gender inequalities; reassessing economic value on work traditionally held by women; seeking women's full and effective participation in leadership and decision-making in the workplace, politics, and public life; recognizing the importance of parental care work; facilitating work-life balance; examining the social responsibility of care and men and women's co-responsibility for care, especially within the family; and abolishing structural pay inequalities.[94] I shall return to a discussion of the Citizens' Assembly on gender equality in chapter 6. The people-centered process of constitutional change in Ireland has highlighted the importance of publicly valuing care to avoid society's overentitlement to women's care work as mothers.[95] In the abortion context, recognizing the losses, risks to life, and inequalities that women sustain because of motherhood and caregiving is central to both the abortion amendment and the Citizens' Assembly's continuing deliberations on gender equality reforms.

RETHINKING MISOGYNY AND THE
LAWS OF REPRODUCTION

Current laws in both Germany and Ireland allow and fund many but not all abortions, rejecting the label and principle of "abortion on demand" because they still recognize the state's duty to protect unborn life. Both legal orders evolved to permit abortions in most reasonable circumstances without jettisoning pro-life commitments. They reached compromises between the absolute protection of unborn life and unfettered rights to abortion on demand that are in sharp contrast to the American compromise of *Roe v. Wade–Harris v. McRae*. The theory of the state underlying German and Irish abortion law is not "bans off our bodies" but rather the state's robust obligation to absorb the costs of reproducing the community. Banning abortion coerces pregnancy and birth and forces women to take on too much of those costs, particularly when the state fails to maintain optimal conditions for healthy and economically secure pregnancies.

Human reproduction—both biological and social—is one process to which women have historically contributed disproportionately compared to men. The joint opinion in *Casey* acknowledged this. Although it takes both a man and a woman to produce a pregnancy as a biological matter, only women can get pregnant. Only the pregnant person can turn an unborn fetus into a baby, and this biological process exacts a far higher price on her than anyone else. The highly publicized deaths of pregnant women in Ireland demonstrated that women do risk their lives and health when they continue a pregnancy and give birth. The process has sacrificed women's lives. Gestation, childbirth, and lactation also exact an economic price from women because they cannot work to the same extent during this process because of the physical toll that these functions take on women's bodies. When a woman continues a pregnancy, wanted or unwanted, she bears an unequal burden for a pregnancy that a man has played an equal part in begetting. When she gives birth to a human being, the child is not only her offspring but also that of a father. But most importantly, children are also future citizens of the society into which they are born, and contributors to the society's continued economic, social, and political survival. The father and the community get a new living member, but the mother has forgone opportunities while doing the most demanding and dangerous essential work to turn the unborn life into a born, live, productive person.

Allowing—and funding—abortion is one way that the state can fulfill its responsibility to the people who would otherwise shoulder the disproportionate costs of reproducing the community. But there are additional ways. The state can also ensure that pregnancy and motherhood do not ruin or diminish women's lives. Often, pregnancy and motherhood impose a lifetime of economic insecurity. Government can implement policies reducing maternal mortality, providing maternity care and paid maternity leave, ensuring that pregnant women and mothers are not deprived of economic opportunities, and providing childcare and education. Enabling mothers to live a decent life with economic security inures to the benefit of the child, both in utero and after birth. The state's duties stem from the benefits the society derives from women staying pregnant and becoming mothers. Failure in these duties is failure to properly value these public benefits flowing from women's sacrifices.

The concepts of overentitlement and unjust enrichment bring the problem into sharper focus, as society is made richer by women's losses and sacrifices in pregnancy and motherhood. The costs borne by women enable the society to perpetuate itself across generations, and there are gains to planning for the multigenerational flourishing of economies, polities, and nations. But instead of treating society's gains at women's disproportionate expense as an injustice to be corrected under the logic of unjust enrichment, some laws treat the dynamic as the normal set of baseline entitlements, what Justice Blackmun referred to in his *Casey* concurrence as the "natural" status and incidents of motherhood.[96] When law protects patriarchal overentitlement as normal and just, it is a legal regime of misogyny. The law authorizes the extraction of gifts from women.

The unjust enrichment frame recasts these "gifts" given by women to the world as socially beneficial losses that should be properly compensated by the public, rather than the "natural" baseline. Proper valuation would result in obligations of restitution, compensation, or support, sometimes by men, but more often by the state. When the community gains from women's losses, it bears some collective responsibility. When the state fails to discharge its duty, it cannot legitimately expect women's continued forbearance and thus cannot stop women from terminating their pregnancies.

Recent developments liberalizing abortion law beyond Europe reflect a similar perspective. Several Latin American countries have recently seen significant shifts from criminal abortion bans to constitutional abortion access. In February 2022, the Constitutional Court of Colombia held that the criminalization of abortions, including elective abortions, prior to twenty-four weeks of gestation was unconstitutional.[97] This landmark decision invalidated the criminal abortion statute. While the court's judgment leaves open the possibility of governmental regulation of abortion prior to twenty-four weeks without criminalization, the unconstitutionality of criminalization ended the regime under which some women choosing to terminate their pregnancies were still being imprisoned.

In September 2021, the Supreme Court of Mexico unanimously rendered a historic decision invalidating the near-total ban on abortion in the Penal Code of Coahuila.[98] While recognizing that the interest in protecting fetal life increased with the time of gestation, a state's measures to protect the fetus had to be limited, to some degree, by the rights of women and gestating persons to reproductive freedom. In 2020, the Argentinian Parliament ended its long-standing criminalization of almost all abortions by adopting a landmark law establishing the right of "women and persons of other gender identity with the ability to gestate" to choose abortion up to fourteen weeks' gestation, to access abortion care in the health system, to receive postabortion services in the health system, and to prevent unwanted pregnancies with access to information, sex education, and effective contraceptives.[99] Beyond the fourteen-week line, the new

Argentinian statute permits abortions if the pregnancy is the result of a criminal violation or if it endangers the life or whole health of the pregnant person.[100]

These developments grew out of earlier judicial decisions that articulated the constitutional stakes of abortion access without enforcing a *Roe*-like negative right to abortion on demand. In 2006, the Constitutional Court of Colombia ruled that the criminal statute prohibiting abortions in all circumstances violated women's fundamental rights.[101] Invoking the 1991 Constitution and international human rights law, the Constitutional Court noted that the state's protection of fetal interests imposed a disproportionate burden on women. The legislature, in enacting a criminal law, "cannot ignore that a woman is a human being entitled to dignity and that she must be treated as such, as opposed to being treated as a reproductive instrument for the human race."[102] Note the emphasis on women's rights not to be used for the benefit of others, which is different from the right to privacy. Therefore, the Colombian Constitutional Court held that abortion could not be criminalized in the following circumstances: when the continuation of the pregnancy presents a risk to the life or physical or mental health of the woman, when there are serious malformations that make the fetus nonviable, and when the pregnancy is the result of rape, incest, unwanted artificial insemination, or unwanted implantation of the fertilized ovule.[103] While the court entertained the possibility that some abortions could remain criminalized, it held that the legislature could not "require a complete sacrifice of any individual's fundamental right in order to serve the general interests of society or in order to give legal priority to other protected values."[104] While acknowledging a privacy interest, the Colombian Constitutional Court emphasized the constitutional problem of requiring disproportionate individual sacrifices for the public good.

In Argentina, abortion became legal in 1921 to prevent danger to the life or health of the mother if the danger could not be avoided by other means, or if the pregnancy resulted from the rape of a mentally deficient or insane woman. This formal rule was not enforced, particularly as antiabortion conservatives effectively established an informal rule of banning all abortions. Over the last two decades, abortion rights advocates deployed new litigation strategies to assert the right to legal abortions under the existing law's formal exceptions. In 2012, the Supreme Court of Argentina took a step toward abortion liberalization by affirming lower courts' refusal to apply criminal sanctions in the case of an abortion performed on a fifteen-year-old girl who had been raped by her stepfather.[105] The existing abortion ban made an exception for rape or sexual assault only in the case of mentally deficient or insane women, thereby calling into question the abortion that took place in that case.[106] By reasonably extending the exception to apply to a non–mentally deficient teenage rape victim, the court opened up a small space from which larger mobilizations could grow. Paola Bergallo argues that the quest to enforce the formal exceptions under the existing abortion law eventually dismantled the informal abortion ban through proceduralization and led to further liberalization culminating in the 2020 law.[107] The court took an incremental step, just as the Irish Supreme Court did in *Attorney General v. X*, allowing abortion in a situation that would draw broad sympathy, even from those who were pro-life.

The Constitutional Court of South Korea has also recently expanded abortion access, in a country that criminalized abortion in 1953 (though perhaps less motivated by public Christian morality and more motivated by a postwar nation-building and population growth agenda). In 2019, the Constitutional Court of South Korea also issued a landmark decision concluding that the criminal abortion statute did not conform to the Constitution. The Korean statute permitted abortions in more circumstances than those at issue in Colombia and Argentina—it authorized abortions for pregnancies that resulted from rape, quasi-rape, or incest; where the putative parents suffered from eugenic or genetic disability or disease; where the pregnant woman or spouse suffered from any specified contagious disease; and when maintaining the pregnancy was likely to severely injure the pregnant woman's health. But the statute was challenged by an abortion provider who asserted the rights of pregnant women to choose abortion, particularly in the early weeks of pregnancy, for broader reasons deriving from the pregnant woman's constitutional right to determine her own destiny.[108]

Article 10 of the South Korean Constitution proclaims human dignity and the right to pursue happiness. The Constitutional Court majority concluded that the constitutional violation occurred in "compelling a pregnant woman to continue her pregnancy and give birth even if she faces the abortion dilemma arising from various and wide-ranging socioeconomic circumstances."[109] The court determined that the abortion bans in the criminal code would become invalid if the legislature failed to remove the unconstitutional elements by December 31, 2020.[110] Pro-choice feminists favored legislative proposals completely repealing the criminal abortion statutes, and others proposed the simple addition of socioeconomic exceptions to existing abortion laws, more closely tracking the logic of the Constitutional Court's decision. But the National Assembly did not pass legislation before the effective date of the court's decision,[111] leading to the invalidation of the criminal code provision on abortion. In the absence of legislative action, questions remain about the legal meaning and effect of existing laws outside the criminal code that regulate abortion and only authorize abortions for indicated reasons up to twenty-four weeks. Nevertheless, the Constitutional Court's primary concern was with protecting women's rights to self-determination, which had to encompass abortion for social and economic reasons, especially in the earlier stages of pregnancy.

These ideas are not alien to the United States. *Casey* acknowledged that the suffering and sacrifices of motherhood were too much for the state to insist upon them, with Justice Blackmun noting that they are uncompensated and Justices O'Connor, Kennedy, and Souter pointing out that only the woman can endure the pregnancy. Historically, in the United States as well as in many societies, mothers' sacrifices include not only enduring the pregnancy for biological reproduction but also forgoing gainful employment to raise children at home—social reproduction. As Justice Blackmun suggests, laws banning abortion assume women's uncompensated sacrifice to be "natural," when the presumption of such an entitlement by men or by the community may violate equal protection. Meanwhile, mothers' forbearance in bearing and raising children contributes to children's eventual abilities, not only to enable the society's continued existence, but also to enlarge its collective prosperity. It is perhaps in recognition of the disproportionate contributions of women to biological and social reproduction, which have tangible collective benefits for the nation, that many constitutions around the world, including those of Germany and Ireland, guarantee an entitlement of mothers to the protection and care of the community.[112]

Before *Dobbs*, the Supreme Court reaffirmed *Roe* in 2016 and 2018 in *Whole Woman's Health v. Hellerstedt* and *June Medical Services v. Russo*.

In those cases, women lawyers and law professors filed amicus briefs urging the Supreme Court to uphold *Roe v. Wade* and the constitutional right to choose an abortion, drawing on their personal experiences to make their legal arguments.[113] These women had undergone abortions at pivotal moments in their educational or professional lives. They told their stories of how their access to abortion had stopped a pregnancy from ruining their lives. Abortions enabled them to keep studying, to become lawyers, to become law professors, to become leaders, to become wealthy, to live the lives that matched their talents, skills, and dreams. Gender equality may require abortion access so that women can pursue economic opportunities unimpeded by unwanted motherhood. But this should not hide the misogyny of a world that makes abortion necessary for women to achieve the same economic opportunities that men enjoy, because the law dooms women who stay pregnant and become mothers to a life of economic hardship and professional inferiority.

An important step in the transition from patriarchy to misogyny to real democracy is a full and fair valuation of society's collective gains and women's individual losses due to pregnancy and motherhood. The Irish experience shows that the process by which public attitudes change over time matters. The dialogue between the court rulings and the people through constitutional referenda and newly created Citizens' Assemblies has been crucial to developing broad-based public consensus on a polarizing issue.

The German and Irish experiences also indicate that resolving these issues is not a job for courts alone. In Germany, the legislature rewrote abortion laws by doing as much as it could with the court's pro-choice dicta about the dignity and equality of mothers. Keeping abortion safe and legal in America will require engaging people who want the law to protect unborn life and save women from life-ruining pregnancies but who feel moral discomfort with abortion on demand. The United States needs to find and create a range of institutions and spaces to deliberate about the as yet unconsidered paths by which a state can protect unborn life, without the excessive burdens that criminalizing abortion places on women. In a world without *Roe v. Wade*, it is necessary to interrogate and expand what it means for government to be pro-life. At the very least, pro-life and pro-choice groups agree that abortions to save the life of the pregnant person should remain legal. Global experience has shown that the line between a threat to life and a threat to health is often unclear. If the law is truly committed to saving pregnant women's lives, it must refrain from punishing abortions necessary to protect women's health. Supporting real access to these life- and health-saving abortions with funding should take priority over litigation seeking to persuade courts to revive *Roe v. Wade*. New spaces of democratic constitutionalism are needed to pave viable paths to overcome the misogyny of banning abortion.

PART II

What to Do about It

REMAKING CONSTITUTIONS AND DEMOCRACY

4 From Patriarchy to Prohibition

RESETTING ENTITLEMENTS THROUGH
CONSTITUTIONAL CHANGE

Women in constitutional democracies have attempted many strategies to overcome the oppressions of patriarchy. This chapter recovers one that is often ignored, as it offers unique insights into the ongoing dynamics of overentitlement and overempowerment.

In the nineteenth century, movements for temperance and Prohibition became a vector for women seeking to temper overempowerment of men and their institutions of toxic masculinity, such as the saloon. Lasting a generation, the temperance movement ultimately demanded a constitutional amendment, which it achieved. Prohibition became an important way for women to attack and reset the legally protected overentitlements of patriarchy in America before the movements for women's rights achieved some later successes. More so than the demands for women's suffrage or equal rights, the women's movement for constitutional Prohibition focused on structural change rather than individual rights. Beyond issues of alcohol, this history shows that constitutional change to reset the power of institutions and industries can matter as much as women's rights for the legal transition from patriarchy to democracy.

The Prohibition Amendment is often depicted as the biggest mistake of American constitution making—the only constitutional amendment that was repealed, and within a very short time span. Prohibition is often repudiated as the constitutional amendment that required the unprecedented intrusion of an expanded government into people's lives. Likewise, it is easy to dismiss the women's temperance movement as a band of hymn-singing church ladies who had nothing but religious fervor and conservative endorsement of women's traditional role in the family to offer. The temperance movement's efforts to impose their moral values and social aspirations on the nation through constitutional law are thought to have been misguided.[1] But this chapter tells a different story about temperance women and their legal strategy, interpreting it as a structural attack on the quotidian effects of patriarchal law. Bringing this lens to the women's movement for constitutional Prohibition—and the later movement for the constitutional repeal of Prohibition—reveals a bright side of feminist constitutionalism in a place where legal feminists seldom look. Women became constitution makers, using the amendment process to reset the entitlements of patriarchal law that enabled drunk men to abuse their rights. The Prohibition Amendment reduced the power of men in relation to women in the home by abolishing spaces of toxic masculinity like the saloon and by reducing the political power of the corporate liquor industry. The successes and failures of Prohibition provide critical insights for future strategies of feminist constitutionalism, far beyond the regulation of alcohol. They suggest, for instance, that changing powerful institutions may be more significant for overcoming misogyny than demanding rights.

DEPENDENCE ON DRUNK HUSBANDS AND THE ABUSE OF PATRIARCHAL RIGHTS

As discussed in the introduction, patriarchy was the law in many states in the nineteenth century. Laws of coverture empowered men over almost all matters affecting women's economic well-being and legal transactions. Husbands controlled their wives' property and earnings; fathers, not mothers, had legal parental authority over their children; men voted on behalf of their families. If men exercised their rights judiciously, the well-being of wives and children would be protected and promoted. But abusive exercises of these rights—whether motivated by malice, extreme self-interest, lack of sufficient regard for women's interests, or bad judgment—could be destructive to married women and often to their children. Husbands who were frequently drunk were prone to exercise poor judgment in the deployment of their rights.

Unlike the Christian temperance movements that began in the earlier part of the century prior to the Civil War, a growing movement of women shifted their focus away from reforming the men who drank too much and toward eradicating the saloons that profited from the moral failings of the men who became alcoholics.[2] Whereas the earlier temperance movement had preached abstinence, responsibility, and self-improvement to men, the women's temperance crusades of 1873 took on the sellers and manufacturers of alcohol. Through women's marches and the establishment of the Woman's Christian Temperance Union (WCTU) the following year, women organized collectively to place blame on the alcohol industry, rather than on their husbands and fathers, for the myriad social costs sustained by women as a result of men's excessive drinking in the nineteenth century.[3] To put it starkly, saloons became rich while women became impoverished when their husbands drank too much.

Historical sources locate the first women's marches against saloons in December 1873 and then through early 1874 throughout the Midwest.[4] The WCTU was founded in late 1874, and the first bill proposing a federal constitutional amendment prohibiting the manufacture, sale, and transportation of alcoholic beverages was introduced in Congress in 1876.[5] Women who participated in these crusades wrote memoirs in the years that followed. Four autobiographical accounts of the women's crusades recount crusaders' encounters with the legal system. Women's advocacy for constitutional Prohibition emerged after decades of less-than-successful efforts to improve their domestic lives and economic security through litigation and political action. The original women's crusades of 1873–74 consisted of women marching to saloons while praying and singing, with the goal of persuading saloonkeepers to shut down operations. The participants in these crusades published autobiographical accounts during the time when WCTU developed its public and vocal support of constitutional Prohibition and women's suffrage. They reveal the failures of existing law of the period, to which a constitutional amendment came to be seen as a solution.

Women's temperance memoirs reveal a vision of Prohibition concerned as much with overcoming the abuses of male power as with legally enshrining a Christian morality of temperance. The Christian morality of temperance was the language by which women demanded that men temper their exercise of the power over their wives and homes. Under the law, men's control over family property, including wages earned by their wives, enabled men to spend the family's resources on alcohol. Saloons deployed the legal protection of their property rights to control and drive out women protesters. The women's temperance movement eventually embraced a federal constitutional amendment prohibiting the sale and manufacture of alcohol in response to this existing legal regime of property rights. It is a case study of feminist democratic constitutionalism, showing how women sought constitutional transformation to challenge their exclusion from power. Relatedly, the women's temperance movement advocated for women's suffrage. They saw women's political empowerment as a crucial means to temper toxic masculinity and its effects on their day-to-day lives.

SUING SALOONS

The agitators of the women's temperance movement believed that saloons were responsible for the injuries that women sustained because of men's excessive drinking habits. These harms included harassment and violence on the streets, as well as domestic violence at the hands of drunken husbands.[6] Saloons bore responsibility stemming from their marketing and sale of alcohol. They lured the husbands in, diverting men's money and time away from their families' needs, and the saloons were significantly enriched as a result. Women were very aware of the costs they absorbed as a result of their husbands' alcohol consumption, from which saloons benefited financially. At the saloon, breadwinning husbands spent earnings that would otherwise go to family expenses—they drank away the family wage. There was less (or no) money for food and new clothing for growing children. Saloons often established relationships with local employers, such that the employer would deduct the debts men accrued on their tab at the saloon from the employee's paycheck and pay it to the saloon.

Saloons often served complimentary snacks with the beer to induce men to drink more. This often meant that men would be fed while spending all their wages on drinks, whereas the wife and children, unwelcome at the saloon, would go hungry.

By the mid-nineteenth century, some states recognized the need for law to remedy these problems by establishing statutory causes of action allowing wives to sue saloons for support after their drunken husbands died or became abusive or unable to work. As the temperance memoirs illustrate, these female plaintiffs often relied on other women in the community who acted informally as advocates in the courtroom, when women were not legally authorized to become lawyers admitted to the bar. As these conflicts escalated, women who protested saloons found themselves named as defendants in civil actions brought by saloon owners to stop their political activities. Saloons obtained civil injunctions and damages against women who sang hymns and protested on or near saloon property. In response to women's legal and political action, saloons organized, hired lawyers, and litigated to stop them, claiming that these women interfered with saloons' property rights and their rights to freely pursue their business. Saloons further claimed that their property and free enterprise rights had constitutional status, and this naturally motivated a constitutional discourse in the response of the women's temperance movement. A constitutional amendment prohibiting the manufacture and sale of alcohol would overcome the judicial constitutionalization of these property and business rights.

In the early 1870s, women tried to use their relatively new statutory rights to sue saloons to hold them legally responsible for their drunken husbands' domestic violence and inability to support their families.[7] The litigation of a "test" case brought on behalf of a drunkard's wife against a saloon is recounted in an 1889 book by Mother Eliza Stewart titled *Memories of the Crusade: A Thrilling Account of the Great Uprising of the Women of Ohio in 1873 against the Liquor Crime.*[8] Although Mother Stewart was not a lawyer, she made opening and closing statements to juries in these trials, and many women in the community filled the courtrooms as spectators and supporters of the plaintiffs. During the break, she tried to rally more women to join her in the courtroom, and interestingly, one of the barriers was the women's "home duties."[9]

128   FROM PATRIARCHY TO PROHIBITION

In the same year of this trial and the beginnings of the women's temperance crusades, the US Supreme Court decided *Bradwell v. Illinois*, holding that a state's refusal to license a married woman to practice law as a member of the bar was not a violation of the Fourteenth Amendment.[10] While the US Supreme Court was legitimizing women's exclusion from the legal profession, Mother Stewart empowered herself by playing the role of lawyer in a county court, insisting that no man could speak for a drunkard's wife challenging a saloon: "I took my law book in my hand, and addressing the jury, said I found myself in a novel position, but I made this attempt to plead the case of my sister, because I knew I could speak for her as no man could."[11]

Mother Stewart's statement to the jury focused on the economic harms of male drunkenness on women and children. "But through the influence of drink furnished by the man now arraigned, he [the husband of plaintiff] had become so worthless and incompetent that the wife and mother, besides her regular domestic duties, was obliged to labor to earn the means of support for her family."[12] This is the narrative that drove many women to support laws prohibiting the sale of alcohol: saloons turned good, responsible, hardworking, wage-earning men into drunkards who could no longer support their wives and children and sometimes even abused them. Alcohol disrupted the traditional roles within the family, forcing women to work and potentially compromise their "regular domestic duties."

According to Mother Stewart's account, in this first "test" case, the jury returned a verdict for the plaintiff of $100 and costs. Characterizing this as a "very fair verdict" in light of it being the first case, and in light of the tremendous efforts of the defendant's lawyer, she notes that the publicity around this case "led the poor women to fancy that I must know a good deal about law, or at least I was a friend that could sympathize with them, and so they came to me to tell their sorrows and ask counsel or assistance."[13] In other words, the women's temperance movement transformed her into a lawyer, thrusting her into a role that had been, until about this moment, restricted to men.

Mother Stewart's account of this and other litigation against saloons highlighted the costs of civil litigation, which were sometimes prohibitive.[14] Furthermore, the plaintiffs' victories were also limited because recovery was delayed by defendants' appeals. Liquor sellers appealed verdicts in favor of plaintiffs, and appellate courts were less likely to tolerate improvised arguments by lay women in lieu of lawyers. Mother Stewart also complained in her memoir that the liquor sellers banded together to help out the saloonkeeper in appealing his case. Despite victorious trial verdicts in the plaintiffs' favor, appeals pursued by saloons and their sophisticated lawyers delayed the certainty of these women's recoveries and raised the costs of litigation for them.

A fair number of civil damage verdicts in favor of women against saloons under these new statutory causes of action in Ohio and other states eventually reached state supreme courts on appeal.[15] The published opinions of state supreme courts in several decisions of the 1870s reveal the fact patterns and legal arguments that were made by the saloons. Saloonkeepers and brewers began organizing into associations to defend themselves against women's legal and political efforts to put them out of business. As the judicial opinions reveal, liquor sellers made arguments on appeal that harped on procedural detail and required some legal training. They invoked stringent pleading standards to try to reverse verdicts that they claimed should never have gone to trial.[16] They attempted modes of statutory construction to try to exclude the specific plaintiffs and specific claims from the scope of the statute.[17] They tried to enforce evidentiary standards to argue that the plaintiff's strongest evidence should have been excluded at trial.[18] While few of these arguments ultimately prevailed, and the verdict against saloons was upheld in most of these cases, these lines of argument highlight the growing strategies by which liquor industry defendants with pooled resources used the professional expertise of the legal profession (from which women were largely excluded) to wear down female plaintiffs. They were able to abuse the power they derived from legal knowledge to prolong the dispute and to raise the costs of litigation.

The Ohio Supreme Court upheld a verdict for a widow under that 1854 liquor statute as early as 1871–72. In *Schneider v. Hosier*, it upheld a civil damage award of $200 to Sarah Hosier, whose husband had died in 1865 after a series of excessive intoxications. The defendant saloonkeeper had appealed the verdict, raising a barrage of procedural arguments. In addition to simply denying having sold the liquor to the deceased husband and suggesting that the husband had gotten intoxicated by his own willful acts, the saloonkeeper urged the court to impose a more stringent pleading standard on the plaintiff and argued that the trial court should have required more specificity in her complaint: "The statement of facts and averments of the second amended petition are such as to leave it uncertain whether the plaintiff below placed her right to recover on the sixth or seventh section of the 'liquor law,' or on the act allowing damages for unlawfully causing the death of her husband."

The defendant also argued that the complaint should have been dismissed for improper joinder if she was invoking both statutes. The defendant further claimed that his demurrer should have been sustained under the liquor statute (what Mother Stewart refers to as the Adair law), because the statutory language created a cause of action for a "wife" and not a "widow" of an intoxicated person. The defendant also argued that the verdict was against the weight of the evidence and excessive, requiring a new trial. This argument was premised on the alleged impropriety of a jury instruction on the "means of support" claimed by the widow. The defendant claimed that "means of support," recoverable under the statute, was a phrase that was "too loose, vague, and uncertain" and could not include "an injury to a thing so intangible as the uncontracted unperformed future labor of the husband." Finally, the defendant argued that it was error to allow the wife and children of the deceased to join as plaintiffs in one civil action.

The Ohio Supreme Court rejected all of the defendant's arguments, and it is worth highlighting some strong statements of law, helpful to women left destitute by drunken husbands, but reinforcing the patriarchal gender roles of husband as breadwinner and wife as dependent:

> Ordinary labor being a means of support, the next question is, whether the labor of the husband, or its proceeds, can be regarded as the wife's means of support.
> A husband is morally and legally bound to supply his wife with the necessaries and comforts of life. If he has no other resource, it is his duty to contribute his labor and its proceeds to her support.[19]

Yet despite the court's rejection of the saloonkeeper's arguments, it is easy to see how defending the verdict against his aggressive and rather technical legal attacks could be burdensome and costly for these women, who were already vulnerable because of their lack of income and employment opportunities. Another case decided by the Ohio Supreme Court in December term 1873 illustrates the difficulties faced by victorious plaintiffs in collecting on their verdicts against saloons. In *Bellinger v. Griffith*, the plaintiff Minnie Bellinger had won a civil damage verdict against the saloonkeeper.[20] A provision of the amended liquor law imposed liability on the property for damages assessed against the occupier. Equipped with the judgment against the saloonkeeper, Bellinger attempted to proceed against the landlords of the saloon to collect on the judgment. But the saloon's landlords had sold the property to a new owner. The Ohio Supreme Court held that, while "the property of every debtor, not exempt by law, is declared by statute to be subject to the payment of his debts, and liable to be taken in the execution," "no lien is created on the property from the fact of such liability."[21] What that meant was that the statute created a cause of action against saloonkeepers and their landlords *in personam* but not against the property itself so as to enable a victorious plaintiff to recover against the new owner of the property. This is another example of the law's limits. Even when women were armed with civil damages judgments against saloons, the legal system ultimately failed to deliver the relief they had won.

BACKLASH: SALOONS FIGHT BACK WITH LEGAL ACTION AND PROPERTY RIGHTS

As women protested saloons and sought to persuade them to go out of business in their communities, saloons fought back with legal action. Saloonkeepers brought civil actions for both injunctions and damages to remove women crusaders from their property. As early as 1856, the New York Court of Appeals had invoked the New York State constitution's due process clause to hold that a state law prohibiting the sale of intoxicating liquors violated the liquor seller's property right.[22] The Indiana Supreme Court had similarly invalidated a Prohibition statute, invoking "certain absolute rights," including "the right to private property."[23] Both of those cases were challenges to the criminal convictions of liquor sellers under state statutes regulating the sale of alcohol.

By 1873, just two months shy of the first women's temperance crusades, the US Supreme Court had decided *Bartemeyer v. Iowa* in favor of

a liquor seller challenging his conviction under an Iowa Prohibition statute. Noting that the defendant's ownership of the liquor was in question
in that case, the Supreme Court suggested that, if a different set of facts
presented the issue fairly to the court, "two grave questions" would arise:
"whether the prohibition statute amounted to a deprivation of the liquor-
seller's property without due process of law, and whether if it were so, the
newly adopted Fourteenth Amendment would be violated."[24] The United
States Brewers' Association, established in 1862, had been developing the
legal theory of property rights belonging to the liquor manufacturer and
saloonkeeper, which they sought to protect as a constitutional liberty that
the state could not take away, pursuant to the Fourteenth Amendment's
Due Process Clause.[25] Often framed as nuisance claims, property rights
formed the basis of saloons' legal actions against the women's temperance
activists who attempted to interfere with liquor sales.

Liquor sellers' property rights lawsuits against women's political pro-
test feature in a history of the women's temperance crusades by Annie
Wittenmyer, the inaugural president of the WCTU.[26] The litigation by
Dunn's Drug Palace against the women who crusaded at his shop in
Hillsboro, Ohio, is discussed in multiple temperance memoirs, including
Mother Stewart's and two other memoirs of the temperance crusades in
Ohio towns that precipitated the founding of the WCTU. According to
Wittenmyer, before marching and singing at saloons, the women had
drafted a pledge to stop selling liquor, which they asked druggists and
saloonkeepers to sign. But drugstore owner Mr. Dunn refused, and the
women responded by erecting a tabernacle next to his store. The ladies
occupied the tabernacle and held a prayer meeting there.

Dunn then took legal action initially demanding an injunction against
this "tabernacle," which was granted. When the temperance women
appealed the injunction, it was dissolved because of a flaw in Dunn's application for the injunction. However, Wittenmyer notes, "Mr. Dunn was not
to be quieted. He now brought a suit for 'trespass' against the Crusaders,
and asked $10,000 damages."[27] Note the picture that emerges: the liquor
seller—in this case a druggist presumably selling alcohol for purportedly
medicinal purposes—relentlessly developed several available legal theories to stop the women from interfering with his business and property
rights. The new lawsuit then proceeded against the women for damages

(five hundred times the amount awarded in verdicts in women's civil damage actions), instead of against the tabernacle for an injunction. Dunn's litigation behavior could easily be characterized as an abuse of right, somewhat reminiscent of later French decisions where an abuse of right was identified, as discussed in chapter 2. French courts determined that litigants who brought claims that they had every right under the law to bring abused their rights when they litigated for the purpose of harassing and coercing the other party.[28]

Wittenmyer's account of the famous Dunn lawsuit included mention of another event of great significance to the temperance cause: the Ohio constitutional convention was going on, concurrent with the Dunn litigation.[29] One of the items up for debate at the state constitutional convention was a provision that would empower the state to permit and regulate the sale of liquor through a licensing scheme. Temperance advocates were generally against the licensing provision, at first preferring constitutional silence on the matter and later advocating constitutional prohibition of the sale and manufacture of liquor.

The Dunn suit against the women crusaders was also recounted in Eliza Thompson's *Hillsboro Crusade Sketches*, a history/memoir that appeared much later, in 1895. Mother Thompson, as she was known, was no stranger to politics or law. She was the daughter of a former Ohio governor and the wife of a county court judge. Mother Thompson's account confirms Dunn's refusal to sign the pledge to stop selling liquor; Dunn replied not personally but through his attorneys. In that reply, the attorneys claimed that the women's "movement" had "forced him into the courts" and demanded that any request be accompanied by "proper concessions to him on the part of the temperance people."[30] Thompson also recounted the women praying and singing next to Dunn's Palace Drugstore and noted that the band included the wife of a former congressman who was a delegate to the Ohio constitutional convention.[31]

In describing the court proceedings in Dunn's first injunction action to remove the tabernacle, Thompson noted that the courthouse was "densely packed." The legal proceeding strengthened temperance sentiments, precisely because the judge ruled against them. "The greatest interest was manifested in the extraordinary proceedings, and temperance sentiment was created, even more rapidly by our court-house experiences than by our saloon visitations; so the world said."[32] A later chapter in Thompson's memoir recounted the other trial, for Dunn's $10,000 trespass action against the women crusaders. Women were not welcome in the courtroom and were out of place amid the "heaps of law-books," where a former judge who had ruled against women crusaders in an earlier proceeding was now representing Dunn as an advocate. Thompson wrote: "Naturally, we 'poor, weak women' felt, Can there be so much against us in those books of doom?"[33]

Mother Thompson drew a poignant contrast between the will of the people and the content of the law: "When the bell rang, hundreds from the outside, willing to shout for the winning side, flocked to the court-house to hear the doom. The jury, obliged to base their decision upon the legal proofs in the case, as allowed by the court, found the defendants guilty of trespass."[34] Nonetheless, the judge determined that because "Mr. Dunn lost the sale of a gallon of coal-oil and some other trifling matter in consequence of the presence of the ladies on his steps and sidewalks, the damages were put at five dollars instead of ten thousand; but that was enough to throw the costs upon the temperance men."[35] Even though the damages were low, and even though Thompson says that "expectation was quite general that the decision would be reversed," the case was never litigated before the Supreme Court of Ohio because Dunn went bankrupt and "his assignee declined to defend the suit in the Supreme Court."[36]

Was this a win or a loss for the temperance women? On the one hand, the women lost on the law, namely the instructions to the jury on proof, which led to the jury's outcome against them. On the other hand, the damages were so low that they can hardly be experienced as a win for the liquor seller. Such low damages would not be a significant incentive to bring future trespass litigation against women activists, nor to defend the victory on appeal. Thus the Ohio Supreme Court did not get the opportunity to make a clear legal statement or rule moving forward. This state of legal uncertainty deterred both sides from aggressively pursuing their goals. In the 1880s, temperance women shifted their focus toward building a national organization that created a robust discourse by which women engaged public policy, debating issues like Prohibition and suffrage rather than crusading at saloons and drugstores. The liquor industry continued to assert property rights and the right to pursue one's business interests, not through lawsuits against crusading women, but through constitutional challenges to the enforcement of state laws prohibiting or regulating the sale of liquor.[37]

In addition, the organization that grew out of these crusades of 1873–74, the WCTU, developed into an effective institution that organized and coordinated women's participation in politics and constitutional democracy. The WCTU grew to become a national organization with many state and regional chapters, drawing the participation of 250,000 women by the turn of the twentieth century.[38] Local chapters had women leaders, and the national organization had legislative and law departments, also led by women. The organizational structure enabled the argument and campaign for a constitutional Prohibition amendment to grow, over two decades, out of the grassroots marches. Local marches grew into a large-scale national effort to reset the entitlements protected by law, particularly with regard to property rights, so as to rebalance power between women, their communities, and the corporate liquor industry that shaped men's toxic social worlds and behavior. Having tried a range of strategies, women lawyers of the WCTU began to argue that changing the federal Constitution would be necessary. Experience showed that other means of weakening the liquor sellers, such as civil damage trials and state licensing schemes, were grossly inadequate. However, trials and state constitutional conventions that took up the possibility of state-based licensing and local options for the regulation of alcohol generated a public discourse in which women participated as litigants, unofficial advocates, and influential spectators. On the one hand, these activities produced limited victories because the appeals process and women's exclusion from the legal profession enabled wealthier liquor sellers to lawyer up and raise the costs of litigation. On the other hand, women empowered through their women's organization began to write and lobby for constitutional change to fight back.

The liquor sellers' legal theories of property rights and business freedom were given constitutional status by the turn of the century. In short, the liquor industry deployed their constitutional property rights to weaken women's political power. The legal uncertainty that remained around civil litigation made public policy and constitutional change the logical next step for women seeking empowerment. The need for women's suffrage became apparent to the leaders of the WCTU—especially Frances Willard, who was its president from 1879 until her death in 1898. But suffrage would not be enough; women sought the vote so that they could then use political power to reset and reduce the business and property entitlements of liquor sellers.

THE FEMINISM OF THE WOMEN'S TEMPERANCE MOVEMENT

Before the Nineteenth Amendment made it unconstitutional to deny the right to vote on account of sex, a step to women's empowerment was made by their entry into the legal profession. Although the Supreme Court's decision in *Bradwell v. Illinois* allowed states to exclude married women from the legal profession consistent with the Fourteenth Amendment, several states, including Illinois, began to admit women to the bar, and the first women lawyers practiced law, often representing women trying to reverse the setbacks they encountered because of their lack of rights and legal status.[39]

Some of these pioneering women lawyers also served as local presidents and legislative counsel to the WCTU. J. Ellen Foster, Ada Kepley, Ada Bittenbender, and Catharine Waugh McCulloch all published books or pamphlets explicitly addressing the need for federal constitutional Prohibition, connecting the issue to women's lack of legal rights within the family and the home, women's economic dependence on men, the lack of women's suffrage, and other sources of women's subordination by law. An increasing number of states adopted constitutional or statutory Prohibition and other forms of regulation during this period, and by the time that the Prohibition Amendment was ratified by the requisite number of states in 1919, fourteen state constitutions included a Prohibition amendment, and fifteen additional states had statutory Prohibition, all of which set the stage for the ratification of the Eighteenth Amendment. The argument for constitutional Prohibition grew out of its female proponents' encounters with the legal system. It was part of a much larger agenda of social and legal reforms to prevent the destitution that could sometimes result from the dynamics of male overentitlement and the overempowerment of the liquor industry.

The WCTU's campaign for a national Prohibition amendment began in 1875.[40] When the Prohibition Amendment was introduced in Congress in 1876, women participated in the political process by testifying in congressional hearings. Even though they could not vote, they became constitution makers by shaping a central narrative leading to the placement of Prohibition in the US Constitution. Frances Willard led the WCTU during the time that it grew to be the largest women's political organization in the United States, advocating not only for the national constitutional Prohibition Amendment but also for women's suffrage and labor rights. Although much has been written about Willard, the most charismatic and well-known president of the WCTU, little attention has been paid to the women lawyers who served as legislative and legal counsel to the WCTU as the organization embraced national constitutional Prohibition. Kepley, Foster, Bittenbender, and McCulloch became lawyers in the decade following the US Supreme Court's decision in *Bradwell v. Illinois*, which allowed but did not rquire married women's exclusion from the legal profession. The writings of these women lawyers shed light on the broader range of social problems women faced as a result of the abuses of legal rights to property and business held by men and by corporations. The WCTU advocated legislative reform on a broad range of related policy issues, in addition to seeking policies to curb or abolish the liquor traffic.

Although she ascended to the presidency of the WCTU to succeed founding president Annie Wittenmyer only a few years after the organization's founding, Willard had not participated in the women's temperance crusades that precipitated the genesis of the WCTU. At the time of the temperance crusades, she was the dean of the women's college at Northwestern University and a professor of aesthetics. She found her path to the WCTU through feminism, not through alcohol. She attended the National Women's Congress of 1873, which met in New York to organize a new society called the Association for the Advancement of Women.[41] While present to give a paper on women's education, she met some temperance leaders and began to pay attention to the temperance activities that were sweeping the nation.

According to Willard's close confidante Anna Gordon, who served as president of the WCTU at the time that the Prohibition Amendment was ratified, Willard's turn to temperance activism was a reaction to men's efforts to put women in their place. When a group of women visited the Chicago City Council to petition for the enforcement of a Sunday-closing law, they were, in Anna Gordon's words, "treated with mocking slight and rudely jostled on the street by a band of rough men, half out for a lark, half ugly." This awakened something in Willard. Gordon continues, "Miss Willard was thoroughly aroused. 'Treat any woman with contumely, and as soon as she hears of it every other woman in the world worth anything feels as if she also were hurt.'"[42] Within days of this episode, Willard wrote a speech in which she publicly declared the temperance cause as "everybody's war," which became the title of one of her most famous and frequent speeches. Willard consciously chose a path that she thought could become the most productive in fighting all the evils that threatened the home, including but not limited to temperance. She could see that temperance was the issue that could organize large numbers of women most effectively in her era.[43]

"Everybody's war" linked the legal regulation of alcohol to women's liberation as well as the flourishing of the nation in the next generation.[44] Willard depicted the saloon as an institution that the law wrongly treated as equal in standing to the church and the school. "And between these two are institutions called saloons, equally guaranteed by our laws, equally fostered by our nation and more than equally patronized by our people." In her narrative description, the saloon was a place where Sunday school teachers would unwittingly enter, invited by male friends, in which they lost control to the overpowerful corporate interests of the liquor industry:

> Let us go in with some friend and see this transaction. Behind the counter stands avarice, before the counter appetite, and between the two a transaction that puts a few dimes into the till of the proprietor and drives voluntary insanity into the brain of the patron. The man goes out, he goes to the primary meeting and election, he loiters away his time, he fritters away his earnings. He goes to the house where he is best beloved, to the best friends he has in the world, where they love him better than they do anybody else. Yet upon that wife that loves him so well and little children clinging about his neck, he inflicts atrocities which imagination cannot picture and no tongue dare describe. Now I am not telling you anything that does not happen in Chicago a hundred times a day.[45]

Willard also engaged in an economic analysis of the costs and benefits of the liquor traffic to argue for stopping it. She asserted that "we use in America forty millions of bushels of nice clean grain [that] is turned over into alcoholic drinks every year. Now a good man has found out by mathematical calculation that we drink enough to pay for paving a good wide street long enough to reach all the way from Chicago to New York."[46] Willard also saw the politics of Prohibition as inextricably linked to women's suffrage:

> In America ballots are bayonets. Every drunkard, every rum seller holds that in his hand which may shake the very President in his chair. In America there are one million drunkards and rum sellers who stagger up to the polls and exercise that sacred right. They are in every ward, in every precinct, and every election district. They stagger up to the polls and drop in their bleared ballots. What fruits can we expect but salary grabbers, [corner?] rings, whiskey rings, post tradership rings, and every sort of ring except the ring of the true metal? Going on at this rate no one needs to be a prophet to see what this thing will lead to.[47]

A year later, the speech was retitled "Home Protection."[48] Excerpted in Willard's *Woman and Temperance* as "My first Home Protection Address," the speech that she began to give in 1876 explicitly made the claim that women's suffrage was needed for public policy to combat the liquor interests that diminished men, compromised the national economy, and corrupted the next generation of citizens.[49] Willard chronicled several failed attempts to pass legislation banning the liquor traffic. The speech also purported to represent more women than those who were formal members of the WCTU. Willard spoke for women who could not be politically active because of "home influence and cares," including "the drunkard's wife and daughters, who from very shame will not come with us."[50] In another call to explicit politicization, Willard said, "Dear Christian women who have crusaded in the rum shops, I urge that you begin crusading in halls of legislation, in primary meetings, and the offices of excise commissioners. Roll in your petitions, burnish your arguments, multiply your prayers."[51] After saloonkeepers asserted their legal property entitlements to stop the women protesting their rum shops, Willard could see that the next step was to reset those legal entitlements by "crusading in halls of legislation."

THE CONSTITUTIONALISM OF THE WOMEN LAWYERS
FOR TEMPERANCE

In the 1880s and 1890s, women lawyers serving as legislative counsel to the WCTU translated Willard's "home protection" themes into arguments justifying the need for a constitutional amendment. As Willard rallied women around "home protection," the first bill proposing a federal constitutional amendment was introduced in Congress.[52] Congressman Henry Blair, in a report in support of the amendment, noted that despite strong public sentiment in favor of addressing the evils wrought by the use of alcohol, temperance efforts had been thwarted because of "the recognition and protection given to alcoholic drink as property, as a legitimate article of manufacture everywhere and for all uses, and of commerce, both interstate and international, by the Constitution and laws of the United States."[53]

By the time the amendment was first proposed, saloonkeepers had asserted their property rights by bringing civil injunction and nuisance damages cases against women who crusaded for temperance. In addition to Willard's charismatic speeches and writings linking Prohibition to suffrage and other reforms to improve women's economic and political status, the women's movement for Prohibition developed intellectual heft through the work of women who were trained in law. Kepley, for instance, was the first woman to graduate from law school in the United States.[54] Most of the women who studied law during this era, including Myra Bradwell and the other women lawyers who were active with the WCTU, obtained their legal educations by privately studying law with their husbands. Kepley's husband was also a lawyer, but Kepley attended law school at what was then the University of Chicago's law department (now Northwestern Pritzker School of Law), spending months away from her husband to do so. Kepley was an active member of the WCTU.[55]

Like Bradwell, Kepley was initially denied admission to the Illinois Bar; she then worked on drafting the bill that banned sex discrimination in professional occupations in Illinois, making it possible despite the US Supreme Court's decision in *Bradwell v. Illinois* for women to be admitted in Illinois. Kepley was admitted to practice in Illinois in 1881, and in that year she ran unsuccessfully as the Prohibition Party candidate for attorney general.[56] When elected officials in her town of Effingham, Illinois, denied the WCTU access to their local buildings to hold meetings, Kepley worked with her husband to purchase a church building and convert it into a public meetinghouse called "The Temple" where the WCTU and churches lacking facilities could meet.[57]

As states continued to prohibit or regulate the sale, manufacture, and transportation of alcohol through statutes and state constitutional provisions, Congress continued to consider a federal constitutional amendment. In 1882, J. Ellen Foster, the superintendent of the Department of Legislation of the WCTU, and the first woman admitted to practice law in Iowa, published *Constitutional Amendment Manual Containing Argument, Appeal, Petitions, Forms of Constitution, Catechism and General Directions for Organized Work for Constitutional Prohibition.* Willard, in her profile of Foster, acknowledged the use of Foster's legal knowledge in the WCTU's advocacy for state constitutional Prohibition amendments.[58] Foster was a popular lecturer and suffragist who also traveled to Europe to study temperance there.

For Foster, the amendment was being proposed not to bring about total abstinence from alcohol, nor to legislate morality. Rather, she argued that the constitutional amendment was needed to curb the excessive economic power of the liquor industry, so that the public interest could be advanced: "'So long as the love of money is the root of all evil,' so long will men argue that prohibitory liquor laws are opposed to the interests of any community, not that they are so opposed, but because the investment of a little capital in manufacturing and selling brings such great returns and because the large revenue to nation and State seem to the careless observer to be a real source of wealth."[59]

Foster believed that the true source of national wealth was land and labor, and she contended that alcohol "destroys the grain that ought to be used as food for man or beast, and lessens or wholly destroys the ability to labor with hand or brain."[60] The argument for a constitutional amendment grew out of a basic analysis of "political economy." Constitutional intervention was needed because efforts to regulate the liquor industry's excessive concentration of power that enabled it to control the true sources of national wealth had failed. Civil and criminal processes had been ineffective. The ineffectiveness of ordinary law, she argued, was due to an oligarchy: "500,000 men engaged in the liquor traffic with their sympathizers and supporters . . . and statutes are not always subjected to the test of right, principle, and beneficial result, but too often to the touch-stone of political expediency and personal gain."[61]

Foster also believed that the liquor industry's excessive wealth and power, protected by law, made women vulnerable in their own homes. In resonance with Willard's "home protection" speeches, Foster wrote, "The home, as the smallest community of individuals, needs protection. Shall any voice attempt to echo the desolations of the home which are the direct and indirect results of this liquor crime? Are not our ears grown deaf with the sad strains of women worse than widowed, and children more than orphaned? Do not our hearts ache to breaking at the ever present sight of so much misery? Has the State any duty to these?"[62] Here we can see the unjust enrichment dynamic in her description of the problem: the saloons got rich, and women got hurt. A constitutional amendment would reset each party's entitlements.

That was essentially Foster's response to skepticism about whether Prohibition was a "proper subject of constitutional law." Foster understood constitutions as "a setting forth of the principles by which [the people] desire to be governed"; constitutional provisions were to be "broad and general," dealing with those subjects that should not be left uncertain or controlled by partisan interests. Prohibition was appropriate according to this understanding, because the evils of intemperance were "broad and general," threatening people, homes, and mothers' ability to raise their children.[63] Foster urged that Prohibition was not different in kind from some existing constitutional provisions, including most analogously, the Thirteenth Amendment's ban on slavery. African slavery was "a crime in which both North and South were partners,"[64] because of the economic interest of the South in producing cotton and the economic need of the North to buy it. The "tears and blood" of slavery were resolved by constitutional amendment, and only after "the agitation of fanatics, and the legislation of enthusiasts, and the battle of warriors, and graves of boys in blue and boys in gray, and the proclamation of Lincoln, the emancipator!" Using the analogy of the constitutional prohibition of slavery, Foster concluded, "The history of our civilization is written in our Constitutions."[65]

A few years later, Foster published another pamphlet titled *The Saloon Must Go*,[66] which focused on three main points. First, she articulated the inadequacies and failures of existing laws, particularly licensing schemes, to reduce the power of the liquor industry. Second, she emphasized women's disempowerment within the home, where they were defenseless against drunken husbands. Third, she described the saloon as an overempowered economic institution that fostered abusive male conduct. What needed to be abolished was the saloon as an institution and a space, not men drinking alcohol as such.

In 1887, Ada Bittenbender's report to the Senate Committee on Education and Labor on behalf of WCTU began, "The real citadel of the rum curse is the National Constitution," denouncing the protection that existing law afforded to liquor manufacturers and sellers, instead of protecting women and their homes. She continued: "The 250,000 women of our Republic, who are banded together in this temperance organization, have petitioned Congress for submission of such an amendment to the Constitution as shall, when ratified, break up this defense and turn the national Government into a home-protection fortress."[67] Her report underscored the effects of alcohol on the national economy that Willard had introduced in her "Home Protection" speech.

The remainder of Bittenbender's report summarized the jurisprudence in which courts had upheld the authority of state legislatures to prohibit and regulate the alcohol trade.[68] But a national constitutional amendment was needed because liquor businesses were successful often enough when they invoked their property rights to limit state and local efforts, led by women, to shut down saloons. Bittenbender presented the constitutional prohibition amendment proposal as a way of directing the police powers of the states toward the promotion of the general welfare. Data from insurance companies and from the medical literature documented the harmful effects of alcohol on health and on men's ability to work. Her defense of the police power predates and resonates with Justice Harlan's widely read *Lochner* dissent.[69]

Bittenbender was also active in the Nebraska Woman Suffrage Association, serving as president of that organization and working on a state constitutional suffrage amendment in Nebraska. She studied law with her husband and became his law partner after being the first woman to be admitted to practice in Nebraska. Willard's biographical sketch notes Bittenbender's role in securing state legislation that required scientific temperance instruction in schools, and a law granting women equal guardianship of her children with the father. She also advocated for legislation establishing an industrial school and home for penitent women and girls, for the purpose of reducing prostitution.[70] In 1888 Bittenbender was admitted to practice before the US Supreme Court, and she was elected attorney for the National WCTU in the same year.[71] During the 1880s, figures like Bittenbender, though based in Nebraska, spent much time in Washington to lobby in favor of Prohibition and related legislation. Beginning in 1895, WCTU had a national superintendent of legislation, Margaret Dye Ellis,[72] who spent every winter while Congress was in session in Washington, D.C., meeting with temperance-friendly legislators and socializing with their wives.

The WCTU continued to advocate for a federal constitutional amendment, working with the Prohibition Party. The Prohibition Party, founded in 1869, was the first American political party to include women as officers and candidates from its inception. Like Kepley in 1881, McCulloch, a woman lawyer, suffragist, and legal adviser to the WCTU, ran as a Prohibition Party candidate in an 1888 election for attorney general of Illinois. In 1899 McCulloch published a book titled *Mr. Lex or The Legal Status of Mother and Child*, exposing several patriarchal features of the common law in many states that were oppressive to married women and mothers, and citing the judicial decisions that enforced coverture. Although she was not elected attorney general, McCulloch nonetheless successfully lobbied the Illinois legislature for statutory reforms to these laws during this period.[73] She was elected justice of the peace in Evanston, Illinois, in 1907.[74]

Mr. Lex exposed the major legal sources of women's subordination, which McCulloch eventually lobbied successfully to change. One was the law's refusal to recognize mothers as legal guardians of their own children. In most states, the common law recognized the authority of fathers over their children, and this left mothers with little control over the raising and upbringing of their children. In *Mr. Lex*, McCulloch illustrates the harmfulness of this scenario for children through the title character, Mr. Lex, a husband and father who always exercises his discretionary rights and powers over his wife and children abusively. Mr. Lex refuses to buy a warm jacket for his daughter in cold weather, refuses to call the doctor for another sick daughter, resulting in her death, forces his children to labor for his own financial benefit, and refuses to allow his very clever son to pursue a good educational opportunity.[75]

Mr. Lex, who is a lawyer by training, is well aware that his choices are legally permitted. In these instances, Mrs. Lex tries to supersede her husband's poor child-rearing choices by, for example, buying a warm winter coat for her daughter and charging it to Mr. Lex.[76] When Mr. Lex refuses to pay the bill and is sued upon it by the store, he relies successfully on an Illinois Supreme Court case clearly establishing the sole authority of the father over the child and hence over what constitutes "family expenses."[77] In response, the store owner then tries to have Mrs. Lex arrested for obtaining the child's coat under false pretenses, and under such a threat, the child herself removes the coat and returns it to the store.[78]

Through the fictional story of Mrs. Lex, McCulloch provided vivid illustrations of the ways in which mothers' lack of legal authority deprived them of the ability to decide matters directly bearing upon the care and well-being of their children and the management of the household, even though married women were expected to devote themselves to raising the children and maintaining the home. Ironically, Justice Bradley had proclaimed in his now-infamous 1873 concurrence in *Bradwell v. Illinois* that "the constitution of the family organization, which is founded in the divine ordinance, as well as in the nature of things, indicates the domestic sphere as that which properly belongs to the domain and functions of womanhood."[79] But the reality of the "separate spheres" tradition, at this moment, was that the domestic sphere did not actually belong to women; women did not have legal authority to raise children and manage the domestic sphere as they saw fit. They were at their husbands' mercy. In 1901, the Illinois legislature passed the Equal Guardian Act, which McCulloch had drafted, and only after McCulloch, who served as legal counsel to the WCTU, had sent a copy of *Mr. Lex* to every Illinois legislator.[80]

Mr. Lex also illustrated law's myriad shortcomings when it came to the seduction of teenage girls leading to their pregnancy and single motherhood. Mary, a fourteen-year-old daughter of Mr. and Mrs. Lex, is seduced and impregnated by a man twice her age.[81] Because the law regarded girls at the age of fourteen as old enough to consent to their own ruin, there was no possibility of prosecuting the man for rape in the absence of evidence of physical violence.[82] Nearly a century before the *Michael M.* case (discussed in chapter 1), advocates for women's rights were committed to establishing a legal presumption of rape—that is, statutory rape—for teenage girls, particularly because of their asymmetric risk of pregnancy. Although it was possible to sue the man for bastardy resulting in an award of child support, the law limited, and all-male juries were unlikely to award, remedies sufficient to support the child.[83] In 1905, also after McCulloch's efforts at lobbying the legislature, a new law in Illinois raised the age of consent to sexual acts from fourteen to sixteen.[84]

Finally, one legal remedy for Mary's situation could stem from a civil cause of action for the family's loss of the daughter's services in the form of work. Mrs. Lex pursues this and ends up winning her suit, but with a damage award of only one dollar.[85] Worse, Mrs. Lex's paltry legal victory is reversed on appeal, on the grounds that a mother has no cause of action, because only the one who would be entitled to the daughter's services would have such a cause of action, and under the patriarchal law then in effect this would be the father only, not the mother.[86] The story of Mary's downfall and Mrs. Lex's inability to pursue legal remedies that would improve Mary's situation clearly reveals a legal regime that prevents women from governing the domain of the family and the home, despite their essential contributions to raising the family and maintaining the home. The law extracts these contributions from mothers and wives but gives them no legal rights to control their destinies.

Mr. Lex also illustrated the vulnerable economic position that married women found themselves in because they were prevented from controlling or enjoying the fruits of their own property. In *Mr. Lex*, much of the family's wealth comes from Mrs. Lex, as the store operated by Mr. Lex comes from the wealth of Mrs. Lex's family. In addition, Mrs. Lex inherits some money from a cousin. Mrs. Lex, now pregnant again, plans to spend the money on flannels, warm shoes, baby clothes, and domestic help with laundry and ironing while she is weakened by pregnancy, but Mr. Lex spends much of it on tobacco. Mrs. Lex attempts without success to refuse to pay.[87] Again, the law clearly established that it was for the father as head of household to determine what constituted a family expense. During this period, many women were in the same situation as Mrs. Lex when their husbands spent the family's income at the saloon on alcohol, including money earned or inherited by the women themselves. McCulloch successfully lobbied the Illinois legislature to adopt a range of reforms that improved the status of married women and mothers, liberating them from the authority of their husbands in many situations detailed in *Mr. Lex*.

Armed with legal education and legal practice, Foster, Bittenbender, Kepley, and McCulloch had a deep understanding of the legal barriers that women faced to controlling their own destinies after the men on whom they depended failed. They saw constitutional Prohibition as one of several necessary reforms to overcome this disempowerment. The liquor economy, working together with the patriarchal legal landscape of rights for men only, led to disastrous lives for many American women. Prohibition would cut the legs off the liquor industry so as to reset the social and economic context in which husbands and wives managed their households. The WCTU lawyers saw the liquor economy as a broad-ranging general subject fit for constitutional intervention because of its effects on citizens' ability to control their lives. These first women lawyers connected Prohibition to a wide range of legal problems that affected women's ability to protect their lives at home.

COMPREHENSIVE LEGAL FEMINISM BEYOND ALCOHOL

The women's temperance movement, guided by women lawyers, imagined Prohibition as reordering the property rights of liquor businesses, with direct consequences for women's power over their lives within the home. For the first time in US history, women lawyers published and staked out a voice in debates about the Constitution and the need for broad-based legal reform. Through the institutional space of the temperance movement, women campaigned for other legal reforms that would reset these entitlements and rebalance power to improve women's lives. They advocated for the eight-hour workday, to facilitate breadwinning fathers' increased involvement in family life in the domestic sphere. They sought to abolish the exclusively male space of saloons, where breadwinning fathers drank away the family wage to recover from a long day of overwork. In place of the saloon, they promoted a family life that included active male participation in child-rearing. And, while assuming that men would remain the main breadwinners, Willard urged the expansion of professional opportunities for women beyond the domestic sphere.

In a 1912 book, *A Farm Philosopher,* Kepley recounted losses women sustained due to local officials' abuses of power. One example was her own absorption of the costs of establishing the WCTU's Temple in Effingham because local officials refused to authorize the organization's use of public space. In another, women organized against the corruption of county officials and juries (all male) who did not enforce existing liquor laws. In the town, women could vote in school board elections, and one of the candidates "had the affliction of a son who was regularly robbed by the saloons of his senses, and his money, and she had a heart, full, for other Mothers who, like herself, were robbed of the sons they risked their lives for."[88] It was well-known in the town that it was nearly impossible to indict saloonkeepers when they operated in violation of liquor laws because "they had a cinch on the County officials and grand juries." But the woman "worked up the evidence" and became "a terror" to the saloonkeepers. She collected evidence that led to indictments of saloonkeepers, and the saloonkeepers "feared and hated her."[89] Although the saloonkeepers tried to organize against her, women mobilized to vote for her for the school board—one thousand voters, rather than the usual fifty, cast votes in this election.[90] The story shows how the movement for Prohibition was intertwined with women's efforts to participate in any democratic processes that were available to them to stop abuses of power by incumbents.

The women's temperance movement began to push for constitutional change through both Prohibition and women's suffrage, made possible by women empowered by law licenses and the ability to form political organizations. Advocacy for constitutional Prohibition grew out of a critique of the liquor industry's excessive economic power, which enabled it to achieve legal and political dominance over women seeking greater control over their domestic and economic well-being. The WCTU gave women a political base and legal counsel, which enabled engagement and progress toward a broader feminist agenda.

HOW PROHIBITION EMPOWERED WOMEN

The nineteenth-century awakening of women's temperance activism culminated nearly a generation after Willard's death, when the Prohibition
Amendment was ratified in 1919. The Eighteenth Amendment to the US
Constitution provided that "after one year from the ratification of this article the manufacture, sale or transportation of intoxicating liquors within,
the importation thereof into, or the exportation thereof from the United
States and all territory subject to the jurisdiction thereof for beverage purposes is hereby prohibited."[91] The amendment gave Congress and the
states concurrent power to enforce Prohibition.

The Prohibition Amendment was short-lived. It was the only constitutional amendment in US history to be repealed and replaced by another
constitutional amendment, the Twenty-First Amendment, ratified in
1933. Given how instrumental women were, across generations, to the
adoption and ratification of the Prohibition Amendment, it may come as
a surprise that they were indispensable to the movement that succeeded
in repealing Prohibition just over a decade later. Indeed, some of the
women leaders of the Women's Organization for National Prohibition
Reform (WONPR) had participated in the temperance movement and
had supported Prohibition before it was enacted. But their experiences of
the 1920s led them to oppose Prohibition and advocate its repeal.

Although the short life span of the Prohibition Amendment leads many
commentators to regard it as a failure or a mistake of American constitutionalism, assessing the amendment from the perspective of the WCTU
women lawyers furnishes different insights. For them, one goal of
Prohibition was to reduce the excessive power of the liquor industry,
because it induced toxic male behavior that imposed hardships on disempowered women. The movement for Prohibition—if not the actual legal
regime of Prohibition—achieved that. From the standpoint of women's
status, Prohibition could be regarded as a relatively successful resetting
tool that was no longer needed by 1933 when it was repealed. Even if
Prohibition did not abolish the drinking of alcohol, it weakened saloons as
the spaces of male overempowerment that they had been. Advocacy for
Prohibition also increased women's political power and enabled women to
pursue reforms that entitled them to certain legal protections. Temperance

activities provided a network and platform for the pursuit of suffrage. The Nineteenth Amendment, prohibiting the denial or abridgment of the right to vote on account of sex, was successfully ratified on the heels of the Prohibition Amendment in 1920, which had just gone into effect when the Nineteenth Amendment became law.

In addition to suffrage, women lawyers of the WCTU, especially McCulloch, advocated simultaneously and successfully for other legal reforms that dismantled the laws of patriarchy and recognized women's rights. Her home state, Illinois, passed a law on mothers' equal guardianship over children in 1901,[92] and another statute raising the age of consent to sex from fourteen to sixteen in 1905,[93] at least a decade after temperance women lawyers had made the case for constitutional Prohibition. These laws tempered the abuses of power facilitated by male overempowerment that McCulloch had detailed in *Mr. Lex.* Other states followed. Whereas in 1880 the age of consent was as low as ten or twelve in most states, by 1920, as Prohibition went into effect, more than half the states (twenty-six) had raised the age to sixteen.

But perhaps the most significant shift in the status of women most directly caused by the Prohibition Amendment stemmed from its effect on the male space of the saloon. As the text of the Eighteenth Amendment makes clear, the Amendment did not prohibit the drinking of alcohol; it prohibited the manufacture, sale, transportation, and importation of intoxicating liquors. It was directed at the liquor industry, not drinkers. The Volstead Act, which implemented Prohibition, permitted the production of wine and cider at home. Therefore, drinking moved from the saloon to the home in the 1920s.[94] Women had control over men's alcohol consumption in their new role as home wine producer and cocktail party host. Women and men drank together as a gender-integrated social activity. Moderate drinking was glamorized to signal a woman's liberation. Even when drinking occurred outside of the home, in cabarets and speakeasies, these illicit drinking spaces provided gender-integrated entertainment and social life.

Historians' accounts of the amendment repealing Prohibition have emphasized the role of women, particularly Pauline Sabin, who founded and led WONPR.[95] Having been active with the Republican Party, which had long supported Prohibition, Sabin abandoned party politics in 1928 largely out of dismay at the growth of Prohibition enforcement. She and the women of WONPR denounced the government's intrusion into the home that had been precipitated by Prohibition enforcement. The privacy of the home and family life were invaded by warrantless searches and wire-tapping. Whereas the men calling for the repeal of Prohibition for years primarily attacked Prohibition on libertarian grounds, embracing the personal freedom to choose to drink, WONPR made headway on the repeal amendment because the women reasoned from "home protection," appropriating the WCTU's rhetoric. Women were the moral guardians of the home, and as such, women, not the government, should decide whether their husbands or sons drank, they argued. The state need not intrude upon the home to enforce temperance, they claimed, because morality would be secured by the woman in the home.

Asserting that women exerted control over life in the home was much more plausible after a decade of Prohibition than it could have been in the years leading up to the Prohibition Amendment's adoption and ratification. The movement for Prohibition nourished the progress toward significant other advances in women's rights, and Prohibition itself altered the culture and social dynamics of drinking that reduced the power of drunk husbands, exclusively male spaces, and the liquor industry. The Prohibition Amendment—and the movement that made it possible—reset the balance of rights, entitlements, and power that had severely subordinated women under a patriarchal legal order. Prohibition illustrates how a constitutional transformation, and the women's political power it inspired and depended upon, can shape the prospects for superseding legal regimes that maintain overentitlement and overempowerment.

In the twenty-first century, legal regimes other than the property and business rights of the liquor industry maintain overentitlement and overempowerment. What the history of Prohibition highlights is the importance and possibility of identifying and targeting those regimes of misogyny. Sometimes the laws and legal initiatives that do not appear to be about women carry the most potential to empower women to reset the baselines of democracy.

5 Rebalancing Power through Parity Democracy

To overcome patriarchal law, women demanded the same entitlements that men enjoyed under the law. Over the last fifty years, the experiences of constitutional democracies around the world show that equal power for women requires more than equal rights under the law. But can women be empowered equally if they are not treated equally?

This puzzle has plagued the effort to replace patriarchy with a democracy where people of all genders enjoy real equality. *United States v. Virginia*, the landmark decision establishing the legal framework for constitutional sex equality, outlawed sex discrimination while permitting men and women to be treated differently. Different treatment was sometimes necessary and therefore constitutionally authorized, Justice Ginsburg wrote, "to compensate women 'for particular economic disabilities [they have] suffered, to 'promot[e] equal employment opportunity,' to advance full development of the talent and capacities of our Nation's people," but not "to create or perpetuate the legal, social, and economic inferiority of women."[1]

That decision forced the Virginia Military Institute (VMI), an old bastion of male power, to open its doors to women. The Supreme Court terminated VMI's policy of excluding women from admission, recognizing VMI as a producer of "citizen-soldiers" and leaders, including military generals, members of Congress, and business executives. VMI also held the "largest per-student endowment of all public undergraduate institutions in the Nation." It should not be difficult to see how reserving such a wealth of advantages and opportunities exclusively to men overempowers them. To rebalance power to render it compatible with democracy rather than patriarchy, constitutional equality law must scrutinize gendered overempowerment, rather than gender classifications. Recent developments in the constitutional law of sex equality in European and Latin American countries illustrate the shift from equal rights to equal power.

THE AMERICAN STRUGGLE TO INTEGRATE MALE INSTITUTIONS

After World War II, American women attempted to use the Equal Protection Clause to challenge unequal power as well as unequal treatment under the law. They litigated to integrate male spaces and institutions, with limited success until the 1970s. The story behind *Goesaert v. Cleary*, a Supreme Court case decided in 1948, illustrates how initial understandings of sex equality under the law remained blind to overentitlement and overempowerment. Female litigants challenged a Michigan law banning women from the bartending profession. That law, enacted in 1945, provided that females could not be licensed as bartenders unless they were wives or daughters of a male owner of the bar.[2] For much of the history of the United States, bars were male spaces.[3] Bars were used as polling stations when only men could vote, and men also gathered there to discuss politics, economics, and other public matters.[4] In some localities at the turn of the century, women were formally excluded by law from entering bars.[5] But Prohibition shut down saloons and the bartending profession. Then, after Prohibition was repealed and during World War II, women worked in many traditionally male jobs, including bartending. The Michigan legislature adopted the law excluding women from bartending just after World War II in response to extensive lobbying by the Bartenders' Union, an exclusively male organization. The members of the Bartenders' Union mingled with judges, attorneys, and legislators; it was an organization with abundant access to political power.

The Michigan Bartenders' Union was not primarily interested in maintaining bars as male social spaces; they were not against bars employing women as waitresses. In addition, the businesses of recreational drinking that emerged after Prohibition were gender-integrated social spaces rather than the distinctly masculine space of the saloon. Nonetheless, the male Bartenders' Union sought to protect their monopoly of higher wages against bar owners inclined to profit from paying less for female barmaids instead of male bartenders. The union did not object to women's presence as customers or waitresses; they objected to women's empowerment through higher wages and the control they could exercise from behind the bar over their own bodies and over men, by denying alcohol to drunk customers.

Women bartenders organized the Michigan Barmaids' Association to assert their employment opportunities, as well to protect their bodies from sexual harassment by bar patrons. Behind the bar, a woman was protected from unwanted pinching and touching,[6] whereas waiting on tables came with greater exposure of working women to toxic and aggressive intrusions by male customers. The Barmaids' Association argued that the statute excluding women from bartending violated the Equal Protection Clause and deprived female bartenders of due process.

The Supreme Court rejected their claim. Justice Frankfurter insisted that "the Fourteenth Amendment did not tear our history up by its roots."[7] Applying a rational basis test, he concluded that the legislature could exclude women on the basis of the judgment that allowing women "behind the bar" would "give rise to moral and social problems." Furthermore, he concluded, "Since the line they have drawn is not without a basis in reason, we cannot give ear to the suggestion that the real impulse behind this legislation was an unchivalrous desire of male bartenders to try to monopolize the calling."[8] To the extent that women's presence as waitresses seemed inconsistent with the purported legislative purpose of preventing "moral and social problems," the Supreme Court defended the legislature's rational basis in "allowing women to be waitresses in a liquor establishment over which a man's ownership provides control."[9] The court could not see legislation to maintain a space where men were in control (empowered), with higher wages (entitled), as a threat to equal protection of the laws. What would it take for the law to recognize this empowerment and entitlement as excessive?

The perpetuation of male control over an institution from which women were historically excluded—the jury—was again upheld by the Supreme Court in *Hoyt v. Florida*. In that case, a woman who was convicted of murdering her husband, on a verdict by an all-male jury, challenged the Florida law that automatically included all male citizens of voting age in the jury pool while including only women who sought out jury service. The practical and perhaps intended effect was that juries that wielded tremendous power over the lives of the accused were largely composed of men. The all-male Supreme Court in 1961 upheld and justified this rule, fully acknowledging the statistics detailing male overrepresentation and female underrepresentation on juries, because "woman is still regarded as the center of home and family life."[10] Women had the privilege of avoiding jury duty unless they really wanted to be included, the court reasoned, so that they could tend to their natural calling as mothers, wives, and homemakers. Women's equal participation in public power did not register on the court's rational basis analysis as a measure of the equal protection of the laws.

In the 1970s and 1980s, the idea that equal protection of the laws required the integration of some bastions of gendered power began to take hold. The insight emerged in part from the cases Ruth Bader Ginsburg litigated challenging laws that treated men and women differently for the purposes of estate administration and social welfare benefits, detailed in chapter 1. In *Seidenburg v. McSorley's Old Ale House, Inc.*, members of the National Organization for Women urged a federal court to find an equal protection violation in the continued operation of a men-only bar in New York, on the theory that a state's continued licensing of a bar that excluded women amounted to a state deprivation of women's equal protection rights. "Once a property, facility, or transaction becomes significantly impregnated with a state character the Equal Protection Clause controls,"[11] the court acknowledged. A bar that benefited from a state-issued liquor license and profited from selling alcohol to the public presented "a pervasive regulation by the state of the activities of the defendant, a commercial enterprise engaged in voluntarily serving the public except for women."[12] The state had acted annually to renew McSorley's liquor license, despite the bar's open discrimination against women. Thus, the court concluded, "The state's participation here is significant" and violated the

Equal Protection Clause. When it came to regulating bars, "sexual separatism" was premised on "outdated images of bars as dens of coarseness and iniquity and of women as peculiarly delicate and impressionable creatures in need of protection from the rough and tumble of unvarnished humanity," views that could no longer be justified.[13]

A concept of unjust enrichment seems to run through the court's analysis of the state's relationship to the bar, in which the state is presumed to represent the interests of all, including women. A license granted to a bar by the state operated to "restrict competition between vendors of alcoholic beverages, thus conferring on license holders a significant state-derived economic benefit" that amounted to state support. For a bar to reap that benefit was an enrichment that was not justified in light of its exclusion of a huge swath of the public. There was no freedom to exclude women because the bar was "voluntarily serving the public, devoted to a business in which volume of patronage is essential to commercial success."[14]

The Supreme Court also began to criticize sexual separatism in several rulings that required male-only institutions to admit women for full and equal participation. But the court was not construing the meaning of the sex equality right under equal protection in those cases; there it simply upheld decisions by lower courts declining to expand male organizations' First Amendment rights to exclude women. In *Roberts v. Jaycees,* the Supreme Court upheld state efforts to require an all-male private civic organization to admit women as members. A state human rights commission had concluded that the exclusion of women according to the organization's bylaws was an unfair discriminatory practice in violation of state law. The organization asserted its federal constitutional right to freedom of association in an effort to preserve its all-male membership rule. But the Supreme Court rejected that challenge and concluded that "by prohibiting gender discrimination in places of public accommodation, the Minnesota Act protects the State's citizenry from a number of serious social and personal harms."[15]

Similarly, in *Rotary International v. Rotary Club of Duarte,* the Supreme Court upheld a California state civil rights law that required California Rotary Clubs to admit women as constitutionally compatible with the Rotary Club's First Amendment rights. The First Amendment rights to freedom of private association could be legitimately limited by a state civil rights law requiring gender integration. The court concluded, "Even if the Unruh Act does work some slight infringement on Rotary members' right of expressive association, that infringement is justified because it serves the State's compelling interest in eliminating discrimination against women."[16]

In more recent years, civil rights laws, including the state and federal constitutional guarantees of equal protection, are standing in the way of efforts to integrate women as equals into male spaces and institutions. Litigation challenging such efforts has seen some preliminary success. In 2018, the California legislature adopted a law, initiated by female legislators, that prohibited corporations from electing boards of directors composed exclusively of men.[17] At the time of the law's adoption, 25 percent of corporate boards of directors in California had no women.[18] The law requires every corporation registered to do business in California to have at least one woman on the board of directors; boards with more than six directors must have at least three. The law is a modest minimum threshold; it requires the inclusion of one to three women on every board but does not require parity or gender balance. However, the law may not survive the litigation challenging its constitutionality in state and federal courts. As of this writing, one federal district court has upheld it, recognizing that California can distinguish between women and men to pursue the important governmental objective of remedying past discrimination against women.[19] But that decision is pending on appeal to the Ninth Circuit,[20] and meanwhile, a state trial court has ruled that the minimum gender diversity requirement violates the equal protection guarantee of the California state constitution.[21]

HOW GENDER PARITY BECAME A REQUIREMENT OF FRENCH DEMOCRACY

By contrast, proposals to require powerful institutions to integrate women, or to meet minimum gender representation requirements, have been legitimized as a constitutional matter in many other countries around the world. Contestation over gender quotas was resolved after decades of struggle by constitutional amendment. In France, for instance, a 1982 law added a provision to the electoral code requiring that, in elections for municipal councilors in some localities, lists of candidates run by political parties "may not contain more than 75% of persons of the same sex."[22] But before it went into effect, the French Constitutional Council, which can review the constitutionality of laws before they go into effect, concluded that the gender quota was unconstitutional. The Constitutional Council invoked Article 3 of the Constitution, which provided that national sovereignty belonged to the people, such that "no section of the people nor any individual may arrogate to itself, or to himself, the exercise thereof."[23] In addition, the Constitutional Council found the gender quota contrary to Article 6 of the Declaration of Rights of Man, which provides: "The Law is the expression of the general will. All citizens have the right to take part, personally or through their representatives, in its making. It must be the same for all, whether it protects or punishes. All citizens, being equal in its eyes, shall be equally eligible to all high offices, public positions and employments, according to their ability, and without other distinction than that of their virtues and talents."[24] The Constitutional Council noted that, in the proposed electoral rule, "a distinction is made between candidates on grounds of sex" and that such a distinction would violate both Article 3 of the Constitution and Article 6 of the Declaration.

The Constitutional Council's decision motivated feminists to zero in on women's lack of political power. As of 1992, only 5.4 percent of the representatives elected to the French Parliament were women.[25] The proportion of women was no larger in 1992 than in 1945, when the first National Assembly was elected to work on the Constitution of France following World War II.[26] Throughout the 1980s and 1990s, women protested the Constitutional Council's interpretation of equality and mobilized to amend the Constitution. How could a constitution stop women from gaining access to political power in a true democracy? Françoise Gaspard, who had served as a mayor of a small town before being elected to the National Assembly in 1981, raised this critical question. Gaspard wrote the manifesto of the movement along with activists Claude Servan-Schreiber and Anne Le Gall, titled *To Power, Women Citizens! Liberty, Equality, and Parity*.[27] Women from across the political spectrum united to enact laws that required women to be represented. Instead of focusing on the rights of women, the movement argued that the legitimacy of French democracy was in crisis.[28] A democracy in which women were equal citizens but were severely underrepresented was no democracy. The parity movement insisted that women were different from interest groups, political parties, and races, because women were half the population and half of humankind. They were the half of humankind without whom the democracy could not reproduce and perpetuate itself.

In 1999, Article 3 of the French Constitution was amended with the following additional language: "The law shall promote the equal access of men and women to electoral authority and elected positions."[29] The supporters of the amendment intended for it to clear the path for electoral rules seeking to increase women's access to elected office after centuries of disfranchisement and decades of underrepresentation. In 2000, the national legislature adopted another law to that effect, requiring equal numbers of men and women on lists for elections to parliamentary seats, by providing that the gap between the number of candidates of each sex could not be greater than one.[30] Although the opponents of the law petitioned the Constitutional Council to review it, the Constitutional Council upheld its constitutionality, pointing to the 1999 amendment.[31]

The 1999 amendment proclaimed women's equal access to power, in the form of the electoral mandate and elected positions. Any existing commitment to equality under the law, presumably prohibiting distinctions between citizens, was revised by this proclamation. In fact, Article 1 of the Declaration of the Rights of Man had always permitted social distinctions based on considerations of the common good. It reads, "Men are born free and equal in rights. Social distinctions may be based only on considerations of the common good."[32] French feminists argued that measures to ensure women's equal access to elected positions, including gender parity requirements in electoral rules, were for the common good. There was something illegitimate, something antidemocratic, if not autocratic, about a polity in which only men exercised public power. The absence of half of humanity from the exercise of state power would undermine the legitimacy of the state and reveal it to be something other than a democracy.[33]

Extending this idea into the economic sphere, the legislature adopted another law in 2006 imposing similar gender parity quotas on corporate boards of directors.[34] But the Constitutional Council invalidated that law, narrowly reading the 1999 amendment as applying only to elected governmental positions, not corporations.[35] Feminists mobilized again to amend the Constitution, and in 2008, the French Constitution was amended once more. This time, new language was inserted into Article 1 of the Constitution, providing, "The law shall promote equal access by women and men to elective offices and posts as well as to positions of professional and social responsibility." Equal power for women, as Pauli Murray had imagined it decades earlier in the United States, was inscribed into France's fundamental law.

This 2008 amendment catalyzed proactive legislation to promote gender equality. Almost immediately, a law requiring gender quotas on corporate boards of directors was reintroduced,[36] very similar to the one that was struck down in 2006.[37] The new statute, adopted in 2011, provided that by 2017 the proportion of board members of each sex could not be less than 40 percent.[38] Several statutes and regulations that imposed gender quotas in many other decision-making bodies followed. For example, a 2012 law provided that various civil service governing bodies could not be less than 40 percent of each sex.[39] A 2013 statute reforming higher education provided that certain committees within higher education institutions had to achieve parity between women and men in composition.[40] Also in 2013, the existing parity rules in regional and municipal elections were strengthened, requiring political parties' candidate lists to strictly alternate male-female in a wider range of elections.[41]

In 2014, the French legislature adopted a comprehensive gender equality statute,[42] asserting a mandate emanating from the 2008 constitutional amendment.[43] The statute, on "real equality between women and men," included the removal of some procedural impediments to abortion access, measures to reduce the gender pay gap, reform of parental leave to incentivize equal caregiving by fathers and mothers, aid to victims of violence against women, and gender balance rules in new institutional settings where they had not previously applied. The 2008 constitutional amendment was cited as a source of a legislative mandate to adopt a comprehensive gender equality agenda, empowering women in many different domains of social, political, and economic life.[44] Several reforms on "professional equality between women and men" were adopted, seeking to reduce the burdens of women's work within families and households and their negative impact on women's careers.[45] The statute also imposed gender parity rules in new domains, such as professional sports organizations, and strengthened the mechanisms for enforcing existing political party quotas.[46] Whereas women constituted less than 20 percent of the elected legislators in the French Parliament at the time that the 2008 amendment was adopted, within a decade women constituted nearly 40 percent of legislators elected to Parliament after the elections of 2017.

With women now constituting more than one-third of the legislature, the French Parliament adopted new legislation in 2018 creating an "equal pay index" for large employers with fifty or more employees.[47] The index consists of five criteria on which the employer receives points for reducing disparities: (1) gaps in salary between women and men; (2) gaps in raises between women and men; (3) gaps in the share of promotions between women and men; (4) percentage of workers who received a raise after maternity leave; and (5) parity between women and men in the top ten earners in the organization. With the first indicator (gaps in salary between women and men) weighted the most heavily, each company receives a score, with the maximum/perfect score being 100 points. The score must be posted on the company's website—with more time for smaller companies to comply with the website posting requirement. All companies to which the law applies were given three years to reach a score of 75 points. At that point, companies failing to achieve a score of 75 would be obligated to devise a plan for reducing the gender gaps, and the labor inspector could fine the company up to 1 percent of payroll.

In France, the last half century has seen two constitutional amendments to legitimize the empowerment of women, followed by a rapid increase in the percentage of women occupying positions of decision-making power in political and economic institutions. This decision-making power has then been deployed to address remaining manifestations of overentitlement and overempowerment in French society. These transformations began with the conflict, similar to the one that courts are still grappling with in the United States, over whether the law can treat women differently to advance their empowerment as equals.

THE MEANING OF EQUAL RIGHTS IN GERMANY: VALUING WOMEN'S CONTRIBUTIONS AND ERADICATING EXISTING DISADVANTAGES

The struggle to constitutionalize women's equal share of political power has a long history in Germany and continues to be the subject of constitutional litigation as of this writing. The constitution adopted at Weimar in 1919 has been influential in twentieth-century constitutionalism; it was among the first that established a modern liberal democracy and guaranteed human rights. Although it was short-lived, many of its articles became part of the German Basic Law that was adopted thirty years later and shaped similar provisions in other twentieth-century constitutions around the world.

The Weimar Constitution of 1919 was also a pivotal event in the history of women's empowerment. It included the first known constitutional provision explicitly guaranteeing the equal rights and responsibilities of men and women. Women participated as elected members of the constituent assembly that adopted the 1919 Constitution; they made up about 10 percent of the constitution-making body. The women constitution makers at Weimar represented political parties from the full range of the political spectrum, from conservative Christian to liberal democratic to socialist and communist. Although they did not agree on a single vision for German women's equality, they made coalitions that successfully entrenched principles that German women's movements had articulated in the late nineteenth and twentieth centuries.[48] The Weimar Constitution's guarantee of equality before the law, analogous to Article 6 of the French Declaration of the Rights of Man and the Fourteenth Amendment to the US Constitution, went one step further: "All Germans are equal before the law. Men and women have basically equal rights and duties of citizenship."[49] An additional provision, like Article 6 of the French Declaration, provided, "All citizens, without distinction, are eligible according to their abilities and accomplishments to open public offices, in accordance with law."[50] But it, too, went one step further to speak explicitly to the status of women. "All regulations making exceptions against female civil servants are abolished," its next sentence provided.[51]

There were extensive debates at Weimar about the inclusion of the word *grundsätzlich* ("basically" or "in principle") in the constitutional declaration of equal rights and duties between men and women. "Basically" equal rights and duties meant not always the same rights and duties. A central issue was whether female citizens should have the same duties as men with regard to military service—an issue that continues to be contested by feminists and misogynists alike with regard to military draft registration in the United States, as we saw in chapter 1. On the one hand, some women expressed concerns that saying "basically equal rights" would dilute the guarantee of women's equality and was unnecessary, even in a legal order that would impose different duties of citizenship on women and men.[52] Some argued that women and men could have equal duties, even if it meant that men would serve the nation in the military and women would serve the nation by raising and educating children at home.[53] Others argued that the question of women in the military was moot because Germany's defeat in World War I had led to treaty obligations that severely restricted German militarization, which would end and prohibit compulsory military service, even for male citizens. Nonetheless, both proponents and opponents of inserting the word *basically* agreed on what they wanted the equality provision to mean: the recognition of women as fully equal citizens under the law, compatible with women occupying different but equal roles.[54]

Nearly three decades later, the women in the Parlamentarischer Rat, the constituent assembly in Bonn convened to write a new constitution for Germany after World War II, had to fight for equal rights anew. In 1948, Elisabeth Selbert was the first woman lawyer ever to participate in the German constitution-making process, as women had been authorized to enter the legal profession only in 1922, after the Weimar Constitution went into effect. A provision that read, "Men and women shall have equal rights" was proposed at Bonn in 1948; the Weimar Constitution's modifier *grundsätzlich* was gone. Male leaders of the liberal and Christian Democratic parties opposed the language "Men and women shall have equal rights," arguing that treating women the same as men would harm women. Equal rights could lead to the denial of spousal support to women in cases of divorce. Equal rights would lead women to work outside the home, the opponents argued, depriving women of fulfillment as mothers and wives. The provision was voted down by the constituent assembly when it was first proposed in December 1948.

That's when Elisabeth Selbert traveled the country to talk directly to the German people about the importance of enshrining women's equality in the nation's Basic Law.[55] As one of the four women in the sixty-five-member constituent assembly selected by the regional governments, Elisabeth Selbert insisted, as her predecessors had done in Weimar, that the principle of equal rights for men and women was compatible with the law treating women and men differently. Selbert believed that women should have the right to pursue work outside the home, but she recognized that many married women would choose full-time marriage and motherhood. Those women also needed rights equal to husbands and fathers, just as women working outside the home and in the public sphere were entitled to equal status. Equality was about placing equal value on women's contributions to society. Women's work in educating the children and running the household should be valued equally to market work and military service. "The work of the housewife is sociologically of the same worth as the work of the woman employed outside the home," Selbert said. What mattered was that women and their contributions were equally valued by law and public institutions. That was the principle—not sameness of treatment above all—that belonged in the Basic Law.

The four women in the constituent assembly united in favor of the provision on the equal rights of women and men and ultimately prevailed. Neither they nor German women as a group agreed on the policy direction that valuing women equally should take, such as encouraging market work or homemaking and child-rearing. Frieda Nadig, like Elisabeth Selbert a member of the Social Democratic Party (SPD), highlighted the demographic reality of the nation after war. There were seven million more women than men. For the nation to reproduce and rebuild itself, single motherhood would be a social reality, and many women would have no choice but to be both breadwinner and caregiver. For the more conservative Helene Wessel, valuing women's contributions meant protecting marriage and the family so that mothers and wives could depend on their husbands to support them and could devote themselves to the valuable work of raising children. But the women of the constituent assembly agreed that whatever women did—whether as workers or as mothers—should be valued through a declaration of women's rights in the Basic Law. The Basic Law that was adopted in 1949 featured two explicit provisions equalizing women's status to that of men. Article 3.2 provides, "Men and women shall have equal rights," and Article 3.3 guarantees, "No person shall be favored or disfavored because of sex, parentage, race, language, homeland, origin, faith or religious or political opinions."

In the initial decades of construing these provisions, the German Constitutional Court's jurisprudence was similar to that of the US Supreme Court in *Goesaert* and *Hoyt*. It refrained from striking down sex distinctions made by the law—even those that kept women subordinate in jobs or public life. In 1953, for instance, the West German Federal Constitutional Court pointed to maternity as a biological difference that justified women's special treatment,[56] and in 1956 it upheld a labor code provision limiting the working hours of women.[57] The cases of the 1950s construed the Article 3.2 equal rights guarantee as doing no more than prohibiting discrimination, and the Article 3.3 antidiscrimination guarantee as permitting different treatment pursuant to review similar to American rational basis review. Within this regime, the Federal Constitutional Court declared in 1959 that men and women were equal in marriage and struck down Civil Code provisions that accorded more weight to fathers than to mothers in the exercise of parental authority over minor children in the event of disagreements between the parents.[58] Ruth Bader Ginsburg cited this particular case over a decade later in her brief to the US Supreme Court in *Reed v. Reed*.[59]

From its establishment in 1951, the German Constitutional Court has always had at least one woman on the court. From 1951 to 1986, there was always exactly one woman judge. (The US Supreme Court got its first woman, Justice Sandra Day O'Connor, in 1981 and its second woman, Justice Ruth Bader Ginsburg, in 1993). From 1986 onwards, the number of female justices on the German Constitutional Court grew steadily, culminating in 2020 in an equal number of male and female justices. In fact, five of the eight female justices sat in the same chamber—the Second Senate—giving women a majority in one of the court's chambers for the first time in history.

In the 1970s, the German Constitutional Court changed its approach to women's traditional caregiving role in justifying sex-based differences in treatment.[60] Applying heightened scrutiny to statutory sex distinctions, it rejected justifications for differential treatment that perpetuated the traditional sex roles that had led to women's inequality.[61] In a widely read decision in 1992, the German Constitutional Court struck down a statute prohibiting women's nighttime employment. The law had been defended as a protection of women, who were assumed to be more susceptible to harm by night work because of their daytime responsibilities for child-rearing. In striking down the ban, the court explained that what rendered the law unconstitutional was not merely the sex classification under Article 3.3 but the law's undermining of women's real prospects for equality on the ground.[62]

The decision recognized the changing roles of men and women in relation to housework and child-rearing and the potential negative effects of the ban on night work on women's economic power. The court framed women's access to employment as a primary concern of Article 3.2's guarantee of equal rights.[63] It explained that the Basic Law's guarantee that "men and women shall have equal rights" was "designed not only to do away with legal norms that base advantages or disadvantages o[n] sex but also to bring about equal opportunity for men and women in the future. It is aimed at the equalization of living conditions."[64] It was "a constitutional mandate to foster equal standing of men and women . . . that extends to social reality."[65]

Two years later, that constitutional mandate on making the equal standing of men and women extend to social reality became more explicit by way of a constitutional amendment. Throughout the 1980s, proactive measures, including gender quotas in regional civil service positions, were introduced to provide more employment opportunities to women. German reunification brought new attention to the unequal participation of women in public institutions, as women in East Germany had been in the workforce in much higher proportions than women in West Germany. The 1990 Unification Treaty declared, "It shall be the task of the all-German legislator to develop further the legislation on equal rights for men and women."[66] That treaty offered a definition of equal rights for men and women that went beyond the commitment to nondiscrimination to empower women economically: "In view of different legal and institutional starting positions with regard to the employment of mothers and fathers, it shall be the task of the all-German legislator to shape the legal situation in such a way as to allow reconciliation of family and occupational life."[67] The Joint Commission on Constitutional Reform proposed an amendment that would nudge the legislature for a newly reunified Germany to adopt public policies toward these goals. That amendment became the second sentence of Article 3.2: "The State shall promote the actual implementation of equal rights for women and men and take steps to eliminate disadvantages that now exist."[68]

Shortly after the 1994 amendment went into effect, the legislature focused on women's share of public positions of power and responsibility. In 2001, the Bundestag adopted the Federal Equality Law on the Equality of Men and Women in Federal Administration and Courts.[69] In departments where women are underrepresented, women with equal qualifications must be given preferential consideration for training, jobs, and promotions, taking individual circumstances into account. The statute also requires gender equality plans within administrative units, including a stipulation that when a unit is downsizing, its proportion of women must be maintained. In 2015, the Bundestag also adopted a law imposing gender quotas on corporate boards of directors, with Germany joining Norway, France, the Netherlands, Italy, Belgium, and Spain in adopting a law requiring some form of gender balance rule for corporate boards.[70] Laws requiring economic and political institutions to guarantee women some share of decision-making power are proliferating in many of the United States' peer democracies as the next step toward realizing the constitutional commitment to equal rights for women. By contrast, in the United States, such laws, even when adopted by only one state to require only one woman on every corporate board, are increasingly likely to be struck down under a constitutional equal protection doctrine that makes gender neutrality its touchstone, rather than ending gendered overempowerment.

The path to women sharing more meaningfully in economic and political power has also met recent resistance in German courts. In 2020, two state-level (Länder) constitutional courts struck down laws adopted by the state-level legislatures to require the political parties to adhere to gender parity in their lists of candidates for legislative elections. Women were underrepresented in the State Parliament of Thuringia, making up 31 percent of the elected representatives while constituting 51.5 percent of the population of those eligible to vote in the state. The Thuringia Parliament thus adopted parity legislation that went into effect in January

2020, only to be challenged by a constitutional complaint from the far-right political party Alternativ für Deutschland (AfD). The Parity Act required political party lists proposed in the proportional voting system to alternate between a man and a woman.[71] But in a 6–3 decision, the state constitutional court for Thuringia struck down the law in July 2020, holding that the parity rule violated both the state constitution and Germany's federal Basic Law.[72] Specifically, the court found that the gender quota violated the right to free and equal elections in the Thuringia constitution, as well as the Basic Law's guarantees of political parties' rights to freedom of activity, freedom to determine the party program, and equal opportunities. Of the nine justices on the Thuringia State Constitutional Court, only two are women. Both women dissented in this ruling, viewing the parity law as being constitutionally sound because the 1994 amendment to Article 3.2 of the Basic Law specifically obligates the state to promote the actual realization of equal rights between women and men and to eliminate disadvantages that now exist.

Similarly, in October 2020 the Constitutional Court of the State of Brandenburg struck down Brandenburg's parity law, which required equal representation of men and women, listed in alternating order, on political party candidate lists for elections to the state parliament. The parity law was adopted when women constituted about one-third of the representatives elected.[73] The Brandenburg court held, similarly to the Thuringia court, that the parity law violated the freedom and equal opportunities of the parties, invoking the guarantee of party freedom in the Brandenburg constitution. The Brandenburg constitution contains a provision similar to the federal Basic Law's Article 3.2, specifically "Women and men shall have equal rights. The Land shall be obligated to take effective measures to provide for the equal status of women and men in work, public life, education and training, the family, and in the areas of social security."[74] The Brandenburg court said that while this provision made the pursuit of gender equality a legitimate goal, the parity law exceeded the framework set by the constitution because it amounted to a fundamental change in constitutional democratic structural principles.[75]

The Federal Constitutional Court has declined to review the Thuringia court's invalidation of its gender parity law, holding the constitutional complaint inadmissible.[76] Both of the state courts advanced very narrow understandings of the scope of the state's legitimate authority to promote women's equality found in Basic Law Article 3.2 and parallel provisions in Länder constitutions. On that general question as to whether Article 3.2 permits the legislature to adopt gender parity quotas despite its limitations on the purported right of political parties to freely choose their candidates, the Federal Constitutional Court issued an opinion addressing the question in an earlier decision dismissing a separate complaint about federal elections as inadmissible.

In the last legislative elections for the German Bundestag, the proportion of women elected had dropped significantly. Although women constitute 51.5 percent of the eligible electorate, they were only 29 percent of the candidates listed by political parties in the 2017 elections. As a result, the proportion of women, previously 36.3 percent, fell to 30.7 percent. Several women brought a constitutional complaint challenging the validity of the election. They argued that the Bundestag gave the political parties too much latitude in their nomination of candidates by allowing them to nominate lists of candidates lacking in gender parity. The complainants argued that the absence of parity in the nomination of candidates by the political parties violated Basic Law Section 3.2, which obligates the state toward the actual realization of equal rights and the elimination of disadvantages that now exist. The complaint also invoked Article 38 of the Basic Law, on elections for the Bundestag. Article 38.1 provides, "Members of the German Bundestag shall be elected in general, direct, free, equal and secret elections. They shall be representatives of the whole people, not bound by orders or instructions and responsible only to their conscience." The problem that the complainants were litigating against was the lack of statutory provisions requiring gender balance in the nomination of candidates for the Bundestag.

The Federal Constitutional Court did not decide the substantive constitutional question, which was essentially the same issue raised by the Thuringia and Brandenburg cases, namely whether a parity rule exceeds the scope of the state's constitutional mandate to implement equality between women and men. Rather, in this case about electing the federal legislature, the court deemed the electoral complaint inadmissible because the litigants were challenging, not a specific legislative act or regulation, but rather the absence of a federal parity requirement.[77] A complaint challenging the absence of federal parity legislation was not justiciable. In the course of explaining this decision, the Federal Constitutional Court brought some clarity to the questions raised by the Thuringia and Brandenburg state court rulings, strongly suggesting the constitutionality of gender parity requirements when they are adopted by legislatures.

The Federal Constitutional Court affirmed the Bundestag's broad latitude to enact laws within its constitutional competence. Article 3.2 clearly authorizes and obligates the legislature to implement equal rights and to eliminate women's existing disadvantages, but it does not require the legislature to act in any particular way.[78] Nonetheless, the court suggested that the legislature could require political parties to adhere to gender parity to fulfill its constitutional mandate to implement equality between women and men, by eliminating existing disadvantages (Basic Law Article 3.2). But it would have to do so while recognizing the equal constitutional standing of the principle of free and equal elections (Basic Law Article 38) and political parties' constitutional freedom (Basic Law Article 21).[79] None of these constitutional principles are absolute, and pursuing one could infringe on another. In the event of these inevitable conflicts between constitutional principles of equal standing, it was appropriate for the legislature to decide on the desired balance as long as it did so in keeping with the Constitutional Court's requirements of proportionality. Nonetheless, the court cited France's experience with parity requirements as evidence that they could achieve the desired goal of overcoming gendered underrepresentation.[80]

The German Constitutional Court's decision, while rejecting the suggestion that gender quotas were constitutionally required, broadly affirmed that the constitutional duty to remove "legal norms that link advantages and disadvantages to gender characteristics" went well beyond the duty not to discriminate "but also aims to harmonize the living conditions of men and women."[81] That meant that "the norm extends the principle of equal rights to social reality, and strives for the actual implementation of gender equality for the future": The structural dynamics that led to men's overempowerment and women's underrepresentation in power were constitutional problems, but future constitutional complaints would have to prove the operation of such dynamics to challenge the validity of specific electoral results.

This measured decision, casting parity as a legitimate response to over-empowerment, on the one hand, but anticipating the possibility of limiting parity because of other important constitutional rights and values, on the other hand, was rendered by the Second Senate of the Federal Constitutional Court shortly after it became, for the first time in German history, a judicial body with a female majority. In Germany, women empowered as constitution makers over a century ago shaped the legal foundations for policies that would eventually overcome their underrepresentation and the overempowerment of men. Although women's empowerment has not reached gender parity in most of Germany's lawmaking bodies, recent efforts to require parity follow decades of progress, with women's representation in the Bundestag close to the one-third threshold that Pauli Murray had suggested in 1970 as an antidote to the dangerous imbalance in the US Congress. (The US Congress, by contrast, has reached its all-time high of women elected at 25 percent, and of the state legislatures only one out of fifty—Nevada—reached gender parity in 2019.)

EMPOWERING WOMEN TO MEND GOVERNMENT: TOWARD A NEW CONSTITUTION FOR ICELAND

Any discussion of women's empowerment and constitutional change would be remiss without attention to Iceland, which has consistently ranked number one in the World Economic Forum's cross-national studies of gender equality for over a decade.[82] Iceland consistently scores 100 percent in the World Bank's annual Women, Business, and the Law index,[83] which assigns scores to nations for the presence and strength of laws and policies that reduce gender gaps. Iceland has also been the site of a major effort at constitutional overhaul, led by women, in the twenty-first century.

In Iceland, the deliberate empowerment of women was a direct response to the financial collapse of 2008, which was largely understood to be caused by overempowered men who had enriched themselves by taking excessive risks, and whose costs were eventually borne by the rest of the nation. Nationwide protests ensued as people took to the streets, outraged by the bankers and politicians whose aggressive behavior they believed to have caused the nation's financial crisis. The incumbent government resigned, and new parliamentary elections were held. The people voted in a new parliament with women elected to nearly half the seats, led by the first female (and openly lesbian) prime minister in 2009. The new government undertook ambitious legal reforms not only to regulate the economy toward greater redistribution but also to ensure women's share of decision-making power. Among the reforms that emerged from this moment, although still unfinished, is a new constitution for Iceland, which the people had demanded during the 2008–09 protests. It was drafted through an innovative process, unprecedented in the world, that included broad popular participation. Although the new constitution won the approval of a supermajority of voters in a 2012 referendum, it has not become law because the existing constitution requires parliamentary adoption of constitutional amendments.

In October 2008, three banks comprising 85 percent of the banking system in Iceland collapsed, leading to the collapse of the rest of the banks and the equity market overnight.[84] The Icelandic people bore the cost of this crisis, with the cost of recapitalizing the failed banks adding up to 64 percent of GDP. The failures were largely understood by the public to have resulted from aggressive and unsustainable strategies of economic liberalization and financialization pursued by a few men who had held economic and political power in the years leading up to the crash.[85] Public outrage was directed at the "new Vikings," the men who reaped profits from their rapid expansion of the banking sector and access to natural resources, enabled by their friends in government, including the prime minister and the former prime minister then heading Iceland's Central Bank.[86] Government had failed to prevent the economic disaster largely because major decisions were made by men in power behind closed doors, lacking democratic transparency. Men holding public power relied on the misguided intuitions of businessmen, who happened to be their friends and neighbors, sidelining the female minister of commerce.[87] Popular discourse suggested that the masculine "Viking" mindset drove the pursuit of daring, aggressive, and risk-taking economic behavior, notwithstanding that these Viking qualities had historically led men to kidnap, rape, and forcibly marry women as well.[88] Icelandic citizens protested outside the Althing (Icelandic Parliament) throughout the winter of 2008–09, making noise with all kinds of kitchenware from their homes and calling for the government's resignation. The "Pots and Pans Revolution" recast the "Viking" mindset as corruption, not democracy. People took to the streets to demand new democratic leadership and eventually a new constitution too. The protests succeeded in making Iceland's government the first in the world to collapse because of the global financial crisis of 2008. In late January 2009, Prime Minister Geir Haarde resigned and called for elections to form a new government by May 2009.[89] Elections in April 2009, in which 85.1 percent of the eligible voters voted,[90] empowered a coalition of the Social Democratic Alliance and the Left-Green Movement, two political parties that had adhered to the principle of gender parity in selecting their candidates for the Althing. Johanna Siggurdardottir was elected the first female prime minister of Iceland, and the world's first openly lesbian head of government.

What followed was feminist democratization—a period of leadership by women focused on reining in the dynamics of overentitlement and overempowerment. The parliament seated in May 2009 included twenty-seven women out of sixty-three members, constituting 43 percent of the body.[91] The previous government had authorized a Special Investigation Commission to report on the causes of the financial crisis.[92] The newly seated government in 2009 then authorized an additional report by feminist scholars analyzing the Special Investigation Commission's findings from a gender perspective.[93] The gender analysis exposed the bad governance that fed the economic bubble and collapse as an abuse of power enabled by the pursuit of "Viking" masculinity. Norms of good governance were not followed because men in power trusted each other and did not follow democratic decision-making processes that would have enabled them to properly value the interests of all the people whose money they were subjecting to unwarranted risk. But in addition to taking outsized risks, they shielded their decision-making from female contributions by sidelining the commerce minister—failing to properly value her authority.[94]

Once women were empowered as an antidote to the economic crisis,[95] the Pots and Pans Revolution revealed itself to be a feminist revolution. The Government Coalition Platform included several gender issues, not only to empower women, but to promote economic recovery. Led by Prime Minister Johanna Sigurdardottir, the Althing adopted legislation requiring gender balance on corporate boards of directors—requiring companies with more than fifty employees to have at least 40 percent of both genders represented on their boards.[96] It then passed legislation making it unlawful to buy the services of a prostitute or to profit from prostitution, without imposing any criminal penalties on prostitutes themselves.[97] Strip clubs—a favorite hangout of the "new Viking" male bankers and entrepreneurs[98]—were also effectively shut down by a new law that made it unlawful for any business to profit from the nudity of its employees.[99] While there is a long-standing debate among feminists as to whether their goals should include the abolition of sex work, Iceland's new laws, instead of banning prostitution and strip clubs outright, seek to regulate the transactions with attention to who is enriched and who is injured by them. They attempt to reduce the effects of male overentitlement and overempowerment on women, particularly those who are most easily exploited.

The new government introduced gender budgeting in 2009. As the government website explains, "Gender budgeting involves combining knowledge about budgeting and gender issues with the aim to encourage cost-effective and equitable distribution of public funds."[100] The gendered impacts of budget allocations are articulated and taken into account, not only for the purpose of promoting women, but because doing so is fair and in the public interest: "Due to different situations of women and men, boys and girls in society, the budget can have different impact on people. Generally, this difference is not clear, however, as the budget appears outwardly to be impartial. Gender budgeting is intended to make existing gender differences visible."[101] Being gender conscious "promotes better economic management and informed decisions, contributing to prosperity and well-being in society." Eventually, the Public Finance Act, passed in 2015, required the formulation of a gender budgeting program, with input by the minister for gender equality. The statute requires the budget bill to outline the effects on gender equality targets.[102]

Finally, Prime Minister Johanna Sigurdardottir introduced a bill, which Parliament adopted, to initiate constitutional reform. Many postcrisis reformers viewed the existing constitution, adopted in 1944 and copied from Denmark's nineteenth-century constitution, as both ill-fitted to the twenty-first century and contributing to the politics that had led to the financial crisis. In June 2010, the Althing passed the Act on a Constitutional Assembly,[103] initiating a constitutional revision process. The bill built on a process initiated by a grassroots organization that had organized a "National Assembly" of 1,200 randomly selected citizens and 300 people representing businesses and organizations to deliberate on the values and priorities that should guide the renewal of government. The parliamentary act authorized the election of a consultative constitutional assembly to review the existing constitution. Eligibility to run for the Constitutional Assembly was open to all who qualified to run for Parliament but excluded those who were current members of Parliament, their alternates, cabinet ministers, members of the Constitutional Commission, or the president of Iceland.[104] To prepare for the Constitutional Assembly's work, the legislation provided that an appointed constitutional committee would organize a "National Gathering" under the following terms: "Participation of approximately one thousand people should be assumed for the National Gathering, selected by means of randomly sampling from the National Population Register, with due regard to a reasonable distribution of participants across the country and an equal division between genders, to the extent possible."[105]

The National Gathering would deliberate on the organization of national government and the Constitution and would deliver information to the Constitutional Assembly, once elected. The constitution-making process in Iceland was unique and unprecedented in including the population at large in the deliberation stage.[106] It is the first constitution in the world to be generated by a deliberative body composed under requirements of random selection and gender balance. It is not surprising that this inclusive and radically democratic procedural design emerged from a legislature empowered to pave a path forward from the messes made by a few men.

The National Forum of 950 randomly selected citizens met for a day that fall, participating in roundtable discussions and small-group deliberations and votes, aided by a company that specialized in crowdsourcing. Groups drafted some recommendations, which formed the basis of a seven-hundred-page report compiled by the Constitutional Committee.

The entire National Forum was live-streamed on the internet.[107] Elections for the Constitutional Assembly—the body that would draft the new Icelandic constitution informed by the National Forum deliberations— were held later that month. Ten women and fifteen men from a range of professional backgrounds were elected.[108]

However, three men who opposed constitutional reform, all members of the Independence Party whose leaders were blamed for the economic crisis, challenged the validity of the election before the Supreme Court of Iceland. The Supreme Court, consisting exclusively at the time of male justices, invalidated the Constitutional Assembly election, holding that the standards and procedures used in other elections to protect ballot secrecy had not been met. In a fairly detailed decision, the Supreme Court considered the physical design of the voting booths, the use of identifying bar codes on ballots, and allegations that voters could not fold their ballots to reach its conclusion that the elections had been conducted contrary to law.[109]

Once the Constitutional Assembly could not function as a legitimately elected body, Parliament resolved to form an appointed Constitutional Council instead and proceeded to appoint the people who had been elected in the election that the Supreme Court invalidated. The Constitutional Council then proceeded to draft a new constitution. With regard to gender issues, Iceland's constitution had already had an explicit guarantee that "men and women shall enjoy equal rights in all respects" since 1995.[110] That provision was retained.[111] The most significant changes in the new draft constitution are the declaration that natural resources that are not in private ownership are the common and perpetual property of the nation,[112] and provisions that empower the people to participate in decision-making, particularly in the amendment of the Constitution.[113]

The new constitution was approved by two-thirds of voters in a 2012 referendum, with about 49 percent voter turnout. However, the referendum was nonbinding, as the draft constitution, by its own terms, would have to be validated under the existing amendment rule. The existing amendment rule, at Article 79 of Iceland's constitution, requires the Althing to adopt a constitutional amendment by a majority, and then to do so again after an intervening election forming a new government.[114] After the referendum, Althing members who opposed the constitutional reform, belonging to the Independence Party, filibustered the bill. Although the majority coalition in Parliament supported the new constitution and would have voted with the requisite majority to adopt it, the opponents prevented it from getting a vote before the next scheduled election in 2013. A new coalition led by the Independence Party prevailed in the 2013 elections and prevented the new, more democratic constitution from being adopted.

There have been renewed efforts to advance the more democratic constitution that was initiated by a gender-balanced parliament with female leadership, deliberated upon at a gender-balanced gathering of randomly selected ordinary citizens, and drafted by a gender-balanced assembly of framers who were not incumbent politicians. A renewed social media campaign, led by the Women's Alliance for the New Constitution, was launched in the fall of 2020, asking "Hvar?" or "Where?," that is, "Where is the new constitution?"[115] The constitutional reform project has returned to the horizon of political possibility because of the support of the second female prime minister of Iceland, Katrin Jakobsdottir, who announced a new effort at constitutional reform in 2018.[116]

Katrin Jakobsdottir became prime minister only when the government was dissolved in 2017 after a controversy involving sexual abuse and potential for abuse of power. Jakobsdottir's Left-Green Party was in coalition with the Independence Party, which held the largest number of seats, and the Bright Future Party. Prime Minister Bjarni Benediktsson of the Independence Party came under fire, however, because his father had written a letter in support of a child sex offender, who had been imprisoned for sexually abusing a girl for many years since she was five years old. The letter was submitted in support of a petition to erase the criminal record of the offender, in a process under Icelandic law that allows restoration to some felons of all their civil and political rights. With the global #MeToo movement drawing attention to the convergence of sexual abuse and abuse of power, Bright Future withdrew from Benediktsson's coalition government. The government was dissolved and new elections were held, after which Katrin Jakobsdottir became prime minister. In the fall of

2020, Katrin Jakobsdottir wrote, in a column in a major national newspaper, "It is my conviction that Althingi owes it to society to complete work on the constitutional amendments."[117]

In the United States, women still make up significantly less than a third of Congress. No woman has served as head of state. And the century-long struggle to change the Constitution to recognize women's status as equal participants, through the Equal Rights Amendment, has stalled again and again. Meanwhile, the idea that women must share fully and equally in the exercise of power and decision-making in a constitutional democracy is taking hold throughout the world. After mass protests with a strong feminist presence, a constituent assembly composed of equal numbers of women and men drafted a new constitution for Chile. The constitution that this inclusive body wrote contained several noteworthy provisions that aimed to reduce gendered overentitlement and overempowerment. For instance, article 6 obligated the state to ensure the participation of "women, men, sexual and gender diversities and dissidences" in substantive equality, including a specific requirement that various branches of government and boards of public companies achieve gender-equal composition, with at least 50 percent women. Article 27 guaranteed "women, girls, adolescents, and people of sexual and gender diversities" "the right to a life free of gender-based violence in all its manifestations." Additional provisions aimed directly to overcome overentitlement and overempowerment. Article 49 recognized that "domestic and care work is socially necessary and indispensable for the sustainability of life and the development of society" and therefore obligated the state to promote "social and gender co-responsibility" for care work, including its redistribution and the prevention of disadvantage to those who perform it. Article 61 declared, "Every person has sexual and reproductive rights," obligating the state to ensure to "all women and persons with the capacity to bear children the conditions for a pregnancy, a voluntary interruption of pregnancy, a voluntary and protected pregnancy and maternity."

While Chilean voters did not adopt this proposed constitution in the September 2022 referendum, the historic process has shifted the world's imagination about who can make a constitution, how a constitution can be made, and what a constitution can be. After decades, if not centuries, of being undervalued, ignored, and invisible, empowered women are transforming the foundations and futures of the political and legal orders that govern them. They are exposing the costs of men's overempowerment and unjust enrichment, borne not only by women but by democracy. As the experiences of constitutional change in France, Germany, and Iceland show, empowering women is necessary, though not sufficient, for recalibrating this overempowerment. Constitutional empowerment is only the beginning; it is the foundation on which an infrastructure can be built to make equality and justice a reality for all.

6 Building Feminist Infrastructures

THE CONSTITUTIONALISM OF CARE

Throughout the spring of 2020, the sounds of clanging pots and pans were heard in New York City at 7 p.m. each evening. They were cheers of appreciation for the essential workers who were sacrificing their time and risking their lives at the onset of the COVID-19 pandemic so that the rest of the population could survive the pandemic-induced lockdown in health and safety.[1] Will the twenty-first century see more kitchenware revolutions beyond Iceland?

Essential work is largely women's work. When the COVID-19 crisis began, one in three jobs held by women was designated as essential.[2] Notwithstanding the appreciation expressed by the jubilant noises of kitchenware, essential workers are undervalued and underpaid. Yet society depends upon their work to survive. Furthermore, the social conditions necessitated by the pandemic magnified our society's dependence on another form of invisible but necessary work that also goes unpaid and underappreciated: motherhood. Because the public health emergency led schools and childcare centers to shut down, mothers stepped in, and millions of working mothers lost or left their jobs to educate and care for their children.[3] As a society, we have been unjustly enriched by the hardships undertaken by low-paid essential workers and working parents—mostly women—which the applause of pots and pans undercompensates. The COVID-19 pandemic exposed the extent to which the law fails to value and support women's essential contributions, on which society depends. A constitutionalism of care can form the basis of infrastructures that are responsive and inclusive. This chapter explores the history of valuing care as a constitutional project, as well as the newest iterations in development. Overcoming twenty-first-century misogyny will require an infrastructure that properly values women's contributions and sacrifices—an infrastructure of care.

SAFETY NETS AND SHOCK ABSORBERS

Many have called for the recognition and compensation of the disproportionate burdens shouldered by working mothers during the pandemic. In the spring of 2021, resolutions were introduced in Congress calling for "a Marshall Plan for Moms to revitalize and restore mothers in the workforce," recognizing that "mothers, especially mothers of color have been pushed to the brink of economic, social, and emotional collapse during COVID-19."[4] But society's dependence on the unpaid work of mothers is nothing new. Since long before the pandemic, working mothers worked an invisible "second shift" at home, caring for family members and performing household work to meet their families' survival needs. Perhaps this, too, was the "violence you don't see" that the global pandemic exposed. Society's overentitlement to women's sacrifices—the misogyny without misogynists—was simply laid bare when the pandemic eliminated the only other element of our inadequate care infrastructure, namely schools. In Iceland, as the previous chapter discussed, the clanging of pots and pans in response to the 2008 financial crisis launched a revolution that became feminist. Can the pots and pans of the COVID-19 crisis be a wake-up call to act against other forms of overentitlement and overempowerment that constitute twenty-first-century misogyny?

In the United States, feminist litigation advanced a vision of women's equality as the right against discrimination based on sex or gender stereotypes. But that right did not ease the burdens of childbearing and childrearing that have disproportionately fallen on women for centuries. American women have trudged along without the support for childbearing and child-rearing that other countries' governments provide. One simple example is parental leave. The majority of American workers have no access to paid parental leave,[5] which makes it all but inevitable that parents—usually mothers—will quit their jobs or get fired because of their children's need for care, as the "she-cession" that followed the onset of the COVID-19 pandemic bore out. In many other countries, paid maternity leave is not only a long-standing public policy, like social security; it is often a constitutional entitlement.

The guarantee of equality for women and men is a nearly universal feature of constitutions around the world that the US Constitution still lacks. But the foundation for laws ensuring paid maternity leave is not equality between women and men but another common feature of twentieth- and twenty-first-century constitutions in Europe, Latin America, and Asia: the constitutional entitlement of mothers to the care and protection of the community. In addition to being a statement of principle, constitutional motherhood clauses have functioned, at least in some countries, to compel public policies that empower women in both the workplace and the family.

Social reproduction—the raising of the next generation of citizen-participants in the economy and polity—became a subject of constitutional intervention when motherhood clauses were introduced to constitutions of the twentieth century. Women who participated in constitution making embraced both sex equality clauses and maternity clauses to constitutionalize a solution to the problem of social reproduction. These clauses grew out of women's movements for suffrage and equal rights that culminated in constitutional amendments at the end of World War I and World War II. The experiences of war amplified the importance of women's contributions to both the economy and the reproduction of the nation.

CONSTITUTIONAL ORIGINS: THE PROTECTION OF MOTHERHOOD IN GERMANY

Language committing to the protection of mothers was first enshrined in the constitution of Germany adopted at Weimar in 1919. Motherhood protection clauses were fairly common in European constitutions adopted in the 1920s and 1930s, including Ireland (1937).[6] After World War II, the motherhood clause was adopted again in the West German Basic Law (1949) and found a place in the constitutions of France (1946) and Italy (1948). These motherhood clauses are part of the constitutions in force today.

The protection of motherhood entered into constitutions at the same moments as the constitutionalization of women's suffrage and of the equal rights of women and men. Their histories establish an important conceptual link between gender equality provisions and maternity clauses. Both gender equality and maternity clauses were the contributions of women who participated in constitution making after World War I and World War II in Europe, and not merely the invention of men who intended to keep women in their place. The protection of mothers was the starting point by which constitutions began to address the problem of social reproduction. In the twenty-first century, women's remaining disadvantages require more nuanced attention to the problem of social reproduction, to engender and sustain a mode of social reproduction that does not depend on the hardships and sacrifices sustained by mothers.

The mere presence of a maternity provision cannot be read in isolation from the constitutional regime it occupies. Many countries at the very bottom of the World Economic Forum's gender gap rankings also have maternity clauses. Yemen, for instance, ranks dead last in the World Economic Forum's cross-national rankings of gender equality, but its constitution has a clause protecting mothers.[7] And Iceland, which has consistently ranked number 1 in the Forum's gender equality rankings for over a decade, lacks a motherhood clause. What matters is not *whether* a constitution has a clause protecting motherhood but *how* such clauses have been used in our peer constitutional democracies. In some cases, they have provided the political or legal foundations for an infrastructure that facilitates women's equal participation in all spheres of life. Germany provides the earliest historical example of a constitutional maternity clause, dating to the Weimar Constitution in 1919. France and Italy's motherhood provisions illustrate how the experience of World War II shaped the constitutional visions of social democracy that valued the public contributions of motherhood. Ireland protected motherhood without gender equality in its 1937 Constitution, and in 2021 a citizen-participatory process considered proposals to amend and improve its constitutional commitment to care through gender equality.

As noted in chapter 5, German women were elected delegates to the constituent assembly that adopted the Weimar Constitution of 1919. The maternity protection clause was debated and embraced by the women members of the Weimar National Assembly that deliberated on the new constitution.[8] These debates were also decades in the making—the women in the constituent assembly had been active in social movements and a wide variety of women's organizations with different views of feminism and women's rights in the decades prior to the adoption of the Weimar Constitution.

While the majority of the Weimar women were from left-wing social democratic parties,[9] there were also several women from the liberal German Democratic Party (Deutsche Demokratische Partei, DDP) who had participated in the bourgeois women's movement in the decades prior to the Weimar Constitution. The provisions in the Weimar Constitution relevant to the status of women grew out of compromises between women who disagreed with one another. Nonetheless, they were able to agree on key provisions that became the template not only for the West German Basic Law that was adopted after World War II but also for many other European constitutions adopted after World War I and World War II.

Article 119 of the Weimar Constitution enshrined principles that survive in Article 6 of the German Basic Law currently in force, and similar provisions can be found in constitutions throughout Europe. Article 119 provided, in full:

> Marriage, as the basis of family life and the preservation and reproduction of the nation, stands under the special protection of the constitution. It is based on the equality of both sexes.
>
> The health, maintenance, and social promotion of the family is the task of the state and the community.
>
> Families with numerous children are entitled to be equalized through support.
>
> Motherhood is entitled to the protection and support of the state.[10]

In addition, the Weimar Constitution offered protection for children born out of wedlock, whose welfare and status had concerned German feminists, particularly during World War I. Article 121 reads, "The same opportunities for physical, psychological, and social development shall be given through the law to children born out of wedlock as to those born within marriage."[11]

Article 119's provision, entitling motherhood to the special protection and support of the state, did not garner extensive debate or discussion in the constituent assembly. But to fully appreciate the meaning of the motherhood clause, one must situate it in the social movement work around motherhood protection engaged in by the women who also participated in the Weimar constituent assembly in the decades preceding this constitutional moment. Gertrud Bäumer, for instance, was the president of the Bund Deutsche Frauenvereine (BDF),[12] a national German women's council consisting of thirty-four women's organizations. German women established the BDF after they returned from the Chicago World's Fair in 1893, where they had encountered American women's organizations whose power inspired them.[13] The BDF was modeled on the National Council of Women in the United States, an organization that had been formed just a few years earlier by Woman's Christian Temperance Union president Frances Willard and suffragist Susan B. Anthony. Gertrud Bäumer, who represented the German Democratic Party in the Weimar constituent assembly, had led the BDF from 1910 until 1919. Bäumer led the organization during World War I and redefined feminism in a more nationalist direction.[14] She defined female emancipation in terms of women as "social" mothers, raising the nation. Women's equality would bring a "richer flow of specifically female forces into the total of the world's activities."[15] While she developed this notion of social motherhood, Bäumer did not bear or raise children herself. She was not married; she spent much of her adult life cohabiting with Helene Lange, a feminist with whom she coauthored the *Handbook on the Women's Movement*.[16]

Nonetheless, the "specifically female forces" Bäumer praised were motherhood and marriage, and she embraced these ideas as some of her contemporaries and allies were establishing the more radical Bund für Mutterschutz (League for the Protection of Motherhood), associated with the feminist writers Helene Stöcker in Germany and Ellen Key in Sweden.[17] However, under Gertrud Bäumer's leadership, the BDF distanced itself from the Mutterschutz League and did not allow the Mutterschutz group to join its federation of German women's organizations. Bäumer wanted the BDF to unite women of all parties in exerting a "motherly" influence over society,[18] but she refused to embrace the Mutterschutz League's advocacy of a "New Morality" that included abortion rights, contraceptives, and sexual liberation. Nonetheless, the women of the German Democratic Party at Weimar shared with the Mutterschutz feminists of the previous decade the belief that the state should help families, and particularly mothers, meet their various obligations.[19] In addition, some of the Socialists who participated in legislating the expansion of social insurance for pregnant workers and abortion liberalization during the Weimar Republic of the 1920s had belonged to the Mutterschutz League and shared in its advocacy of the rights of single mothers and children born outside of marriage.[20]

Throughout the 1920s, the legislative agendas promoted by the Social Democratic Party in the Reichstag overlapped with those promoted by the Mutterschutz feminists of 1905–19. The Social Democrats promoted legislation reforming abortion, marriage, and divorce.[21] They promoted the expansion of pregnant women's rights to paid maternity leave and legislation authorizing longer periods of time off and higher rates of pay.[22] Socialist women also advocated the decriminalization of abortion, particularly in the first trimester. They believed that most abortions occurred because of social and economic circumstances, not because women were rejecting the desire to be mothers. They assumed that the longing for motherhood was deeply ingrained in women but that social and economic conditions drove women to abort.[23] Thus the campaign for abortion rights went hand in hand with the campaign for motherhood protection. Feminists from left-leaning political parties advocated for maternity insurance and other policies by which women would be compensated for the socially productive labor of motherhood.[24]

When the constituent assembly of sixty-five delegates selected by the German states convened at Bonn after World War II to adopt a new constitution, the provisions of Article 119 from the Weimar Constitution were put into Article 6 of the Basic Law of 1949, with slight revisions. Article 6 remains in force, and reads, in its entirety:

(1) Marriage and the family shall enjoy the special protection of the state.

(2) The care and upbringing of children is the natural right of parents and a duty primarily incumbent upon them. The state shall watch over them in the performance of this duty.

(3) Children may be separated from their families against the will of their parents or guardians only pursuant to a law and only if the parents or guardians fail in their duties or the children are otherwise in danger of serious neglect.

(4) Every mother shall be entitled to the protection and care of the community.

(5) Children born outside of marriage shall be provided by legislation with the same opportunities for physical and mental development and for their position in society as are enjoyed by those born within marriage.[25]

Article 6 creates several obligations on the part of the state to protect families and marriages and to support and collaborate with parents in the raising of children. The state must care for children when parents fail and must ensure children's development regardless of the marital status of their parents. The protection of motherhood is embedded in this larger package of governmental duties to ensure the well-being of families and children. It is a recognition of the enormous contributions that mothers make to family life and the raising of children, such that the community is then indebted through a constitutional obligation to care for mothers.

SUPPORTING MOTHERS TO REBUILD THE NATION:
FRANCE AND ITALY AFTER WORLD WAR II

Unlike Germany, France and Italy extended the suffrage to women no earlier than this post–World War II moment. In France, Paragraph 3 of the 1946 Preamble declares, "The law guarantees women equal rights to those of men in all spheres." Paragraph 11 provides, "It [the nation] guarantees to all, especially to the child, the mother, and to old workers, the protection of health, material security, rest, and leisure." Article 37 of the Italian Constitution adopted in 1948 provides, "The woman worker has the same rights, and equality of work, and the same compensation, paid to male workers. The conditions of work must permit the fulfillment of her essential functions in the family and assures to the mother and to the child a special and adequate protection."

The French Constitution of 1946 was adopted by a constituent assembly, which, like that at Weimar, contained the first women legislators in

France. A 1944 decree extended the vote to women, and their participation in the October 1945 elections led to the election of thirty-three women delegates to the parliamentary assembly charged with task of drafting a new constitution. They constituted only 7 percent of the French Constituent Assembly. Nonetheless, some of these women were vocal on the questions of women's equality and motherhood protection. Over two-thirds of the women elected—twenty two of the thirty-three—belonged to the Communist or Socialist parties.

Gilberte Roca, a Communist Party deputy, framed Paragraph 11 of the Preamble, which protects mothers and children, as a concrete realization of the abstract declaration of equal rights for women in Paragraph 3. Having mentioned the constitutionalization of woman's suffrage, she explained:

> But, in our opinion, the right to vote is only the beginning of equality. It is not enough to give woman the right to vote, and to make her a citizen, if, in all her actions in life, she remains a diminished citizen, if, to take a few examples, she cannot, because she is married, open a bank account, sell her own belongings without the consent of her husband, if she does not have access to all the careers and she cannot freely engage in commerce or a profession because her husband is opposed to it, ultimately, if she does not have the same rights as the father over her children.[26]

State protection of motherhood represented the next, more advanced phase of women's equality. "If women rejoice that their rights are being recognized, they know that it is not enough to grant women equality of rights, but that it is also necessary to give her the possibility of exercising them." During the war, eight million women worked in industry, surpassing the number of men working in these jobs. In addition, there were by that moment many female-dominated jobs, such as teaching. Given how many women participated in market work, Roca observed: "Today, it is difficult for a woman to, at the same time, perform her tasks as a worker, as a mother, and then to find time to engage the problems of national life, ultimately, to fully exercise her role as a citizen."

Recognizing the need to reproduce the French nation, Roca defended the new Preamble's language protecting mothers and children, specifically: "The Nation guarantees to all, especially to the child, the mother, and older workers the protection of health and material security." The protection of mothers combined women's equal rights as citizens with the collective project of rebuilding the postwar nation. Roca noted that the Preamble merely articulated the framework and that the principles articulated on paper should lead legislatures to realize them by regulating work, improving housing, and instituting a system of nurseries, childcare centers, afterschool programs, cafeterias, and basically "all the undertakings that will allow the woman to be no longer a servant but the guardian of her household and to participate with all of the might of her intelligence and her heart in the French rebirth."[27] Remaking the Constitution was the necessary first step toward building the infrastructure that would affirm and support women's control over their own households as well as their equal participation in the new French republic emerging after the defeat of Nazism.

In Italy, as in Germany and France, the constituent assembly that was charged with the drafting of a postwar constitution in 1945 included women. Of the 556 elected members of the Constituent Assembly, 21 were women, from across the political spectrum. Nine were from the Christian Democratic Party, 9 from the Communist Party, 2 from the Socialist Party, and 1 from the Uomo Qualunque party.[28] Of the twenty-one women who participated in the Constituent Assembly of the Italian Republic, four were elected by the assembly to join a "Committee of 75," tasked with drafting the constitution to be debated and voted on by the larger assembly. Nilde Iotti, Teresa Noce, Lina Merlin, and Maria Federici participated in the Committee of 75 and played a significant role in advocating for the specific mention of sex in the equality guarantee in Article 3, spousal equality in Article 29, and the rights of women workers in Article 37. Iotti and Noce represented the Communist Party and were particularly vocal about the rights of women workers.

It was these Communist women, on behalf of women workers, who favored a constitutional protection of women's "essential family function" in Article 37, which also guarantees equal pay for women. They advanced a revolutionary vision of female citizenship in which women could choose how and when to work, as well as how and when to have children.[29] Maria Federici, a Christian Democrat and a Catholic, insisted that the Constitution should entitle single mothers to support, particularly as they became heads of families after losing their husbands in war. Federici was concerned about creating the conditions by which these women could raise and educate their children, even though circumstances made it necessary for them to work.

In Italy, postwar women constitution makers from all points on the political spectrum viewed the protection of maternity as a vehicle to women's full equality, autonomy, and citizenship. When the Committee for the Constitution met to discuss economic and social rights to family support, Angelina Merlin noted that the woman "had a decisive importance in the formation of the family." "A woman, even if she is not married, if she has children, can constitute a proper family." She also argued that the protection of mothers was not merely a question that concerned women and their right to equality but also an important investment in the nation: "Note, then, that the recognition of the social function of maternity interests not only the woman, or the man, or the family, it interests all of society. Protecting the mother means protecting society at its roots, because around all mothers that constitute the family and, through the mother, one guarantees the future of society."[30] Immediately after the adoption of the Italian Constitution, these women went to work as lawmakers to advance the policies that would deliver on the Constitution's promises. In 1950 Noce sponsored legislation in Parliament, known as the "Legge Noce," that instituted paid mandatory maternity leave and paid nursing breaks from work for mothers who had recently given birth, in addition to regular paid break times.

The inclusion of Italy in a chapter about getting beyond misogyny may appear puzzling, as Italy ranks poorly on most indicators of gender equality and ranks low by comparison to the other countries discussed thus far. In the World Economic Forum cross-national annual study of gender equality, France and Germany consistently perform better than the United States in measurements of gender gap reduction, whereas Italy consistently ranks well behind the United States. In 2021, for instance, the World Economic Forum ranked the United States thirtieth, as compared with Germany at eleventh and France at sixteenth. Italy was ranked sixty-third.[31] Nordic countries dominate the top ten, with Iceland consistently number one. Despite Italy's legal protections for women workers, including a paid mandatory maternity leave much longer than that available in Germany and France, Italian women's labor force participation even before the pandemic was significantly lower than that of Germany, France, and the United States.[32] It is often feared in the United States that the legal protection of motherhood, like the Italian Constitution's embrace of women's "essential role" in the family, reinforces gender stereotypes and perpetuates traditional gender roles that keep women subordinate.

In a legal order that makes the rejection of gender stereotypes the touchstone of legal gender equality, the constitutional entrenchment of motherhood appears to violate the principle of gender equality.[33] Indeed, several US Supreme Court opinions, including some by Justice Ginsburg, predicted that laws requiring employers to extend special treatment or generous protections to pregnant women or mothers would likely intensify employers' incentives to discriminate against all women in hiring.[34] Since women workers of childbearing age may get pregnant, whereas male hires are certain not to get pregnant or become mothers, the rational employer could avoid the costs of accommodating pregnancy by never hiring anyone who might get pregnant. It was because of such dynamics that Ginsburg, in her many briefs to the Supreme Court as a feminist lawyer in the 1970s, depicted the special protection of mothers as a cage, not a pedestal. But the context in which mothers obtain the special protection of the state matters to its meaning and effect on women's empowerment, which can change over time.

A "LIFE WITHIN THE HOME"? AMBIVALENCE AND AMBIGUITY IN IRELAND

The Irish Constitution's protection of motherhood is an excellent example. In recent years, Ireland has usually ranked within the World Economic Forum's top ten for gender equality, including ninth in 2021. But the Constitution adopted in 1937 did not explicitly guarantee equal rights to women. Furthermore, the Irish Constitution included a motherhood protection clause similar to Italy's in its reference to women's special role as mothers. Article 41.2 of the Irish Constitution provides:

2.1° in particular, the state recognises that by her life within the home, woman gives to the state a support without which the common good cannot be achieved.

2.2° the state shall, therefore, endeavour to ensure that mothers shall not be obliged by economic necessity to engage in labour to the neglect of their duties in the home.[35]

In addition, Article 45 of the Irish Constitution, which lists "Directive Principles of Social Policy" to guide the legislature, without giving rise to any judicially enforceable rights, appears to discourage women's work outside the home. That language from Article 45.4.2, also still in force, reads:

The State shall endeavor to ensure that the strength and health of workers, men, and women, and the tender age of children, shall not be abused and that citizens shall not be forced by economic necessity to enter avocations unsuited to their sex, age, or strength.

When these clauses were introduced in 1937, many women's groups criticized them and expressed concern that they would diminish women's status and opportunities to work outside the home.[36] Furthermore, the 1922 Constitution of the Irish Free State had specifically guaranteed the privileges of citizenship to "every person, without distinction of sex."[37] The 1937 Constitution declined to use any "without distinction of sex" language and created these special protections for mothers and women.

Eamonn De Valera, who presided over the assembly (Dáil Eirann) considering the new constitution, and who is largely recognized to be the primary father of the 1937 Constitution,[38] denied that Article 41.2 would take rights away from women. To the contrary, the protection of mothers was a necessary "part of our social programme."[39] He said, "We state here that mothers in their homes give to the State a support which is essential. Is there anybody who denies it? Is it not a tribute to the work that is done by women in the home as mothers?"[40] De Valera was recognizing that women's work raising children was "essential" to society and the state, a truth that should be constitutionally enshrined. Putting it in the constitution would make clear an aspiration that De Valera acknowledged to be challenging for societies to reach: "We may not succeed, it is true. It is a very difficult thing to bring about. But the present social system, inasmuch as it compels mothers to leave their natural duties as mothers and go out and become breadwinners when their husbands are idle and cannot get work, is a system which we ought to try to reform."[41] This included public support for widows, so that they could raise their children without having to work to support them.

But opponents of the constitution in the Dáil took aim at this provision. Deputy John Marcus O'Sullivan alleged that De Valera was out to "destroy . . . the constitutional bulwark of women's rights."[42] Noting that women already had the vote, and access to the professions, the opponents suggested that the new constitution "makes possible laws that will do away with these things and that will still be in conformity with the Constitution." Indeed, in opposing the Constitution and De Valera more generally, O'Sullivan warned his colleagues against becoming "that Party of Yes-men."[43]

To which Helena Concannon, one of three women in the Dáil at the time, piped back, "There is a woman here, too."[44] Like the women constitution makers in Germany, France, and Italy, Concannon supported the motherhood clauses and responded directly to the fears, which she had shared initially, that these clauses would undermine women's rights. She began, "So much of the discussion . . . has turned on its possible effect on the status of women that it seems to me it would be unfitting that this debate should close without a woman's voice being heard in connection with the matter." She presented the criticisms that several women's groups had publicly made against proposed Articles 41 and 45 and their advancement of a guarantee of equal rights and opportunities without distinction of sex.

Then Deputy Concannon challenged De Valera to reaffirm that Articles 41.2 and 45 would strengthen, rather than undermine, women's rights. "I would be glad if the President would give us an assurance that he will look once more into these Articles and satisfy himself that by no error of draftsmanship, by no ambiguity in the Irish or English versions, could any interpretation be given by future courts that would lessen the status of women."[45] In her interpretation, the state's duty to ensure that mothers would not be obliged by economic necessity to engage in labor to the neglect of their duties in the home was the principle animating legislation supporting widows and orphans. In its defense, she said:

> I think it is due to women who have so bravely carried on the battle for civilization, and who have had to bear the hardest part, that the State should give them this recognition. Do we not all know that the price of each human

life is some woman's agony? Do we not know that the rearing of each child is purchased at the cost of some woman's sleepless nights and hardworking days, and are we not all aware of the life of sacrifice that each woman has to experience to launch her family on the world? Why, then should we begrudge to women that the State should honour them for their contribution to the State's support and its common good?[46]

Concannon insisted, for the record, that Article 41 "does not mean— and I for one would protest most actively against it if it did mean—to close the door to work for women in any other sphere. That is not the intention at all."[47] Then she argued that recognizing women's contributions to the state through their work in the home should lead to the expansion of educational opportunities for women: "Women will work better in the homes if they have been educated and if they have had contact with outside life."[48] Therefore, she hoped that "women will avail of" Article 41, that "they will insist that the education of girls shall have some relation to the work they will have to do for the 'common good' in the home.'"[49] The woman in the home was a doctor, a cook, a dressmaker, a nurse, a carpenter, and "above all, she has to be an educator, and so on."

Concannon's defense of Article 41.2, as a constitution maker and framer, was decidedly feminist. She wanted it to be the new bulwark against government and society's undervaluing of the tremendously valuable and difficult work that women did, using the language of sacrifice and hard work to explain De Valera's identification of mothers' work as "essential." Notwithstanding what a feminist framer of Article 41.2 intended, the Oireachtas adopted legislation restricting women's employment opportunities after the 1937 Constitution went into effect. The Local Government Act of 1941 authorized the minister for local government to disqualify married women from certain public-sector jobs.[50] And, prior to 1937, there had been marriage bars requiring women to resign upon marriage from public-sector jobs, including teaching, which remained operative until 1973.[51]

THE EVOLUTION OF MOTHERHOOD PROTECTION

In both Germany and Ireland, the constitutional protection of motherhood has evolved through judicial interpretation so as to support policies that value mothers' socially beneficial sacrifices and to mitigate the disadvantages that such sacrifices could cause. Because the German Basic Law clearly obligates the community, and by extension the state, to protect mothers, it has been assumed to be compatible with the constitutional guarantee of equality between men and women in Article 3.2, as well as the guarantee of nondiscrimination on grounds of sex in Article 3.3. A comprehensive maternity protection statute was enacted in West Germany in 1952,[52] guaranteeing paid maternity leave, protecting pregnant employees and those who had recently given birth from dismissal, and regulating conditions and hours of work for pregnant women and nursing mothers. The law has been reformed several times, including, most recently, in 2017. Paid maternity leave of eighteen weeks is now guaranteed, with six weeks before childbirth and twelve weeks afterwards.[53] A woman may not be employed during the eight weeks immediately following childbirth;[54] maternity leave is therefore mandatory during that time. Pregnant women cannot be terminated throughout the pregnancy and for four months following childbirth.[55] In the workplace, pregnant women are entitled to accommodations; they are not permitted to perform any heavy physical labor or be exposed to elements that could be hazardous to them or the fetus. The statute prohibits night work (8 p.m. to 6 a.m.), overtime work, and Sunday and holiday work by pregnant women and nursing mothers,[56] even though the Constitutional Court held in 1992 that the equality guarantee did not allow the law to prohibit all women from night work.

Although there have been several changes with regard to lengths of time and specific entitlements over the past several decades, the basic framework (maternity leave, job security, and accommodations) is understood to be constitutionally required by Article 6.4's declaration of mothers' entitlement to the special care of the community. In 1979, the Federal Constitutional Court invoked Article 6.4 to invalidate a provision of the Maternity Protection Law for insufficiently protecting a pregnant employee from dismissal.[57] The statute generally prohibited the dismissal of pregnant employees and made such dismissals void only if the employer knew of the pregnancy or was informed of it within two weeks of the pregnant worker's dismissal. A terminated female employee had informed her employer immediately after she found out that she was pregnant (but more than two weeks after the dismissal), in an effort to invalidate her dismissal. In 1991, in the context of German reunification, a law abolishing various civil service positions in the former East Germany was held unconstitutional on the grounds that it failed to sufficiently protect pregnant employees from dismissal and was therefore contrary to Article 6(4).[58] These cases makes clear that a near-absolute ban on firing a pregnant employee is constitutionally required.

A more recent case suggests that the mandatoriness of maternity leave is also constitutionally required. Reading the maternity clause, which requires this strong protection of maternity leave, along with the substantive equality clause added to the Basic Law in 1994, the Federal Constitutional Court has required the state to compensate for the disadvantaging effects of taking mandatory maternity leave. In 2006, the Federal Constitutional Court brought together the maternity protection guarantee of Article 6(4) with the duty to reduce existing disadvantages of Article 3(2), diminishing the formal guarantee of equality before the law in Article 3(1). The 2006 decision held that mothers' constitutional entitlement to protection of the state was violated when their time on mandatory maternity leave was not taken into account in calculating the qualifying period for their statutory unemployment insurance.[59] In Germany, the maternity leave statute required pregnant women to take maternity leave for six weeks before and eight weeks after childbirth, during which they received maternity pay with contributions from both the employer and the state. However, this time was not treated as time worked for purposes of calculating unemployment insurance eligibility. The Constitutional Court noted that this framework violated the equality guarantee of Article 3(2) and 3(3). Because mandatory maternity leave only affected women, "Article 3(2) of the Basic Law imposes on the legislature an obligation to pass provisions that put women during the prohibition of employment in the same position as if there were no prohibition of employment."[60] Read together with the guarantee of equal rights for men and women, the German protection of motherhood functions as a constitutional shield for laws that compensate for the burdens of pregnancy and maternity. That shield is needed because special treatment for women is often subject to legal challenge based on men's rights to nondiscrimination.

In Ireland, judges relied on the "woman in the home" clause, as Article 41.2 has come to be known, to uphold the exemption of women from jury duty. In a case similar factually to *Hoyt v. Florida* in the US Supreme Court, female criminal defendants challenged a law that required women to opt in to jury service. As the US Supreme Court upheld such exemptions so as to enable women to prioritize their household duties, the Irish Supreme Court in 1976 concluded that a woman was entitled under Article 41.2 "to decide for herself, in accordance with her own circumstances and special responsibilities, whether service on a jury is a right she ought to exercise or a burden she ought to undertake." Citing *Hoyt v. Florida* favorably as compared with subsequent Supreme Court cases invalidating sex distinctions in jury service, Chief Justice O'Higgins noted that "the American Constitution has no article similar to Article 41, s.2, of our Constitution."[61] In some cases in the 1990s, the Irish courts upheld the preferential treatment of women for the purposes of public benefits available to widows and deserted wives.[62]

In the 1980s, feminist lawyers argued in divorce cases that women who had not contributed financially to marital property were nevertheless entitled to a share of the property because of Article 41.2's recognition of the value created by women's work in the home. In the case of *L. v. L.*, a High Court judge attempted to justify this expansion of Article 41.2 to promote women's equality in divorce, reasoning as follows:

> In my view the judiciary has a positive obligation to interpret and develop the law in a way which is in harmony with the philosophy of Article 41 as to the status of woman in the home. It is also in harmony with that philosophy of Article 41 as an equal partnership in which a woman who elects to adopt the full-time role of wife and mother in the home may be obligated to make a sacrifice, both economic and emotional, in doing so. In return for that voluntary sacrifice, which the Constitution recognises as being in the interest of the common good, she should receive some reasonable economic security within the marriage.[63]

This approach reads the constitutional protection of motherhood as remedying the injustice of society's enrichment from women's sacrifices. But the Supreme Court of Ireland rejected this expansion as legislating beyond the permissible limits of judicial interpretation, and reversed.[64]

Later in that year—1992—the Supreme Court of Ireland got its first female judge, Susan Denham. (Incidentally, the second female judge, appointed in 2000, was Catherine McGuiness, the lawyer who had litigated on behalf of the divorced wife in the case of *L. v. L.*). In 2001, Judge Denham reaffirmed the High Court's interpretation of Article 41.2, albeit in an opinion with which her male colleagues disagreed. In a case challenging the state's discriminatory failure to educate a mentally disabled child, Judge Denham would have upheld the lower court's additional damages award for the child's mother on the basis of Article 41.2. The lower courts had justified her damages because she was a "de facto single parent" and the primary carer for several children. Under those circumstances, the state's failure to educate her disabled child caused independent injuries to her. Whereas the majority of the Supreme Court rejected this theory and held damages to be appropriate only for the child, Judge Denham put forth a twenty-first-century construction of the "woman in the home" clause beginning with a citation to the above passage from *L. v. L*. Judge Denham continued:

> The second case in this appeal is grounded on a fundamental concept—even more so perhaps—that our society is built on the family. Further, that within the family the special benefit given by women in the home, is recognised. It is acknowledged that that benefit is not just for the particular home, family, and children, but for the common good.
>
> This special recognition is of the 21st century and belongs to the whole of society. . . .
>
> Thus, in Ireland, in relation to the family and the home, women have a constitutionally recognised role which is acknowledged as being for the common good. This gives to women an acknowledged status in recognition not merely of the physical aspect of home making and family building, but of the emotional, social, physical, intellectual, and spiritual work of women and mothers. . . .
>
> Article 41.2 does not assign women to a domestic role. Article 41.2 recognises the significant role played by wives and mothers in the home. This recognition and acknowledgment does not exclude women and mothers from other roles and activities. It is a recognition of the work performed by women in the home. The work is recognised because it has immense benefit for society. This recognition must be construed harmoniously with other Articles of the Constitution when a combination of Articles fall to be analyzed.[65]

This jurisprudence, developed by the first female Irish Supreme Court judge, who later became that court's first female chief justice, lays a normative foundation for damages to compensate the invisible work of mothers, especially when the state fails its educational duties to a child. As societies consider the invisible work largely shouldered by mothers when the state stopped educating children during the COVID-19 pandemic, a constitutional provision like Ireland's Article 41.2 can provide the constitutional anchor for plans like the proposed Marshall Plan for Moms.

Nonetheless, in the twenty-first century, the "woman in the home" constitutional language seems sexist on its face. As one commentator put it, it is "a stunning example of linguistic gender stereotyping and an appeal to a false universal notion of womanhood."[66] As academic commentators have pointed out for decades, it entrenches 1937 assumptions that only women *should* do household work and that only mothers (not fathers) have duties in the home that conflict with paid work.[67] Some Supreme Court judges have tried to overcome the sexism of Article 41.2 by suggesting that it protects the person, male or female, who does socially valuable unpaid care work in the home (shorthand verb: *mothering*).

In *T. v. T.*, the Irish Supreme Court upheld a large lump sum payment, in the context of a divorce, from a wealthy husband to a wife who had worked in "low-key" medical posts as a physician throughout the marriage because she was the primary caregiver for their three children. Whereas the husband's total assets, accumulated during a successful legal career, were £20 million, the wife's total assets were £1 million. The court's decision primarily concerned the application of a 1996 divorce statute that instructed courts to consider, inter alia, "the degree to which the future earning capacity of a spouse is impaired by reason of that spouse having relinquished or foregone the opportunity of remunerative activity in order to look after the home or care for the family." In her opinion, Judge Denham did not resist the opportunity to note that the statute was consistent with "express recognition within the Constitution of the work done by women in the home," quoting Article 41.2 in its entirety.[68]

In his opinion, Judge Murray also recognized the relevance of Article 41.2 and urged, consistent with precedents, that the Constitution be interpreted as a living document consistent with contemporary conditions. He noted, "In acknowledging the nature and status of marriage and the family in society, the Constitution reflects its historical, cultural, and social role underpinned by values common to all religious traditions." The family had endured as a valuable social institution, but the contributions and roles of husbands and wives had evolved:

> The Constitution views the family as indispensable to the welfare of the State. Article 41.2.1 recognises that by her life in the home the woman gives to the State a support without which the common good cannot be achieved. No doubt the exclusive reference to women in that provision reflects social thinking and conditions at the time. It does however expressly recognise that work in the home by a parent is indispensable to the welfare of the State by virtue of the fact that it promotes the welfare of the family as a fundamental unit of society. A fortiori it recognises that work in the home is indispensable for the welfare of the family, husband, wife, and children, where there are children. . . .
>
> I would observe in passing that the Constitution, as this court has stated on a number of occasions, is to be interpreted as a contemporary document. The duties and obligations of spouses are mutual and, without elaborating further since nothing turns on this point in this case, it seems to be that it implicitly recognises similarly the value of a man's contributions in the home as a parent.[69]

Judge Murray's approach suggests that on the basis of a living constitutionalist interpretation, if a future case presented the claims of a stay-at-home father, Article 41.2 should protect him. To date, however, courts have not invoked Article 41.2 to protect a caregiving man.[70]

THE IRISH CITIZENS' ASSEMBLY RECOMMENDATIONS: A GENDER-EQUAL CONSTITUTIONALISM OF CARE

Chapter 3 explored the evolution of constitutional abortion law in Ireland, highlighting the citizens' assembly as a significant legitimizing institution for twenty-first-century constitutional change. The abortion amendment of 2018 was part of a larger constitutional transformation about women's contributions to Irish life, both private and public. It may be an accident of history that Savita Halappanavar died because she was denied an abortion in October 2012, a few months before the Constitutional Convention began deliberations on Article 41.2 of the Irish Constitution. Nonetheless, there are significant links between the constitutional debate about valuing mothers' care work and the constitutional status of abortion.

The 2013 debates about mothers' duties in the home were not about abortion. But the two subjects are causally connected. The report of the Constitutional Convention noted that 86 percent of childcare was carried out by women,[71] only 55 percent of women were in employment,[72] and the absence of childcare prevented women from becoming more active in public affairs.[73] A few years later, 72 percent of the Citizens' Assembly convened in 2017 supported the legality of abortion for "socio-economic" reasons,[74] understanding that having a baby can disrupt gainful employment and lead to joblessness or poverty. The Constitutional Convention that met in 2013 did not lead to a referendum to amend Article 41.2 at the time, but the concerns about the socioeconomic effects of motherhood and the inadequacy of state support returned in constitutional conversations about legalizing abortion.

As De Valera and Concannon both articulated, Article 41.2 of the Irish Constitution recognizes that women's work within the home is a sacrifice that is essential for the common good. Constitutional Convention deliberations in 2013 revealed that a vast majority (88 percent) favored changing these provisions, even though many saw the value of a constitutional provision that acknowledged the value of care work within the home, including childrearing. Many citizens therefore supported gender-neutral language protecting carers, parents, or guardians. But no specific recommendation for a constitutional amendment emerged from the convention at the time.

Meanwhile, since the abortion referendum of 2018, proposals to amend Article 41.2 have returned to the constitutional amendment process. In 2018, at a hearing before the Joint Oireachtas Committee on Justice and Equality, the Stay-at-Home Parents Association of Ireland supported replacing Article 41.2 with gender-neutral language protecting all parents and carers. They explicitly built their case for replacing, rather than repealing, Article 41.2 by connecting their goals to the constitutional reform of abortion: "When we voted yes on May 25th, we were voting not only for the choice to end pregnancies, but also to being supported with the continuation of pregnancies and for parenthood."[75] This statement reflects a step in the Irish constitutional discourse toward integrating abortion rights into a broader vision of reproductive autonomy. This vision includes but is not limited to the ability to access an abortion. Its more significant component is state support for those who choose parenthood, in recognition of the benefits to the state and society that accrue from some citizens bearing the costs of bearing and raising children.

In July 2019, the Oireachtas passed a resolution launching the Citizens' Assembly on Gender Equality, which would include deliberations on Article 41.2. Deciding what to do about the "woman in the home" clause of the Constitution would be embedded in a series of deliberations about other gender equality issues, including social norms and attitudes that facilitate gender discrimination; economic and salary norms that lead to gender inequality, such as the low economic value placed on work traditionally held by women; barriers to women's full and effective participation in leadership and decision-making in the workplace, politics, and public life; care and work-life balance; social responsibility for care;, and the overrepresentation of women in low-pay work. At the constitutional level, consideration was to be given not only to the "woman in the home" provisions but also to whether the general equal protection guarantee should be amended to explicitly refer to sex or gender equality.

After the first weekend meeting of the Citizens' Assembly in February 2020, the COVID-19 pandemic changed both its procedure and its substance. A meeting had been scheduled for late March 2020, but it was canceled, since the government prohibited meetings of larger than one hundred people. After consultation with the members of the assembly, a decision was made to hold the next meeting virtually over the Zoom videoconferencing platform. A successful pilot virtual meeting led to the remainder of the Citizens' Assembly sessions on gender equality being held virtually, through April 2021, with the final report being published in June 2021. A group of experts was also engaged to study the design of the process, with attention to the unanticipated and unprecedented virtual format. The report observed that some members saw an advantage to "less time away from family, particularly for those who have further to travel in order to participate in Dublin-based meetings and for those with young children, or as one member pointed out, for lone parents or carers."[76] For an assembly that deliberated on constitutional and policy changes affecting caregivers, the significance of this procedural pivot to the question of whose voices were enabled cannot be overstated.

The COVID-19 pandemic also changed the content of the discussions, since the pandemic economy amplified existing gender inequalities and created new burdens for people with caregiving responsibilities within the home, often mothers. As the final report of the Citizens' Assembly observed, "The outbreak of Covid-19 not only delayed the Assembly and changed its working methods, it also shone a strong spotlight on care, its importance in our society and the gendered nature of its provision. The topic of care therefore permeated all the work of the Assembly and was seen as relevant to all the other items set out in the resolution."[77] The pandemic put the spotlight not only on mothers but on paid care workers, who emerged as a core example of lower-paid and undervalued workers, demonstrating the lower economic value generally placed on work traditionally done by women. Thus the need to rethink and rebuild the country's care infrastructure, and the state's role in it, took on a renewed sense of urgency in the Citizens' Assembly deliberations.

Ultimately, the assembly made thirty-six recommendations for action by the Oireachtas. They began with three significant proposals for constitutional change. The first was to amend the existing guarantee of equality before the law at Article 40.1 "to refer explicitly to gender equality and non-discrimination."[78] Second, the assembly favored keeping the constitutional protection of the family as a fundamental unit group of society in Article 41.1 but recommended an amendment that "would protect private and family life, with the protection afforded to the family not limited to the marital family."[79] Although the Citizens' Assembly did not propose any specific text, this would most likely require a deletion or alteration of existing Article 41.3.1, which pledges the state "to guard with special care the institution of Marriage."

The third constitutional amendment proposal was specifically to delete Article 41.2 and replace it "with language that is not gender specific and obliges the State to take reasonable measures to support care within the home and wider community."[80] The proposal drew the support of a sizable supermajority of the Citizens' Assembly. 94.4 percent of the members favored changing Article 41.2 in some way; 84.3 percent favored deleting the provision and replacing it with a provision relating to care that would not be gender specific; and 80.9 percent favored further language obliging the state to support care within the home and wider community.[81] Although there may be disagreements about how and to what extent the family and caregiving should be constitutionally protected, the overwhelming majority embraced care as a value that deserves constitutional enshrinement rather than deletion in the twenty-first century. In July 2022, the Oireachtas Joint Committee on Gender Equality issued an interim report on constitutional change, suggesting specific language for the Citizens' Assembly's constitutional amendment proposals and recommending a referendum in 2023 on all three of the amendments supported by the Citizens' Assembly.[82]

The next set of recommendations grew out of the assembly deliberations about the laws and public policies most directly related to the convergence of gender equality and care. The majority's recommendation—that the state be constitutionally obligated to support care, both in the home and in the wider community—would be toothless without a legislative program to implement such support. The Citizens' Assembly recommended, by close to 100 percent of the vote, policies to improve the terms and conditions of work for paid carers.[83] Specifically, carers "should have a pay structure and benefits . . . that reward their level of skill and training," and "They should have a career structure, including access to training and professional registration."[84] More specific policy proposals were made regarding improving carers' pensions and pay.

With regard to policies supporting parents raising children, the Citizens' Assembly recommended, by 96.7 percent of the vote, to move over the next decade to a "publicly funded, accessible and regulated model of quality, affordable early years and out of hours childcare," including by increasing "the State share of GDP spent on childcare, from the current 0.37% of GDP to at least 1% by no later than 2030."[85] In addition, it recommended an expansion of paid parental leave so as to mirror the policies that were pioneered in Sweden and other Scandinavian countries and adopted by Germany and France following their most recent sex equality constitutional amendments. Specifically, the Citizens' Assembly recommended that paid leave for parents should "cover the first year of a child's life" and "be non-transferable to encourage sharing of childcare between parents." Consistent with the recommendation to amend the Constitution to recognize the value of all families, not only marital ones, the assembly also recommended providing "lone parents with the same total leave period as a couple." Finally, aware of the gender disparities in take-up rate, often due to the dynamics of the pay gap between women and men,[86] the assembly recommended that paid parental leave be "incentivised by increasing payment levels to encourage increased take up."[87]

The remainder of the Citizens' Assembly recommendations concerned the full range of gender equality policy areas, with an eye to reducing the burdens women shoulder for the public good and increasing women's share of public power.

Social Protections and Decision-Making Power

The assembly suggested improving social protections with sensitivity to gendered impacts;[88] expanding gender quotas, with penalties, to achieve gender balance in elected lawmaking positions; and enacting legislation requiring gender parity on corporate boards.[89] It also recommended making public funding to various sports, cultural, and media organizations contingent on increasing the representation of women on governing bodies to 40 percent by 2030.[90] Finally, supplementing these mechanisms to achieve gender parity in leadership and decision-making positions of power were recommendations to "improve family-friendly practices for elected representatives in public office, and to hold "technology and social media companies accountable for immediately removing online content that constitutes sexual harassment, bullying, stalking, sexually violent or abusive content."[91] These proposals combine the goal of gender equality in the exercise of public power with thoughtful interventions to address the barriers likely to hinder achievement of gender parity.

Education, Work, and Gender-Based Violence

The Citizens' Assembly also recommended education reforms to reduce gender stereotyping, including curriculum review and development, and funding to encourage women in male-dominated careers like STEM and men in female-dominated careers such as caring professions.[92] The recommendations on pay and workplace conditions focused on addressing women's disproportionate concentration in low-wage work. Interventions would include setting legislative targets to reduce the hourly gender gap gradually from 14 percent (current) to 9 percent (by 2025), then to 4 percent (by 2030), and finally eliminating it by 2035. Increasing the minimum wage, establishing the right to collective bargaining, and introducing the right to flexible working were also recommended. In addition, on domestic, sexual, and gender-based violence, which were topics not included in the Oireachtas resolution but introduced to the assembly by its chair, the Citizens' Assembly made general recommendations to improve awareness through education, increase support for victims and punishment for perpetrators, and fund beds, shelters, and accommodation for survivors of violence.[93]

Institutional Infrastructure for Gender Equality

The final set of proposals, perhaps carrying the most potential for lasting change after amending the Constitution, would institutionalize gender equality. The Citizens' Assembly recommended the establishment of a statutory body for gender equality with a cabinet minister in charge of cross-governmental coordination of gender equality issues, with adequate resources and powers to deliver gender equality across government and implement the Citizens' Assembly recommendations. To institutionalize gender equality, the government would have to gather and publish data on gender equality issues, require gender impact assessments of all proposed legislation, require equality budgeting across all governmental entities, review antidiscrimination laws, and require antidiscrimination training.

The recommendations of the 2021 Irish Citizens' Assembly on Gender Equality, formed in the midst of the global COVID-19 pandemic's gendered effects, provide a model worth engaging, not only for Ireland, but for all twenty-first-century constitutional democracies seeking to overcome misogyny through law. The broad-ranging blueprint seeks to overcome the patriarchal and paternalistic assumptions in early twentieth-century constitutions' protections of motherhood, as well as the baseline overentitlements and overempowerments neutralized by late twentieth-century constitutions' enforcement of gender equality under the law. A renewed commitment to valuing care as a public good, entitling people of all genders who engage in it to proper respect and compensation, forms a new, inclusive constitutionalism of care. Inclusive constitutionalism is taking shape not only through the substantive pluralistic approach to families and carers within both the home and the community but also through the procedural people-powered citizens' assembly mechanism by which the transformative changes to public law are delivered.

BRINGING CARE CONSTITUTIONALISM HOME

Women participated as founders and framers of the constitutions that protected motherhood and committed to gender equality in the twentieth century. In the twenty-first century, constitutional democracies are increasingly experimenting with citizen participation in constitutional and major policy change on the problems that most shape citizens' lives.[94] France, the United Kingdom, and Germany held citizens' assemblies on climate policy in 2019, 2020, and 2021, following the Icelandic experiment with crafting a "crowdsourced" constitution in 2012 where environmental issues were debated, and Irish citizens also deliberated on climate during the Convention on the Constitution in 2012.

This book has shown that misogyny has endured in law and society, long after the law rejected the violence and hatred of misogynists, because the law did not reset society's overentitlement to women's sacrifices or develop a legal vocabulary for redressing the abuses that flowed from men's overempowerment. Institutional transformations—of the sort often achieved by constitutional change—can reset the baseline for entitlements and rebalance power in a democracy. The American experience with the Prohibition Amendment illustrates that it's fraught and contested but not impossible in the United States. Some organizations have called for Congress to convene citizens' assemblies to guide and legitimize the major changes in policy that are needed in the twenty-first century.[95] And in January 2021, the state of Washington became the first US state to hold a state-level citizens' assembly on climate pollution.[96] The need to inject American democracy with a dose of the more innovative features of twenty-first-century constitutionalism is more urgent than ever. It has been difficult to update the United States' eighteenth-century Constitution to address twenty-first century problems such as climate change, gun violence, and abortion. The constitutional amendment process under the US Constitution is no longer feasibly functional, with no amendments since 1992. Recent decisions of the Supreme Court interpret the Constitution on the basis of meanings from the time of each provision's adoption in the eighteenth and nineteenth centuries—before women were recognized as rights bearers.[97]

In several European nations, a constitutionalism of care shapes a critical perspective on the overentitlement of society to women's sacrifices by explicitly recognizing the public value of those sacrifices and entitling mothers to the protection of the community in return. The COVID-19 pandemic, with its particularly destructive effects on working mothers' careers, drew new attention to the urgent need for a care infrastructure in the United States. A year into the pandemic, Congress passed and President Biden signed the American Rescue Plan,[98] which created an expansion of the child tax credit and $40 billion funding for childcare, including block grants to help childcare providers operate safely, increase pay and benefits for childcare workers, and reduce childcare costs for parents. It also extended paid family leave, allocated $150 million for maternal, infant, and early childhood programs, and created an option for states to extend postpartum Medicaid coverage to reduce maternal mortality.

All of these elements of the care infrastructure were temporary pandemic recovery measures, passed through the budget reconciliation process, which does not require a supermajority of the Senate to overcome a threatened filibuster. The House subsequently passed the Pregnant Workers' Fairness Act, which requires reasonable accommodations for pregnant workers on the job, of the sort that the law of most European countries protected after World War II, but the Senate did not follow. The lawmakers committed to constitutionalizing women's equality have also tried to pass statutes that would guarantee paid parental leave and support for childcare and maternal health extending indefinitely, beyond a one-off budget act. But such legislation has failed to garner the supermajority (and therefore bipartisan) support required to pass the Senate. Childcare and paid parental leave were initially part of President Biden's infrastructure plan,[99] but the bipartisan negotiation that procured Senate support abandoned care as part of the infrastructure package.

These roadblocks are a reminder that overentitlement and overempowerment operate together. Overcoming the injustice of undervaluing women's care work is difficult when women hold less than a third of the Senate seats and operate in a severe imbalance of power. Yet polling indicates that an overwhelming supermajority of American voters want more affordable childcare options,[100] and three-fourths support enshrining women's equality in the Constitution.[101]

In 2020, Americans defeated misogynists like Harvey Weinstein by enforcing the criminal law. They defeated other misogynists like Donald Trump by voting against him. But a much more inclusive and representative constitutional structure, beyond the guarantee of equality under the law, may be required to reset entitlements and rebalance power.

Conclusion

TOWARD A FEMINIST REMAKING OF
CONSTITUTIONAL DEMOCRACY

This book has journeyed around the world to moments of feminist constitutional change, within and beyond the United States. By amending
constitutions, challenging baseline entitlements, and resetting the balance of power in institutions of lawmaking and economic influence, feminists have taken on the problems of overentitlement and overempowerment and are remaking constitutional democracy for the twenty-first
century. Episodes from American legal history and global constitutionalism illustrate what women have contributed to overcome the failures of
law, not only for themselves, but for the future that their children will
inherit.

Where do we go from here? Can the global innovations of feminist lawmaking direct the law to realize and value the contributions of women in
the United States? This book has answered "yes," but it remains to be seen
whether the forces of feminism or the forces of backlash (which tracks
modern misogyny) will prevail.

COMPARATIVE LESSONS: FROM TRANSPLANT
TO TRANSLATION

American lawyers, judges, and scholars are often skeptical of comparative constitutional learning. Justice Scalia excoriated his colleagues on the court for deploying global legal norms against criminalization of gay sex in *Lawrence v. Texas*;[1] Justice Roberts said that "looking at foreign law for support is like looking out over a crowd and picking out your friends."[2] Skeptics of comparative law warn against cherry-picking to support one's prior beliefs.

Yet picking cherries is a valuable scholarly inquiry, if not a judicial strategy; scholars pick cherries and pick them apart under a magnifying glass when we select the most ambitious models, to understand and develop their logic for further development and future use. This book has selected the brightest spots in the world of feminist lawmaking to consider a fuller range of possibility than what has been attempted in the United States. This focus aims at illuminating the conceptual underpinnings, ideals, and aspirations that are most helpful toward shifting the legal paradigms in the long transition from the laws of patriarchy to the laws of inclusive democracy and feminism.

In presenting the histories and ideas of women's long struggles for full inclusion and voice in constitutional democracies across the globe, I have encountered a fair dose of skepticism from my fellow American feminists, who express plenty of reasonable doubt about whether US law can take any lessons from feminist constitution making throughout the world, given the different and unique legal and political context of the United States. I conclude that it can, but not by simple transplant. The more nuanced work of translation is needed, and this concluding chapter attempts it. It draws concrete lessons for the future of law and feminism from the theoretical account of misogyny advanced in this book, and the global efforts by women to confront it, in the United States and beyond.

Yes, the United States is unique and different. But that should not excuse cynicism or closed-mindedness. Nevertheless, a meaningful engagement of global innovations requires significant work to arrive at feasible normative recommendations. This scholarly project is different from recent comparative constitutional law scholarship that employs empirical methods for assessing constitutional performance across a range of national and cultural contexts.[3] International organizations, including the World Economic Forum and the World Bank, have produced studies that attempt to draw causal links between the presence of certain laws, including constitutional provisions, and measurable indicators of gender equality or women's economic opportunities.[4] Mila Versteeg and Adam Chilton have employed several empirical methods to study the effect of constitutional gender equality clauses and found no evidence that constitutionalizing the right to gender equality improves de facto gender equality.[5] Furthermore, they have found that constitutional clauses guaranteeing maternity leave and protecting motherhood may be associated with improved gender equality. Such studies raise questions about whether generalizable insights can be drawn from the effects of legal provisions and constitutional change on the lives of women on the ground, across vastly different national, cultural, economic, political, and legal contexts.[6]

My purpose here in studying episodes of feminist lawmaking, particularly to achieve constitutional change, is somewhat different. My primary goal is not to make scientific predictions about what works and doesn't work in the long run for women everywhere, or for constitutional democracies in general. Rather, this book presents textured portraits of the legal theories and normative propositions underlying the strategies that are moving law forward in the transition from patriarchy to democracy. The most significant milestones in this trajectory involve the confrontation of overentitlement and overempowerment. Constitutional efforts to reset entitlements, rebalance power, and build new infrastructures have been as significant as the demand for equal rights in the transition from patriarchy to real democracy.

Some legal scholars may see their job as gathering information to predict the future of law. That is different from an equally important function of legal scholarship: the development of new paradigms. The success of new paradigms cannot be accurately predicted with empirical methods because the future will never be exactly like the past; the new contexts in which new ideas are introduced will never be exactly like the old ones. In a democracy, the success of new ideas will depend on the persuasion and cooperation of the people and the institutions they occupy, more so than successes or failures elsewhere or in the past. This book elaborates upon approaches to institutions and legal reasoning more ambitious than those inherited from the languishing regimes of American gender equality and sex discrimination law, because scholars must never take the ignorance of the people as fixed and unchangeable. That assumption, more than any scientific predictions, explains the resistance to new ideas and the change they could bring about.

Scholars of comparative law have been debating about the desirability and methods of legal transplant for generations, largely because the development of the Western legal tradition can be described as a series of legal transplants.[7] Taxonomies and text have been cut and pasted from the classical texts of Roman law to modern civil codes; constitutions of the twentieth and twenty-first centuries contain a fair share of ideas, provisions, and clauses that were transplanted from the constitutions of other polities. There is a rhetorical simplicity that is undeniably appealing if the study of global law can be reduced to "Countries X, Y, and Z do A with great success; why don't we?" To that it is easy enough to reply, "It didn't happen here,"[8] perhaps meaning "It can't happen here,"[9] consistent with a long tradition of American exceptionalism that has resisted European transplants or has assumed that resistance on the part of the American people or their institutions is fixed.

Law and society scholar Robert Kagan has suggested that the proper medical metaphor for comparative law is psychotherapy rather than major organ transplant. Like psychotherapy, comparative analysis "attempts to reveal roads not taken, unconsciously maintained patterns, and sources of resistance to change."[10] What is gained from cross-national study of legal feminism is not specific transplant proposals but a creative translation. As Vicki Jackson has put it, the transnational era we now inhabit calls for constitutional "engagement," which is different from complete immersion and copying.[11] Engaged translation entails solving puzzles within the opportunities and constraints of US law. Can we give effect to the values and ideas of feminist constitutionalism that have been differently expressed in other contexts? Below I sketch short-term doctrinal possibilities for bringing an overentitlement perspective to American constitutional law, as well as a more ambitious long-term vision of constitutional change, for which persuasion of the citizenry is the necessary first step.

RESPONDING TO OVERENTITLEMENT AND UNJUST
ENRICHMENT THROUGH TAKINGS DOCTRINE

We can begin with abortion, and the protection of access to legal, safe, and free abortion by the laws of many countries that face strong pro-life political forces and legal doctrines. Women in many countries that have recently liberalized abortion access have more meaningful access to abortions that are legal, safe, and free than US women do. Women in these countries never had the constitutional right to abortion protected by the logic of *Roe v. Wade,* but in many of these constitutional democracies, mothers have the right to the protection of the state. Their contributions to the public good, through the bearing and raising of children, are publicly valued, including in cases that assess the burdens of forced maternity to adjudicate abortion access. Because the US Supreme Court has ended the regime of *Roe,* the paths toward abortion access in countries that protect unborn life must inform new strategies of reproductive justice under US law.

The success of both the antiabortion constitutional amendment in Ireland in 1983 and the repeal of that amendment to pave the way for abortion access in 2018, as detailed in chapter 3, should not suggest that constitutional amendments against or for abortion access are plausible or desirable in the United States, given significant differences in constitutional amendment rules and the subjects that constitutional provisions tend to address in the two nations. It's also hard to imagine the transplant of a constitutional amendment guaranteeing the protection of mothers and caregivers—even in the gender-neutral way that Ireland is now contemplating—in the United States. But there are other ways that US law can give effect to the public, rather than private, dimensions of pregnancy that have been amply theorized by feminists, judges, and lawmakers throughout the world.

A full appreciation of the state's interest in pregnancy and parenthood might guide the formulation of new constitutional arguments, not under the Fourteenth Amendment's Due Process and Equal Protection Clauses, but under the Takings Clause of the Fifth Amendment, or the Thirteenth Amendment ban on involuntary servitude. Takings doctrine, in particular, is an untapped source of legal claims compensating the burdens of unwanted pregnancy. Indeed, the idea that motherhood is undervalued and uncompensated is not new to public policy debates in the United States: from the drive for mothers' pensions during the Progressive Era,[12] to the wages for housework movement of the 1970s,[13] to the pandemic-era calls for a Marshall Plan for Moms,[14] some American feminists have long demanded public compensation for the collective benefits conferred on society and the nation by women's disproportionate childbearing and child-rearing load. When a state bans abortion, it requires the pregnant person to endure a physically demanding bodily change for nine months and then imposes legal parenthood on her for the next eighteen years, with all of its legally enforceable responsibilities. A law banning abortion effectively extracts physical and mental labor from women for the benefit of others, often for the collective public good. This extraction resembles a regulatory taking, requiring compensation by the state.

The Fifth Amendment does not prohibit government from taking property from people entirely; it simply requires "just compensation" when private property is "taken for public use." Scholars have long grappled with the line between substantive due process (*Roe*'s constitutional home for abortion access) and takings.[15] A governmental action that causes property loss can be either a legitimate exercise of the police power or a taking.[16] If the latter, a governmental duty of just compensation arises, owed to those from whom private property is taken for public use.[17] As one property scholar has put it, a regulation registers as a taking when it goes too far, and the determination often focuses on the property interest that is being affected.[18]

Abortion bans can be framed as regulatory takings requiring the state to compensate the people who have sustained losses or made personal sacrifices to carry an unwanted pregnancy to term. To fit within the takings paradigm, a property interest should be identified, which belongs to the pregnant person, and which is adversely affected when the state forbids abortion. Do women have a property interest in their wombs? If so, a state that bans abortion uses an individual's womb for a public purpose, namely procuring the birth of future members of the community who cannot survive without access to a receptive womb. The fact that only this particular individual—the pregnant person—is able to keep the unborn life viable does not absolve the state of responsibility for the rental of the womb. Even if the state is permitted by the Constitution to borrow the woman's womb temporarily for its own purposes in this way, Takings Clause jurisprudence has robustly developed the insight that the government must compensate the private property owner even when the taking of property for a public purpose is justified. By this logic, compensation is owed to a person who stays pregnant subject to a regulation that effectively occupies the pregnant person's womb until fetal viability. Staying pregnant involves physical changes to the body that often prevent women from continuing to engage in lucrative employment.[19] Black women who stay pregnant face risks of maternal mortality that are unreasonable in an economically advanced society.[20]

The constitutions of many of our peer democracies, including those of Germany, Ireland, France, Italy, South Korea, Mexico, Argentina, and Colombia, either authorize or obligate the state or public policy to protect pregnant women or mothers.[21] Ireland's clauses about the "woman in the home"[22] and "mothers"[23] are efforts—albeit excessively gendered by twenty-first-century standards—to recognize the valuable contributions of pregnancy and motherhood to the public and collective good. The collective benefits include the gestation, birth, and raising of a new generation of citizens and workers, concretely speaking, as well as the state's ability to protect life, more abstractly, by promoting a culture of life.

The American states that are banning abortion are asserting a public interest in the protection of unborn life, even before fetal viability.[24] In Texas, Senate Bill 8 empowers everyone to sue an abortion provider who performs an abortion after the detection of fetal cardiac activity, in an apparent departure from the typical legal requirement that civil plaintiffs themselves suffer a concrete injury. Underlying this widely distributed enforcement power is the implicit assumption that everyone is injured when these unborn lives are prevented from developing into born persons. The statutory design presumes a strong community interest in the gestation of unborn life that overrides the pregnant woman's interest in her own health and well-being in determining the course of her life. Other constitutional democracies also embrace this public interest in protecting unborn life, but over the decades they have come to acknowledge that there is a serious constitutional problem with requiring the only class of citizens who are capable of getting and staying pregnant to absorb the full costs and sacrifices necessary to enable the state to protect and gestate unborn life, for the benefit of the community that gains a new generation of workers and citizens. The US Constitution views other situations involving the extraction of public benefits from private individuals as problems worthy of a governmental solution. The Takings Clause provides the constitutional anchor for such grievances.[25]

The risks, costs, burdens, and sacrifices of continuing an unwanted pregnancy may not, at first glance, seem like a taking of private property. Yet three significant changes that have occurred in the legal landscape since *Roe v. Wade* make it feasible in the twenty-first century to view the legally compelled continuation of an unwanted pregnancy as a taking of private property: (1) the recognition of property rights in body parts and tissue (including embryos); (2) the enforceability of commercial surrogacy contracts by which a woman is entitled to compensation for the renting of her womb; and (3) changes in parentage law, including safe haven laws, that have weakened the presumption, in some cases, that the woman who gives birth to a child is that child's legal mother. These legal developments, taken together, make it reasonable to interpret a legally compelled pregnancy as the state's rent-free tenancy in the pregnant person's womb.

This proposition construes the womb as private property. In 1988, a California court of appeal opened up the possibility of treating body parts as private property for the purposes of advancing the common-law claim of conversion.[26] The California Supreme Court did not embrace this theory of private property in one's own human tissue *once it was removed from one's body* but allowed the case to proceed on other grounds. It left open the question of whether the law might enforce a property right in tissue that remains within one's own body.

Furthermore, courts have inched toward recognizing ownership interests in reproductive material. A California court of appeal recognized a man's ownership interest in his own sperm and authorized his right to bequeath it as property upon his death to his girlfriend.[27] Courts have also treated frozen embryos as marital property in the context of divorce[28] and have enforced contractual agreements about their distribution upon divorce. Dicta in these cases assume a property interest in body parts that remain in one's own living body. It is not a radical stretch to treat the womb as private property. Property rights in the womb would include the right to control its use, including excluding use by others. Such right of control has never encompassed the right to injure, destroy, or kill others in the course of controlling and enjoying one's property. But it does entail the right to exclude and/or profit from others' use of the property.

The rise of commercial gestational surrogacy in the decades since *Roe* exemplifies a person's exercise of such rights over her womb. In gestational surrogacy arrangements, a person agrees to become pregnant with the child of another and to carry that pregnancy to term, allowing the use of her womb for the period of gestation in exchange for remuneration. The pregnant person is merely the gestational carrier of the unborn life, which transitions from embryo to fetus to infant within her uterus; the gestational carrier is usually not the infant's legal parent after the child is born. Typically, the gestational carrier is not the genetic parent of the child either, since the embryo is often formed with the egg donated or purchased from another party. The evolution of reproductive technology and surrogacy law have made it possible, if not normal, that neither the genetic mother (i.e., the woman from whom the egg originates) nor the birth mother (i.e., the woman who gestates and delivers the baby) becomes the child's legal mother.[29] The unique legal status of the gestational carrier— increasingly common in surrogacy arrangements for childbearing and child-rearing—has transformed modern understandings of pregnancy and parenthood. In today's legal landscape, there is nothing radical about the proposition that a pregnant person who gestates an infant for the benefit of others deserves just compensation.

Gestational surrogacy assigns legal parenthood to other private individuals or couples, which makes it easy to understand that the pregnant person is gestating an infant for the benefit of others. But even in the absence of gestational surrogacy, every state has a "safe haven" law that also determines the legal parenthood of a child born of an unwanted pregnancy. Typically, the "safe haven" law relieves a person carrying an unwanted pregnancy to term of parental rights and responsibilities. These laws tell the pregnant person that she does not have to be a legal mother when she delivers the baby. Safe haven laws liberate pregnancy from legal parental responsibilities to the newborn infant and from any liability to the state, so long as the infant is safely delivered to public authorities,

typically at a police or fire station.[30] Safe haven laws relieve the birth parents of the duties and burdens of legal parenthood. Justice Amy Coney
Barrett suggested during the oral argument in *Dobbs v. Jackson Women's
Health* that while "forced parenting, forced motherhood, would hinder
women's access to the workplace and to equal opportunities," "the safe
haven laws take care of that problem."[31] Because safe haven laws extin-
guish parental rights and responsibilities shortly after the child's birth,[32]
these laws theoretically make it possible for a woman facing an unwanted
pregnancy to carry the pregnancy to term without really occupying, intending, or even entertaining the role of legal parent. In overruling *Roe v. Wade*,
the Supreme Court majority referenced these laws to suggest that
Americans do not regard unwanted pregnancy as the significant burden
that it once was.[33] If safe haven laws effectively terminate the pregnant
woman's parental rights and responsibilities almost immediately upon
birth, in the same way that gestational surrogacy arrangements assign
legal parenthood to the intended parents rather than to the pregnant and
birthing woman, characterizing every unwanted pregnancy as a tenancy of
the womb by the child of another becomes an accurate legal description.

The safe haven laws implicitly make the state the legal guardian or parent of the embryo/fetus/infant who is occupying the unwilling pregnant
woman's womb, and who is being housed for survival, rent-free. The state,
on behalf of the life-affirming society, owes compensation to the pregnant
person in these circumstances. This obligation is even more acute in jurisdictions that fail to protect pregnant women from the economic insecuri-
ties stemming from pregnancy discrimination and the failure to accom-
modate pregnancy in remunerative employment, and from high rates of
maternal mortality that are exacerbated by lack of access to affordable
health care and/or health insurance.[34] The United States has higher rates
of maternal mortality than countries similar in wealth and development,[35]
and many of the states that are instituting near-total bans on abortion
have some of the highest rates of maternal mortality.[36] Within this landscape, maternal mortality rates are higher for poor women[37] and Black
women.[38]

Regarding the pregnancy as a coerced and uncompensated physical
occupation of the pregnant individual's body to optimize the public inter-

est may recall the famous violinist hypothetical in philosopher Judith Jarvis Thomson's seminal 1971 article, "A Defense of Abortion."[39] There Thomson famously raised the question of whether a person would be morally obligated to limit her own bodily freedom for nine months in order to save the life of a famous violinist whom she discovered attached to her by medical tubes for life support.[40] The hypothetical assumes, for the sake of argument, that the life that is dependent on the woman's forbearance is that of an actual person with full rights and capacities, unlike an embryo or fetus, whose human rights and capacities are arguably different and ambiguous.[41] Thomson pointed out that "the body that houses the child is the mother's body," resonating with my suggestion that the pregnant woman facing unwanted pregnancy, who intends not to become a legal mother, is providing rent-free housing to a person who belongs not solely to her but primarily to society at large, and over whom the state is the legal guardian. If the state, by threatening the pregnant woman or the abortion provider with criminal sanctions or civil damages, prevents the pregnant woman from evicting the fetus before viability by way of a safe and legal abortion, the Takings Clause obligates the state to compensate her for the public use of her womb.

The takings theory is related to another proposal, by some constitutional scholars including Andrew Koppelman, to challenge abortion restrictions as involuntary servitude in violation of the Thirteenth Amendment.[42] Forced pregnancy and parenthood are involuntary servitude, and if the state, through enacted laws, is forcing these services out of women, it appears to be a straightforward violation of the ban on involuntary servitude. Challenging an abortion ban under a Thirteenth Amendment theory would likely lead to its abolition, whereas a successful takings claim could leave the abortion ban intact as long as the state compensated women for the use of their wombs. Of course, compensation to carry a pregnancy to term would likely weaken the characterization of that pregnancy as slavery or involuntary servitude, which are, by definition, unpaid forced labor. Successful takings claims against abortion restrictions, requiring the state to fully cover the significant expenses of every pregnancy and parenthood, might well lead states to rethink the economic viability and political wisdom of banning abortion.

OVEREMPOWERMENT AND THE SHIFTING DOCTRINE
OF GENDER-BASED AFFIRMATIVE ACTION

Chapter 5 detailed the evolution of gender parity laws in several European countries. These requirements have made a significant difference to women's participation as lawmakers and decision makers in institutions of power. When constitutional courts struck down these gender quotas, enforcing a constitutional vision of formal equality, lawmaking bodies were willing not only to reinstate parity rules but also to amend constitutions to definitively resolve the question of whether constitutional equality required or permitted laws to rebalance decision-making power to end male overempowerment. A constitutional amendment explicitly authorizing or even requiring gender parity in positions of power would be helpful toward ending gendered overempowerment if it could possibly be transplanted in the United States. Laws requiring women's inclusion are probably necessary to increase women's actual share of decision-making positions, as decades of prohibiting sex discrimination and relying on voluntary diversity efforts have not led to gender parity. However, as with any constitutional amendment protecting abortion, motherhood, or caregiving, transplanting a constitutional amendment requiring parity in the exercise of power is hard to imagine in the United States, largely because Article V of the US Constitution sets nearly impossible hurdles for constitutional amendment by comparison to all the other constitutions that have had such amendments.

However, some states are passing legislation requiring women's inclusion in positions of power, in contexts where their historic and persistent exclusion is clear. New legal arguments about their constitutional validity are needed to ensure their survival against litigation seeking to enforce a vision of equal protection that bans sex distinctions in the law. The California law requiring minimum gender diversity on corporate boards has been upheld by a federal court and struck down by a state court, indicating that the law of equal protection is unclear and capable of being remade with regard to gendered empowerment. The statute requires every corporation registered to do business in California to have at least one woman on the board; a board with more than six directors must have at least three. The statute can be viewed as a modest legal transplant; its legislative findings, as stated, included a reference to the many European countries that have legislated more ambitious gender parity quotas. The legislature found:

> (d) Other countries have addressed the lack of gender diversity on corporate boards by instituting quotas mandating 30 to 40 percent of seats to be held by women directors. Germany is the largest economy to mandate a quota requiring that 30 percent of public company board seats be held by women; in 2003, Norway was the first country to legislate a mandatory 40 percent quota for female representation on corporate boards. Since then, other European nations that have legislated similar quotas include France, Spain, Iceland, and the Netherlands.[43]

In June 2022, after a decade of debate, the European Union announced that it would soon adopt a new law requiring listed companies to have at least 40 percent of their non–executive director positions held by members of the underrepresented sex.[44]

In California, anti–affirmative action groups immediately brought litigation challenging the corporate board gender representation requirement, arguing that it was a "woman quota" that violated the Equal Protection Clause of the Fourteenth Amendment as well as similar state constitutional provisions on equality. In December 2021, a federal court declined to enjoin the minimum gender diversity requirement, finding the doctrine in Supreme Court jurisprudence striking down racial quotas to be inapplicable to gender quotas and other efforts to empower women.[45] The district court was persuaded by the evidence in the legislative record establishing that the severe underrepresentation of women on boards (with 25 percent of California boards still having no women whatsoever on them) was due to discrimination against women in board selection. Remedying that discrimination was a sufficiently important governmental interest supporting the constitutionality of the minimum gender diversity requirement.

As this decision was simply a preliminary injunction denial, which is being appealed to the Ninth Circuit and perhaps eventually the Supreme Court, and many additional lawsuits are being brought to challenge this minimum gender diversity requirement, there will be more significant opportunities in the future for lawyers and judges to develop the law against overempowerment. In this preliminary decision, the focus is on discrimination against women in board selection processes. But the

California legislature made several findings about the problems with the excessive concentration of power in men, which go beyond the animus against and exclusion of women. The legislature cited numerous studies concluding that public companies perform better when their boards are not all male. The presence of at least one woman consistently led firms to higher returns on equity and price-to-book values as compared to "zero-women boards."[46] The legislature instituted a rule that attempted to address the problems correlated with male overempowerment on boards, citing a finding that companies with women on their boards were more likely to institute strong governance structures with a high level of transparency and that they tended to be risk averse and carry less debt.[47]

Yet the heightened intermediate scrutiny framework to root out gender-unequal protection under the Fourteenth Amendment makes these findings of overempowerment constitutionally suspect. Deploying the equal-treatment, nondiscrimination, and antistereotyping paradigms that have dominated constitutional gender equality law, the litigants challenging the minimum gender diversity rule point to these precise findings to argue that the legislature generalized about how women and men behave in a manner that perpetuated constitutionally problematic gender stereotypes, treating men and women differently without a substantial public purpose.[48] The legislature drew the general conclusion, using data, that a governance regime with zero women, consisting 100 percent of men, the historically advantaged gender, led to bad governance. A law of constitutional gender equality that would prohibit such generalizations about power stands little chance of overcoming the dynamics by which concentrations of power lead to its misuse and abuse.

Shifting what is scrutinized in equal protection analysis from gender classification to gendered overempowerment, and from gender stereotyping to gender underrepresentation (the "inexorable zero"), would go a long way to remedy discrimination against women, a governmental purpose that the district court recognized as legitimate and important. And, beyond remedying past discrimination, promoting democracy in the institutions that exercise economic and political power is and should be recognized by constitutional doctrine as an important governmental purpose. Seeing how gender quotas have evolved in other countries can provide some clarity in any future efforts to reframe the constitutional problems and solutions involved in litigation challenging affirmative action for women. Even without transplanting constitutional amendments authorizing or requiring gender parity, overempowerment and the democratic legitimacy of governance institutions provide crucial perspectives on the path that can lead to the legal order that replaces patriarchy and misogyny.

PROCESS MATTERS: DEMOCRATIZING OUR CONSTITUTION

All of the efforts to dismantle patriarchal law and reset entitlements appropriate to a truly inclusive constitutional democracy point to the importance of the processes by which this transition occurs. Chapter 1 highlighted an institutional story that made a huge difference to the implementation of transformative sex role thinking in Sweden. The major constitutional reform in Sweden of the 1960s was not the addition of an equal rights guarantee for women but the redesign of the legislative branch. A bicameral parliament became obsolete because of a newly designed unicameral body. The redesign of the legislature in Sweden made it more representative of the people and more responsive to their needs. Concurrent with the sex role debates of the 1960s were debates about the institutional design of the legislature, resulting in the profoundly consequential constitutional reform that transformed the Riksdag from a bicameral legislature to a unicameral body. Unicameralism, prevalent in the Scandinavian countries known as pioneers in feminist lawmaking, cleared the path to adopting bold legislation involving major resource allocation.[49] These constitutional reforms in Sweden also included the adoption of proportional representation in the electoral system,[50] which facilitated the election of a greater proportion of women to the legislature.[51] The normative vision of gender emancipation—that women should be liberated from the home and that men should be liberated from the workplace—could become a reality only with strong governmental intervention. These constitutional reforms enabled government to act decisively to reshape social and economic life. That institutional change likely did more than antidiscrimination law, which was adopted in Sweden in 1980, to reset men's and women's entitlements to household and market work.

The implications of the Swedish story should be obvious for the United States. Consider all the examples of feminist legislation at the federal level that have been passed by the House but filibustered by the Senate. They would be much more likely to be adopted by Congress if the House and the Senate were merged into one body, with a proportional-representation electoral system in place to elect its members. But even if the Senate is not abolished the way its counterpart was in Sweden, its most antidemocratic aspects should be redesigned. The Senate filibuster is not a rule that the Constitution requires or even authorizes the Senate to use; yet it has been used in the Senate for the past generation to stop legislation that the House has passed, even if a majority of the Senate supports that legislation.[52] Because the filibuster rule empowers a forty-senator minority to prevent any measure from proceeding to a vote by closing debate on that measure, it has become a tool for empowering a minority of senators to block several pieces of legislation passed in the House that would redress the problems of societal overentitlement to women's forbearance and male overempowerment to society's detriment. Even when legislation is not officially filibustered by an official cloture vote, politicians' simple knowledge that sixty votes are necessary to get a vote on any bill in the Senate shapes their choices about the allocation of political resources toward proposed laws; it essentially determines the political agenda.

Proposed legislation to compensate women's contributions to the economy and relieve the burdens women bear to gestate, birth, and raise the next generation of citizens has been passed by the House, only to disappear into the legislative graveyard of the Senate. If such bills could become law, the vast differences that make the United States exceptionally resistant to the proactive welfare state interventions supporting women and other vulnerable populations would diminish. In the 117th Congress (2021–23), as of this writing, the House passed two such bills, one on equal pay and the other protecting abortion access, which the Senate officially filibustered by official cloture vote, supported by a majority but short of the sixty votes necessary to advance the bill to a vote. The Paycheck Fairness Act has been proposed in Congress for over twenty years, recognizing the inadequacies of existing equal pay laws, under which women still make eighty-two cents to the man's dollar. The law would make it harder for employers to defend unequal pay practices, limiting the employer's permitted justifications only to bona fide job-related factors in wage discrimination claims. It would also provide employees complaining of unequal pay stronger legal protection from retaliation and would prohibit employers from requiring contracts by which employees agree not to disclose information about their own wages. The bill would increase civil penalties for employer violations of equal pay provisions.[53]

The Women's Health Protection Act would protect access to abortion, protecting both abortion providers and patients.[54] It would prohibit restrictions on abortion before viability and would ban other regulations that tend to burden abortion access, such as requirements of surgical hospital admission privileges for abortion providers and requirements of in-person visits to the health care provider beyond those medically necessary. The legislation would in effect codify legal protections for abortion access that have emanated from Supreme Court decisions like *Roe v. Wade*, *Planned Parenthood v. Casey*, and *Whole Woman's Health v. Hellerstedt*. The House passed the bill in September 2021, but the Senate cloture vote to advance consideration of the bill got only forty-nine votes in February 2022.[55] Then, in early May 2022, the Supreme Court draft majority opinion in *Dobbs* that overruled *Roe v. Wade* was leaked to the press, leading to protests and public upheaval. The Senate majority leader then scheduled another cloture vote, this time on the Senate's Women's Health Protection Act bill. The legislation was filibustered again, with only forty-nine votes to close debate and move to a vote.[56]

Even when antimisogyny legislation is not officially filibustered by formal cloture votes, the filibuster rule has tremendous influence on shaping the horizons of lawmaking possibility. As of this writing, the House has passed additional legislation that would reset men's and society's entitlements to women's sacrifices for their gain. But such bills are often not on the Senate's agenda when it is known that fewer than sixty senators support them. Even without a cloture vote to kill a legislative proposal that has been passed by the House, many feminist laws die under the invisible power of the filibuster rule. In the 117th Congress, the House passed, for the second time, with bipartisan support, the Pregnant Workers Fairness Act.[57] The legislation would protect pregnant workers from being terminated or adversely treated in the workplace because of their need for a reasonable accommodation of their pregnancies. As highlighted in chapter 3, women who stay pregnant face risks, not only to their health, but also to their economic security, because the law fails to protect the reasonable accommodations that are often necessary for their continued employment. A legal order that refuses to guarantee reasonable accommodations of pregnancy implicitly assumes that society is entitled to women sacrificing their livelihoods and absorbing the costs of bringing children into the world. Such observations are explicit in other constitutional democracies' abortion jurisprudence and efforts to reform and rebuild the constitutional protection of motherhood. However, the procedural rules and composition of the Senate have prevented US law at the federal level from changing the obsolete assumptions of patriarchal law.

Similarly, the House passed the Violence Against Women Act (VAWA) Reauthorization Act in 2019, but the Senate stalled it until 2022. The VAWA Reauthorization Act would have reauthorized federal programs to prevent domestic violence, sexual assault, dating violence, and stalking, after the previous VAWA sunsetted by its own terms. The Reauthorization Act also proposed new programs, including housing for victims, to respond to violence against women. The Senate finally adopted a version of it, but without the provisions that the House had adopted to prohibit domestic violence offenders from purchasing firearms. Violence against women, especially sexual violence in the presence of guns, enforces men's overentitlement to women's sexual availability and can be traced to patriarchal laws protecting male control over female sexual activity and husbands' legal authority to chastise their wives and coerce them into unwanted sex. While it is easy to see how stronger gun legislation would reset the overentitlements and rebalance the overempowerments of misogyny, this is another bill that languished in the Senate.

The Senate's failures to make feminist law are only partly explained by the filibuster rule, which theoretically could be abandoned without a constitutional amendment. But the filibuster rule has not been repealed for the same reason that only forty-nine, rather than fifty, Democratic senators voted to advance the Women's Health Protection Act: the Democratic senator from West Virginia votes with Republicans more often than most members of his party, representing a state that has consistently given its electoral votes to Republican presidential candidates in every presidential election of the twenty-first century. The people of West Virginia, a state populated by

1.8 million people, are entitled to elect the same number of senators as the people of, say, New York, who are ten times greater in number, with a state population of 19 million. To put the point more starkly, the least populous state—Wyoming, population 579,000—gets the same number of votes in the Senate as the most populous state—California, population 39 million.

Indeed, the much more significant barrier to Senate action that would complete the long legal transition from patriarchy to real democracy is that the Constitution entrenches a Senate composition that is deeply unrepresentative of the American people and antidemocratic. Not only does Article II, Section 3 prescribe two senators from each state, Article V immunizes that rule from the normal process of constitutional amendment. While Article V allows the Constitution to be amended by a two-thirds vote by Congress and ratification by three-fourths of the state legislatures (and by a constitutional convention procedure that has never been used to date), it also provides that "no State, without its consent, shall be deprived of its equal Suffrage in the Senate." Any effort to make the Senate more representative, by, for instance, allowing the most populous states to have more senators than the least populous states, would require every state to consent, not three-fourths. Underpopulated states have elected senators who are overempowered to stop legislation that most American people support, such as the Women's Health Protection Act.[58]

Within the context of our Constitution's overempowerment of underpopulated states in its own enumerated amendment process, the last fifty years wreaked an unprecedented controversy about the validity of a constitutional amendment guaranteeing equal rights to women. Many participants in the Equal Rights Amendment (ERA)'s legislative history viewed the amendment as securing equal power for women, through the guarantee of equal rights unabridged on account of sex.[59] The ERA was adopted by two-thirds of Congress in 1972 and was ratified by three-fourths of the states from 1972 to 2020. But its status as a constitutional amendment remains contested because Congress imposed a seven-year ratification deadline on the states, which three of the thirty-eight states missed by several decades in delivering their ratifications, notwithstanding a three-year deadline extension in the 1970s.[60] Ongoing debates in litigation and in Congress have raised questions about the legal validity and meaning of the ERA's ratification deadline, which was itself inserted into the ERA proposal by a vocal minority of ERA opponents who had already established a reputation for filibustering civil rights legislation.[61]

Not surprisingly, the path to legitimizing the ERA in the twenty-first century is obstructed anew by the specter of filibuster in the Senate. After Nevada, Illinois, and Virginia ratified the ERA in 2017, 2018, and 2020, over three decades past Congress's extended deadline, the House passed resolutions retroactively removing the ratification deadline in 2020 and 2021. And, even though the Senate deadline removal bill has enough bipartisan support to be passed by a majority, it lacks the support of the sixty senators required to overcome a filibuster. Accordingly, even the ERA's supporters in Senate leadership have declined to put the ERA deadline removal up for a cloture vote. If Congress did act to remove the deadline, the ERA's legitimacy as part of the Constitution would have a stronger likelihood of being left undisturbed by the Supreme Court, in light of established separation-of-powers precedents treating the question of ratification validity as a political question. A majority of the court, as evidenced by the majority opinion in *Dobbs*, appears inclined to respect the policy decisions of democratically elected legislatures, particularly on issues that come within the political question doctrine.

Nonetheless, this struggle to add the ERA to the Constitution shows how difficult it is to amend the US Constitution, particularly in ways that change who exercises lawmaking power. Shortly before the ERA was adopted by Congress, with the seven-year deadline insisted upon by filibuster-prone Senate opponents, that same group of senators successfully filibustered another constitutional amendment that would have abolished the electoral college as a means of choosing presidents.[62] Critics of the electoral college, then and now, claim that it is not democratic, since it allows the election of presidents who have failed to win the popular vote. But our Constitution's amendment process—and its design of lawmaking and electoral systems— makes it nearly impossible to change the Constitution to empower those who have previously been excluded from power, such as women.

The American resistance to constitutional change comes into sharper focus as an abnormal dysfunction within modern constitutionalism, rather than the charming genius of our (slaveholding) founding fathers, when compared to the processes of constitutional amendment in other countries that have adopted amendments to address overentitlement and overempowerment. In Germany and France, each constitution's rule for amendment set lower thresholds than Article V and was effectively deployed by women's movements in the late twentieth and early twenty-first centuries to add gender parity provisions that rebalanced the exercise of public power. The German constitution can be amended when both houses of the federal legislature adopt proposed amendments by a two-thirds vote,[63] with no additional ratification by the regional Land legislatures. The French Constitution empowers the legislature to adopt an amendment by a majority, subject to majority approval in a referendum of the people. It also allows amendments to be proposed by the president to the legislature, in which case a three-fifths vote by both houses obviates the need for a referendum.[64] Operating under these rules, amendments that obligated lawmakers to implement actual equality, or to promote equal access to power, succeeded after a robust public debate between courts, the legislature, and the people.

Ireland, a country where the influence of Catholicism looms large, has seen recent constitutional amendments guaranteeing same-sex marriage, liberalizing divorce, and authorizing the legislature to liberalize abortion access only because the amendment process was designed to identify the people's will and gauge their readiness for these changes. The Irish Constitution's amendment rule requires adoption by a majority of both houses of Parliament followed by majority approval in a referendum by a vote of the people.[65] While there is no mention in the Constitution of citizens' assemblies, Parliament further democratized the amendment process by creating these institutions to deliberate on potential amendment proposals on divisive social issues, including abortion and state support for mothers and caregivers. Citizens' assemblies did not displace Parliament's constitutional role as the proposer of constitutional amendments, as Parliament created these institutions on an advisory basis, to recommend amendments that it was not bound to adopt. Nonetheless, the citizens' assembly processes have created an important public space by which Parliament can identify the will of the people, which buttresses the democratic legitimacy of the proposals it considers, adopts, and sends for a referendum vote. In a society where public opinion is divided, such processes can facilitate the identification of potential points of compromise and convergence.

There may be ways to make the American constitutional amendment process more responsive to the will of the people, particularly when it comes to women's emancipation and reproductive justice. Polls indicate that a significant majority of Americans support the Equal Rights Amendment. On abortion, several polls reveal that more than 60 percent of Americans want abortion to be generally legal in the first three months of pregnancy but that they favor restrictions in the second and third trimesters.[66] The views of the American people on abortion match up with the results of the Irish Citizens' Assembly process that led the way to repealing the constitutional abortion ban. But the United States, unlike Ireland, has not had an official process by which the American people have been able to deliberate, persuade, compromise, and establish a constitutional direction. After the Supreme Court issued its *Dobbs* decision overruling *Roe*, supporters of abortion rights protested in the streets throughout the nation. But a more deliberative path for legitimizing the people's support for abortion access is also needed, without dependence on the Supreme Court (the least democratic branch of federal government).

Article V of the US Constitution does not mention citizens' assemblies, but that should not be a barrier to congressional creativity in the amendment process. Article V does not mention ratification deadlines either. With the latter, Congress has simply imposed deadlines as a necessary and proper procedural element of its constitutional power to propose amendments. By this logic, there is no constitutional barrier to innovation on Congress's part—beyond deadlines—in designing the process it uses to exercise its Article V power to propose amendment. Congress can create new mechanisms to improve its work; it can seek the advice of the people by holding citizens' assemblies as the Irish Parliament did, or by appointing an advisory council as the Icelandic Parliament did, to explore national public opinion in a transparent and deliberative way, and to assess the possible models of compromise and convergence on difficult issues like gender relations and the transition from patriarchy to feminist equality. This process would be extremely useful for legitimizing paths forward. Once the people are able to speak through these new institutional frameworks, it would be more difficult for senators to use the filibuster to stop legislative proposals after a transparent process reveals them to be supported by the people. In 2021, a Citizens' Assembly on Climate Change gathered in Washington State to deliberate on the issues and make recommendations to the legislature.[67] Organizations that have designed these processes, learning from the assemblies authorized by legislatures in Europe, could hold citizens' assemblies on issues like gender equality, abortion, and care to make recommendations to Congress, even in the absence of an initiative initially authorized or driven by Congress.

In Chile, the constitutional reform process began with the people. After the wave of demonstrations that included the feminist flash mobs chanting their anthem against patriarchy, the Chilean Parliament authorized the referendum that set off a process of writing a new constitution for Chile. It legislated the election of a constitution-making assembly that would follow requirements of gender parity as well as provide seats for the representation of indigenous groups in proportion to their population. A surprising outcome of the elections for the constituent assembly was that grassroots independent candidates, rather than those belonging to established political parties, prevailed to form a majority. By the terms of the parliamentary plan for the Constitutional Convention (the constituent assembly), every provision in the draft constitution that was put to referendum in September 2022 had to attain the approval of two-thirds of the Constitutional Convention.

The proposed constitution that this body generated included ambitious and unprecedented provisions relating to gender equality, women's empowerment, and reproductive justice. Beyond the provisions explicitly addressing gender parity and the rights of women, the 387-article document revamped almost every existing institution and contained expansive and detailed guarantees of social, economic, political, and human rights. The September 2022 referendum rejecting this proposal indicated that Chilean voters were not yet willing to embrace such a massive overhaul of existing entitlements and institutions. But the vision of inclusive constitutionalism that this process engendered is continuing to mobilize efforts to reform the constitution. Although this feminist constitution has not become the nation's fundamental law, the Chilean process of feminist protest and women's empowerment has redefined the terms of the nation's constitutional future. It marks a significant milestone in the ongoing transition from patriarchy to inclusive constitutional democracy.

Having begun with the patriarchy—men controlling women through law—we end with women increasing their share of control of law and society. Throughout the world, misogyny's engine of overempowerment has been slowed by democratic constitutionalism, with women making their constitutions change to establish new foundations of equality and inclusion for twenty-first-century democracies. Instead of seeking individual justice against misogynists, new movements have focused on establishing comprehensive legal orders that reset entitlement and power. Misogyny will be overcome when women's contributions and sacrifices are visibly valued.

Constitutional movements around the world are adding a new stanza to the feminist anthem with which this book began. After "patriarchy is our judge / that judges us for being born" the transition to full democracy will require the law to value women for the burdens they have borne. Can we imagine the day when "the cops, the judges, the state, the president" are no longer "the rapist in your path"? Instead, the cops, the judges, the state, and the president will be women who are entitled and empowered by democracy to do justice themselves.

Acknowledgments

Although this book was written during the period of abnormal isolation imposed by the COVID-19 pandemic, the research, conferences, workshops, teaching, and conversations that shaped it spanned over two decades, during which I accumulated many intellectual debts on several continents.

It is a book that grew out of years of studying and teaching law outside the United States, particularly in Europe. Long before I came to focus on patriarchy and feminism, many teachers, friends, and colleagues introduced me to the myriad institutions and legal frameworks that can shape the prospects for real equality. Over time, these interlocutors helped me arrive at the central insight of this book—that true equality and inclusion for women in twenty-first century democracies must entail changing institutions and processes of legal change, both within and beyond constitutionalism. For establishing my global and comparative mindset, I am grateful to my teachers at Yale Law School, especially Bruce Ackerman, Owen Fiss, Judith Resnik, Reva Siegel, James Q. Whitman, and Kenji Yoshino. I am also grateful to the many scholars, lawyers, and judges in or of Europe who have enriched me with extended conversation about equality in both public and private law over many years, namely Susanne Baer, Fabrizio Cabrizzi, Gwénaële Calvès, Graínne De Burca, Jeanne Fagnani, Sandra Fredman, Stéphanie Hennette-Vauchez, Tarunabh Khaitan, Sophie Latraverse, Pierre Legrand, Eléonore Lépinard, Kasper Lippert-Rasmussen, Susanna Mancini, Ruth Rubio-Marín, Christopher McCrudden, Marie Mercat-Bruns, Hans Micklitz, Marie-Ange Moreau, Pap Ndiaye, Colm O'Cinneiade, Diane Roman,

Daniel Sabbagh, Bernhard Schlink, and Patrick Weil. Their generous insights and friendship nourished the ideas that grew into this book.

The research upon which the arguments in this book are based was presented in many forms at various conferences, faculty workshops, and seminars in the past decade. Some of my earlier published articles or essays drew on this research, specifically "A World without Roe: The Constitutional Future of Unwanted Pregnancy" (*William and Mary Law Review* 64, no. 2 [2022]); "An Equal Rights Amendment for the Twenty-First Century: Bringing Global Constitutionalism Home" (*Yale Journal of Law and Feminism* 28, no. 2 [2017]); "Are Gender Stereotypes Bad for Women? Rethinking Antidiscrimination Law and Work-Family Conflict" (*Columbia Law Review* 110, no. 1 [2010]); "Gender Equality and the Protection of Motherhood in Global Constitutionalism" (*Journal of Law and Ethics of Human Rights* 12, no. 1 [2018]), and "Gender Parity and State Legitimacy: From Public Office to Corporate Boards" (*International Journal of Constitutional Law* 10, no. 2 [2012]). Presenting these papers helped me update the research, expand on it, and develop the larger theory of misogyny at the heart of this book.

I presented early drafts of papers about motherhood protection, work-family conflict, and comparative quotas and affirmative action, Prohibition and constitutional amendment at the International Society of Public Law (ICON-S) conferences from the inaugural one in Florence in 2014 and from New York in 2015, Berlin in 2016, Copenhagen in 2017, Hong Kong in 2018, and Santiago in 2019. My co-panelists and the audiences at these conferences contributed tremendously to the new ideas that the research spawned. The pleasant surprise of a "standing-room-only" turnout at our "mothers in law" panel in Berlin 2018 and my encounter with David Kenny's work on the Irish constitutional referendum on the comparative reproductive rights panel that I chaired in Hong Kong in 2018 were especially generative. I also benefited from presenting my work on Prohibition and abortion at the American Society of Legal History in 2018 and 2019 and at the Law and Society conference in 2019.

In Paris, the research team REGINE, formed by Stéphanie Hennette-Vauchez and Diane Roman to pursue a government grant exploring gender and the law, hosted two extremely productive conferences in 2012 and 2014, where my presentations of research on comparative work-family conflict and gender equality law helped point me in new directions. Judith Resnik at Yale Law School also hosted two conferences in 2012 and 2013 devoted to gender parity in global context, supported by the Gruber Program there, which were also extremely valuable to developing the new research questions that eventually became this book.

Draft chapters at all stages of development benefited from being put under the microscope at various law school faculty workshops, including ones at Cardozo, University of Connecticut, Duke, Emory, Fordham, Humboldt University (in Berlin), New York Law School, and Northwestern. Specialized seminars with faculty and students also provided valuable and helpful insights on one or more of these chapters: Anu Bradford's seminar on comparative and international law at Columbia Law School, Ruth Rubio-Marín's seminar on gender and constitutions at NYU Law School, Dan Hulsebosch and David Golove's legal history seminar at NYU Law School, Jed Shugerman and Saul Cornell's legal history seminar at Fordham Law School, Richard Albert's comparative constitutional law seminar at the University of Texas, and Sarah Song and Josh Cohen's Kadish seminar at UC-Berkeley Law. The Texas and Berkeley seminars were particularly helpful for making me realize that my work on comparative abortion law belonged in a different book than the one I was writing at the time.

The New-York Historical Society's Center for Women's History hosted an excellent public conference in 2019 entitled "Ninety-Nine Years since Prohibition," where I presented an early version of chapter 4. I am grateful to the N-YHS, the panelists and audience members, and particularly Alice Kessler-Harris, who moderated the session, for deepening my knowledge of Prohibition history.

At the City University of New York (CUNY) Graduate Center, I worked with Sarah Covington, director of the Master's Program in Biography and Memoir, and the Irish Studies Program at Queens College to help organize and present at the conference "Reproductive Rights in Ireland and the U.S.," in May 2019. It was a pivotal and eye-opening experience for me to talk with Ailbhe Smyth, Una Mulally, and Maeve Higgins about the evolution of abortion discourse in Ireland. I am grateful to all of the participants and organizers.

The New York Public Library also made it possible for me to research the nineteenth- and early twentieth-century history in this book (both US and European). I am grateful for the many months that I spent in the Wertheim Study. The NYPL's microform and electronic copies of the German Constituent Assembly debates at Weimar and Bonn made my research much easier to conduct during the teaching semester.

I would also like to thank the European University Institute in Florence and LUISS-Guido Carli for hosting me as a visiting scholar, to former judge András Sajó for hosting me at the European Court of Human Rights, and to the Honorable Olivier Dutheillet de la Mothe for enabling access that helped me learn about the workings of the Conseil d'Etat and the Conseil constitutionnel during my stays in Paris. The Italian Constitutional Court library and librarians helped me access many of the Italian Constituent Assembly materials from the post–World War II era during my period of residence in Rome in 2016. I'm particularly grateful to Justices Marta Cartabia and Silvana Sciarra for generously hosting me at the court and affording me access to their library.

As a central insight of this book is that institutions matter, I should thank the institutions that I have been lucky to call home during the time that this book came to fruition. The research began when I was a professor at Cardozo Law School, my intellectual home from 2005 to 2018. I was blessed with summer research grants every year during my time there, and the support of Deans David Rudenstine, Matthew Diller, and Melanie Leslie. My senior colleagues Michel Rosenfeld, Martin Stone, Suzanne Stone, and Richard Weisberg deserve special mention for supporting my comparative and interdisciplinary work as an entry-level junior faculty member. I then spent three years at the Graduate Center of the City University of New York (CUNY), as a professor of sociology and liberal studies and as a dean for master's programs. Provost Joy Connolly encouraged the administrator-scholar-teacher model with generous research funding that enabled work on this book to continue during my time as a dean. Since Fall 2021, I have had the good fortune to have joined the faculty at Fordham University School of Law, and I am grateful to Dean Matthew Diller for supporting my research. The faculty at Fordham have forged one of the most rigorous and dynamic scholarly communities in the country, and I am thankful to my brilliant colleagues for their sincere commitment to maintaining it.

Many students have contributed to the making of this book. I taught several courses over the past decade that directly engaged the ideas in this book: Comparative Law and Antidiscrimination Law at Cardozo Law School; Comparative Law: Western Legal Orders and Discrimination: Theoretical and Comparative Perspectives at Harvard Law School; Mothers in Law, at the Graduate Center at CUNY (team-taught with the amazing medieval historian Sara McDougall); Constitutions and Constitutional Design and Gender Law and Policy at Fordham Law School. My attention to the processes by which feminists have attempted legal change, and the limits of litigation, would not be possible without my students of civil procedure since 2005, first at Cardozo Law School and now at Fordham, and the many civil procedure sections I taught as a visiting professor at UCLA, Columbia, Harvard, and Yale Law Schools. My students Samantha McCarthy at Fordham Law School and Varshini Parasarathy and Angela Lulu Zhang, both at Yale Law School, provided critical research assistance.

At UC Press, Maura Roessner has been amazing. She read an early paper on Prohibition and encouraged me to develop a book project about toxic masculinity, connecting it to the ongoing global history of women in constitution making. I am grateful for her insight and encouragement. The three anonymous reviewers provided incredibly helpful feedback that helped reframe the introduction and conclusion of the book. Sam Warren, Stephanie Summerhays, Jeff Anderson, and Elisabeth Magnus provided crucial editorial support. Thanks to all of you for making this book happen.

Within and beyond the many institutional settings mentioned above, some colleagues and friends deserve special mention for the comments and questions they raised upon reading earlier draft chapters that became this book, at various stages. They are: Bruce Ackerman, Richard Albert, Julian Arato, Joseph Blocher, Deborah Dinner, Rosalind Dixon, Guy-Uriel Charles, Mathilde Cohen, Erin Delaney, David Fontana, Jennifer Gordon, Clare Huntington, Alice Kessler-Harris,

Suzanne Kim, Ethan Leib, Serena Mayeri, Sara McDougall, Samuel Moyn, Melissa Murray, Ruth Rubio-Marín, Nicholas Parillo, Elizabeth Sepper, Jed Shugerman, Reva Siegel, Sarah Song, Gila Stopler, Kirsten Swinth, Deborah Tuerkheimer, and Kimberly Yuracko.

I am also lucky to have a family that offers both emotional support and intellectual engagement. My sister Jeannie Suk Gersen and my brother-in-law Jacob Gersen have provided encouragement and an informal sounding board for many of the ideas in this book. It has been pretty remarkable to watch my sons, Emile and Niccolo, grow into adolescence through dinner conversations about socialism, equality, and democracy. And I am most indebted to my spouse, Youngjae Lee, for his patience, forbearance, and genuinely insightful feedback as an intellectual companion, as this book took up so much of our family's space during the quarantine and postquarantine of the COVID-19 pandemic. If this book contributes to making the world better, one indicator will be the reduced need to obsess about injustice and inequality, and the increased time to enjoy our loved ones, for whom I am eternally grateful.

My parents, who left their hometowns as children during the Korean War, and then left their native country as immigrants to the United States in the 1970s, have long inspired and supported my global and comparative work. My mother has always thought critically out loud about what women can and should do as she raised me and my two sisters and worked with many organizations to support women and girls in her community and globally. Her character always speaks to my work, for which I owe a lifetime of gratitude.

I dedicate this book to all the women of the world, who struggle invisibly to make the world more just, not only for themselves, but for everyone. It has been challenging, but new paths lie ahead.

Notes

Throughout the notes, citations of non-US cases, laws, constitutions, and similar sources use abbreviations as defined here. Consult *The Bluebook* for definitions of all abbreviations used for US legal citations.

BGB	Bürgerliches Gesetzbuch (Civil Code) (Germany)
BGBl.	*Bundesgesetzblatt* (Federal Law Gazette) (Germany)
BGH	Bundesgerichtshof (Federal Court of Justice) (Germany)
BGHZ	*Entscheidungen des Bundesgerichtshofes in Zivilsachen* (Decisions of the Federal Court of Justice in Civil Matters) (Germany)
Burr.	Burrow's Reports, King's Bench (England)
BvC	Case number of the Bundesverfassungsgericht, for electoral complaints
BVerfG	Bundesverfassungsgericht (Federal Constitutional Court) (Germany)
BVerfGE	*Entscheidungen des Bundesverfassungsgerichts* (decisions of the Federal Constitutional Court) (Germany)

BvF	Case number of the Bundesverfassungsgericht, for abstract judicial review of statutes
BvL	Case number of the Bundesverfassungsgericht, for specific judicial review of statutes
BvR	Case number of the Bundesverfassungsgericht, for constitutional complaints
CA	Cour d'appel (regional court of appeal) (France)
Cass.	Cour de cassation (Supreme Court for Judicial Matters) (France)
Cass. 1e civ.	Cour de cassation, Chambre civile 1 (France)
Cass. req.	Cour de cassation, Chambre des requêtes (France)
CC	Conseil Constitutionnel (Constitutional Council) (France)
C.C.	Corte Constitucional (Constitutional Court, Colombia)
C. civ.	Code civil (France)
Cód. Pen.	Código Penal (Argentina)
Const. Ct.	Constitutional Court (South Korea)
Const. Nac.	Constitución Nacional (Argentina)
Cost.	Costituzione (Italy)
C.P.	Constitución Política de los Estados Unidos Mexicanos (Mexico) or Constitución Política de Colombia (Colombia)
CSJN	Corte Suprema de Justicia de la Nación (National Supreme Court of Justice) (Argentina)
Dáil Deb.	Dáil Debates (Ireland)
Eng. Rep.	English Reports
Eur. Ct. H.R.	European Court of Human Rights
GG	Grundgesetz (Basic Law) (Germany)
GVBl.	Gesetz- und Verordnungsblatt (law gazette [for a state]) (Ger.).
IESC	Supreme Court of Ireland
IR	*Irish Reports*
J.O.	*Journal Officiel de la République Française* (Official Gazette of France)
J.O.A.N.	*Journal Officiel Assemblée Nationale* (Official Journal of the National Assembly)

M. & W.	Meeson & Welshy's Reports (UK)
Mutterschutzgesestz	Mutterschutzgesestz, Gesetzes vom 23. Mai 2017 (Mothers' Protection Law of May 23, 2017) (Germany)
SCJN	Suprema Corte de Justicia de la Nación (National Supreme Court of Justice) (Mexico)
ThVerfGH	Thüringer Verfassungsgerichtshof (Thurinigia Constitutional Court) (Germany)
VfGBbg	Verfassungsgericht des Landes Brandenburg (Constitutional Court of the State of Brandenburg) (Germany)

INTRODUCTION

1. Laurie Timmers, "The Rapist in Your Path: This Chilean Feminist Anthem Is Spreading around the World," December 12, 2019, www.euronews.com /2019/12/07/a-rapist-in-your-path-this-chilean-feminist-anthem-is-spreading -around-the-world. For footage of the protest, see "Un violador en tu camino," by feminist collective Lastesis during the protests in Santiago de Chile, November 28, 2019, www.youtube.com/watch?v=VZWHua6PHa8.

2. See Jane Sherron DeHart, *Ruth Bader Ginsburg: A Life* (New York: Knopf, 2018), 119.

3. See Simone de Beauvoir, *The Second Sex*, trans. Constance Borde and Sheila Malovany-Chevallier (New York: Vintage, 2011), 71.

4. De Beauvoir, *Second Sex*, 85.

5. De Beauvoir, *Second Sex*, 87, 90.

6. De Beauvoir, *Second Sex*, 77. She explains:

Once woman is dethroned by the advent of private property, her fate is linked to it for centuries: in large part, her history is intertwined with the history of inheritance. The fundamental importance of this institution becomes clear if we keep in mind that the owner alienated his existence in property; it was more important to him than life itself; it goes beyond the strict limits of a mortal lifetime, it lives on after the body is gone, an earthly and tangible incarnation of the immortal soul; but this continued sur-vival can occur only if property remains in the owner's hands: it can remain his after death only if it belongs to individuals who are extensions of himself and recognized, who are *his own*. Cultivating paternal lands and worshipping the father's spirit are one and the same obligation for the heir: to ensure the survival of ancestors on earth and in the underworld. Man will not, therefore, agree to share his property or his children with woman. He will never really be able to go that far, but at a time when patriarchy is powerful, he strips woman of all her rights to hold and transmit property. It seems log-ical, in fact, to deny her these rights. If it is accepted that a woman's children do not belong to her, they inevitably have no link with the group the woman comes from. (90)

7. De Beauvoir, *Second Sex*, 80. See Friedrich Engels, *The Origins of the Family, Private Property, and the State*, ed. Tristram Hunt, reissue ed. (New York: Penguin Classics 2010), 61, 84.

8. Economist Nancy Folbre notes that "patriarchal rules typically enforce a harsh sexual double standard, ostensibly in order to allow men to guarantee paternity." Nancy Folbre, *The Rise and Decline of Patriarchal Systems: An Intersectional Political Economy* (London: Verso 2021), 27.

9. Engels, *Origins of the Family*, 104.

10. See Gerda Lerner, *The Creation of Patriarchy* (Oxford: Oxford University Press, 1986), 23.

11. August Bebel, *Woman under Socialism*, trans. Daniel De Leon (New York: New York Labor News Press 1904), 28 (emphasis in the original).

12. John Andrew Crouch, "Woman in Early Roman Law," *Harvard Law Review* 9, no. 1 (1894–95): 39–50.

13. See Barry Nicholas, *An Introduction to Roman Law* (Oxford: Clarendon Press, 1962), 65.

14. See generally Eva Cantarella, "Women and Patriarchy in Roman Law," in *The Oxford Handbook of Roman Law and Society*, ed. Paul du Plessis, Clifford Ando, and Kaius Tuori (Oxford: Oxford University Press, 2016), chap. 32.

15. See Jane Gardner, *Women in Roman Law and Society* (London: Routledge, 1991), 5.

16. Gardner, *Women in Roman Law*, 127.

17. William Blackstone, *Commentaries on the Laws of England*, Book 1, Chapter 15, § III (Boston: Beacon Press, 1962).

18. Catharine Waugh McCulloch, in the first generation of women lawyers admitted to practice, depicted the consequences of these legal rules in a fictional story based upon the court decisions that established these rules. Catharine Waugh McCulloch, *Mr. Lex or the Legal Status of Mother and Child* (Chicago: F. H. Revell, 1899), 16–23, 41.

19. Hendrik Hartog provides a nuanced history of patriarchy and misogyny in the nineteenth-century US legal orders that governed marriage and married persons, as well as judges' and lawyers' efforts to improvise solutions in an inherited and changing legal order. See Hendrik Hartog, *Man and Wife in America: A History* (Cambridge, MA: Harvard University Press, 2000).

20. For an account of this virtual representation theory of democracy in the family, see Reva B. Siegel, "The Nineteenth Amendment and the Democratization of the Family," *Yale Law Journal Forum* 129 (January 20, 2020): 450–95.

21. See Reva B. Siegel, "Home as Work: The First Woman's Rights Claims Concerning Wives' Household Labor, 1850–1880," *Yale Law Journal* 103, no. 5 (1994): 1073–1217.

22. "But the husband cannot be guilty of a rape committed by himself upon his lawful wife, for by their mutual matrimonial consent and contract the wife

hath given herself into this kind unto her husband, which she cannot retract." Matthew Hale, *Historia Placitorum Coronae: The History of the Pleas of the Crown* (London, 1736), 1:629.

23. Bradwell v. Illinois, 83 U.S. 130 (1873).

24. *Bradwell,* 83 U.S. at 139, 141 (Bradley, J., concurring).

25. See Reva B. Siegel, "'The Rule of Love': Wife Beating and Prerogative and Privacy," *Yale Law Journal* 105, no. 8 (1996): 2117, 2122.

26. Elizabeth Cady Stanton, *Declaration of Sentiments*, Seneca Falls Convention, July 1848, www.nps.gov/wori/learn/historyculture/declaration-of -sentiments.htm.

27. Stanton, *Declaration of Sentiments,* para. 4.

28. U.S. Const. amend. XIX.

29. For a history of the ERA, including the conflicts that prevented its adoption when initially proposed, and the long and ongoing struggle for ratification since the 1970s, see Julie C. Suk, *We the Women: The Unstoppable Mothers of the Equal Rights Amendment* (New York: Skyhorse, 2020).

30. Reed v. Reed, 404 U.S. 71 (1971).

31. *Reed,* 404 U.S. at 76.

32. See, for example, Frontiero v. Richardson, 411 U.S. 677 (1973); Weinberger v. Wiesenfeld, 420 U.S. 636 (1975); Missouri v. Duren, 439 U.S. 357 (1979).

33. *Frontiero,* 411 U.S. at 685.

34. Maggie Doherty, "The Philosopher of #MeToo," *Chronicle of Higher Education,* November 13, 2019, www.chronicle.com/article/the-philosopher -of-metoo/.

35. Kate Manne, *Down Girl: The Logic of Misogyny* (Oxford: Oxford University Press, 2017), 19.

36. See Kate Manne, *Entitled: How Male Privilege Hurts Women* (New York: Crown, 2020), chaps. 3–4 (entitlement to sex and entitlement to consent) and chap. 7 (entitlement to domestic labor).

37. Catharine A. MacKinnon, "Feminism, Marxism, Method, and the State: Toward Feminist Jurisprudence," *Signs* 8, no. 4 (1983): 635, 644.

38. See Catherine A. MacKinnon, *Toward a Feminist Theory of the State* (Cambridge, MA: Harvard University Press, 1991), 172.

39. MacKinnon, "Feminism, Marxism," 648.

40. Mackinnon, *Toward a Feminist Theory,* 173.

41. MacKinnon, "Feminism, Marxism," 653.

42. Catharine A. MacKinnon, *Sexual Harassment of Working Women* (New Haven, CT: Yale University Press, 1979), 175.

43. Siegel, "'Rule of Love,'" 2178, 2182. Siegel shows how a status regime can be modernized. An earlier legal regime protected the rights of husbands to beat their wives as "chastisement." After this regime was repudiated and reformed,

judges in the more enlightened regime protected the rights of husbands to privacy in matters of family life, which did not formally authorize wife beating but instead rendered it invisible to the law.

44. See MacKinnon, *Sexual Harassment*, 220–21.

45. Robin West, "Relational Feminism and Law," in *Research Handbook on Feminist Jurisprudence*, ed. Robin West and Cynthia Bowman (Cheltenham, UK: Edward Elgar, 2019), 66.

46. West, "Relational Feminism and Law," 67–68.

47. West, "Relational Feminism and Law," 67–68.

48. West, "Relational Feminism and Law," 67–68.

49. West, "Relational Feminism and Law," 67–68.

50. See Joan Williams, *Unbending Gender: Why Family and Work Conflict and What to Do about It* (Oxford: Oxford University Press, 2000).

51. Williams, *Unbending Gender*, 6.

52. Williams, *Unbending Gender*, 7.

53. See Ellen Key, "Motherliness," *Atlantic Monthly*, October 1912, 567–68.

54. Key, "Motherliness," 569–70.

55. Key, "Motherliness," 570.

56. See Helen Stöcker, *Bund für Mutterschutz* (Berlin: Pan-Verlag, 1905); Helene Stöcker, *Zehn Jahre Mutterschutz* (Berlin: Oesterheld, 1915). For an excellent contemporaneous account in English by an American feminist, see Katherine Anthony, *Feminism in Germany and Scandinavia* (New York: Holt, 1915).

57. Torborg Lundell, "Ellen Key and Swedish Feminist Views on Motherhood," *Scandinavian Studies* 56, no. 5 (1984): 354 (discussing Ellen Key's *The Renaissance of Motherhood*).

58. Ann Taylor Allen, "Mothers of a New Generation: Adele Schreiber, Helene Stöcker, and the Evolution of a German Idea of Motherhood, 1900–1914," *Signs* 10, no. 3 (Spring 1985): 423.

59. See Alexandra Kollontai, "Working Woman and the Mother" (1914), in *Alexandra Kollontai: Selected Writings*, ed. and trans. Alix Holt (New York: Lawrence Hill, 1980), 127, 132.

60. Kollontai, "Working Woman," 135.

61. Kollontai, "Working Woman," 136.

62. See generally Suk, *We the Women*, 9–42.

63. See, for example, Coleman v. Court of Appeals of Maryland, 566 U.S. 30, 47, 57 (2012) (Ginsburg, J., dissenting) (suggesting that a California maternity leave, because it provided benefits only to women, would lead employers to discriminate against women in hiring).

64. See Martha Albertson Fineman, *The Autonomy Myth: A Theory of Dependency* (New York: New Press, 2004), 171.

65. Fineman, *Autonomy Myth*, 172.

66. Fineman, *Autonomy Myth*, 175.

67. See Anne Helen Petersen, "Other Countries Have Social Safety Nets. The U.S. Has Women," Culture Study Substack, November 11, 2020, https:// annehelen.substack.com/p/other-countries-have-social-safety (quoting sociologist Jessica Calarco). Jessica Calarco's studies of pandemic-related childcare disruptions and working mothers' experiences during the pandemic include Jessica Calarco, Elizabeth Anderson, Emily Meanwell, and Amelia Knopf, "'Let's Not Pretend It's Fun': How COVID-19-Related School and Childcare Closures Are Damaging Mothers' Well-Being," SocArXiv Papers, preprint, November 1, 2020, https://osf.io/preprints/socarxiv/jyvk4/; Jessica McCrory Calarco, Emily Meanwell, Elizabeth Anderson, and Amelia Knopf, "'My Husband Thinks I'm Crazy': COVID-19 Related Conflict in Couples with Young Children," SocArXiv Papers, preprint, September 23, 2020, https://osf.io/preprints/socarxiv/cpkj6/.

68. See Jessica Grose, "Mothers Are the 'Shock Absorbers' of Our Society," *New York Times*, October 14, 2020 (quoting Dharushana Muthulingam), www .nytimes.com/2020/10/14/parenting/working-moms-job-loss-coronavirus.html.

69. Pauli Murray and Mary O. Eastwood, "Jane Crow and the Law: Sex Discrimination and Title VII," *George Washington Law Review* 34, no. 2 (1965): 242.

70. Pauli Murray, "The Negro Woman's Stake in the Equal Rights Amendment," *Harvard Civil Rights-Civil Liberties Law Review* 6, no. 2 (1971): 253. Dorothy Roberts spells out, more than Pauli Murray, the commercial value of Black women to white enslavers because of their ability to produce children who could be enslaved. See Dorothy E. Roberts, *Killing the Black Body: Race, Reproduction, and the Meaning of Liberty*, rev. ed. (New York: Vintage, 2017), 24. For a more detailed account of Pauli Murray's ERA testimony, see Julie C. Suk, "A Dangerous Imbalance: Pauli Murray's Equal Rights Amendment and the Path to Equal Power," *Virginia Law Review Online* 107 (2021): 3–26; see also Equal Rights 1970: Hearings on S.J. Res. 61 and S.J. Res. 231 Before the S. Comm. on the Judiciary, 91st Cong., 427-33 (1970) (statement of Pauli Murray).

71. Murray, "Negro Woman's Stake," 254.

72. Angela Y. Davis, *Women Race, and Class*, rev. ed. (New York: Vintage Books, 1983), 7.

73. Kimberlé Crenshaw, "Mapping the Margins: Intersectionality, Identity Politics, and Violence against Women," *Stanford Law Review* 43, no. 6 (1991): 1262–63.

74. Roberts, *Killing the Black Body*, 212–13.

75. Dorothy E. Roberts, "Critical Race Feminism," in West and Bowman, *Research Handbook*, 124.

76. Khiara M. Bridges, "Privacy Rights and Public Families," *Harvard Journal of Law and Gender* 34, no. 1 (2010): 122. Bridges elaborates the argument that poor women do not enjoy the privacy rights that constitutional law generally

protects, in Khiara M. Bridges, *The Poverty of Privacy Rights* (Stanford, CA: Stanford University Press, 2017).

77. Martha Albertson Fineman, *The Neutered Mother, the Sexual Family, and Other Twentieth Century Tragedies* (New York: Routledge, 1995), 177–93.

CHAPTER 1. THE EQUAL PROTECTION OF FEMINISTS AND MISOGYNISTS

1. The book was published as Ruth Bader Ginsburg and Anders Bruzelius, *Civil Procedure in Sweden* (The Hague: M. Nijhoff, 1965).

2. "RBG's Early Days in Sweden Shaped Her Fight for Women's Equality," *The World*, September 21, 2020 (interviewing now-judge Karin Bruzelius, the daughter of Ginsburg's Swedish coauthor), www.pri.org/stories/2020-09-21/rbg -s-early-days-sweden-shaped-her-fight-women-s-equality.

3. Petula Devorak, "Ruth Bader Ginsburg Had to Leave America to See How Unfairly It Treated Women," *Washington Post*, September 24, 2020.

4. Alva Myrdal and Viola Klein, *Women's Two Roles: Home and Work* (London: Routledge, 1962).

5. See Ruth Bader Ginsburg, Gillian Metzger, and Abbe Gluck, "A Conversation with Justice Ruth Bader Ginsburg," *Columbia Journal of Law and Gender* 25, no. 1 (2013): 8.

6. Olof Palme, "The Emancipation of Man," address presented at the Women's National Democratic Club, Washington, DC, June 8, 1970, www.olofpalme.org /wp-content/dokument/700608_emancipation_of_man.pdf.

7. Palme, "Emancipation of Man," 5.

8. Palme, "Emancipation of Man," 6–7.

9. See Edmund Dahlström, *The Changing Roles of Men and Women* (Boston: Beacon Press 1971), 172.

10. Dahlström, *Changing Roles*, 179.

11. Dahlström, *Changing Roles*, 179.

12. Dahlström, *Changing Roles*, 179.

13. Government of Sweden, "The Status of Women in Sweden: Report to the United Nations" (1968), in Dahlström, *Changing Roles*, 209–302.

14. Government of Sweden, "Status of Women," 235–40.

15. Dahlström, *Changing Roles*, 180.

16. Dahlström, *Changing Roles*, 181.

17. Reed. v. Reed, 404 U.S. 71 (1971); Brief for the Appellant, Reed v. Reed., 404 U.S. 71 (1971) (No. 70-4), 15, 55. Forty years later, Ginsburg said, "I regard *Reed v. Reed* as the grandparent brief. We had many other cases before the Court in the seventies. They were all variations on the same theme. A law that provides males must be preferred to females does not recognize women's equal citizenship

stature." Transcript, "*Reed v. Reed* at 40: Equal Protection and Women's Rights," *American University Journal of Gender, Social Policy and the Law* 20, no. 2 (2012): 317.

18. Brief for the Appellant, Reed v. Reed, 55n52.

19. Brief for the Appellant, Reed v. Reed, 6.

20. Brief for the Appellant, Reed v. Reed, 34.

21. *Reed,* 404 U.S. at 76.

22. Moritz v. Commissioner of Internal Revenue, 469 F.2d 466 (10th Cir. 1972) (reversing 55 T.C. 113 (1970)).

23. *On the Basis of Sex,* directed by Mimi Leder (Los Angeles: Focus Features, 2018).

24. Brief for Petitioner-Appellant, Moritz v. Commissioner of Internal Revenue, 469 F.2d 466 (10th Cir. 1972) (No. 71-1127), 31.

25. *Moritz,* 469 F.2d at 470.

26. *Reed,* 404 U.S. at 76; *Moritz,* 469 F.2d at 470.

27. Cary Franklin, "The Anti-stereotyping Principle in Constitutional Sex Discrimination Law," *New York University Law* Review 85, no. 1 (2010): 83–173.

28. Frontiero v. Richardson, 411 U.S. 677 (1973).

29. *Frontiero,* 411 U.S. at 685 (citing Bradwell v. Illinois).

30. *Frontiero,* 411 U.S. at 687.

31. Kahn v. Shevin, 416 U.S. 351, 353 (1974).

32. Weinberger v. Wiesenfeld, 420 U.S. 636 (1975).

33. *Wiesenfeld,* 420 U.S at 645.

34. *Wiesenfeld,* 420 U.S at 652 (citing Stanley v. Illinois).

35. Califano v. Goldfarb, 430 U.S. 199 (1977).

36. *Goldfarb,* 430 U.S. at 202.

37. *Goldfarb,* 430 U.S. at 216.

38. *Goldfarb,* 430 U.S. at 236 (Rehnquist, J., dissenting).

39. *Goldfarb,* 430 U.S. at 231.

40. *Goldfarb,* 430 U.S. at 235.

41. Mississippi Univ. for Women v. Hogan, 458 U.S. 718, 723 (1982).

42. *Hogan,* 458 U.S. at 724.

43. *Hogan,* 458 U.S. at 729.

44. Craig v. Boren, 429 U.S. 190 (1976).

45. *Craig,* 429 U.S. at 194.

46. *Craig,* 429 U.S. at 199.

47. Walker v. Hall, 399 F. Supp. 1304 (W.D. Okla. 1975).

48. *Craig,* 429 U.S. at 201.

49. *Craig,* 429 U.S. at 202–3.

50. *Craig,* 429 U.S. at 204.

51. *Craig,* 429 U.S. at 210n24.

52. R. Darcy and Jenny Sanbrano, "Oklahoma in the Development of Equal Rights: The ERA, 3.2% Beer, Juvenile Justice, and *Craig v. Boren*," *Oklahoma City Law Review* 22, no. 3 (1997): 1023.

53. Darcy and Sanbrano, "Oklahoma," 1036.

54. Darcy and Sanbrano, "Oklahoma," 1025.

55. National Minimum Drinking Age Act of 1984, 23 U.S.C. § 158.

56. See Ruth Bader Ginsburg, "Sexual Equality under the Fourteenth and Equal Rights Amendments," *Washington University Law Quarterly* 1979, no. 1 (1979): 168 (characterizing the case as "gossamer," in contrast with *Califano v. Goldfarb*, a weighty case because of public cost considerations).

57. Michael Graham, "*Craig v. Boren*: Sex Discrimination, 3.2% Beer, and the Clash between Oklahoma Law and the Equal Protection Clause," *Oklahoma Politics* 8 (October 1999): 44.

58. I explore this in greater depth in chapter 4.

59. See Bill Scher, "After Kavanaugh, #MeToo Should Launch a New Temperance Movement," *Politico*, October 9, 2018, www.politico.com/magazine/story /2018/10/09/kavanaugh-metoo-temperance-suffragettes-221141/.

60. See Stephanie K. Baer, "Here Are All the Times Brett Kavanaugh Said He Likes Beer at His Senate Hearing on Sexual Assault Allegations," BuzzFeed News, September 27, 2018, www.buzzfeednews.com/article/skbaer/brett -kavanaugh-likes-beer.

61. See, for example, Michael J. Cleveland, Maria Testa, and Liana S. E. Hone, "Examining the Roles of Heavy Episodic Drinking, Drinking Venues, and Sociosexuality in College Men's Sexual Aggression," *Journal of Studies on Alcohol and Drugs* 80, no. 2 (2019): 177–85.

62. Bianca DiJulia, Mira Norton, Peyton Craighill, Scott Clement, and Molyann Brodie, Survey of Current and Recent College Students on Sexual Assault, Kaiser Family Foundation/Washington Post Poll, June 12, 2015, reported in Emma Brown, Steve Hendrix, and Susan Svriuga, "Drinking Is Central to College Culture—and to Sexual Assault," *Washington Post*, June 14, 2015.

63. Ginsburg's former clerks, law professors Abbe Gluck and Gillian Metzger, confirm that "for Justice Ginsburg, equality did not mean special—she would say 'pedestal'—treatment for women. Equality meant the *same* treatment for women and men." See Abbe Gluck and Gillian Metzger, "Her Black Coffee Always Brewed Strong," *New York Times*, September 20, 2020.

64. See Michael M. v. Superior Court, 450 U.S. 464, 466 (1981) (citing § 261.5 of the Cal. Penal Code).

65. In 2014, California enacted the "Yes Means Yes" law, requiring colleges in California to have sexual assault policies in which sexual acts are presumed nonconsensual unless there is an "affirmative, unambiguous, and conscious decision

by each participant to engage in mutually agreed-upon sexual activity." Cal. Educ. Code § 67386(a)(1).

66. See Cal. Penal Code Ann. § 261.5 (2011). See Crimes—Unlawful Sexual Intercourse, 1993 Cal. Legisl. Serv. Ch. 596 (S.B. 22) (1993) (explaining the need for gender-neutral language in the statute).

67. *Michael M.*, 450 U.S. at 470.

68. *Michael M.*, 450 U.S. at 471.

69. *Michael M.*, 450 U.S. at 464.

70. *Michael M.*, 450 U.S. at 481 (Blackmun, J., concurring).

71. *Michael M.*, 450 U.S. at 483.

72. *Michael M.*, 450 U.S. at 483.

73. *Michael M.*, 450 U.S. at 483.

74. *Michael M.*, 450 U.S. at 483.

75. *Michael M.*, 450 U.S at 484–85.

76. These accounts are discussed in the Introduction. See Catherine MacKinnon, *Toward a Feminist Theory of the State* (Cambridge, MA: Harvard University Press, 1991), 172; Robin West, "Relational Feminism and Law," in *Research Handbook on Feminist Jurisprudence*, ed. Robin West and Cynthia Bowman (Cheltenham, UK: Edward Elgar, 2019), 65–66.

77. For example, a Yale student who was accused of nonconsensual sex with a severely intoxicated female, with bruises and other evidence of aggression, was criminally prosecuted for rape, but the jury acquitted him. See Vivian Wang and Cheryl P. Weinstock, "Yale Student Found Not Guilty in Rape Trial," *New York Times*, March 7, 2018.

78. *Michael M.*, 450 U.S. at 489 (Brennan, J., dissenting).

79. *Michael M.*, 450 U.S. at 490.

80. *Michael M.*, 450 U.S. at 496.

81. See 1993 Cal. Legis. Serv. Ch. 596 (S.B. 22) (West).

82. Cal. Penal Code § 261.5.

83. *Michael M.*, 450 U.S. at 501 (Stevens, J., dissenting).

84. *Michael M.*, 450 U.S. at 501.

85. Hyde amend., Pub. L. 96-123, § 109, 93 Stat. 926. The Hyde Amendment was upheld over a constitutional challenge in Harris v. McRae, 448 U.S. 297 (1980). I discuss it in more depth in chapter 3.

86. "Paternity Fraud: Father by Default," A Voice for Men, last modified January 3, 2015, https://avoiceformen.com/mens-rights/paternity-fraud-father-by-default/. For a feminist argument against the concept of paternity fraud, see Melanie B. Jacobs, "When Daddy Doesn't Want to Be Daddy Anymore: An Argument against Paternity Fraud Claims," *Yale Journal of Law and Feminism* 16, no. 2 (2004): 193–240.

87. J.E.B. v. State of Alabama ex rel. T.B., 511 U.S. 127 (1994).

88. *J.E.B.*, 511 U.S. at 128.

89. *J.E.B.*, 511 U.S. at 131–33.

90. Following the US Supreme Court's decision, the Alabama Court of Civil Appeals reversed and set aside the paternity judgment. J.E.B. v. State ex rel. T.B., 641 So. 2d 821 (Ala. Ct. Civ. App. 1994).

91. Deborah Tuerkheimer, *Credible: Why We Doubt Accusers and Protect Abusers* (New York: HarperCollins, 2021).

92. See "National Coalition for Men Helps Pass Paternity Fraud Legislation," National Coalition for Men Successes, last accessed June 1, 2022, https://ncfm .org/ncfm-home/national-coalition-for-men-ncfm-samples-of-success/.

93. See Introduction, text accompanying notes 3–25.

94. United States v. Virginia, 518 U.S. 515 (1996).

95. An expert testified at the district court level, "'Males tend to need an atmosphere of adversativeness,' while "Females tend to thrive in a cooperative atmosphere." *Virginia*, 518 U.S. at 541.

96. *Virginia*, 518 U.S. at 522.

97. *Virginia*, 518 U.S. at 523.

98. *Virginia*, 518 U.S. at 534.

99. *Virginia*, 518 U.S. at 550.

100. *Virginia*, 518 U.S. at 550.

101. *Virginia*, 518 U.S. at 570 (Scalia, J., dissenting).

102. *Virginia*, 518 U.S. at 531.

103. *Virginia*, 518 U.S. at 533 (citing California Fed. Sav. & Loan Assn v. Guerra, 479 U.S. 272, 289 (1987). Reva Siegel argues that the citation to *Guerra* in *United States v. Virginia* was recognizing the regulation of pregnancy as a sex-based classification worthy of heightened scrutiny. Reva B. Siegel, "The Pregnant Citizen, from Suffrage to the Present," *Georgetown Law Journal* 108 (2020): 205.

104. *Virginia*, 515 U.S. at 534.

105. Rostker v. Goldberg, 453 U.S. 57 (1981).

106. *Rostker*, 453 U.S. at 80–82.

107. *Rostker*, 453 U.S. at 75.

108. See Secretary of Defense, Memorandum, Implementation Guidance for the Full Integration of Women in the Armed Forces, December 3, 2015, https:// dod.defense.gov/Portals/1/Documents/pubs/OSD014303-15.pdf; "Carter Opens All Military Occupations, Positions to Women," U.S. Department of Defense News, December 3, 2015, www.defense.gov/Explore/News/Article /Article/632536/carter-opens-all-military-occupations-positions-to-women/.

109. National Coalition for Men v. Selective Service System, 355 F. Supp. 568 (S.D. Tex. 2019).

110. National Coalition for Men v. Selective Service System, 969 F.3d 546 (5th Cir. 2020).

111. See National Coalition for Men v. Selective Service System, 141 S. Ct. 1815 (Mem.) (Statement of Justice Sotomayor) ("It remains to be seen, of course, whether Congress will end gender-based registration under the Military Selective Service Act. But at least for now, the Court's longstanding deference to Congress on matters of national defense and military affairs cautions against granting review while Congress actively weighs the issue").

112. The most thorough intellectual defense of the men's rights movement is found in the writings of Warren Farrell, who started out as a supporter of 1970s feminist organizations such as the National Organization for Women (NOW). In his 1974 book *The Liberated Man*, Farrell embraced feminist accounts of male emancipation similar to the Swedish approach litigated by Ruth Bader Ginsburg in the 1970s. Warren Farrell, *The Liberated Man: Beyond Masculinity; Freeing Men and Their Relationships with Women* (New York: Random House, 1974). In the 1990s, Farrell argued that men are the undervalued sex, pointing to higher rates of suicide, occupational death (including in the military), incarceration, and other indicators. Warren Farrell, *The Myth of Male Power: Why Men Are the Disposable Sex* (New York: Simon and Schuster, 1993). In 2005, Farrell argued that men therefore should be paid more than women and rejected the suggestion that the gender pay gap could be explained by bias against women. See Warren Farrell, *Why Men Earn More: The Startling Truth behind the Pay Gap—And What Women Can Do about It* (New York: NY AMACOM, 2005). For an interview with Farrell, see Mariah Blake, "Mad Men: Inside the Men's Rights Movement—and the Army of Misogynists and Trolls It Spawned," *Mother Jones*, January–February 2015, www.motherjones.com /politics/2015/01/warren-farrell-mens-rights-movement-feminism-misogyny-trolls/.

113. Woods v. Horton, 167 Cal. App. 4th 658 (Cal. Ct. App. 2008). For a more sustained discussion of efforts by fathers' rights groups to undermine battered women's shelters and services, see Molly Dragiewicz, *Equality with a Vengeance: Men's Rights Groups, Battered Women, and Antifeminist Backlash* (Boston: Northeastern University Press, 2011). Similar litigation had been brought in federal court by other litigants in Minnesota, which was dismissed for lack of standing. Booth v. Hvass, 302 F.3d 849 (8th Cir. 2002).

114. Cal. Const. art. I, § 31.

115. Cal. Gov't Code § 11139.

116. See *Woods*, 167 Cal. App. 4th at 664.

117. *Woods*, 167 Cal. App. 4th at 665–66.

118. *Woods*, 167 Cal. App. 4th at 678.

119. One in five women and one in seven men have been victims of severe physical violence by an intimate partner in their lifetime. Ten percent of women, and 2 percent of men, report having been stalked by an intimate partner. "Fast Facts: Preventing Intimate Partner Violence," Centers for Disease Control

and Prevention, last accessed June 1, 2022, www.cdc.gov/violenceprevention /intimatepartnerviolence/fastfact.html.

120. See Katherine Rosman, "A Fight for Men's Rights, in California Courts," *New York Times*, July 18, 2018 (describing the NCFM's litigation against ladies' nights, women's career seminars, and paternity fraud).

121. Unruh Civil Rights Act Cal. Civ. Code §§ 51–52. The statute prohibits discrimination on various grounds, including sex, by business establishments in California.

122. Complaint, Allison v. FS-ISAC, Case No. 37-2018-00029403 (Cal. Super. Ct., filed June 14, 2018).

123. Class Action Complaint, Allison v. Sony Electronics, Case No. 37-2019-00052970 (Cal. Super. Ct., filed October 4, 2019).

124. Complaint, Allison v. Red Door Epicurean & Ladies Get Paid, Case No. 37-2017-00036282 (Cal. Super. Ct. 2017).

125. See Melissa Batchelor Warnke, "There Are No Safe Spaces for Women," Girl Boss, May 24, 2018, www.girlboss.com/read/ladies-get-paid-lawsuit.

126. See Claire Wasserman, "It's Been One Year since Ladies Got Sued," Ladies Get Paid, May 8, 2019, https://ladiesgetpaid.com/blog/2019-5-8-its -been-one-year-since-ladies-got-sued/.

127. Answer, Allison v. Sony Electronics, Case No. 37-2019-00052970 (Cal. Super. Ct., filed December 5, 2019).

128. See "Ladies Get Paid: We Need Your Help to Keep Our Business Open and Grow Our Programming," last accessed June 1, 2022, https://ifundwomen .com/projects/ladies-get-paid.

129. Sara Ashley O'Brien, "Women-in-Tech Events Are Anti-male, Say Men's Rights Activists," CNN Business, August 12, 2015, https://money.cnn .com/2015/08/11/technology/mens-rights-activist-chic-ceo/; Hannah Levintova, "These Men's Rights Activists Are Suing Women's Groups for Meeting without Men," *Mother Jones*, January 15, 2016, www.motherjones.com /politics/2016/01/men-rights-unruh-act-women-discrimination/.

130. See Alan Watson, *Legal Transplants: An Approach to Comparative Law* (Edinburgh: Scottish Academic Press, 1993).

131. See Gunther Teubner, "Legal Irritants: Good Faith in British Law or How Unifying Law Ends Up in New Divergencies," *Modern Law Review* 61, no. 1 (1998): 11–32; Otto Kahn-Freund, "On the Uses and Misuses of Comparative Law," in *Selected Writings* (London: Stevens, 1978); Pierre Legrand, "The Impossibility of 'Legal Transplants,'" *Maastricht Journal of European and Comparative Law* 4, no. 2 (1997): 111–24; William Ewald, "Comparative Jurisprudence I: What Was It Like to Try a Rat?," *University of Pennsylvania Law Review* 143, no. 6 (1995): 1889–2150.

132. Government of Sweden, "Status of Women," 268–69.

133. Sweden Government Offices, Ministry of Employment, *Gender Equality Policy in Sweden: A Feminist Government*, March 7, 2019, www.government.se/information-material/2019/03/gender-equality-policy-in-sweden/. See also Hilda Scott, *Sweden's "Right to Be Human: Sex-Role Equality: The Goal and the Reality* (London: Routledge, 1982), 72.

134. See Anita Nyberg, "Gender Equality Policy in Sweden: 1970s-2010s," *Nordic Journal of Working Life Studies* 2, no. 4 (2012): 67, 71.

135. Nyberg, "Gender Equality Policy," 68.

136. Sweden Government Offices, "Gender Equality Policy," 3.

137. One scholar notes that when parental leave was made available to fathers, only 2 percent of fathers took advantage of the opportunity in the first year. By the fifth year, 12 percent of fathers took parental leave. Scott, *Sweden's "Right to Be Human,"* 62–63.

138. Roger Congleton, *Improving Democracy through Constitutional Reform: Some Swedish Lessons* (Boston: Springer, 2003), 158; David Arter, "The Swedish Riksdag: The Case of a Strong Policy-Influencing Assembly," *West European Politics* 13, no. 3 (1990): 120.

139. Arter, "Swedish Riksdag," 120.

140. Arter, "Swedish Riksdag," 122.

141. Congleton, *Improving Democracy*, 160.

142. See Sveriges Riksdag, *The Constitution of Sweden: The Fundamental Laws and the Riksdag Act* (Stockholm: Sveriges Riksdag, 2016), www.riksdagen.se/globalassets/07.-dokument--lagar/the-constitution-of-sweden-160628.pdf.

143. I explore this idea in Julie C. Suk, "Are Gender Stereotypes Bad for Women? Rethinking Antidiscrimination Law and Work-Family Conflict," *Columbia Law Review* 110, no. 1 (2010): 1.

144. An Act on Equality between Women and Men, The Equal Opportunities Act, SFS 1991:433 (Swed.).

145. The Instrument of Government, Part 4, art. 13 (Swed.). The provision explicitly provides protection against "unfavourable treatment of anyone on grounds of gender," "unless the provision forms part of efforts to promote equality between men and women or relates to compulsory military service or other equivalent official duties."

146. Sessions v. Morales-Santana, 137 S. Ct. 1678 (2017). For an account of the remedy in this case, see Cary Franklin, "Biological Warfare: Constitutional Conflict over 'Inherent Differences' between the Sexes," *Supreme Court Review* 2017 (2017): 202–4; Kristin Collins, "Equality, Sovereignty, and the Family in *Morales-Santana*," *Harvard Law Review* 131, no. 1 (2017): 171.

147. *Morales-Santana*, 137 S. Ct. at 1687 (citing 8 U.S.C. § 1401).

148. *Morales-Santana*, 137 S. Ct. at 1689.

149. *Morales-Santana*, 137 S. Ct. at 1698.

150. *Morales-Santana*, 137 S. Ct. at 1698.

151. Petition for a Writ of Certiorari, National Coalition for Men v. Selective Service System, 141 S. Ct. 1815 (Mem.) (No. 20-928), 36–37.

CHAPTER 2. OVERENTITLEMENT AND
OVEREMPOWERMENT

1. Johnny Diaz, Maria Cramer, and Cristina Morales, "What to Know about the Death of Vanessa Guillén," *New York Times*, April 30, 2021.

2. See Secretary of the Army, "Report of the Fort Hood Independent Review Committee," November 6, 2020, www.army.mil/forthoodreview/.

3. Li Zhou, "The Atlanta Spa Shootings Can't Be Divorced from Racism and Misogyny," Vox, March 18, 2021.

4. Teo Armus, "The Atlanta Suspect Isn't the First to Blame 'Sex Addiction' for Heinous Crimes. But Scientists Are Dubious," *Washington Post*, March 18, 2021.

5. Erica Schwiegershausen, "Gunman Who Killed 6 Asian Women Was 'Having a Bad Day,' Police Say," The Cut, March 17, 2021, www.thecut.com/2021/03/atlanta-spa-shooting-police-say-gunman-was-having-bad-day.html.

6. See Joe Walsh, "FBI Director Says Atlanta Shooting 'Does Not Appear' Racially Motivated," Forbes, March 18, 2021, www.forbes.com/sites/joewalsh/2021/03/18/fbi-director-says-atlanta-shooting-does-not-appear-racially-motivated/?sh=2fb219fc1a0d.

7. Anne Anlin Cheng, "The Dehumanizing Logic of All the 'Happy Ending' Jokes," *The Atlantic*, March 23, 2021, www.theatlantic.com/culture/archive/2021/03/atlanta-shootings-racist-hatred-doesnt-preclude-desire/618361/.

8. Cheng, "Dehumanizing Logic."

9. Cathy Park Hong addresses this particular dynamic with regard to Asian Americans: "Minor feelings are the emotions we are accused of having when we decide to be difficult—in other words, when we decide to be honest. When minor feelings are finally externalized, they are interpreted as hostile, ungrateful, jealous, depressing, affects ascribed to racialized behavior that whites consider *out of line*" (emphasis in original). Cathy Park Hong, *Minor Feelings: An Asian American Reckoning* (New York: One World, 2020), 57.

10. See, for example, In re African-American Slave Descendants Litigation, 304 F. Supp. 1027 (N.D. Ill. 2004) (dismissing reparations lawsuit, including unjust enrichment claim). Some commentators have suggested that restitution for unjust enrichment provides a stronger basis for slavery reparations than compensation; see, for example, Eric A. Posner and Adrian Vermeule, "Reparations for Slavery and Other Historical Injustices," *Columbia Law Review* 103, no. 3 (2003): 700–701; Hanoch Dagan, "Restitution and Slavery: On Incomplete

Commodification, Intergenerational Justice, and Legal Transitions," *Boston University Law Review* 84, no. 5 (2004): 1139–76. Others, however, have argued against such an unjust enrichment claim in this context; see Emily Sherwin, "Reparations and Unjust Enrichment," *Boston University Law Review* 84, no. 5 (2004): 1443–66; Anthony J. Sebok, "Two Concepts of Injustice in Restitution for Slavery," *Boston University Law Review* 84, no. 5 (2004): 1405–42.

11. At least one federal appeals court has acknowledged the viability of the unjust enrichment theory. Shaffer v. George Washington University, 27 F.4th 754 (D.C. Cir. 2022).

12. See "Unjust Enrichment: Introduction, Developments in the Law," *Harvard Law Review* 133, no. 6 (2020): 2062 ("Unjust enrichment has struggled to establish a consistent place for itself within American legal thought").

13. See John Dawson, *Unjust Enrichment: A Comparative Analysis* (Boston: Little, Brown, 1951), 3; Ernest Weinrib, *Corrective Justice* (Oxford: Oxford University Press, 2012), 188.

14. See generally Jack Beatson and Eltjo Schrage, eds., *Cases, Materials, and Texts on Unjustified Enrichment* (Oxford: Hart, 2003) (studying the doctrine across jurisdictions, including England, France, Germany, Netherlands, South Africa).

15. American Law Institute, *Restatement of the Law of Restitution: Quasi-Contracts and Constructive Trusts as Adopted and Promulgated by the American Law Institute at Washington, D.C., May 8, 1936. Together with Notes on Restatement of Restitution by the Reporters W. A. Seavey and A. W. Scott* (St. Paul, MN: American Law Institute, 1937), 12; Dawson, *Unjust Enrichment*, 3.

16. Dawson, *Unjust Enrichment*, 5.

17. Barry Nicholas, *An Introduction to Roman Law* (Oxford: Clarendon Press, 1962), 229–31.

18. Savigny's "Historical School" reclaimed Roman legal history to guide German law in the nineteenth century and envisioned academic essays and treatises as the principal sources of law, rather than judicial precedent. James Q. Whitman, *The Legacy of Roman Law in the German Romantic Era: Historical Vision and Legal Change* (Princeton, NJ: Princeton University Press, 1990), 129.

19. Friedrich Carl von Savigny, *System of the Modern Roman Law,* vol. 2, trans. W. H. Rattigan (London: Wildy and Sons, 1884). For a discussion of Savigny's approach to unjust enrichment, see Reinhard Zimmerman and Jacques du Plessis, "Basic Features of the German Law of Unjustified Enrichment," *Restitution Law Review* 2 (1994): 14–43.

20. Zimmerman and du Plessis, "Basic Features," 17.

21. BGB § 812.

22. Section 138 of the German Civil Code provides that "a legal transaction which is contrary to public policy [*gute Sitten* or literally, good morals] is void" BGB § 138 (Ger.).

23. Zimmerman and Du Plessis, "Basic Features," 18–19.

24. Moses v. Macferlan, [1760] 2 Burr. 1005, 97 Eng. Rep. 676.

25. Dawson, *Unjust Enrichment,* 13.

26. *Macferlan,* 2 Burr. 1005.

27. *Macferlan,* 2 Burr. at 1012.

28. Kelly v. Solari, [1841] 9 M. & W. 54, 152 Eng. Rep. 24. See Peter Birks's discussion of the case in Peter Birks, *Unjust Enrichment* (Oxford: Oxford University Press, 2005), 5.

29. *Kelly,* 9 M. & W. at 55.

30. Lord Parke wrote, "I think that where money is paid to another under the influence of a mistake, that is, upon the supposition that a specific fact is true, which would entitle the other to the money, but which fact is untrue, and the money would not have been paid if it had been known to the payer that the fact was untrue, an action will lie to recover it back, and it is against conscience to retain it." *Kelly,* 9 M. & W. at 58.

31. Birks writes: "Your purse is now empty. You no longer have the money which you received. But your wealth, abstractly regarded as a single fund, is still swollen. . . . You would otherwise have gone to the cash machine or paid by credit card. It is evident that in these situations the strict liability from which we recoil is actually the only acceptable regime." Birks, *Unjust Enrichment,* 7.

32. See Nicholas, *Introduction to Roman Law,* 227.

33. See Francesco Giglio, "A Systematic Approach to 'Unjust' and 'Unjustified' Enrichment," *Oxford Journal of Legal Studies* 23, no. 3 (2003): 455, 458. Giglio describes the law of enrichment as addressing "situations of misplacing wealth."

34. See C. civ. art. 1371–81 (Fr.).

35. Cour de cassation [Cass.] [supreme court for judicial matters] req., June 15, 1892 (Fr.) (Julien Patureau c/Boudier).

36. Cass. req., June 15, 1892.

37. Am. Jur. Restitution 2d., § 11.

38. On the 1938 merger, see Thomas O. Main, "Traditional Equity and Contemporary Procedure," *Washington Law Review* 78, no. 2 (2003): 480.

39. See Douglas Laycock, "Restoring Restitution to the Canon," *Michigan Law Review* 110, no. 6 (2012): 931.

40. See, for example, Abraham v. WPX Energy Production, LLC, 20 F. Supp. 3d 1244, 1276, 1277 (D. New Mexico) (construing applicable Colorado law of unjust enrichment).

41. See Laycock, "Restoring Restitution," 932.

42. American Law Institute, *The Restatement Third: Restitution and Unjust Enrichment,* ed. Charles Mitchell and William Swadling (London: Bloomsbury, 2011), § 25. See, for example, Kalkowski v. Nebraska National Trails Museum Foundation, 290 Neb. 798 (Neb. 2015) (rejecting unjust enrichment claim by

tenant who claimed to improve the leased property, making restitution unavailable for unrequested benefits that are in effect forced exchanges). Dawson noted that courts were hostile to "intermeddlers" who conferred benefits on others to pursue their own self-interest and sought to protect people from forced exchanges. See John P. Dawson, "The Self-Serving Intermeddler," *Harvard Law Review* 87, no. 7 (1974): 1409–58.

43. See Saul Levmore, "Explaining Restitution," *Virginia Law Review* 71, no. 1 (1985): 67 (viewing restitution cases as presenting courts with the question of whether to create bargains where parties have not done so).

44. Laycock, "Restoring Restitution," 933–34.

45. Laycock, "Restoring Restitution," 933.

46. American Law Institute, *Restatement Third*, § 28.

47. Cour de cassation [Cass.] [supreme court for judicial matters] civ., January 9, 1979, No. 77-12.991 (Fr.).

48. Cour de cassation [Cass.] [supreme court for judicial matters] 1e civ., October 26, 1982, No. 81-14.824.

49. Marvin v. Marvin, 557 P.2d 106 (Cal. 1976).

50. *Marvin*, 557 P.2d. at 122.

51. See Robert C. Casad, "Unmarried Couples and Unjust Enrichment: From Status to Contract and Back Again?," *Michigan Law Review* 77, no. 1 (1978): 50. See also Candace Saari Kovacic-Fleischer, "Cohabitation and the Restatement (Third) of Unjust Enrichment," *Washington and Lee Law Review* 68, no. 3 (2011): 1407, 1439.

52. Marvin v. Marvin, 122 Cal. App. 3d 871 (Cal. Ct. App. 1981).

53. American Law Institute, *Restatement Third*, § 28, cmt. D.

54. Salzman v. Bachrach, 996 P.2d 1263 (Colo. 2000).

55. I discuss Justice Bradley's concurring opinion in Bradwell v. Illinois, 83 U.S. 130, 139, 141 (1873) (Bradley, J., concurring), in the introduction.

56. Anna di Robilant argues, however, that while abuse of right as an explicit doctrine is absent from common law, including US law, there are "functional equivalents" in property law to curb similar conduct in the common law. See Anna di Robilant, "Abuse of Rights: The Continental Drug and the Common Law," *Hastings Law Journal* 61, no. 3 (2010): 687.

57. Di Robilant, "Abuse of Rights," 695–710.

58. C. civ. art. 552 (Fr.).

59. Cour d'appel [CA] [regional court of appeal] Colmar, May 2, 1855, D.1856.2.9 (Fr.) ("Arrêt Doerr").

60. Cour d'appel [CA] [regional court of appeal] Lyon, April 18, 1856 (Fr.) ("Affaire St. Galmier").

61. See H. C. Gutteridge, "Abuse of Rights," *Cambridge Law Journal* 5, no. 1 (1933): 22–45.

62. Louis Josserand, *De L'abus des droits* (Paris: Arthur Rousseau, 1905), 6.

63. Cour de cassation [Cass.] [supreme court for judicial matters] civ., August 3, 1915 (Fr.) ("Affaire Clément-Bayard").

64. Cass. civ., August 3, 1915.

65. See Vera Bolgár, "Abuse of Rights in France, Germany, and Switzerland: A Survey of a Recent Chapter in Legal Doctrine," *Louisiana Law Review* 35, no. 5 (1975): 1016.

66. BGB art. 226 (Ger.).

67. BGB art. 138 and 242 (Ger).

68. For a comparative analysis of the duty of good faith in contract negotiations, see Friedrich Kessler and Edith Fine, "Culpa in Contrahendo, Bargaining in Good Faith, and Freedom of Contract: A Comparative Study," *Harvard Law Review* 77, no. 3 (1964): 401–49.

69. Bundesverfassungsgericht [BVerfG] [Federal Constitutional Court], October 19, 1993, BVerfGE 89, 214 (Ger.).

70. BVerfGE 89, 214, ¶ 50. Here the basic right being invoked was Article 2.1 of the Basic Law, which provides, "Every person shall have the right to free development of his personality insofar as he does not violate the rights of others or offend against the constitutional order or the moral law." German Basic Law, art. 2.1.

71. BVerfGE 89, 214, ¶ 52.

72. BVerfGE 89, 214, ¶ 56

73. BVerfGE 89, 214, ¶ 42.

74. BVerfGE 89, 214, ¶43.

75. BVerfGE 89, 214, ¶ 56.

76. BVerfGE 89, 214, ¶ 56.

77. Bundesgerichtshof [BGH] [Federal Court of Justice] February 21, 1952, 5 BGHZ 186 (Ger.).

78. Cour de cassation [Cass.] [supreme court for judicial matters] 2e civ., April 21, 1982, No. 81-11.775 (Fr.).

79. Cass. 2e civ., April 21, 1982.

80. Cour de cassation [Cass.] [supreme court for judicial matters] 2e civ., November 21, 1990, No. 89-17.659 (Fr.) (finding malicious motive in abuse of right for failure to deliver the get).

81. See Michelle Kariyeva, "Chained against Her Will: What a Get Means for Women under Jewish Law," *Touro Law Review* 34, no. 3 (2018): 772.

82. Cour de cassation [Cass.] [supreme court for judicial matters] 2e civ., February 28, 2013, No. 12-18.856 (Fr.) (abuse of right for failure to deliver the get in absence of legitimate reason). Nonetheless, the wife's damages for abuse of right were nullified on procedural grounds, as the lower court had not sufficiently considered the husband's claim that the get is ordinarily delivered after the dis-

tribution of property in the civil divorce, which had not been finalized, with the husband alleging that the wife had delayed and obstructed the process.

83. Jean-Marie Hisquin, "Le refus de délivrer le guet sanctionné par les juges," *Revue des Droits et Libertés Fondamentaux*, no. 10 (2013), www.revuedlf .com/personnes-famille/le-refus-de-delivrer-le-guet-sanctionne-par-les-juges -commentaire/.

84. See Irving Breitowitz, "The Plight of the Agunah: A Study in Halacha, Contract, and the First Amendment," *Maryland Law Review* 51, no. 2 (1992): 324–25.

85. Breitowitz, "Agunah," 324.

86. By contrast, the State of New York passed a law in 1983 to address the problem of extortionist demands being made in return for the get. The law requires any party initiating a civil divorce in New York courts to certify that he or she has removed any "barrier to remarriage." N.Y.S. Domestic Relations Law § 253. Since its adoption, commentators and courts have questioned whether the legislation, or court interference with the terms of the get, is compatible with the First Amendment's religion clauses. Breitowitz, "Agunah," 381. See also Tanina Rostain, note, "Permissible Accommodations of Religion: Reconsidering the New York State *Get* Statute," *Yale Law Journal* 96, no. 5 (1986): 1149. See, for example, Masri v. Masri, 55 Misc. 3d 487 (Sup. Ct., Orange County, NY 2017) (holding that increasing the amount of husband's maintenance obligation because of his refusal to give his wife the get would interfere with his free exercise of religion).

87. See Cass. 2e civ., February 28, 2013.

88. See John Curran, "Ius Vitae Necisque: The Politics of Killing Children," *Journal of Ancient History* 6, no. 1 (2018): 112.

89. See Raymond Westbrook, "Vitae Necisque Potestas," *Historia: Zeitschrift für Alte Gischichte* 48, no. 2 (1999): 207.

90. William V. Harris, "The Roman Father's Power of Life and Death," in *Studies in Roman Law in Memory of A. Arthur Schiller*, ed. Roger S. Bagnali and W. V. Harris (Leiden: E. J. Brill, 1986), 86.

91. Curran, "Ius Vitae Necisque," 115 (quoting Polybius).

92. Westbrook, "Vitae Necisque Potestas," 206.

93. Harris, "Roman Father's Power," 84.

94. Harris, "Roman Father's Power," 84.

95. Gardner, *Women in Roman Law*, 7.

96. Gardner, *Women in Roman Law*, 129.

97. Curran, "Ius Vitae Necisque," 117.

98. Westbrook, "Vitae Necisque Potestas," 221.

99. See D. J. Devine, "Some Comparative Aspects of the Doctrine of Abuse of Rights," *Acta Juridica* 1964 (1964): 150n6 (1964) (quoting Gaius).

CHAPTER 3. MISOGYNY AND MATERNITY

1. Dobbs v. Jackson Women's Health, 143 S.Ct. 2228 (2022) (overruling Roe v. Wade, 410 U.S. 113 (1973)).

2. The court's draft majority opinion in *Dobbs*, authored by Justice Alito, was leaked to *Politico* and made widely available over a month before the decision was officially published. See Josh Gerstein and Alexander Ward, "Supreme Court Has Voted to Overturn Abortion Rights, Draft Opinion Shows," *Politico*, May 2, 2022. *Politico* made the draft opinion available at www.politico.com /news/2022/05/02/read-justice-alito-initial-abortion-opinion-overturn-roe-v-wade-pdf-00029504.

3. Moira Donegan, "The Texas Abortion Ban Is a Performance of Misogyny. But It Might Get Worse," *The Guardian*, May 23, 2021.

4. Reilly Neill, an unsuccessful candidate for Montana governor, tweeted that the abortion ban was "about keeping women in the place your God wants them: under your boot," and called it "simple misogyny." See Gustaf Kilander, "'Simple Misogyny': Three Bills Restricting Abortion Signed by Montana Governor," *The Independent*, April 27, 2021, www.independent.co.uk/news/world/americas/us -politics/montana-abortion-bill-greg-gianforte-b1838434.html. Caitlin Borgmann, executive director of the ACLU of Montana, warned that these bills were the first step toward making abortion completely unavailable, concluding, "These bills represent the worst kind of government overreach—placing the government between patients and the medical care they deserve." Iris Samuels, "Montana Governor Signs 3 Bills Restricting Abortion Access," Associated Press, April 26, 2021, https://apnews.com/article/health-business-government-and -politics-montana-abortion-901c2d7fdd0d5427b094bfde3a660032.

5. For an account of Catholic constitutionalism and abortion, including in Colombia, see Julieta Lemaitre, "Catholic Constitutionalism on Sex, Women, and the Beginning of Life," in *Abortion Law in Transnational Perspective: Cases and Controversies*, ed. Rebecca J. Cook, Joanna N. Erdman, and Bernard M. Dickens (Philadelphia: University of Pennsylvania Press, 2014), 239–57.

6. *Roe*, 410 U.S. at 152.

7. *Roe*, 410 U.S. at 163.

8. On compelled medical exams, see Union Pac. Ry. Co. v. Botsford, 141 U.S. 250 (1891) ("To compel any one, and especially a woman, to lay bare the body, or to submit it to the touch of a stranger, without lawful authority, is an indignity"). On privacy and involuntary sterilization, see Skinner v. Oklahoma, 316 U.S. 535 (1942). On privacy and child-rearing, see Pierce v. Society of Sisters, 268 U.S. 510 (1925). On privacy in the home, see Olmstead v. United States, 277 U.S. 438, 478 (Brandeis, J., dissenting) (1928). On privacy and marriage, see Loving v. Virginia, 388 U.S. 1 (1967). On privacy and birth control, see Griswold v. Connecticut, 381 U.S. 479 (1965).

9. Eisenstadt v. Baird, 405 U.S. 438, 453 (1972).

10. *Roe*, 410 U.S. at 170 (Stewart, J., concurring, citing *Pierce* and Meyer v. Nebraska, 262 U.S. 390 (1923).

11. Cleveland Bd. of Educ. v. Lafleur, 414 U.S. 632, 639 (1974).

12. Harris v. McRae, 448 U.S. 297, 316 (1980).

13. *McRae*, 448 U.S. at 318.

14. Robin West has criticized *Roe*'s negative rights framing, arguing that the right to abortion protected by *Roe* is at odds with a capacious understanding of reproductive justice because *Roe*'s abortion right is fundamentally a negative right that rhetorically keeps the state out of family life. See Robin West, "From Choice to Reproductive Justice: De-constitutionalizing Abortion Rights," *Yale Law Journal* 118, no. 7 (2009), 1394–1433.

15. Dorothy E. Roberts, "Critical Race Feminism," in *Research Handbook on Feminist Jurisprudence*, ed. Robin West and Cynthia Bowman (Cheltenham, UK: Edward Elgar, 2019), 124.

16. Dorothy E. Roberts, *Killing the Black Body: Race, Reproduction, and the Meaning of Liberty*, rev. ed. (New York: Vintage, 2017), 300.

17. Khiara M. Bridges, "Privacy Rights and Public Families," *Harvard Journal of Law and Gender* 34, no. 1 (2010): 122.

18. See Geduldig v. Aiello, 417 U.S. 484 (1974).

19. Deborah Dinner points out that the majority opinion reflected a concern about the threat that the claim for paid maternity leave would pose to the solvency of the Calfiornia disability insurance program. For Dinner, this case and others related to pregnancy discrimination and parental leave reveal ambivalences about sharing and redistributing the costs of reproduction. See Deborah Dinner, "The Costs of Reproduction: History and the Legal Construction of Sex Equality," *Harvard Civil Rights-Civil Liberties Law Review* 46, no. 2 (2011): 415–96.

20. DeShaney v. Winnebago County Dep't of Social Services, 489 U.S. 189, 195 (1989).

21. *Roe*, 410 U.S. at 113, 153.

22. See Planned Parenthood v. Casey, 505 U.S. 833, 877 (1992).

23. *Casey*, 505 U.S. at 887–95.

24. *Casey*, 505 U.S. at 852.

25. *Casey*, 505 U.S. at 852.

26. *Casey*, 505 U.S. at 852.

27. *Casey*, 505 U.S. at 928 (emphasis added).

28. *Casey*, 505 U.S. at 928.

29. *Dobbs*, 143 S.Ct. at 2244–58.

30. See Reva B. Siegel, "Prochoicelife: Asking Who Protects Life and How—and Why It Matters in Law and Politics," *Indiana Law Journal* 93, no. 1 (2018): 217.

31. Bundesverfassungsgericht [BVerfG] [Federal Constitutional Court], February 25, 1975, BVerfGE 39, 1 (Ger.) ("Abortion I"). The quoted text in English references the following translation: Robert E. Jonas and John D. Gorby, "West German Abortion Decision: A Contrast to *Roe v. Wade*," *John Marshall Journal of Practice and Procedure* 9, no. 3 (1976): 605–84.

32. BVerfG, Abortion I, 647.

33. BVerfG, Abortion I, 647.

34. BVerfG, Abortion I, 647.

35. BVerfG, Abortion I, 648.

36. BVerfG, Abortion I, 653.

37. BVerfG, Abortion I, 653.

38. BVerfG, Abortion I, 649.

39. Fifteenth Criminal Law Amendment Act of May 18, 1976.

40. Fifteenth Criminal Law Amendment Act of May 18, 1976 (language previously inserted into Section 218 of Criminal Code).

41. See generally Rachel Rebouché, "Comparative Pragmatism," *Maryland Law Review* 72, no. 1 (2012): 85.

42. Fifteenth Criminal Law Amendment Act of May 18, 1976 (formerly Section 218(a)(1) of the Criminal Code).

43. Albin Eser, "Reform of German Abortion Law: First Experiences," *American Journal of Comparative Law* 34, no. 2 (1986): 381. In 1977, 37 percent of the medical certifications for abortion were for a "medical" justification (physical or mental), and 57 percent of the certifications were for based on the "danger of distress"—known as the "social" indication for abortion. But by 1982, nearly 77 percent of abortions were certified on the basis of the "social" indication.

44. Eser, "Reform," 382.

45. See Katherine Kortsmit, Michele G. Mandel, Jennifer A. Reeves, Elizabeth Clark, Pamela Pagano, Antoinette Nguyen, Emily E. Petersen, and Maura K. Whiteman, "Abortion Surveillance—United States, 2019," *Surveillance Summaries* 70, no. 9 (November 26, 2021): 1–29, Centers for Disease Control and Prevention, www.cdc.gov/mmwr/volumes/70/ss/ss7009a1.htm#methods.

46. Pregnancy and Family Assistance Act, July 27, 1992, BGBl. I (1992), 1398.

47. Planned Parenthood of Southeastern Pennsylvania v. Casey, 505 U.S. 833 (1992); Bundesverfassungsgericht [BVerfG] [Federal Constitutional Court], May 28, 1993, BvF 2/90 (Ger.) ("Abortion II") (quoted English text from official translation available on German Federal Constitutional Court website, www.bundesverfassungsgericht.de/SharedDocs/Entscheidungen/EN/1993/05/fs19930528_2bvf000290en.html).

48. BVerfG, Abortion II, ¶ 166.

49. BVerfG, Abortion II, ¶ 167.

50. BVerfG, Abortion II, ¶ 167.

51. BVerfG, Abortion II, ¶ 168.

52. BVerfG, Abortion II, ¶ 170.

53. BVerfG, Abortion II, ¶ 170.

54. BVerfG, Abortion II, ¶ 170.

55. BVerfG, Abortion II, ¶ 171.

56. BVerfG, Abortion II, ¶ 172.

57. BVerfG, Abortion II, ¶ 182.

58. BVerfG, Abortion II, ¶ 182.

59. BVerfG, Abortion II, ¶ 184.

60. See M. Antonia Biggs, Heather Gould, and Diana Greene Foster, "Understanding Why Women Seek Abortions in the US," *BMC Women's Health* 13 (2013): art. no. 29, https://bmcwomenshealth.biomedcentral.com/track /pdf/10.1186/1472-6874-13-29.pdf (finding that 40 percent of women have abortions for financial reasons, and 29 percent because they need to focus on their other children); Lawrence B. Finer, Lori F. Frohwirth, Lindsay A. Dauphinee, Susheela Singh, and Ann M. Moore, "Reasons U.S. Women Have Abortions: Quantitative and Qualitative Perspectives," *Perspectives on Sexual and Reproductive Health* 37, no. 3 (2005): 110–18 (finding that primary reasons for abortion are that having a child would interfere with a woman's education, work, or ability to care for dependents and/or that the woman could not afford to have a baby).

61. For a more detailed discussion of the adoption of this amendment, the issues it intended to address, and jurisprudence construing it, see Julie C. Suk, "An Equal Rights Amendment for the Twenty-First Century: Bringing Global Constitutionalism Home," *Yale Journal of Law and Feminism* 28, no. 2 (2017): 412–18.

62. See Rebouché, "Comparative Pragmatism," 131–35.

63. See Pregnancy and Family Allowance Act, August 21, 1995, BGBl. I 1995 § 1050, art. 5 (Ger.).

64. Pregnancy and Family Allowance Act § 1050, art. 5 (Ger.).

65. See Mary Anne Case, "Perfectionism and Fundamentalism in the Application of the German Abortion Laws," *Florida International University Law Review* 11, no. 1 (2015): 157n23.

66. Gesetz zum Elterngeld und zur Elternzeit (Bundeselterngeld- und Elternzeitgesetz—BEEG), December 5, 2006, BGBl. I 2748 (Ger.).

67. Bundesverfassungsgericht [BVerfG] [Federal Constitutional Court], June 6, 2011, 1 BvR 2712/09 (Ger.).

68. In 1974, the Irish Supreme Court had cited *Griswold v. Connecticut* to strike down a statute banning contraceptives in McGee v. Attorney General [1974] IR 284 (Ir.), so antiabortion groups feared that favorable citation of *Roe v. Wade* could be next. Neighboring European countries, such as France, had liberalized abortion by statute, with some courts upholding those statutes, Conseil

Constitutionnel [CC] [Constitutional Council] decision No. 74-54DC, January 15, 1975 (Fr.). See also Abortion Act 1967 (UK); Termination of Pregnancy Act 1984 (Netherlands); Abortion Act, 1974:595 (Sweden); Act on Counseling and Education regarding Sex and Childbirth and on Abortion and Sterilization, May 22, 1975, no. 22 (Iceland).

69. The initial proposal for the antiabortion amendment was worded, "Nothing in this Constitution shall be invoked to invalidate, or to deprive of force or effect, any provision of a law on the ground that it prohibits abortion." See Eighth Amendment of the Constitution Bill, 341 Dáil Deb. col. 10 (April 27, 1983) (Ir.), www.oireachtas.ie/en/debates/debate/dail/1983-04-27/5/.

70. See Lindsay Earner-Byrne and Diana Urquhart, *The Irish Abortion Journey, 1920-2018* (Basingstoke, UK: Palgrave Macmillan, 2019), 78.

71. Dáil Deb., April 27, 1983.

72. Dáil Deb., April 27, 1983 (remarks of Mr. Michael Noonan, Minister for Justice).

73. Dáil Deb., April 27, 1983 (remarks of Dr. Michael Woods, Deputy).

74. Attorney General v. X, [1992] IESC 1; [1992] 1 IR 1, ¶ 40 (Ir.).

75. *Attorney General v. X*, ¶ 65.

76. See Earner-Byrne and Urquhart, *Irish Abortion Journey*, 86–87.

77. Government of Ireland, *Referendum Results, 1937–2019*, 46, last accessed June 2, 2022, www.gov.ie/en/publication/32ea7-1937-2019-referendum -results/.

78. Byrne and Urquart, *Irish Abortion Journey*, 87.

79. A, B, & C v. Ireland, [2010] Eur. Ct. H.R. 2032.

80. For an extended narrative account, see Kitty Holland, *Savita: The Tragedy That Shook a Nation* (Dublin: Transworld Ireland, 2013).

81. Protection of Life During Pregnancy Act, No. 35 of 2013, July 30, 2013 (Ir.).

82. Resolution of the Houses of Oireachtas of July 2012 (Ir.), www .constitutionalconvention.ie/Documents/Terms_of_Reference.pdf.

83. For detailed information about the selection and recruitment process, see "Constitutional Convention—Members of the Public Recruitment Process," last accessed June 2, 2022, www.constitutionalconvention.ie/Documents /BehaviourAndAttitudes.pdf.

84. Resolution of the Houses of Oireachtas of July 2012, www.constitutional-convention.ie/Documents/Terms_of_Reference.pdf.

85. See *Third Report of the Convention on the Constitution: Amending the Constitution to Provide for Same-Sex Marriage*, December 17, 2013, last accessed June 2, 2022, www.constitutionalconvention.ie/AttachmentDown load.ashx?mid=c90ab08b-ece2-e211-a5a0=005056a32ee4. Although the Convention on the Constitution also recommended a constitutional amendment guaranteeing gender equality (see Ireland Convention on the Constitution, *Sec-*

ond Report of the Convention on the Constitution, (i) Amending the clause on the role of women in the home and encouraging greater participation of women in public life; and (ii) Increasing the participation of women in politics, May 2013, www.constitutionalconvention.ie/AttachmentDownload.ashx?mid=268d9308-c9b7-e211-a5a0-005056a32ee4), that proposal was not adopted by the Oireachtas for a referendum.

86. Resolution of Dáil Éireann Approving Establishment of the Citizens' Assembly, July 2016.

87. See generally Ireland Citizens' Assembly, *First Report and Recommendations of the Citizens' Assembly, The Eighth Amendment to the Constitution*, June 29, 2017, https://2016-2018.citizensassembly.ie/en/The-Eighth-Amendment-of-the-Constitution/.

88. Ireland Citizens' Assembly, *First Report and Recommendations*, 50–53.

89. See Ireland Citizens' Assembly 2016–2018, *Eighth Amendment, Recommendations*, https://2016-2018.citizensassembly.ie/en/The-Eighth-Amendment-of-the-Constitution/.

90. Paper of National Women's Council of Ireland, Citizens' Assembly, March 5, 2017, https://2016-2018.citizensassembly.ie/en/Meetings/NWCI-s-Paper.pdf; Ireland Citizens' Assembly, *Paper of Parents for Choice*, March 5, 2017, https://2016-2018.citizensassembly.ie/en/Meetings/Parents-for-Choice-s-Paper.pdf.

91. Ireland Citizens' Assembly, *Paper of Parents for Choice*, 1.

92. See Ireland Citizens' Assembly 2016–2018, *Eighth Amendment, Recommendations*.

93. Ireland Citizens' Assembly 2016–2018, *Eighth Amendment, Recommendations*.

94. Seanad Eireann, Resolution of 11th July, 2019, www.oireachtas.ie/en/debates/debate/dail/2019-07-11/31/.

95. See Ireland Citizens' Assembly, "Citizens' Assembly Begins Discussions on Gender Equality," press release, February 13, 2020, www.citizensassembly.ie/en/news-publications/press-releases/citizens-assembly-begins-discussions-on-gender-equality.html.

96. See *Casey*, 505 U.S. at 928 (1992) (Blackmun, J., concurring in part and dissenting in part).

97. Corte Constitucional [C.C.] [Constitutional Court], February 21, 2022, Sentencia C-055/22 (Colom.).

98. Aborto. Suprema Corte de Justicia de la Nación [SCJN] [Supreme Court], Acción de inconstitucionalidad 148/2017, September 21, 2021 (Mex.).

99. Law No. 27.610, December 30, 2020, art. 2, 4. (Arg.).

100. Law No. 27.610, December 30, 2020, art. 4 (Arg.). For a detailed account of the movement that culminated in this legislative change, see Kim D. Ricardo, "Was Justice Ginsburg Roe-Ght? Reimagining U.S. Abortion Discourse in the

Wake of Argentina's Marea Verde," *Mitchell Hamline Law Review* 48, no. 1 (2022): 128–209.

101. Corte Constitucional [C.C.] [Constitutional Court], May 10, 2006, Sentencia C-355/06 (Colom.).

102. C.C. Sentencia C-355/06, English quotations from Manuel José Cepeda Espinosa and David Landau, eds. and trans., *Colombian Constitutional Law: Leading Cases* (Oxford: Oxford University Press, 2017), 73, 75.

103. C.C. Sentencia C-355/06, *Colombian Constitutional Law*, 77–79.

104. C.C. Sentencia C-355/06, *Colombian Constitutional Law*, 75.

105. Corte Suprema de Justicia de la Nación [CSJN] [National Supreme Court of Justice], March 13, 2012, "F., A. L. s/ medida autosatisfactiva," Fallos (2012-335-197) (Arg.).

106. Cód. Pen. art. 86 (Arg. 2012). For a discussion of this case in the context of liberalization of abortion access by other Latin American courts, see Paola Bergallo and Agustina Ramón Michel, "Constitutional Developments in Latin American Abortion Law," *International Journal of Gynecology and Obstetrics* 135 (2016): 228–331.

107. Paola Bergallo, "The Struggle against Informal Rules on Abortion in Argentina," in Cook, Erdman, and Dickens, *Abortion Law in Transnational Perspective*, 143–65.

108. Constitutional Court [Const. Ct.], 2017 Hun-Ba 127, April 11, 2019 (S. Kor.). Official English translation in *Constitutional Court Decisions 2019* (Seoul: Constitutional Court of the Republic of Korea, 2020), 1–64.

109. Const. Ct., 2017 Hun-Ba 127, 26–27.

110. Const. Ct., 2017 Hun-Ba 127, 28.

111. See Bak Chae-yeong, "Abortion No Longer a Crime, and Debates on the Right to Terminate a Pregnancy Have Come to a Halt," *Kyunghang Shinmun*, December 23, 2020, http://english.khan.co.kr/khan_art_view.html?code=7101 00&artid=202012231911467.

112. See, for example, German Basic Law art. 6.4 and Ir. Const. art. 41.2. For an account of the history and jurisprudence of motherhood protection clauses in some western European countries, see Julie C. Suk, "Gender Equality and the Protection of Motherhood in Global Constitutionalism," *Journal of Law and Ethics of Human Rights* 12 (2018): 141; Julie C. Suk, "Feminist Constitutionalism and the Entrenchment of Motherhood," *Studies in Law, Politics, and Society* 75 (2018): 107 (special issue, "Law and the Imagining of Difference").

113. Whole Women's Health v. Hellerstedt, 579 U.S. 582 (2016); June Medical Services v. Russo, 140 S. Ct. 2103 (2020); Whole Woman's Health v. Hellerstedt, 579 U.S. 582 (2016) (No. 15-274), Brief of Janice Macavoy, Janie Schulman, and Over 110 Other Women in the Legal Profession Who Have Exercised Their Constitutional Right to an Abortion as Amici Curiae in Support of Petitioners; June Medical Services v. Gee, 140 S. Ct. 2103 (2020) (No. 8-1323 and No. 18-1460),

Brief for Michele Coleman Mayes, Claudia Hammerman, Charanya Krishnas-wami, and 365 Other Legal Professionals Who Have Exercised Their Constitu-tional Right to an Abortion as Amici Curiae Supporting Petitioners.

CHAPTER 4. FROM PATRIARCHY TO PROHIBITION

1. See Richard Hamm, *Shaping the Eighteenth Amendment: Temperance Reform, Legal Culture, and the Polity, 1880-1920* (Chapel Hill: University of North Carolina Press, 1995), 3 ("The prohibitionist Mosaic conception of law assumed that the purpose of government was to foster morality"); Norman Clark, *Deliver Us from Evil: An Interpretation of American Prohibition* (New York: W. W. Norton, 1976); Lisa McGirr, *The War on Alcohol: Prohibition and the Rise of the American State* (New York: W. W. Norton, 2016); Daniel Okrent, *Last Call: The Rise and Fall of Prohibition* (New York: Scribner, 2010).

2. See Jack S. Blocker Jr., *American Temperance Movements: Cycles of Reform* (Boston: Twayne, 1988), 39-46.

3. Barbara Leslie Epstein, *The Politics of Domesticity: Women, Evangelism, and Temperance in Nineteenth-Century America* (Middletown, CT: Wesleyan University Press, 1981); Jed Danenbaum, *Drink and Disorder: Temperance Reform in Cincinnati from the Washingtonian Revival to the WCTU* (Urbana: University of Illinois Press, 1984), 70.

4. See Jack S. Blocker Jr., *Give to the Winds Thy Fears: The Women's Temper-ance Crusade, 1873-1874* (Westport, CT: Greenwood Press, 1985).

5. Joint Resolution for a Federal Prohibition Amendment to the U.S. Consti-tution, 44th Cong. (1876).

6. Blocker, *Give to the Winds*, 96, 100.

7. Elaine Frantz Parsons provides an excellent account, based on trial court records, of the narratives that emerged in these cases. See Elaine Frantz Parsons, *Manhood Lost: Fallen Drunkards and Redeeming Women in the Nineteenth-Century United States* (Baltimore: Johns Hopkins University Press, 2003).

8. Mother Stewart, *Memories of the Crusade: A Thrilling Account of the Great Uprising of the Women of Ohio in 1873, against the Liquor Crime* (Columbus, OH: Wm. G. Hubbard, 1888).

9. Mother Stewart, *Memories of the Crusade*, 33.

10. Bradwell v. Illinois, 83 U.S. 130 (1873).

11. Mother Stewart, *Memories of the Crusade*, 35.

12. Mother Stewart, *Memories of the Crusade*, 35-36.

13. Mother Stewart, *Memories of the Crusade*, 37, 39.

14. Not only did Mother Stewart refer to the contingency fee, but in the second suit, the plaintiff's attorney wondered out loud "what we should do for our juror's fees." When it became apparent that these fees would be taken out of the

plaintiff's recovery, the jurors immediately, one by one, volunteered to donate their fees.

15. An 1881 treatise provides a good discussion of these cases. See R. Vashon Rogers Jr., *Drinks, Drinkers, and Drinking, or The Law and History of Intoxicating Liquors* (Albany, NY: Weed, Parsons 1881), 184–208.

16. See, for example, Fountain v. Draper, 49 Ind. 441 (Ind. 1874).

17. See Friend v. Dunks, 37 Mich. 25 (Mich. 1877) (arguing that plaintiff could not join mental anguish claims with claims for refund for intoxicating liquors against saloon); Brantigan v. While, 73 Ill. 561 (Ill. 1874) (arguing that wives could recover only for injuries to person and property, and not for mental suffering).

18. For example, Hackett v. Smelsley, 77 Ill. 109 (Ill. 1875).

19. Schneider v. Hosier, 21 Ohio St. 98, 102 (Ohio 1871).

20. Bellinger v. Griffith, 23 Ohio St. 619 (Ohio 1873).

21. *Bellinger*, 23 Ohio St. at 621.

22. Wynehamer v. People, 13 N.Y. 378 (N.Y. 1856).

23. Beebe v. State, 6 Ind. 501 (Ind. 1855).

24. Bartemeyer v. Iowa, 85 U.S. 129, 133 (1873).

25. Hamm, *Shaping the Eighteenth Amendment*, 48.

26. Annie Wittenmyer, *History of the Woman's Temperance Crusade: A Complete Official History of the Wonderful Uprising of the Christian Women of the United States against the Liquor Traffic, Which Culminated in the Gospel Temperance Movement* (Philadelphia: The Christian Woman, 1878).

27. Wittenmyer, *History*, 43.

28. For example, Cour de cassation [Cass.] [supreme court for judicial matters] req., June 21, 1926 (Kirsch c/Davoust).

29. Wittenmyer, *History*, 44.

30. Mrs. Eliza Jane Trimble Thompson, Her Two Daughters, and Frances E. Willard, *Hillsboro Crusade Sketches and Family Records* (Cincinnati, OH: Jennings and Graham, 1906), 90.

31. Thompson, *Hillsboro Crusade Sketches*, 95.

32. Thompson, *Hillsboro Crusade Sketches*, 103.

33. Thompson, *Hillsboro Crusade Sketches*, 134.

34. Thompson, *Hillsboro Crusade Sketches*, 134.

35. Thompson, *Hillsboro Crusade Sketches*, 134.

36. Thompson, *Hillsboro Crusade Sketches*, 136.

37. In *Mugler v. Kansas*, the Supreme Court upheld the Kansas prohibition statute against a Fourteenth Amendment due process challenge, holding that the Fourteenth Amendment "has never been regarded as compatible with the principle . . . that all property in this country is held under the implied obligation that the owner's use of it shall not be injurious to the community." Mugler v. Kansas, 123 U.S. 623, 665 (1887) (citing Beer Co. v. Massachusetts, 97 U.S. 32 (1877)).

38. Ruth Bordin, *Woman and Temperance: The Quest for Power and Liberty, 1873–1900* (Philadelphia: Temple University Press, 1981).

39. See Jill Norgren, *Rebels at the Bar: The Fascinating, Forgotten Stories of America's First Women Lawyers* (New York: New York University Press, 2016).

40. See Elizabeth Putnam Gordon, *Women Torch-Bearers: The Story of the Woman's Christian Temperance Union 134* (Evanston, IL: Women's Christian Temperance Union Publishing House, 1924).

41. Ruth Bordin, *Frances Willard: A Biography* (Chapel Hill: University of North Carolina Press, 1986), 71.

42. Anna A. Gordon, *The Beautiful Life of Frances Willard* (Chicago: Woman's Temperance Publishing Association, 1898), 94–95.

43. Bordin, *Frances Willard*, 73.

44. Frances E. Willard, "Everybody's War" (1874), in *Let Something Good Be Said: Speeches and Writings of Frances E. Willard*, ed. Carolyn de Swarte Gifford and Amy R. Slagell (Urbana: University of Illinois Press, 2007), 4.

45. Willard, "Everybody's War," 5.

46. Willard, "Everybody's War," 5.

47. Willard, "Everybody's War," 7.

48. Bordin, *Frances Willard*, 99.

49. Frances E. Willard, *Woman and Temperance, or, The Work and Workers of the Woman's Christian Temperance Union* (Chicago: J. S. Goodman, 1883), 454.

50. Willard, *Woman and Temperance*, 456.

51. Willard, *Woman and Temperance*, 456.

52. See Henry William Blair, *The Temperance Movement, or The Conflict between Man and Alcohol* (Boston: William E. Smuthe, 1888), 374–75J (excerpting the joint resolution the author introduced to the 44th Congress in 1876 as a representative from New Hampshire).

53. S. Rep. No. 1653, 49th Cong., 1st Sess.

54. See Virginia Drachman, *Women Lawyers and the Origins of Professional Identity in America: The Letters of the Equity Club, 1887 to 1890* (Ann Arbor: University of Michigan Press, 1993), 235.

55. See Frances E. Willard and Mary A. Livermore, *American Women: Fifteen Hundred Biographies with Over 1,400 Portraits: A Comprehensive Encyclopedia of the Lives and Achievements of American Women during the Nineteenth Century* (New York: Mast, Crowell and Kirkpatrick, 1897), 433.

56. Drachman, *Women Lawyers*, 236.

57. Drachman, *Women Lawyers*, 236–37.

58. Willard and Livermore, *American Women*, 296.

59. J. Ellen Foster, *Constitutional Amendment Manual, Containing Argument, Appeal, Petitions, Forms of Constitution, Catechism and General Directions for Organized Work for Constitutional Prohibition* (New York: National Temperance Society and Publication House, 1882).

60. Foster, *Constitutional Amendment Manual*, 12.

61. Foster, *Constitutional Amendment Manual*, 14–15.

62. Foster, *Constitutional Amendment Manual*, 15–16.

63. Foster, *Constitutional Amendment Manual*, 23–24.

64. Foster, *Constitutional Amendment Manual*, 32.

65. Foster, *Constitutional Amendment Manual*, 32.

66. J. Ellen Foster, *The Saloon Must Go* (New York: National Temperance Society and Publication House, 1889).

67. Ada M. Bittenbender, "National W.C.T.U. Argument," in *The National Prohibitory Amendment Guide*, ed. Ada M. Bittenbender (Chicago: Woman's Temperance Publication Association, 1889), 19 (reproducing her testimony to the Senate Committee on Education and Labor for the Woman's Christian Temperance Union).

68. See, for example, *Mugler v. Kansas*, in which the Supreme Court upheld Kansas's statutory and constitutional prohibition laws as within the police power of the state, against a Fourteenth Amendment due process-based challenge.

69. See Lochner v. New York, 198 U.S. 45 (Harlan, J., dissenting) (citing, inter alia, *Mugler v. Kansas*).

70. See Willard and Livermore, *American Women*, 87.

71. Willard and Livermore, *American Women*, 87.

72. See Mrs. John A. Logan, *The Part Taken by Women in American History* (Wilmington, DE: Perry-Nalle, 1912), 667.

73. For example, Illinois Equal Guardian Act of 1901. See Adade Mitchell Wheeler, "Conflict in the Illinois Women Suffrage Movement of 1913," *Journal of the Illinois State Historical Society* 76, no. 2 (1983): 98.

74. Norgren, *Rebels at the Bar*, 153.

75. Catharine Waugh McCulloch, *Mr. Lex or the Legal Status of Mother and Child* (Chicago: F. H. Revell, 1899), 16, 20, 22–23, 50.

76. McCulloch, *Mr. Lex*, 16.

77. McCulloch, *Mr. Lex*, 17.

78. McCulloch, *Mr. Lex*, 18.

79. Bradwell v. Illinois, 83 U.S. at 141 (Bradley, J., concurring).

80. See Wheeler, "Conflict," 98.

81. McCulloch, *Mr. Lex*, 26.

82. McCulloch, *Mr. Lex*, 27.

83. McCulloch, *Mr. Lex*, 29–30.

84. See "Catharine McCulloch: Illinois Suffragist and Lawyer," *Illinois History and Lincoln Collections* (blog), March 14, 2019, https://publish.illinois.edu/ihlc-blog/2019/03/14/catharine-mcculloch-illinois-suffragist-and-lawyer/.

85. McCulloch, *Mr. Lex*, 33.

86. McCulloch, *Mr. Lex*, 33.

87. McCulloch, *Mr. Lex*, 41.

88. Ada H. Kepley, *A Farm Philosopher: A Love Story* (Teutopolis, IL: Worman's Printery, 1912), 68.

89. Kepley, *Farm Philosopher*, 68.

90. Kepley, *Farm Philosopher*, 68.

91. U.S. Const. amend. XVIII.

92. Wheeler, "Conflict," 98.

93. See "Catharine McCulloch: Illinois Suffragist."

94. See generally Catherine Gilbert Murdock, *Domesticating Drink: Women, Men, and Alcohol in America, 1870–1840* (Baltimore: Johns Hopkins University Press, 2002), 88–133; Lori Rotskoff, *Love on the Rocks: Men, Women, and Alcohol in Post-World War II America* (Chapel Hill: University of North Carolina Press, 2002), 38. Indeed, Murdock notes that this was a lasting change. Before Prohibition, most alcohol that was sold in America was sold in saloons, but as of 1941, most alcohol sold in the country was for off-premises home consumption. Murdock, *Domesticating Drink*, 165.

95. See generally Kenneth D. Rose, *American Women and the Repeal of Prohibition* (New York: New York University Press, 1996). See also David Kyvig, *Repealing National Prohibition*, 2nd ed. (Kent, OH: Kent State University Press, 2000).

CHAPTER 5. REBALANCING POWER THROUGH PARITY DEMOCRACY

1. United States v. Virginia, 518 U.S. 515, 534 (1996).

2. Goesaert v. Cleary, 335 U.S. 464, 465 (1948).

3. See Lori Rotskoff, *Love on the Rocks: Men, Women, and Alcohol in Post-World War II America* (Chapel Hill: University of North Carolina Press, 2002), 17–18 ("The subculture of the saloon was central to the formation of gender identity for its male patrons. . . . The avid saloongoer epitomized 'dissolute manhood,' . . . [which] defined the untrammeled, pleasure-seeking male as the epitome of manliness").

4. See Amy Holtman French, "Mixing It Up: Michigan Barmaids Fight for Civil Rights," *Michigan Historical Review* 40, no. 1 (2014): 29–30.

5. French, "Mixing It Up," 31 (detailing a Flint ordinance that was upheld by the Michigan Supreme Court despite a constitutional challenge based on discrimination against women).

6. French, "Mixing It Up," 34.

7. *Goesaert*, 335 U.S. at 465.

8. *Goesaert*, 335 U.S. at 467.

9. *Goesaert*, 335 U.S. at 467.

10. Hoyt v. Florida, 368 U.S. 57, 62 (1961).

11. Seidenburg v. McSorley's Old Ale House, Inc., 317 F. Supp. 593, 597 (S.D.N.Y. 1970).

12. *Seidenburg*, 317 F. Supp. at 599.

13. *Seidenburg*, 317 F. Supp. at 606.

14. *Seidenburg*, 317 F. Supp. at 604.

15. Roberts v. Jaycees, 468 U.S. 609, 625 (1984).

16. Bd. of Dir. of Rotary International v. Rotary Club of Duarte, 481 U.S. 537, 549 (1987).

17. Cal. Corp. Code § 301.3.

18. Cal. Corp. Code § 301(b)(1)-(3).

19. Meland v. Weber, No. 2:19-cv-02288-JAM-AC, 2021 WL 6118651 (E.D. Cal. December 27, 2021).

20. Meland v. Weber, No. 22-15149 (9th Cir. 2022).

21. Crest v. Padilla, Verdict, No. 19STCV27561 (Cal. Super. Ct. May 13, 2022).

22. See Conseil Constitutionnel [CC] [Constitutional Council] decision No. 82-146 DC, November 18, 1982 (Fr.) (citing proposed section L.260bis of the Electoral Code).

23. Const. art. 3 (Fr.).

24. 1789 Declaration of the Rights of Man art. 6 (Fr.).

25. Françoise Gaspard, Claude Servan-Schreiber, and Anne Le Gall, *Au pouvoir, citoyennes! Liberté, egalité, parité* [To power, women citizens! Liberty, equality, parity] (Paris: Seuil, 1992). A timeline shows the percentage of women in the Senate and the National Assembly from 1952 to 2017, with rapid growth beginning in 1999, when the Constitution was amended. See Proportion of Women Progresses at the Assembly and the Senate, December 4, 2018, www .inegalites.fr/paritefemmeshommespolitique?id_theme=22.

26. Of 586 members elected to the Constituent Assembly, 33 were women. *Portraits et biographies des 33 femmes élues députées pour la première fois en 1945* [Portraits and biographies of the 33 women elected deputies for the first time in 1945], French National Assembly, http://www2.assemblee -nationale.fr/decouvrir-l-assemblee/histoire/le-suffrage-universel/la-conquete-de -la-citoyennete-politique-des-femmes/les-33-femmes-elues-deputees-en-1945.

27. Gaspard, Servan-Schreiber, and Le Gall, *Au pouvoir, citoyennes!*

28. For an account of parity and its emergence as a broadly accepted tool to renew democratic representation in institutions that were in crisis, see Eléonore Lépinard, *L'egalité introuvable: La parité, les féministes et la République* (Paris: Presses de Sciences Po, 2007).

29. Loi constitutionnelle 99-569 du 8 juillet 1999 relative a l'egalite entre les hommes et les femmes, art. 1, *Journal Officiel de la République Française* [J.O.] [Official Gazette of France], July 8, 1999, at 10175 (Fr.).

30. Loi 2000-493 du 6 juin 2000, art. 1, J.O., June 7, 2000, at 8560 (Fr.).

31. Conseil Constitutionnel [CC] [Constitutional Council] decision No. 2000-429, May 30, 2000 (Fr.), ¶ 7.

32. 1789 Declaration of the Rights of Man art. 1.

33. See Gaspard, Servan-Schreiber, and Legall, *Au pouvoir, citoyennes!*. See also Sylviane Agacinski, *Parity of the* Sexes, trans. Lisa Walsh (New York: Columbia University Press, 1998); Joan Scott, *Parité! Sexual Equality and the Crisis of French Universalism* (Chicago: University of Chicago Press, 2005).

34. Projet de loi relatif à l'égalité salariale entre les femmes et les hommes, adopté, dans les conditions prévues à l'article 45, alinéa 3, de la Constitution par l'Assemblée nationale le 23 février 2006 (Fr.), www.assemblee-nationale.fr/12 /dossiers/egalite_salariale_femmes_hommes.asp.

35. Conseil Constitutionnel [CC] [Constitutional Council] decision No. 2006-533DC, March 16, 2006 (Fr.).

36. Loi 2011-103 du 27 janvier 2011 relative à la représentation équilibrée des femmes et des hommes au sein des conseils d'administration et de surveil-lance et à l'égalité professionnelle (1), [Law 2011-103 of January 27, 2011, on the balanced representation of women and men on administrative and supervisory boards and on professional equality], J.O., January 28, 2011, p. 1680.

37. See Projet de loi relatif à l'égalité salariale entre les femmes et les hommes.

38. See Loi 2011-103 du 27 janvier 2011, art. 1.

39. Loi 2012-347 du 12 mars 2012 relative à l'accès à l'emploi titulaire et à l'amélioration des conditions d'emploi des agents contractuels dans la fonction publique, à la lutte contre les discriminations et portant diverses dispositions relatives à la fonction publique [Law 2012-347 of March 12, 2012, on tenured employment and the improvement of employment conditions of contractual agents in the civil service, on the fight against discrimination and imposing vari-ous measures relating to the civil service], J.O., March 13, 2012, p. 5598, at art. 52–56.

40. Loi 2013-660 du 22 juillet 2013 relative à l'enseignement supérieur et à la recherche (1), [Law 2013-660 of July 22, 2013, on Higher Education and Research (1)], J.O., July 23, 2013, p. 12235, at art. 50.

41. Loi 2013-403 du 17 mai 2013 relative à l'élection des conseillers départe-mentaux, des conseillers municipaux et des conseillers communautaires, et mod-ifiant le calendrier électoral [Law 2013-403 of May 17, 2013, on the election of regional council members, municipal council members, and community council members, and modifying the electoral calendar], J.O., March 18, 2013, p. 8242, art. 3.

42. Loi 2014-873 du 4 août 2014 pour l'égalité réelle entre les femmes et les hommes (1) [Law 2014-873 of August 4, 2014 for real equality between women and men (1)], J.O., August 5, 2014, p. 12949.

43. France, Sénat, *Etude d'impact, Projet de loi pour l'égalité entre les femmes et les hommes*, § I.1.1 NOR: DFEX1313602L/Bleue-1 (July 1, 2013), www.senat .fr/leg/etudes-impact/pjl12-717-ei/pjl12-717-ei.html (justifying the bill that was eventually adopted in 2014 as an implementation of the 2008 constitutional amendment).

44. France, Sénat, *Étude d'impact*, 15.

45. Loi 2014-873 tit. I.

46. Loi 2014-873 tit. V.

47. Loi No. 2018-771 du 5 septembre 2018 pour la liberté de choisir son avenir professionnel I (Law No. 2018-771 for the freedom to choose one's professional future I) (Fr.).

48. For an account of the women elected to the Constituent Assembly and the parties and political agendas they represented, see Renate Pore, *A Conflict of Interest: Women in German Social Democracy, 1919–1933* (Westport, CT: Greenwood Press, 1981), 39–45.

49. Const. art. 109 (Weimar 1919) (Ger.).

50. Const. art. 128 (Weimar 1919) (Ger.).

51. Const. art. 128 (Weimar 1919) (Ger.).

52. *Deutsche Nationalversammlung im jahre 1919 in ihrer Arbeit für den Aufbau des neuen deutschen Volksstaates* [German National Assembly in 1919 in their work for the establishment of a new German republic], July 15, 1919, 57. Sitzung, 3804.

53. *Deutsche Nationalversammlung*, vol. 6, at 3806.

54. *Deutsche Nationalversammlung*, vol. 6, at 3808.

55. For a fuller account of Elisabeth Selbert's work in the Constituent Assembly at Bonn, and the contributions of the four women who were in the assembly, see Robert G. Moeller, *Protecting Motherhood: Women and the Family in the Politics of Postwar West Germany* (Berkeley: University of California Press, 1993), 38–75. In Germany, a made-for-television movie dramatized these debates. See *Sternstunde ihres Lebens*, directed by Erica von Moeller (Germany: Camino Filmverleih, 2014).

56. Bundesverfassungsgericht [BVerfG] [Federal Constitutional Court], December 18, 1953, BVerfGE 3, 225 (Ger.) ¶ 42.

57. Bundesverfassungsgericht [BVerfG] [Federal Constitutional Court], May 25, 1956, 1 BvR 53/54 (Ger.). For a discussion of regulation of women's work during this period, see Dagmar Schiek, "Lifting the Ban on Women's Night Work in Europe: A Straight Road to Equality in Employment?" *Cardozo Women's Law Journal* 3, no. 2 (1996): 309–34.

58. Bundesverfassungsgericht [BVerfG] [Federal Constitutional Court], July 29, 1959, BVerfGE 10, 59 (Ger.).

59. Brief for the Appellant, Reed v. Reed, 404 U.S. 71 (1971) (No. 70-4), 55.

NOTES TO CHAPTER 5

60. See Anne Peters, *Women, Quotas, and Constitutions: A Comparative Study of Affirmative Action for Women under American, German, EC, and International Law* (The Hague: Kluwer Law International, 1999), 159.

61. See Renate Jaeger, "The Federal Constitutional Court: Fifty Years of the Struggle for Gender Equality," *German Law Journal* 2, no. 9 (2001): art. no. 35.

62. "Not every inequality based on sex offends Article 3(3)." See Bundesverfassungsgericht [BVerfG] [Federal Constitutional Court], January 28, 1992, BVerfGE 85, 191 (Ger.) (trans. Donald Kommers, German Law Archive), www .iuscomp.org/wordpress/?p=79. The court noted:

> Insofar as investigations show that women are more seriously harmed by night work, this conclusion is generally traced to the fact that they are also burdened with housework and child rearing. . . . Women who carry out these duties in addition to night work outside the home . . . obviously suffer the adverse consequences of nocturnal employment to an enhanced degree. . . . But the present ban on night work for all female labourers cannot be supported on this ground, for the additional burden of housework and child rearing is not a sufficiently gender specific characteristic. BVerfGE 85, 191, ¶ 58.

63. The court explained:

> The infringement of the discrimination ban of Article 3(3) is not justified by the equal opportunity command of Article 3(2). The prohibition of night work . . . does not promote the goals of this provision. It is true that it protects a number of women . . . from nocturnal employment that is hazardous to their health. But this protection is coupled with significant disadvantages: Women are thereby prejudiced in their search for jobs. They may not accept work that must be done even in part at night. In some sectors this has led to a clear reduction in the training and employment of women. In addition, women labourers are not free to dispose as they choose of their own working time. One result of all this may be that women will continue to be more burdened than men by child rearing and housework in addition to work outside the home, and that the traditional division of labour between the sexes may be further entrenched. To this extent the prohibition of night work impedes the elimination of the social disadvantages suffered by women. BVerfGE 85, 191, ¶ 62.

64. BVerfGE 85, 191, ¶ 62.

65. BVerfGE 85, 191, ¶ 62. For a discussion of how this case read actual implementation of equal rights into Article 3(2), even before the 1994 amendment, see Jaeger, "Federal Constitutional Court."

66. 1990 Unification Treaty at art. 31(1).

67. 1990 Unification Treaty at art. 31(2).

68. Grundgesetz [GG] [Basic Law], art. 3(2). Nonetheless, conflicts about the permissibility of gender quotas continued through references and litigation before the European Court of Justice. The European Court initially invalidated a civil service gender quota adopted in the German Land of Bremen but later upheld preferences for the underrepresented sex as long as the candidate was equally qualified and the rejected male candidate had an opportunity to show

that special circumstances tilted the balance in his favor. See Kalanke v. Freie Hansestadt Bremen, 1995 E.C.R. I-03051; Marschall v. Land Nordrhein -Westfalen, 1997 E.C.R. I-06363; Badeck v. Hessen, 2000 E.C.R. I-01875.

69. Gesetz zur Gleichstellung von Frauen und Männern in der Bundesverwaltung und in den Gerichten des Bundes (Bundesgleichstellungsgesetz—BGleiG), November 30, 2001, BGBl. I 3234, www.bgbl.de/xaver/bgbl/start.xav?start= %2F%2F*%5B%40attr_id%3D%27bgbl101s3234.pdf%27%5D#__bgbl__%2F %2F*%5B%40attr_id%3D%27bgbl101s3234.pdf%27%5D__1478738905246.

70. For accounts of corporate board gender quota laws, see Aaron Dhir, *Challenging Boardroom Homogeneity* (Cambridge: Cambridge University Press, 2015); Julie C. Suk, "Gender Parity and State Legitimacy: From Public Office to Corporate Boards," *International Journal of Constitutional Law* 10, no. 2 (2012): 449–64.

71. Gesetz zur Änderung des Thüringer Landeswahlgesetzes-Einführung der paritätischen Quotierung vom 30. Juli 2019 [Law on Changes to Thurinigia Regional Election Regulations on Parity Quotas of July 30, 2019] (GVBl. 2019, S. 322) (Ger.).

72. Thüringer Verfassungsgerichtshof [ThVerfGH] [Thurinigia Constitutional Court], July 15, 2020, VerfGH 2/20 (Ger.).

73. "Verfassungsgericht kippt Paritätgesetz in Brandenburg," *Frankfurter Allgemeine Zeitung*, October 24, 2020.

74. Verfassung Brandenburg [Constitution of Brandenburg], art. 12(3) (Ger.).

75. Verfassungsgericht des Landes Brandenburg [VfGBbg] [Constitutional Court of the State of Brandenburg], VfGBbg 9/19, October 23, 2020, ¶ 165 (Ger.).

76. BVerfG, December 6, 2021, 2 BvR 1470/20, ¶¶ 1–61.

77. BVerfG, December 15, 2020, 2 BvC 46/19, ¶ 87.

78. The Constitutional Court noted that positive state duties to protect and act can be achieved through various possible solutions, with the legislature retaining freedom of design. Positive legislative duties are, by their nature, indefinite. See BVerfG, December 15, 2020, ¶¶ 42–44.

79. BVerfG, December 15, 2020, ¶ 30.

80. BVerfG, December 15, 2020, ¶ 31e.

81. BVerfG, December 15, 2020, ¶ 92.

82. See World Economic Forum, *Global Gender Gap Report 2021*, March 2021, https://www3.weforum.org/docs/WEF_GGGR_2021.pdf, 6 ("Iceland is the most gender-equal country in the world for the 12th time").

83. World Bank Group, *Women, Business, and the Law 2022*, March 1, 2022, https://wbl.worldbank.org/en/reports, 14.

84. See Thorvaldur Gylfason, "Constitutions: Financial Crisis Can Lead to Change," *Challenge* 55, no. 5 (2012): 108.

85. See Jane Kelsey, "A Gendered Response to Financial Crisis: What Can Others Learn from Iceland?" *Oñati Socio-Legal Series* 6, no. 1 (2016): 8–25.

86. See Daniel Chartier, *The End of Iceland's Innocence* (Ottawa: University of Ottawa Press, 2011), 119–20.

87. See Thorgerdur Einarsdottir and Gyda Margret Petursdottir, "An Analysis of the Report of Althing's Special Investigation Commission from a Gender Perspective," September 2010, https://rm.coe.int/16806ccff4, § 5.1.

88. See Janet Elise Johnson, Thorgedur Einarsdottir, and Gyda Margret Petursdottir, "A Feminist Theory of Corruption: Lessons from Iceland," *Politics and Gender* 9 (2013): 176, 188–90.

89. See Valur Gunnarsson and Mark Tran, "Icelandic PM Becomes World's First Leader to Step Down over Banking System Crisis," *The Guardian*, January 26, 2009.

90. See Jafnréttisstofa, *Gender Equality in Iceland* (Akureyri: Center for Gender Equality Iceland, 2012), 18.

91. See Thora Kristin Thorsdottir, "Iceland: From Feminist Governance to Gender-Blind Austerity?" *Gender, Sexuality and Feminism* 1, no. 2 (2014): 28, table 2.

92. Act No. 142/2008 (Iceland). The commission included a Supreme Court judge, the parliamentary ombudsman of Ireland, and an economist who was on the faculty at Yale.

93. Kelsey, "A Gendered Response," 12.

94. See Einarsdottir and Pettursdottir, "Special Investigation Commission from a Gender Perspective," § 7.6.

95. See Chartier, *End of Iceland's Innocence*, 129. As the *Financial Times* predicted, "Icelandic Women Will Clean Up the Young Men's Mess." *Financial Times*, October 14, 2008.

96. Act Respecting Amendment to Act on Public Limited Companies and Act on Private Limited Companies (Ownership, Sex Ratios and Acting Chairmen of Boards of Directors), Law No. 13/2010, March 8, 2010 (Iceland); English translation available at www.government.is/publications/legislation/lex/2018/02/06/TRANSLATION-OF-RECENT-AMENDMENTS-OF-ICELANDIC-PUBLIC-AND-PRIVATE-LIMITED-COMPANIES-LEGISLATION-2008-2010-including-Acts-13-2010-sex-ratios-and-68-2010-minority-protection-remuneration/.

97. See Jafnréttisstofa, *Gender Equality in Iceland*, 37.

98. See Janet Elise Johnson, "The Most Feminist Place in the World," *The Nation*, February 3, 2011.

99. See Jafnréttistofa, *Gender Equality in Iceland*, 38.

100. "Gender Budgeting," accessed August 4, 2021, www.government.is/topics/economic-affairs-and-public-finances/gender-budgeting/.

101. "Gender Budgeting," accessed August 4, 2021, www.government.is/topics/economic-affairs-and-public-finances/gender-budgeting/.

102. Public Finance Act, Law No. 123/2015, art. 18 (2015) (Iceland).

103. Act on a Constitutional Assembly No. 90/2010, June 10, 2010 (Iceland).

104. Act on a Constitutional Assembly, art. 6.

105. Act on a Constitutional Assembly, Interim Provision.

106. See Hélène Landemore, "Inclusive Constitution-Making: The Icelandic Experiment." *Journal of Political Philosophy* 23, no. 2 (2015): 166–91.

107. Case 130, Icelandic National Forum 2010, Participedia, https://participedia.net/case/130.

108. See Björg Thorarensen, "The Impact of the Financial Crisis on Icelandic Constitutional Law, Legislative Reforms, Judicial Review and Revision of the Constitution," in *Constitutions in the Global Financial Crisis: A Comparative Analysis*, ed. Xenophon Contiades (Farnham, Surrey: Ashgate, 2013), 63–283.

109. Supreme Court of Iceland, Complaints by Odin Sigthorsson, Skafti Hardarson, Thorgrimur S. Thorgrimsson, Decision of January 25, 2011 (Iceland), English translation available at http://stjornarskrarfelagid.is/wp-content/uploads/2011/07/Decision_of_the_Supreme_Court.pdf. For a commentary on the decision by a member of the Constitutional Society (an organization founded in 2010 to support the drafting of a new constitution), see Reynir Axelsson (a math professor at the University of Iceland), "Comments on the Decision of the Supreme Court to Invalidate the Election of the Constitutional Assembly," July 2011, http://stjornarskrarfelagid.is/wp-content/uploads/2011/07/Article_by_Reynir_Axelsson.pdf.

110. Const. art. 65 (Iceland).

111. Stjórnlagaráð [Constitutional Council], *A Proposal for a New Constitution for the Republic of Iceland*, July 29, 2011, www.stjornlagarad.is/other_files/stjornlagarad/Frumvarp-enska.pdf.

112. Stjórnlagaráð, *Proposal*, art. 34.

113. See, for example, Stjórnlagaráð, *Proposal*, art. 113.

114. Const. art. 79 (Iceland).

115. Andie Sophia Fontaine, "Where Is the New Constitution? A Nation Still Waits for Iceland 2.0," *Reykjavik Grapevine*, November 9, 2020, https://grapevine.is/mag/feature/2020/11/09/where-is-the-new-constitution/.

116. See Alexander Hudson, "Will Iceland Get a New Constitution? A New Revision Process Is Taking Shape," *International Journal of Constitutional Law*, I-CONnect Blog, October 23, 2018, www.iconnectblog.com/2018/10/will-iceland-get-a-new-constitution-a-new-revision-process-is-taking-shape/#:~:text=In%20January%202018%2C%20Prime%20Minister%20Jakobsd%C3%B3ttir%20announced%20a,the%20new%20revision%20process%20Parliament%20will%20be%20central.

117. See Jelena Ciric, "Icelandic Parliament 'Owes Society' an Updated Constitution, Says Prime Minister," *Iceland Review*, October 8, 2020, www.icelandreview.com/politics/icelandic-parliament-owes-society-an-updated-constitution-says-prime-minister/.

CHAPTER 6. BUILDING FEMINIST
INFRASTRUCTURES

1. See Steven Reinberg, "Nearly 74 Million Essential Workers at High Risk for COVID in U.S.," *US News and World Report*, November 9, 2020, www.usnews .com/news/health-news/articles/2020-11-09/nearly-74-million-essential-workers -at-high-risk-for-covid-in-us.

2. Campbell Robertson and Robert Gebeloff, "How Millions of Women Became the Most Essential Workers in America," *New York Times*, April 18, 2020, www.nytimes.com/2020/04/18/us/coronavirus-women-essential-workers .html.

3. See Betsey Stevenson, "The Initial Impact of COVID-19 on Labor Market Outcomes across Groups and the Potential for Permanent Scarring," Essay 2020-16, The Hamilton Project, July 2020, www.hamiltonproject.org/assets /files/Stevenson_LO_FINAL.pdf?_ga=2.16007601.608379579.1628178750- 1815969472.1628178750; Misty L. Heggeness, "Estimating the Immediate Impact of the COVID-19 Shock on Parental Attachment to the Labor Market and the Double Bind of Mothers," *Review of Economics of the Household* 18, no. 4 (2020): 1053–78.

4. H. Res. 121, S. Res. 87, 117th Cong. (2021). The "Marshall Plan for Moms" was first a publicity campaign started by Reshma Saujani, founder and CEO of Girls Who Code, in a paid advertisement in the *New York Times* urging a plan to pay mothers for their unseen, unpaid labor. See Reshma Saujani, "COVID Has Decimated Women's Careers—We Need a Marshall Plan for Moms, Now," *The Hill*, December 7, 2020.

5. Twenty-three percent of private industry employees have access to paid parental leave. US Dept. of Labor, Bureau of Labor Statistics, "Employee Benefits in the United States—March 2021," news release, USDL-21-1690, September 23, 2021.

6. Motherhood clauses were written into new constitutions in Estonia (1920), Czechoslovakia (1920), the Kingdom of the Serbs, Croats, and Slovenes (1921), Poland (1921), Spain (1931), and Portugal (1931).

7. Const. art. 30 (Yemen).

8. For an account of cross-party coalitions by women in the Weimar Reischstag, particularly around issues such as protective labor legislation, see Claudia Koonz, "Conflicting Allegiances: Political Ideology and Women Legislators in Weimar Germany," *Signs* 1, no. 4 (1976): 663.

9. Twenty-two of the forty-one women were members of the Social Democratic Party (Sozialdemokratische Partei Deutschland, SPD), and many had been active in the social democratic women's movement of early twentieth-century Germany. By that point, the far-left Bolshevik Independent Social Democratic

Party (Unabhängige Sozialdemokratische Partei Deutschlands, USPD) had split off from the SPD and elected notable women to the Constituent Assembly as well. See Ute Frevert, *Women in German History: From Bourgeois Emancipation to Sexual Liberation*, trans. Stuart McKinnon-Evans, Terry Bond, and Barbara Norden (Oxford: Berg, 1997), 169–70.

10. 1919 Const. art. 119 (Ger.).

11. 1919 Const. art. 119. (Ger.).

12. See Richard Evans, *The Feminist Movement in Germany, 1894–1933* (London: Sage Publications, 1976), 153.

13. See Kathryn Kish Sklar, Anja Schüler, and Susan Strasser, *Social Justice Feminists in the United States and Germany: A Dialogue in Documents, 1994–1933* (Ithaca, NY: Cornell University Press, 1998), 26.

14. See Evans, *Feminist Movement in Germany*, 154.

15. Evans, *Feminist Movement in Germany*, 155 (quoting and translating article in *Die Frau*).

16. Helene Lange was "the leading German feminist between 1890 and 1914," who "more than any other single individual held together the coalition of conservative and progressive women activists during the first decade of the twentieth century." Lange was an admirer of American feminist Elizabeth Cady Stanton. See Sklar, Schüler, and Strasser, *Social Justice Feminists*, 24–25.

17. Ellen Key's essay "Motherliness," published in the United States in 1912, is discussed in the introduction. Key was also the author of several books, contemporaneously translated into English, about the women's movement and the need for greater public attention to the needs of mothers and children. See Ellen Key, *The Morality of Woman, and Other Essays*, trans. Mamah Bouton Borthwick (Chicago: Ralph Fletcher Seymour, 1911); Ellen Key, *The Woman Movement*, trans. Mamah Bouton Borthwick (New York: Putnam, 1912); Ellen Key, *The Renaissance of Motherhood*, trans. Anna E. B. Fries (New York, Putnam, 1914). For a more detailed account of the Mutterschutz movement and Helene Stöcker, see Ann Taylor Allen, *Feminism and Motherhood in Germany* (New Brunswick, NJ: Rutgers University Press, 1991).

18. See Evans, *Feminist Movement in Germany*, 237.

19. See Frevert, *Women in German History*, 170.

20. See Renate Pore, *A Conflict of Interest: Women in German Social Democracy, 1919–1933* (Westport, CT: Greenwood Press, 1981), 44.

21. See Mannfred Georg, "The Right to Abortion" (1922), in *The Weimar Republic Sourcebook*, ed. Anton Kaes, Martin Jay, and Edward Dimendberg (Berkeley: University of California Press, 1994); Cornelie Usborne, *Cultures of Abortion in Weimar Germany* (Oxford: Berghahn, 2007).

22. Pore, *Conflict of Interest*, 65–80.

23. See Usborne, *Cultures of Abortion*.

24. Pore, *Conflict of Interest,* 80–84. For an account of the evolution of socialist women's views on these questions, see Jean H. Quataert, *Reluctant Feminists in German Social Democracy, 1885–1917* (Princeton, NJ: Princeton University Press, 1979).

25. Grundgesetz [GG] [Basic Law] art. 6 (Ger.).

26. Journal Officiel Assemblée Nationale [official journal] [J.O.A.N.], Débats Parlementaires de la 4ème République et Constituantes, August 27, 1946, No. 83, at 3332.

27. J.O.A.N. No. 83, at 3332.

28. Biblioteca del Senato, *Le donne della Costituente* (October 2008), 1, www.senato.it/application/xmanager/projects/leg18/file/repository/relazioni/biblioteca/emeroteca/Donnedellacostituente.pdf.

29. See Molly Tambor, *The Lost Wave: Women and Democracy in Postwar Italy* (New York: Oxford University Press, 2014), 79.

30. Assemblea Costituente della Repubblica Italiana [Constituent Assembly of the Italian Republic], Commissione per la Costituzione [Commission for the Constitution] vol. VIII (September 13, 1946): 2105.

31. See World Economic Forum, *The Global Gender Gap Report 2021*, March 30, 2021, www.weforum.org/reports/global-gender-gap-report-2021/.

32. See World Bank Group, *Women, Business, and the Law 2022*, March 1, 2022, https://wbl.worldbank.org/en/reports; World Bank, "Labor Force Participation Rate, Female (% of Female Population Ages 15-64) (modeled ILO estimate)—Italy," data as of June 2021, https://data.worldbank.org/indicator/SL.TLF.ACTI.FE.ZS?locations=IT.

33. See Julie C. Suk, "Are Gender Stereotypes Bad for Women?," *Columbia Law Review* 110, no. 1 (2010): 1–69.

34. See, for example, Coleman v. Court of Appeals of Maryland, 566 U.S. 30, 47, 57 (2012) (Ginsburg, J., dissenting). See also Nevada v. Hibbs, 538 U.S. 721, 732 (2003).

35. Ir. Const., 1937, art. 41.2.

36. See Laura Cahillane, "Revisiting Article 41.2," *Dublin University Law Journal* 40, no. 2 (2017): 113.

37. Ir. Const., 1922, art. 3.

38. See generally Brian Farrell, ed., *De Valera's Constitution, and Ours* (Dublin: Gil and Macmillan, 1988); Tim Pat Coogan, *De Valera: Long Fellow, Long Shadow* (London: Hutchinson, 1993).

39. Dáil Deb., May 11, 1937 (Ir.), www.oireachtas.ie/en/debates/debate/dail/1937-05-11/29/ (remarks of Eamonn De Valera).

40. Dáil Deb., May 11, 1937.

41. Dáil Deb., May 11, 1937.

42. Dáil Deb., May 12, 1937 (Ir.), www.oireachtas.ie/en/debates/debate/dail/1937-05-12/12/.

43. Dáil Deb., May 12, 1937 (remarks of John Marcus O'Sullivan).

44. Dáil Deb., May 12, 1937 (remarks of Helena Concannon).

45. Dáil Deb., May 12, 1937.

46. Dáil Deb., May 12, 1937.

47. Dáil Deb., May 12, 1937.

48. Dáil Deb., May 12, 1937.

49. Dáil Deb., May 12, 1937.

50. See Yvonne Scannell, "The Constitution and the Role of Women," in *De Valera's Constitution and Ours*, ed. Brian Farrell (Dublin: Gil and Macmillan, 1988), 128.

51. Scannell, "Constitution," 98.

52. Gesetz zum Schutze der erwerbstätigen Mutter (Mutterschutzgesetz), January 24, 1952, (Ger).

53. Mutterschutzgesestz, Gesetzes vom 23. Mai 2017 [Mothers' Protection Law of May 23, 2017] BGBl. I 1228 (Ger.).

54. Mutterschutzgesestz § 6.

55. Mutterschutzgesestz § 8a-d.

56. Mutterschutzgesestz § 8.

57. Bundesverfassungsgericht [BVerfG] [Federal Constitutional Court], November 13, 1979, BVerfGE 52, 357 (Ger.).

58. Bundesverfassungsgericht [BVerfG] [Federal Constitutional Court], April 24, 1991, 1 BvR 1341/90 (Ger.).

59. Bundesverfassungsgericht [BVerfG] [Federal Constitutional Court], March 26, 2006, 1 BvL 10/01 (Ger.).

60. BVerfG, 1BvL 10/01, ¶ 49.

61. De Burca v. Attorney General, [1976] IR 38, 57 (Ir.).

62. See Dennehy v. Minister for Social Welfare, 1983 WJSC-HC 2007 (Ir.); Lowth v. Minister for Social Welfare, [1993] IR 339 (Ir.).

63. L. v. L., [1992] 2 IR 77, 88–89 (citing the 1988 High Court opinion by Judge Barr).

64. L. v. L., [1992] 2 IR 77, 107 (Finlay, CJ).

65. Sinnott v. Minister for Education, [2001] 2 IR 545, 664–65 (Ir.).

66. See Alan D. P. Brady, "Gender and the Irish Constitution: Article 41.2, Symbolism and the Limitation of Courts' Approach to Substantive Gender Inequality," in *Law and Gender in Modern Ireland: Critique and Reform*, ed. Lynsey Black and Peter Dunne (Oxford: Hart, 2019), 211.

67. Brady, "Gender," 212–13.

68. T. v. T., [2002] IESC 68 (Ir.) (Denham, J.).

69. T. v. T., [2002] IESC 68 (Ir.) (Murray, J.).

70. In his presentation to the Convention on the Constitution in 2013, Professor Gerry Whyte discussed all the cases in which Article 41.2 has been at issue and remarked that courts are unlikely to interpret Article 41.2.2 to improve

social protections, whether for mothers or for parents, given extreme judicial caution by judges when litigants raise economic, social, and cultural rights in the superior courts. See Gerry Whyte, Advisory Panel presentation "Amending the Clause on the Role of Women in the Home," Convention on the Constitution, February 16, 2013. Whyte also cited T. D. v. Minister for Education, [2001] 4 IR 259, a Supreme Court case that explicitly warned judges against implying constitutional rights in litigation that would encroach upon the legislative province of allocating public expenditures.

71. Ireland Convention on the Constitution, *Second Report of the Convention on the Constitution, (i) Amending the clause on the role of women in the home and encouraging greater participation of women in public life; and (ii) Increasing the participation of women in politics*, May 2013, at 15, www .constitutionalconvention.ie/AttachmentDownload.ashx?mid=268d9308-c9b7 -e211-a5a0-005056a32ee4.

72. Ireland Convention on the Constitution, *Second Report.*

73. Ireland Convention on the Constitution, *Second Report*, 23.

74. See Ireland Citizens' Assembly 2016–2018, *Eighth Amendment, Recommendations*, https://2016-2018.citizensassembly.ie/en/The-Eighth-Amendment -of-the-Constitution/.

75. Ireland Houses of the Oireachtas, Joint Committee on Justice and Equality, *Report on Pre-legislative Scrutiny of the General Scheme of the 38th Amendment of the Constitution (Role of Women) Bill, 32/JAE/31*, December 2018, 77.

76. Jane Suiter, Kirsty Park, Yvonne Galligan, and David M. Farrell, *Evaluation Report of the Irish Citizens' Assembly on Gender Equality 2021*, Independent Researchers Report, DCU Institute of Future Media, Democracy, and Society, 2021, www.citizensassembly.ie/en/previous-assemblies/2020-2021 -citizens-assembly-on-gender-equality/news-publications/publications/independent -researchers-report-on-the-process.pdf.

77. Ireland Citizens' Assembly, *Report of the Citizens' Assembly on Gender Equality*, June 2021, 63, www.citizensassembly.ie/en/previous-assemblies /2020-2021-citizens-assembly-on-gender-equality/about-the-citizens-assembly /report-of-the-citizens-assembly-on-gender-equality.pdf.

78. Ireland Citizens' Assembly, *Report*, 50.

79. Ireland Citizens' Assembly, *Report*, 50.

80. Ireland Citizens' Assembly, *Report*, 53.

81. Ireland Citizens' Assembly, *Report*, 116–17.

82. Oireachtas, Joint Committee on Gender Equality, Interim Report on Constitutional Change, 33/GE/02, July 2022, https://data.oireachtas.ie /ie/oireachtas/committee/dail/33/joint_committee_on_gender_equality/reports /2022/2022-07-13_interim-report-on-constitutional-change_en.pdf.

83. Ireland Citizens' Assembly, *Report*, 118.

84. Ireland Citizens' Assembly, *Report*, 60.

85. Ireland Citizens' Assembly, *Report*, 61, 120.

86. See Children's Rights Alliance Submission to the Citizens' Assembly, January 2021, 2–3.

87. Ireland Citizens' Assembly, *Report on Gender Equality*, 61.

88. Ireland Citizens' Assembly, *Report*, 66–67.

89. Ireland Citizens' Assembly, *Report*, 69.

90. Ireland Citizens' Assembly, *Report*, 70.

91. Ireland Citizens' Assembly, *Report*, 70.

92. Ireland Citizens' Assembly, *Report*, 75–76.

93. Ireland Citizens' Assembly, *Report*, 81–82.

94. See Hélène Landemore, *Open Democracy: Reinventing Popular Rule for the Twenty-First Century* (Princeton, NJ: Princeton University Press, 2020).

95. See American Academy of Arts and Sciences, Commission on the Practice of Democratic Citizenship, "Responsive Government Strategy 3.3, Create Citizens' Assemblies," www.amacad.org/ourcommonpurpose/recommendation -3-3.

96. See the Washington Climate Assembly's website, www.waclimate assembly.org/. After weekend meetings listening to presentations and deliberating, the Washington Climate Assembly produced its final report in March 2021. See Washington Climate Assembly, *Washingtonians Finding Solutions Together*, https://81a84cbc-5f71-4d22-9287-6f567df5d228.filesusr.com/ugd/d6c986_9 495356c240c4f1a976524905f9bf421.pdf.

97. See, for instance, Dobbs v. Jackson Women's Health, 597 U.S. __ (2022), slip opinion, p. 25 ("The inescapable conclusion is that a right to abortion is not deeply rooted in the Nation's history and traditions"). See also New York State Rifle & Pistol Association, Inc. v. Bruen, 597 U.S. __ (2022) (striking down a New York State regulation limiting the public carrying of guns on the basis of eighteenth-century meanings of the Second Amendment); West Virginia v. Environmental Protection Agency, 597 U.S. __ (2022) (striking down an environmental regulation on emissions reduction).

98. American Rescue Plan Act of 2021, H. Res. 1319.

99. White House, "The American Families Plan," fact sheet, April 2021, www .whitehouse.gov/wp-content/uploads/2021/04/American-Families-Plan-Fact-Sheet-FINAL.pdf.

100. Seventy-three percent of Republican voters support free universal early childcare programs, and 93 percent of Democrats do. See Elisabeth Buchwald, "Americans Want More Affordable Child Care Options—Republican Voters Included," *Marketwatch*, April 30, 2021 (citing December 2020 polling conducted by the First Five Years Fund).

101. "Three in Four Americans Support Equal Rights Amendment, Poll Shows," Associated Press, February 24, 2020.

CONCLUSION

1. Lawrence v. Texas, 539 U.S. 558, 598 (2003) (Scalia, J., dissenting).

2. S. Hrg. 109-158, Confirmation Hearing on the Nomination of John G. Roberts, Jr. to be the Chief Justice of the United States, Hearing Before the Senate Committee on the Judiciary, 109th Cong., September 12–15, 2005, at 201.

3. For example, Tom Ginsburg and Aziz Huq, *Assessing Constitutional Performance* (Chicago: University of Chicago Press, 2016); Adam Chilton and Mila Versteeg, *How Constitutional Rights Matter* (Oxford: Oxford University Press, 2020); David S. Law, ed., *Constitutionalism in Context* (Cambridge: Cambridge University Press, 2022).

4. See World Economic Forum, *The Global Gender Gap Report 2021*, www .weforum.org/reports/global-gender-gap-report-2021/; World Bank Group, *Women, Business and the Law 2022*, https://wbl.worldbank.org/en/reports.

5. See Adam Chilton and Mila Versteeg, "The Effect of Constitutional Gender Equality Clauses," preprint, SSRN, October 27, 2021, http://dx.doi .org/10.2139/ssrn.3789365.

6. See Madhav Khosla, "Is A Science of Comparative Constitutional Law Possible?," *Harvard Law Review* 135, no. 8 (2022), https://harvardlawreview .org/2022/06/is-a-science-of-comparative-constitutionalism-possible/.

7. See generally Alan Watson, *Legal Transplants: An Approach to Comparative Law* (Edinburgh: Scottish Academic Press, 1974).

8. This is the title of an important work in political science that explores the reasons why the United States has resisted the transplant of socialism. See Seymour Martin Lipset and Gary Marks, *It Didn't Happen Here: Why Socialism Failed in the United States* (New York: W. W. Norton, 2000). Nearly a century earlier, German sociologist Werner Sombart's book *Why Is There No Socialism in the United States?* suggested that the two-party system made the emergence of a workers' party impossible in the United States. See Werner Sombart, *Why Is There No Socialism in the United States?* (1906), trans. Patricia M. Hocking and C. T. Husbands (London: Macmillan 1976).

9. Sinclair Lewis's 1935 dystopian novel depicted the rise of a dictator in the United States similar to Adolf Hitler, satirizing Americans' belief in America's immunity to European political ideas and dynamics. See Sinclair Lewis, *It Can't Happen Here* (1936; repr., New York, Signet Classics, 2014).

10. Robert Kagan, *Adversarial Legalism: The American Way of Law*, 2nd ed. (Cambridge, MA: Harvard University Press 2019), 6.

11. Vicki Jackson, *Constitutional Engagement in a Transnational Era* (Oxford: Oxford University Press, 2010).

12. See Theda Skocpol, *Protecting Soldiers and Mothers: The Political Origins of Social Policy in the United States* (Cambridge, MA: The Belknap Press of Harvard University Press, 1992), 424, 429–79.

13. See Silvia Federici, "Wages against Housework" (1975), reprinted in *Revolution at Point Zero: Housework, Reproduction, and Feminist Struggle* (New York: PM Press, 2020), 15–22.

14. See H. Res. 121, S. Res. 87 (117th Cong. 2022).

15. See Richard Epstein, *Takings: Private Property and the Power of Eminent Domain* (Cambridge, MA: Harvard University Press, 1985), 111; Eduardo M. Peñalver and Lior Jacob Strahilevitz, "Judicial Takings or Due Process?," *Cornell Law Review* 97, no. 2 (2012): 305.

16. See Abraham Bell and Gideon Parchomovsky, "Takings Reassessed," *Virginia Law Review* 87, no. 2 (2001): 283.

17. See Joseph L. Sax, "Takings and the Police Power," *Yale Law Journal* 74, no. 1 (1964): 36–77.

18. In 1922, in *Pennsylvania Coal Co. v. Mahon*, Justice Holmes said that if a regulation goes too far, it is a taking. Joseph Blocher observes that the court's subsequent regulatory takings jurisprudence can be understood through a functional lens, whereby a largely factual inquiry is undertaken to assess the impact of the regulation on the property interests, and ultimately focuses on the property interests themselves. See Joseph Blocher, "Bans," *Yale Law Journal* 129, no. 2 (2019): 337.

19. Under the federal Pregnancy Discrimination Act, federal courts have held that employers may terminate or place on unpaid leave pregnant workers when pregnancy renders them unable to perform the job without an accommodation. See, for example, Troupe v. May Dep't Stores, 20 F.3d 734 (7th Cir. 1994); Young v. United Parcel Service, 575 U.S. 206 (2015).

20. Khiara Bridges, "Racial Disparities in Maternal Mortality," *New York University Law Review* 95, no. 5 (2020): 1229–1318.

21. See Grundgesetz [GG] [Basic Law] § 6.4 (Ger.); Ir. Const., 1937, art. 41.2; 1946 Const. Preamble ¶ 11 (Fr.); Art. 37 Costituzione [Cost.] (It.); Daehan Minkuk Hunbeob [Constitution] art. 36(2) (S. Kor.); Constitución Política de los Estados Unidos Mexicanos [C.P.]. art. 123(B)(XI)(c) (Mex.); Art. 75(23), Constitución Nacional [Const. Nac.] (Arg.); Constitución Política de Colombia [C.P.] art. 43 (Colom.). For an account of the origins of maternity clauses in European constitutions, see Julie C. Suk, "Gender Equality and the Protection of Motherhood in Global Constitutionalism," *Journal of Law and Ethics of Human Rights* 12 (2018): 151–80.

22. Ir. Const., 1937, art. 41.2.1.

23. Ir. Const., 1937, art. 41.2.2.

24. The supporters noted, "Enforcing the Texas Heartbeat Act only through civil enforcement by private citizens, not the state, would strengthen citizens' ability to hold violators accountable for a practice that many Texans find morally objectionable." See Texas House Research Organization, S.B. 8 (2d reading), Bill Analysis (May 5, 2021): 9.

25. Shortly after *Casey* was decided, one scholar suggested that abortion regulations should be approached through a takings theory. See Susan E. Looper-Friedman, "Keep Your Laws off My Body: Abortion Regulation and the Takings Clause," *New England Law Review* 29, no. 2 (1995): 253–84. More recently, a student note suggests that abortion providers could challenge targeted regulation of abortion providers (TRAP) laws, such as those requiring abortion providers to have admitting privileges at surgical hospitals, under a takings theory. See Hope Silberstein, "Taking on TRAP Laws: Protecting Abortion Rights through Property Rights," *University of Chicago Legal Forum* 2017 (2017): 737–66.

26. See Moore v. Regents of the University of California, 249 Cal. Rptr. 494, 498–499 (Cal. Ct. App. 1988).

27. Hecht v. Superior Court, 59 Cal. Rptr. 2d 222, 226 (Cal. Ct. App. 1996).

28. See, for example, Bilbao v. Goodwin, 217 A.3d 977 (Conn. 2019); Patel v. Patel, 99 Va. Cir. 11 (Circuit Ct. Va. 2017).

29. See generally Douglas NeJaime, "The Nature of Parenthood," *Yale Law Journal* 126, no. 8 (2017): 2305–6.

30. See generally Carol Sanger, "Infant Safe Haven Laws: Legislating the Culture of Life," *Columbia Law Review* 106, no. 4 (2006) 753–829.

31. Jackson Women's Health v. Dobbs, No. 19-1392, Oral Argument Transcript (December 1, 2021), 56.

32. For example, Texas's "Baby Moses" law, which was the first safe haven law enacted in the nation in 1999, provides that a court may terminate the parent-child relationship if the parent voluntarily delivers a child younger than thirty days old to an emergency medical services provider, who is to take possession of the child. See H.B. 3423, An Act Relating to the Emergency Possession of and Termination of the Parent-Child Relationship of Certain Abandoned Children (Tex. 1999).

33. *Dobbs v. Jackson Women's Health*, 597 U.S. __ (2022), slip op. at 34.

34. See Siegel, "Prochoicelife," 217–20.

35. See Gianna Melillo, "U.S. Ranks Worst in Maternal Care, Mortality Compared with 10 Other Developed Nations," *American Journal of Managed Care,* December 3, 2020, www.ajmc.com/view/us-ranks-worst-in-maternal-care-mortality-compared-with-10-other-developed-nations. See also J. Phillip Gingery, "Maternal Mortality: A US Public Health Crisis," *American Journal of Public Health* 110, no. 4 (2020): 462–64.

36. Alabama, Mississippi, Louisiana, Tennessee, Arkansas, Texas, Oklahoma, and South Carolina have the highest risk of maternal death. In southern states, one in five women of reproductive age live in counties with high risk of death and other poor maternal health outcomes, such as postpartum hemorrhage, preeclampsia, and preterm birth. See Sema Sgaier and Jordan Downey, "What We See in Shameful Trends on U.S. Maternal Health," *New York Times,* November 17, 2021.

37. Maternal Health Task Force, Harvard Chan School, Center of Excellence in Maternal and Child Health, "Maternal Health in the United States," accessed July 17, 2022, www.mhtf.org/topics/maternal-health-in-the-united-states.

38. Michele Goodwin, *Policing the Womb: Invisible Women and the Criminalization of Pregnancy* (Cambridge: Cambridge University Press, 2020), 7–8.

39. Judith Jarvis Thomson, "A Defense of Abortion," *Philosophy and Public Affairs* 1, no. 1 (1971): 47–66.

40. Thomson, "Defense of Abortion," 48–49.

41. "I propose, then, that we grant that the fetus is a person from the moment of conception," she wrote, in introducing the hypothetical of the famous violinist. Thomson, "Defense of Abortion," 48.

42. Andrew Koppelman, "Forced Labor: A Thirteenth Amendment Defense of Abortion," *Northwestern University Law Review* 84, no. 2 (1989): 480–535; Andrew Koppelman, "Originalism, Abortion, and the Thirteenth Amendment," *Columbia Law Review* 112, no. 7 (2012): 1917–48.

43. S.B. 826 § 1(d) (California, October 10, 2018), codified at Cal. Corp. Code § 301.

44. Council of the European Union, "Council and European Parliament Agree to Improve Gender Balance on Company Boards," press release, June 7, 2022, www.consilium.europa.eu/en/press/press-releases/2022/06/07/council-and-european-parliament-agree-to-improve-gender-balance-on-company-boards/.

45. Meland v. Weber, No. 2:10-vb-03388-JAM-AC, 2021 WL 6118651, at *7. ("Yet whether SB 826 is or is not a quota is not the dispositive issue; even if it were a quota, no case brought forward by Plaintiff supports a per se rule that gender quotas are unconstitutional.")

46. S.B. 826 § 1(c).

47. S.B. 826 § 1(c)(3); § 1(c)(5)(C).

48. See Meland v. Weber, No. 22-15149, Appellant's Opening Brief, at 26.

49. See Roger Congleton, *Improving Democracy through Constitutional Reform: Some Swedish Lessons* (Boston: Springer, 2003), 158; David Arter, "The Swedish Riksdag: The Case of a Strong Policy-Influencing Assembly," *West European Politics* 13, no. 3 (1990): 120.

50. Arter, "Sweidsh Riksdag," 120.

51. Arter, "Swedish Riksdag," 122.

52. See generally Erwin Chemerinsky and Catherine L. Fisk, "The Filibuster," *Stanford Law Review* 49, no. 2 (1997): 181–254. For a more recent general-audience account of the antidemocratic uses of the Senate filibuster, see Adam Jentleson, *Kill Switch: The Rise of the Modern Senate and the Crippling of American Democracy* (New York: Liveright, 2021).

53. Paycheck Fairness Act, H.R. 7, 117th Cong. (2021). The report on the legislation specifically acknowledged that wage inequality experienced by mothers, in particular, "threatens the stability of families across the United States." See

House Committee on Education and Labor, H. Rept. 117-13, Paycheck Fairness Act (April 5, 2021), 23. In a roll call vote on May 28, 2021, the Senate voted, 49 in favor and 50 opposed, not to proceed on the bill.

54. Women's Health Protection Act, H.R. 3755, 117th Cong. (2021).

55. In a roll call vote on February, the Senate voted, 49 in favor and 50 opposed, not to proceed on the bill.

56. Women's Health Protection Act of 2022, S. 4132, Roll Call Vote No. 170, 168 Cong. Rec. S.2439 (May 11, 2022).

57. Pregnant Workers' Fairness Act, H.R. 1065.

58. A majority of Americans support legalizing abortion in all or most cases. See Hannah Hartig, "About Six-in-Ten Americans Say That Abortion Should Be Legal in All or Most Cases," Pew Research Center, May 6, 2021, www.pewresearch.org/fact-tank/2021/05/06/about-six-in-ten-americans-say-abortion-should-be-legal-in-all-or-most-cases/.

59. See Equal Rights 1970: Hearings on S.J. Res. 61 and S.J. Res. 231 Before the S. Comm. on the Judiciary, 91st Cong. 427–33 (1970) (statement of Pauli Murray). ("Underlying the issue of equal rights for women is the more fundamental issue of equal power for women. No group in power has surrendered its power without a struggle. Many male opponents of equal rights for women recognize the more fundamentally revolutionary nature of the changes which a genuine implementation of such an amendment would bring about.") Pauli Murray's "equal power" vision of the ERA has resonances in the legislative histories of the recent ratifications, in which Black state legislators played central roles. See Julie C. Suk, "A Dangerous Imbalance: Pauli Murray's Equal Rights Amendment and the Path to Equal Power," *Virginia Law Review Online* 107 (2021): 3.

60. See generally Julie C. Suk, *We the Women: The Unstoppable Mothers of the Equal Rights Amendment* (New York: Skyhorse, 2020).

61. Suk, *We the Women*, 84–89.

62. Proposing an Amendment to the Constitution Relating to the Election of the President and Vice President, H.J. Res. 681, 91st Cong. (1971). See "Electoral College Reform Victim of Senate Filibuster," in *CQ Almanac 1970*, 26th ed., 05-840-05-845 (Washington, DC: Congressional Quarterly, 1971), http://library.cqpress.com/cqalmanac/cqal70-1291702.

63. GG art. 79.

64. 1958 Const. art. 89 (Fr.).

65. Ir. Const. 1937, art. 46.

66. See Jerusalem Demsas, "The Abortion Policy Most Americans Want," *The Atlantic*, May 13, 2022 (citing polls by Gallup/CNN/USA Today and Associated Press/NORC from 1996 to 2021).

67. See Washington Climate Assembly, Final Report 2021, www.waclimateassembly.org/_files/ugd/09fdff_7123b8b71d304311b075bd5d8460eb06.pdf.

Selected Bibliography

This bibliography is a selected list of the primary and secondary sources that were of significant use in the making of this book. The list is not a complete record of all the relevant works and sources consulted, and is intended to serve as a resource for those who wish to study the bodies of law and scholarly literature that shaped this book's arguments. The themes of these sources include patriarchal law, feminist legal theory, US constitutional sex equality jurisprudence, the private-law doctrines of unjust enrichment and abuse of right, abortion and reproductive justice, the legal and social movement history of Prohibition, comparative law and method, gender parity in Europe, motherhood and care, and democratic constitutionalism. This list includes some but not all the sources that are specifically referenced in the notes. It also includes many additional sources that helped form my thinking about the ideas developed here, even though not specifically cited in the notes. The sources are organized by category: Cases, Constituent Assembly Debates, Pending Constitutional Reforms, Reports by Government Entities, Reports by Nongovernmental Organizations, and Secondary Sources.

CASES

A, B, & C v. Ireland, [2010] Eur. Ct. H.R. 2032.
Aborto. Suprema Corte de Justicia de la Nación [SCJN] [Supreme Court], Acción de inconstitucionalidad 148/2017, September 21, 2021 (Mex.) (decriminalization of abortion).

Attorney General v. X, [1992] 1 IR 1 (Ir.).

Bartemeyer v. Iowa, 85 U.S. 129 (1873).

Beer Co. v. Massachusetts, 97 U.S. 32 (1877).

Bellinger v. Griffith, 23 Ohio St. 619 (Ohio 1873).

Bilbao v. Goodwin, 217 A.3d 977 (Conn. 2019).

Board of Directors of Rotary International v. Rotary Club of Duarte, 481 U.S. 537 (1987).

Bradwell v. State of Illinois, 83 U.S. 130 (1873).

Brantigan v. While, 73 Ill. 561 (Ill. 1874).

Bundesgerichtshof [BGH] [Federal Court of Justice] February 21, 1952, 5 BGHZ 186 (Ger.) (husband's abuse of right to divorce his wife when his only purpose is to marry another woman).

Bundesverfassungsgericht [BVerfG] [Federal Constitutional Court], December 18, 1953, BVerfGE 3, 225 (Ger.) (equal rights of men and women in marriage and family).

Bundesverfassungsgericht [BVerfG] [Federal Constitutional Court], May 25, 1956, 1 BvR 53/54 (Ger.) (labor protections for women).

Bundesverfassungsgericht [BVerfG] [Federal Constitutional Court], July 29 1959, BVerfGE 10, 59 (1959) (equal parental authority of mothers and fathers).

Bundesverfassungsgericht [BVerfG] [Federal Constitutional Court], February 25, 1975, BVerfGE 39, 1 (Ger.) (Abortion I).

Bundesverfassungsgericht [BVerfG] [Federal Constitutional Court], November 13, 1979, BVerfGE 52, 357 (Ger.) (ban on terminating pregnant employee).

Bundesverfassungsgericht [BVerfG] [Federal Constitutional Court], April 24, 1991, 1 BvR 1341/90 (Ger.) (unification treaty and ban on terminating pregnant employee).

Bundesverfassungsgericht [BVerfG] [Federal Constitutional Court], January 28, 1992, BVerfGE 85, 191 (Ger.) (ban on women's night work).

Bundesverfassungsgericht [BVerfG] [Federal Constitutional Court], May 28, 1993, BvF 2/90 (Ger.) (Abortion II).

Bundesverfassungsgericht [BVerfG] [Federal Constitutional Court] October 19, 1993, BVerfGE 89, 214 (Ger.) (bank abuse of rights in surety contract with single mother).

Bundesverfassungsgericht [BVerfG] [Federal Constitutional Court], March 26, 2006, 1 BvL 10/01 (Ger.) (mandatory maternity leave counts as time worked).

Bundesverfassungsgericht [BVerfG] [Federal Constitutional Court], June 6, 2011, 1 BvR 2712/09 (Ger.) (parental leave and parental allowance).

Bundesverfassungsgericht [BVerfG] [Federal Constitutional Court], December 15, 2020, 2 BvC 46/19, ¶ 87 (Ger.) (inadmissibility of complaint for lack of gender parity rule at federal level).

Bundesverfassungsgericht [BVerfG] [Federal Constitutional Court], December 6, 2021, 2 BvR 1470/20 (Ger.) (inadmissibility of complaint against Thuringia parity law).

Califano v. Goldfarb, 430 U.S. 199 (1977).

California Federal Savings & Loan Association v. Guerra, 479 U.S. 272.

Cleveland Board of Education v. Lafleur, 414 U.S. 632 (1974).

Coleman v. Court of Appeals of Maryland, 566 U.S. 30 (2012).

Conseil Constitutionnel [CC] [Constitutional Council] decision No. 74-54DC, January 15, 1975 (Fr.) (upholding the statute decriminalizing abortion).

Conseil Constitutionnel [CC] [Constitutional Council] decision No. 82-146DC, November 18, 1982 (Fr.) (gender quota for political party candidate lists in municipal elections).

Conseil Constitutionnel [CC] [Constitutional Council] decision No. 2000-429, May 30, 2000 (Fr.) (gender quota for political party candidate lists in parliamentary elections).

Conseil Constitutionnel [CC] [Constitutional Council] decision No. 2006-533DC, March 16, 2006 (Fr.) (gender quota for corporate boards).

Constitutional Court [Const. Ct.], 2017Hun-Ba127, April 11, 2019 (S. Kor.). Official English translation at Constitutional Court Decisions 2019, at 1 (Republic of Korea 2019).

Corte Constitucional [C.C.] [Constitutional Court], May 10, 2006, Sentencia C-355/06. (Colom.) (constitutionally required exceptions to abortion criminalization.

Corte Constitucional [C.C.] [Constitutional Court], February 21, 2022, Sentencia C-055/22. (Colom.) (decriminalization of abortion).

Corte Suprema de Justicia de la Nación [CSJN] [National Supreme Court of Justice], 13/3/2012 "F., A. L. s/ medida autosatisfactiva," Fallos (2012-335-197) (Arg.) (permitting abortion in case of rape).

Cour d'appel [CA] [regional court of appeal] Colmar, May 2, 1855, D.1856.2.9 (Fr.) ("Arrêt Doerr," dummy chimney case).

Cour d'appel [CA] [regional court of appeal] Lyon, April 18, 1856 (Fr.). ("Affaire St. Galmier," spring water pump case).

Cour de cassation [Cass.] [supreme court for judicial matters] req., June 15, 1892 (Fr.) (Julien Patureau c/Boudier) (unjustified enrichment involving fertilizer).

Cour de cassation [Cass.] [supreme court for judicial matters] civ., August 3, 1915 ("Affaire Clément-Bayard," neighboring hangar case) (Fr.).

Cour de cassation [Cass.] [supreme court for judicial matters] civ. January 9, 1979, No. 77-12.991 (Fr.). (restitution for unpaid work during cohabitation).

Cour de cassation [Cass.] [supreme court for judicial matters] 2e civ., April 21, 1982, No. 81-11.775 (Fr.) (abuse of right for failure to deliver the get).

Cour de cassation [Cass.] [supreme court for judicial matters] 1e civ., October 26, 1982, No. 81-14.824 (restitution for unpaid work for husband's business during marriage).

Cour de cassation [Cass.] [supreme court for judicial matters] 2e civ., November 21, 1990, No. 89-17.659 (Fr.) (finding malicious motive in abuse of right for failure to deliver the get).

Cour de cassation [Cass.] [supreme court for judicial matters] 2e civ., February 28, 2013, No. 12-18.856 (Fr.). (abuse of right for failure to deliver the get in absence of legitimate reason).

Craig v. Boren, 429 U.S. 190 (1976).

De Burca v. Attorney General, [1976] IR 38 (Ir.).

DeShaney v. Winnebago County Dep't of Social Services, 489 U.S. 189 (1989).

Eisenstadt v. Baird, 405 U.S. 438 (1972).

Fountain v. Draper, 49 Ind. 441 (Ind. 1875).

Friend v. Dunks, 37 Mich. 25 (Mich. 1877).

Frontiero v. Richardson, 411 U.S. 677 (1973).

Geduldig v. Aiello, 417 U.S. 484 (1974).

Goesaert v. Cleary, 335 U.S. 464 (1948).

Griswold v. Connecticut, 381 U.S. 479 (1965).

Harris v. McRae, 448 U.S. 297 (1980).

Hecht v. Superior Court, 59 Cal. Rptr. 2d 222 (Cal Ct. App. 1996).

Hoyt v. Florida, 368 U.S. 57 (1961).

J.E.B. v. Alabama ex rel. T.B., 511 U.S. 127 (1994).

June Medical Services v. Russo, 140 S. Ct. 2103 (2020).

Kelly v. Solari, [1841] 9 M. & W. 54, 152 ER. 24 (Eng.).

L. v. L., [1992] 2 IR 77 (Ir.).

Lawrence v. Texas, 539 U.S. 558 (2003).

Lochner v. New York, 198 U.S. 45 (1905).

Loving v. Virginia, 388 U.S. 1 (1967).

Lowth v. Minister for Social Welfare, [1993] IR 339 (Ir.).

Marvin v. Marvin, 557 P.2d 106 (Cal. 1976).

Masri v. Masri, 55 Misc. 3d 487 (N.Y. Sup. Ct. Orange County 2017).

McGee v. Attorney General [1974] IR 284 (Ir.).

Meland v. Weber, 2021 WL 6118651 (E.D. Cal. 2021).

Meyer v. Nebraska, 262 U.S. 390 (1923).

Michael M. v. Superior Court, 450 U.S. 464 (1981).

Mississippi Univ. for Women v. Hogan, 458 U.S. 718 (1982).

Moore v. Regents of the University of California, 249 Cal. Rptr. 484 (Cal. Ct. App. 1988).

Moritz v. Commissioner of Internal Revenue, 469 F.2d 466 (10th Cir. 1972).

Moses v. Macferlan, [1760] 2 Burr. 1005, 97 Eng. Rep. 676. (Eng.).

Mugler v. Kansas, 123 U.S. 623 (1887).

National Coalition for Men v. Selective Service System, 141 S. Ct. 1815 (Mem.) (2021).

Nevada v. Hibbs, 538 U.S. 721 (2003).

Olmstead v. United States, 277 U.S. 438 (1928).

Pennsylvania Coal Co. v. Mahon, 260 U.S. 393 (1922).

Pierce v. Society of Sisters, 268 U.S. 510 (1925).

Planned Parenthood of Southeastern Pennsylvania v. Casey, 505 U.S. 833 (1992).

Reed v. Reed, 404 U.S. 71 (1971).

Roberts v. Jaycees, 468 U.S. 609 (1984).

Roe v. Wade, 410 U.S. 113 (1973).

Rostker v. Goldberg, 453 U.S. 57 (1981).

Salzman v. Bachrach, 996 P.2d 1263 (Colo. 2000).

Schneider v. Hosier, 21 Ohio St. 96 (Ohio 1871).

Seidenburg v. McSorley's Old Ale House, Inc., 317 F. Supp. 593 (S.D.N.Y. 1970).

Sessions v. Morales-Santana, 137 S. Ct. 1678 (2017).

Sinnott v. Minister for Education, [2001] 2 I.R. 545 (Ir.).

Skinner v. Oklahoma, 316 U.S. 535 (1942).

Struck v. Secretary of Defense, 480 F.2d 1372 (9th Cir. 1971).

Supreme Court of Iceland, Complaints by Odin Sigthorsson, Skafti Hardarson, Thorgrimur S. Thorgrimsson, Decision of January 25, 2011 (Iceland).

T. v. T., [2002] IESC 68 (Ir.).

Thüringer Verfassungsgerichtshof [ThVerfGH] [Thuringia Constitutional Court], July 15, 2020, VerfGH 2/20 (Ger.) (state law requiring gender parity in political party candidate lists for legislature).

Troupe v. May Department Stores, 20 F.3d 734 (7th Cir. 1994).

United States v. Virginia, 518 U.S. 515 (1996).

Verfassungsgericht des Landes Brandenburg,[VfGBbg] [Constitutional Court of the State of Brandenburg], VfGBg 9/19, October 23, 2020, ¶ 165 (Ger.) (state law requiring gender parity in political party candidate lists for state legislature).

Weinberger v. Wiesenfeld, 420 U.S. 636 (1975).

Whole Women's Health v. Hellerstedt, 136 S. Ct. 2292 (2016).

Woods v. Horton, 167 Cal. App. 4th 658 (Cal. Ct. App. 2008).

Wynehamer v. People, 13 N.Y. 378 (N.Y. 1856).

Young v. United Parcel Service, Inc., 575 U.S. 206 (2015).

CONSTITUENT ASSEMBLY DEBATES

France (1946)
Journal Officiel de la République Française [Official Journal], Assemblée
Nationale, Débats Parlementaires de la 4ème République et Constituantes,
June–October 1946. http://4e.republique.jo-an.fr/.

Germany (Weimar, 1919)
*Deutsche Nationalversammlung im jahre 1919 in ihrer Arbeit für den Aufbau
des neuen deutschen Volksstaates* [German National Assembly in 1919 in
their work for the establishment of a new German republic]. Vols. 1–9.
Berlin: Norddeutsche buchdruckerei und verlagsanstalt 1920.

Germany (Bonn, 1948–49)
Parlamentarischer Rat, Verhandlung des Hauptausschusses [Constituent
Assembly debates]. Bonn: Bonner Universitäts-Buchdr, 1949.

Ireland (1937)
Bunreacht na hÉireann, Dáil, May 11, 1937. www.oireachtas.ie/en/debates
/debate/dail/1937-05-11/29/.

Italy (1947–48)
*Assemblea Costituente della Repubblica Italiana, June 2, 1946–January 31,
1948.* Rome: Segretariato generale della Camera dei deputati, Uficio studi
legislative, 1949.

PROPOSED CONSTITUTIONAL REFORMS

Chile
Propuesta Constitución Política de la República de Chile, July 4, 2022. www
.chileconvencion.cl/wp-content/uploads/2022/08/Texto-CPR-2022-
entregado-al-Pdte-y-publicado-en-la-web-el-4-de-julio.pdf. Translation
by Progressive International available at https://act.progressive
.international/newchile/.

Iceland
Constitutional Council. *A Proposal for a New Constitution for the Republic of
Iceland.* 2011. http://stjornlagarad.is/other_files/stjornlagarad/Frumvarp-
enska.pdf.

REPORTS BY GOVERNMENT ENTITIES

France

Sénat. *Etude d'impact, Projet de loi pour l'égalité entre les femmes et les hommes,* NOR: DFEX1313602L/Bleue-1. July 1, 2013. www.senat.fr/leg/etudes-impact/pjl12-717-ei/pjl12-717-ei.html.

Iceland

Iceland Special Investigation Commission. *Antecedents and Causes of the Collapse of the Icelandic Banks in 2008 and Related Events.* April 12, 2010. English translation excerpts at www.rna.is/eldri-nefndir/addragandi-og-orsakir-falls-islensku-bankanna-2008/skyrsla-nefndarinnar/english/.

Ireland

Ireland Citizens' Assembly. *First Report and Recommendations of the Citizens' Assembly, The Eighth Amendment to the Constitution.* June 29, 2017. https://2016-2018.citizensassembly.ie/en/The-Eighth-Amendment-of-the-Constitution/.

———. *Report of the Citizens' Assembly on Gender Equality.* June 2021. www.citizensassembly.ie/en/previous-assemblies/2020-2021-citizens-assembly-on-gender-equality/about-the-citizens-assembly/report-of-the-citizens-assembly-on-gender-equality.pdf.

Ireland Citizens' Assembly 2016–2018. *Eighth Amendment, Recommendations.* https://2016-2018.citizensassembly.ie/en/The-Eighth-Amendment-of-the-Constitution/.

Ireland Convention on the Constitution. *Second Report of the Convention on the Constitution, (i) Amending the clause on the role of women in the home and encouraging greater participation of women in public life; and (ii) Increasing the participation of women in politics.* May 2013. www.constitutionalconvention.ie/AttachmentDownload.ashx?mid=268d9308-c9b7-e211-a5a0-005056a32ee4.

Ireland Houses of the Oireachtas, Joint Committee on Justice and Equality. *Report on Pre-Legislative Scrutiny of the General Scheme of the 38th Amendment of the Constitution (Role of Women) Bill, 32/JAE/31.* December 2018.

Sweden

Government Offices, Ministry of Employment. *Gender Equality Policy in Sweden: A Feminist Government.* March 7, 2019. www.government.se/information-material/2019/03/gender-equality-policy-in-sweden/.

Sveriges Riksdag. *The Constitution of Sweden: The Fundamental Laws and the Riksdag Act* ((Stockholm: Sveriges Riksdag, 2016). www.riksdagen.se /globalassets/07.-dokument—lagar/the-constitution-of-sweden-160628 .pdf.

REPORTS BY NONGOVERNMENTAL ORGANIZATIONS

Centre for Gender Equality Iceland. *Gender Equality in Iceland*. February 2012. www.althingi.is/pdf/wip/Gender_Equality_in_Iceland_2012 .pdf.

Einarsdottir, Thorgerdur, and Gyda Margret Petursdottir. "An Analysis of the Report of Althing's Special Investigation Commission from a Gender Perspective." September 2010. https://rm.coe.int/16806ccff4.

Stevenson, Betsey. "The Initial Impact of COVID-19 on Labor Market Outcomes across Groups and the Potential for Permanent Scarring." Essay 2020-16, The Hamilton Project, July 2020. www.hamiltonproject.org/assets/files/Stevenson _LO_FINAL.pdf?_ga=2.16007601.608379579.1628178750-1815969472 .1628178750.

World Bank. "Labor Force Participation Rate, Female (% of Female Population Ages 15-64) (modeled ILO estimate)—Italy." Data as of June 2021. https:// data.worldbank.org/indicator/SL.TLF.ACTI.FE.ZS?locations=IT.

World Bank Group, *Women, Business, and the Law 2022*. March 1, 2022. https://wbl.worldbank.org/en/reports.

World Economic Forum. *Global Gender Gap Report 2021*. March 2021. www .weforum.org/reports/global-gender-gap-report-2021/.

SECONDARY SOURCES

Agacinski, Sylviane. *Parity of the* Sexes. Translated by Lisa Walsh. New York: Columbia University Press, 1998.

Alexy, Robert. *A Theory of Constitutional Rights*. Oxford: Oxford University Press, 2002.

Allen, Ann Taylor. *Feminism and Motherhood in Germany*. New Brunswick, NJ: Rutgers University Press, 1991.

Ambrose, Hugh. *Liberated Spirits: Two Women Who Battled over Prohibition*. New York: Penguin Random House, 2018.

Anthony, Katherine. *Feminism in Germany and Scandinavia*. New York: Holt, 1915.

Arenberg, Richard A., and Robert B. Dove. *Defending the Filibuster: The Soul of the Senate*. Bloomington: Indiana University Press, 2014.

Arter, David. "The Swedish Riksdag: The Case of a Strong Policy-Influencing Assembly." *West European Politics* 13, no. 3 (1990): 120–142.

Barsotti, Vittoria, Paolo G. Carozza, Marta Cartabia, and Andrea Simoncini. *Italian Constitutional Justice in Global Context*. Oxford: Oxford University Press, 2016.

Bebel, August. *Woman under Socialism*. Translated by Daniel De Leon. New York: New York Labor News Press, 1904.

Beienburg, Sean. *Prohibition, the Constitution, and States' Rights*. Chicago: University of Chicago Press, 2019.

Bergallo, Paola. "The Struggle against Informal Rules on Abortion in Argentina." In *Abortion Law in Transnational Perspective: Cases and Controversies*, edited by Rebecca J. Cook, Joanna N. Erdman, and Bernard M. Dickens, 143–65. Philadelphia: University of Pennsylvania Press, 2014.

Biggs, M. Antonia, Heather Gould, and Diana Greene Foster. "Understanding Why Women Seek Abortions in the U.S." *BMC Women's Health* 13 (2013): art. no. 29.

Birks, Peter. *Unjust Enrichment*. Oxford: Oxford University Press, 2005.

Bittenbender, Ada. *The National Prohibitory Amendment Guide*. Chicago: Woman's Temperance Publication Association, 1889.

Black, Lynsey, and Peter Dunne. *Law and Gender in Modern Ireland: Critique and Reform*. Oxford: Hart, 2019.

Blocher, Joseph. "Bans." *Yale Law Journal* 129, no. 2 (2019): 308–77.

Blocker, Jack S., Jr. *American Temperance Movements: Cycles of Reform*. Boston: Twayne, 1988.

———. *"Give to the Winds Thy Fears": The Women's Temperance Crusade, 1873–74*. Westport, CT: Greenwood Press, 1985.

Bolgár, Vera. "Abuse of Rights in France, Germany, and Switzerland: Survey of a Recent Chapter in Legal Doctrine." *Louisiana Law Review* 35, no. 5 (1975): 1015–36.

Bordin, Ruth. *Frances Willard: A Biography*. Chapel Hill: University of North Carolina Press, 1986.

———. *Woman and Temperance: The Quest for Power and Liberty, 1873–1900*. Philadelphia: Temple University Press, 1981.

Bridges, Khiara. *The Poverty of Privacy Rights*. Stanford, CA: Stanford University Press, 2017.

———. "Racial Disparities in Maternal Mortality." *New York University Law Review* 95, no. 5 (2020): 1229–1318.

Cahill, Maria, Colm Ó Cinnéide, Seán Ó Conaill, and Conor O'Mahony. *Constitutional Change and Popular Sovereignty: Populism, Politics, and the Law in Ireland*. London: Routledge, 2021.

Cahillane, Laura. "Revisiting Article 41.2." *Dublin University Law Journal* 40, no. 2 (2017): 107–26.

Cantarella, Eva. "Women and Patriarchy in Roman Law." In *The Oxford Handbook of Roman Law and Society*, by Paul DuPlessis, Clifford Ando, and Kaius Tuori, chap. 32. Oxford: Oxford University Press, 2016.

Case, Mary Anne. "Perfectionism and Fundamentalism in the Application of German Abortion Laws." *Florida International University Law Review* 11, no. 1 (2015): 149–62.

Chartier, Daniel. *The End of Iceland's Innocence: The Image of Iceland in the Foreign Media during the Crisis*. Ottawa: University of Ottawa Press, 2011.

Clark, Norman H. *Deliver Us from Evil: An Interpretation of American Prohibition*. New York: Norton, 1976.

Congleton, Roger D. *Improving Democracy through Constitutional Reform: Some Swedish Lessons*. Boston: Springer, 2003.

Coogan, Tim Pat. *De Valera: Long Fellow, Long Shadow*. London: Hutchinson, 1993.

Cott, Nancy F. *The Grounding of Modern Feminism*. New Haven, CT: Yale University Press, 1987.

Crenshaw, Kimberlé. "Mapping the Margins: Intersectionality, Identity Politics, and Violence against Women." *Stanford Law Review* 43, no. 6 (1991): 1241–99.

Crittenden, Ann. *The Price of Motherhood: Why the Most Important Job in the World Is Still the Least Valued*. New York: Henry Holt, 2001.

Dahlström, Edmund. *The Changing Roles of Men and Women*. Boston: Beacon Press, 1967.

Davis, Angela Y. *Women, Race, and Class*. New York: Knopf Doubleday, 1983.

Dawson, John P. *Unjust Enrichment: A Comparative Analysis*. Boston: Little, Brown, 1951.

De Beauvoir, Simone. *The Second Sex*. Translated by Constance Borde and Sheila Malovany Chevallier. New York: Vintage, 2011. Originally published as *Le deuxième sexe* (Paris: Gallimard, 1949).

Degler, Carl N. *At Odds: Women and the Family in America from the Revolution to the Present*. Oxford: Oxford University Press, 1981.

Dhir, Aaron. *Challenging Boardroom Homogeneity: Corporate Law, Governance, and Diversity*. New York: Cambridge University Press, 2015.

Di Robilant, Anna. "Abuse of Rights: The Continental Drug and the Common Law." *Hastings Law Journal* 61, no. 3 (2010): 687–748.

Dinner, Deborah. "The Costs of Reproduction: History and the Legal Construction of Sex Equality." *Harvard Civil Rights–Civil Liberties Law Review* 46, no. 2 (2011): 415–96.

Doyle, Oran. *The Constitution of Ireland: A Contextual Analysis*. Oxford: Hart, 2018.

Drachman, Virginia. *Women Lawyers and the Origins of Professional Identity in America: The Letters of the Equity Club, 1887 to 1890*. Ann Arbor: University of Michigan Press, 1993.

Earner-Byrne, Lindsey, and Diana Urquhart. *The Irish Abortion Journey, 1920–2018*. Basingstoke: Palgrave Macmillan, 2019.

Eichner, Maxine. *The Free-Market Family: How the Market Crushed the American Dream (and How It Can Be Restored)*. Oxford: Oxford University Press, 2020.

Engels, Friedrich. *The Origins of the Family, Private Property, and the State*. Edited by Tristram Hunt. 1884. Reprint, New York: Penguin, 2010.

Epstein, Barbara Leslie. *The Politics of Domesticity: Women, Evangelism, and Temperance in Nineteenth-Century America*. Middletown, CT: Wesleyan University Press, 1981.

Epstein, Richard A. *Takings: Private Property and the Power of Eminent Domain*. Cambridge, MA: Harvard University Press, 1984.

Eser, Albin. "Reform of German Abortion Law." *American Journal of Comparative Law* 34, no. 2 (1986): 369–83.

Esping-Andersen, Gosta. *The Incomplete Revolution: Adapting to Women's New Roles*. Cambridge: Polity Press, 2009.

Evans, Richard J. *The Feminist Movement in Germany, 1894–1933*. London: Sage Publications, 1976.

Ewald, William. "Comparative Jurisprudence I: What Was It Like to Try a Rat?" *University of Pennsylvania Law Review* 143, no. 6 (1995): 1889–2150.

Farrell, Brian, ed. *De Valera's Constitution and Ours*. Dublin: Gil and Macmillan, 1988.

Farrell, Warren. *The Myth of Male Power: Why Men Are the Disposable Sex*. New York: Simon and Schuster, 1993.

Federici, Silvia. *Patriarchy of the Wage: Notes on Marx, Gender, and Feminism*. New York: PM Press, 2021.

———. *Revolution at Point Zero: Housework, Reproduction, and Feminist Struggle*. New York: PM Press, 2020.

Fineman, Martha Albertson. *The Autonomy Myth: A Theory of Dependency*. New York: New Press, 2004.

———. *The Neutered Mother, the Sexual Family, and Other Twentieth Century Tragedies*. New York: Routledge, 1995.

Fisk, Catherine, and Erwin Chemerinsky. "The Filibuster." *Stanford Law Review* 49, no. 2 (1997): 181–254.

Folbre, Nancy. *The RIse and Decline of Patriarchal Systems*. London: Verso, 2021.

Foster, J. Ellen. *Constitutional Amendment Manual, Containing Argument, Appeal, Petitions, Forms of Constitution, Catechism and General Directions for Organized Work for Constitutional Prohibition*. New York: National Temperance Society and Publication House, 1882.

———. *The Saloon Must Go*. New York: National Temperance Society and Publication House, 1889.

Franklin, Cary. "The Anti-stereotyping Principle in Constitutional Sex Discrimination Law." *New York University Law Review* 85, no. 1 (2010): 83–173.

Frevert, Ute. *Women in German History: From Bourgeois Emancipation to Sexual Liberation*. Oxford: Berg, 1989.

Friedan, Betty. *The Feminine Mystique*. New York: Norton, 1963.

Gardner, Jane F. *Women in Roman Law and Society*. London: Routledge, 1996.

Gaspard, Françoise, Claude Servan-Schreiber, and Anne Le Gall. *Au pouvoir, citoyennes! Liberté, Egalité, Parité*. Paris: Editions du Seuil, 1992.

Gifford, Carolyn de Swarte, and Amy R. Slagell. *Let Something Good Be Said: Speeches and Writings of Frances E. Willard*. Urbana: University of Illinois Press, 2007.

Gilman, Charlotte Perkins. *Women and Economics: A Study of the Economic Relation between Men and Women as a Factor in Social Evolution*. Boston: Small, Maynard, 1898.

Ginsburg, Ruth Bader. *Justice, Justice Thou Shalt Pursue*. Berkeley: University of California Press, 2021.

Ginsburg, Ruth Bader, and Anders Bruzelius. *Civil Procedure in Sweden*. The Hague: M. Nijhoff, 1965.

Ginsburg, Tom, and Aziz Huq. *Assessing Constitutional Performance*. Cambridge: Cambridge University Press, 2016.

Glendon, Mary Ann. *Abortion and Divorce in Western Law: American Failures, European Challenges*. Cambridge, MA: Harvard University Press, 1987.

Goldin, Claudia. *Career and Family: Women's Century-Long Journey toward Equity*. Princeton, NJ: Princeton University Press, 2021.

Goodwin, Michele. *Policing the Womb: Invisible Women and the Criminalization of Motherhood*. Cambridge: Cambridge University Press, 2020.

Gordon, Anna. *The Beautiful Life of Frances E. Willard*. Chicago: Woman's Temperance Publishing Association, 1898.

Gordon, Elizabeth Putnam. *Women Torch-Bearers: The Story of the Woman's Christian Temperance Union*. Evanston, IL: National Woman's Christian Temperance Union Publishing House, 1924.

Grace, Fran. *Carry A. Nation: Retelling the Life*. Bloomington: Indiana University Press, 2001.

Gusfeld, Joseph R. *Symbolic Crusade: Status Politics and the American Temperance Movement*. Urbana: University of Illinois Press, 1963.

Gutteridge, H. C. "Abuse of Rights." *Cambridge Law Journal* 5, no. 1 (1933): 22–45.

Hamm, Richard. *Shaping the Eighteenth Amendment: Temperance Reform, Legal Culture, and the Polity, 1880–1920.* Chapel Hill: University of North Carolina Press, 1995.

Hartog, Hendrik. *Man and Wife in America: A History.* Cambridge, MA: Harvard University Press, 2000.

Hesketh, Tom. *The Second Partitioning of Ireland? The Abortion Referendum of 1983.* Dublin: Brandsma Books, 1990.

Hochschild, Arlie Russell. *The Second Shift.* New York: Penguin Books, 1989.

Holland, Kitty. *Savita: The Tragedy That Shook a Nation.* Dublin: Transworld Ireland, 2013.

Jackson, Vicki. *Constitutional Engagement in a Transnational Era.* Oxford: Oxford University Press, 2010.

Jaeger, Renate. "The Federal Constitutional Court: Fifty Years of the Struggle for Gender Equality." *German Law Journal* 2 (2001): art. no. 35.

Jentleson, Adam. *Kill Switch: The Rise of the Modern Senate and the Crippling of American Democracy.* New York: Liveright, 2021.

Johnson, Janet Elise, Thorgadur Einarsdóttir, and Gyda Margrét Pétursdóttir. "A Feminist Theory of Corruption: Lessons from Iceland." *Politics and Gender* 9 (2013): 174–206.

Kagan, Robert A. *Adversarial Legalism: The American Way of Law.* Cambridge, MA: Harvard University Press, 2001.

Kanowitz, Leo. *Equal Rights: The Male Stake.* Albuquerque: University of New Mexico Press, 1981.

Kelsey, Jane. "A Gendered Response to Financial Crisis: What Can Others Learn from Iceland?" *Oñati Socio-Legal Series* 6, no. 1 (2016): 8–25.

Kepley, Ada. *A Farm Philosopher: A Love Story.* Teutopolis, IL: Worman's Printery, 1912.

Kerber, Linda. *No Constitutional Right to Be Ladies: Women and the Obligations of Citizenship.* New York: Hill and Wang, 1998.

Kessler, Friedrich, and Edith Fine. "Culpa in Contrahendo, Bargaining in Good Faith, and Freedom of Contract: A Comparative Study." *Harvard Law Review* 77, no. 3 (1964): 401–49.

Key, Ellen. "Motherliness." *Atlantic Monthly,* October 1912, 562–70.

Kollontai, Alexandra. *Selected Writings.* New York: Lawrence Hill, 1980.

Koppelman, Andrew. "Forced Labor: A Thirteenth Amendment Defense of Abortion." *Northwestern University Law Review* 84, no. 2 (1989): 480–535.

Kristmundsdóttir, Sigrídur Dúna. *Doing and Becoming: Women's Movements and Women's Personhood in Iceland 1870–1990.* Reykjavík: Social Science Research Institute, University Press, University of Iceland, 1997.

Kyvig, David. *Repealing National Prohibition.* Kent, OH: Kent State University Press, 2000.

Landau, David, and Manuel José Cepeda Espinosa. *Colombian Constitutional Law: Leading Cases*. Oxford: Oxford University Press, 2017.

Landemore, Hélène. "Inclusive Constitution-Making: The Icelandic Experiment." *Journal of Political Philosophy* 23, no. 2 (2015): 166–91.

———. *Open Democracy: Reinventing Popular Rule for the Twenty-First Century*. Princeton, NJ: Princeton University Press, 2020.

Laycock, Douglas. "Restoring Restitution to the Canon." *Michigan Law Review* 110, no. 6 (2012): 929–52.

Lemaitre, Julieta. "Catholic Constitutionalism on Sex, Women, and the Beginning of Life." In *Abortion Law in Transnational Perspective: Cases and Controversies*, edited by Rebecca J. Cook, Joanna N. Erdman, and Bernard M. Dickens, 239–57. Philadelphia: University of Pennsylvania Press, 2014.

Lerner, Gerda. *The Creation of Feminist Consciousness*. Oxford: Oxford University Press, 1993.

———. *The Creation of Patriarchy*. Oxford: Oxford University Press, 1987.

Levmore, Saul. "Explaining Restitution." *Virginia Law Review* 71, no. 1 (1985): 65–124.

Luker, Kristin. *Abortion and the Politics of Motherhood*. Berkeley: University of California Press, 1984.

MacKinnon, Catharine. "Feminism, Marxism, Method, and the State: Toward Feminist Jurisprudence." *Signs* 8, no. 4 (1983): 635–58.

———. *Feminism Unmodified: Discourses on Life and Law*. Cambridge, MA: Harvard University Press, 1987.

———. *Sexual Harassment of Working Women*. New Haven, CT: Yale University Press, 1979.

———. *Toward a Feminist Theory of the State*. Cambridge, MA: Harvard University Press, 1991.

Manne, Kate. *Down Girl: The Logic of Misogyny*. Oxford: Oxford University Press, 2017.

———. *Entitled: How Male Privilege Hurts Women*. New York: Crown, 2020.

Mayeri, Serena. *Reasoning from Race: Feminism, Law and the Civil Rights Revolution*. Cambridge, MA: Harvard University Press, 2014.

McCulloch, Catharine Waugh. *Mr. Lex, or the Legal Status of Mother and Child*. Chicago: F. H. Revell, 1899.

McGirr, Lisa. *The War on Alcohol: Prohibition and the Rise of the American State*. New York: Norton, 2016.

Moeller, Robert G. *Protecting Motherhood: Women and the Family in the Politics of Postwar West Germany*. Berkeley: University of California Press, 1993.

Monopoli, Paula. *Constitutional Orphan: Gender Equality and the Nineteenth Amendment*. Oxford: Oxford University Press, 2020.

Mullally, Una. *Repeal the 8th*. London: Unbound, 2018.

Murdock, Catherine Gilbert. *Domesticating Drink: Women, Men, and Alcohol in America, 1870–1940*. Baltimore: Johns Hopkins University Press, 2002.

Murray, Melissa. "Race-ing Roe: Reproductive Justice, Racial Justice, and the Battle for Roe v. Wade." *Harvard Law Review* 134, no. 6 (2021): 2025–2101.

Murray, Pauli. "The Negro Woman's Stake in the Equal Rights Amendment." *Harvard Civil Rights–Civil Liberties Law Review* 6, no. 2 (1971): 253–59.

Murray, Pauli, and Mary O. Eastwood. "Jane Crow and the Law: Sex Discrimination and TItle VII." *George Washington Law Review* 34, no. 2 (1965): 232–56.

Myrdal, Alva, and Viola Klein. *Women's Two Roles: Home and Work*. London: Routledge, 1956.

NeJaime, Dougla. "The Nature of Parenthood." *Yale Law Journal* 126, no. 8 (2017): 2260–2381.

Nicholas, Barry. *An Introduction to Roman Law*. Oxford: Oxford University Press, 1962.

Norgren, Jill. *Rebels at the Bar: The Fascinating, Forgotten Stories of America's First Women Lawyers*. New York: New York University Press, 2013.

———. *Stories from Trailblazing Women Lawyers*. New York: New York University Press, 2018.

Okin, Susan Moller. *Justice, Gender, and the Family*. New York: Basic Books, 1989.

———. *Women in Western Political Thought*. Princeton, NJ: Princeton University Press, 1979.

Okrent, Daniel. *Last Call: The Rise and Fall of Prohibition*. New York: Scribner, 2010.

Palme, Olof. "The Emancipation of Man." Address by Mr. Olof Palme, Swedish Prime Minister at the Women's National Democratic Club, Washington, DC, June 8, 1970. www.olofpalme.org/wp-content/dokument/700608_emancipation_of_man.pdf.

Parsons, Elaine Frantz. *Manhood Lost: Fallen Drunkards and Redeeming Women in the Nineteenth-Century United States*. Baltimore: Johns Hopkins University Press, 2003.

Pateman, Carole. *The Disorder of Women: Democracy, Feminism, and Political Theory*. Stanford, CA: Stanford University Press, 1989.

Peñalver, Eduardo M., and Lior Jacob Strahilevitz. "Judicial Takings or Due Process?" *Cornell Law Review* 97, no. 2 (2012): 305–68.

Peters, Anne. *Women, Quotas, and Constitutions: A Comparative Study of Affirmative Action for Women under American, German, EC, and International Law*. The Hague: Kluwer Law International, 1999.

Piscopo, Jennifer, and Peter Siavelis. "Chile's Constitutional Moment." *Current History* 120, no. 823 (2021): 43–49.

Pore, Renate. *A Conflict of Interest: Women in German Social Democracy, 1919–1933*. Westport: Greenwood Press, 1981.

Quataert, Jean H. *Reluctant Feminists in German Social Democracy*. Princeton, NJ: Princeton University Press, 1979.

Reagan, Leslie J. *When Abortion Was a Crime: Women, Medicine and Law in the United States, 1867–1973*. Berkeley: University of California Press, 1997.

Rebouché, Rachel. "Comparative Pragmatism." *Maryland Law Review* 72, no. 1 (2012): 85–155.

Rich, Adrienne. *Of Woman Born: Motherhood as Experience and Institution*. New York: Norton, 1986.

Roberts, Dorothy. *Killing the Black Body: Race, Reproduction, and the Meaning of Liberty*. New York: Penguin Random House, 1997.

Rogers, R. Vashon, Jr. *Drinks, Drinkers, and Drinking, or, The Law and History of Intoxicating Liquors*. Albany, NY: Weed, Parsons, 1881.

Rose, Kenneth D. *American Women and the Repeal of Prohibition*. New York: New York University Press, 1996.

Rotskoff, Lori. *Love on the Rocks: Men, Women, and Alcohol in Post-World War II America*. Chapel Hill: University of North Carolina Press, 2002.

Rubio-Marín, Ruth. "The (Dis)establishment of Gender: Care and Gender Roles in the Family as a Constitutional Matter." *International Journal of Constitutional Law* 13, no. 4 (2015): 787–818.

Rubio-Marín, Ruth, and Beverly Baines. *The Gender of Constitutional Jurisprudence*. New York: Cambridge University Press, 2004.

Rubio-Marín, Ruth, and Blanca Rodriguez-Ruiz. "Constitutional Justification of Parity Democracy." *Alabama Law Review* 60, no. 5 (2009): 1171–96.

Rudolphy, Marcela Prieto. "Symposium on Chilean Referendum Part III: A Feminist Rethinking of the Chilean Constitution?" *International Journal of Constitutional Law Blog*, November 2020. www.iconnectblog.com/2020/11/symposium-on-chilean-referendum-part-iii-a-feminist-rethinking-of-the-chilean-constitution/.

Rudolphy, Marcela, and Sergio Verdugo. "Understanding Chile's Constitution-Making Procedure." *International Journal of Constitutional Law* 19, no. 1 (2021): 1–5.

Sanger, Alexander. *Beyond Choice: Reproductive Freedom in the 21st Century*. New York: PublicAffairs, 2004.

Sanger, Carol. *About Abortion: Terminating Pregnancy in Twenty-First Century America*. Cambridge, MA: The Belknap Press of Harvard University Press, 2017.

———. "Infant Safe Haven Laws: Legislating the Culture of Life." *Columbia Law Review* 106, no. 4 (2006): 753–829.

Sax, Joseph L. "Takings and the Police Power." *Yale Law Journal* 74, no. 1 (1964): 36–77.

Scales, Ann. *Legal Feminism: Activism, Lawyering, and Legal Theory*. New York: New York University Press, 2006.

Scannell, Yvonne. "The Constitution and the Role of Women." In *De Valera's Constitution and Ours*, edited by Brian Farrell, 123–36. Dublin: Gil and Macmillan, 1988.

Schrad, Mark Lawrence. *Smashing the Liquor Machine: A Global History of Prohibition*. Oxford: Oxford University Press, 2021.

Scott, Hilda. *Sweden's "Right to Be Human": Sex Role Equality: The Goal and the Reality*. London: Routledge, 1982.

Scott, Joan Wallach. *Parité! Sexual Equality and the Crisis of French Universalism*. Chicago: University of Chicago Press, 2005.

Sherwin, Emily. "Reparations and Unjust Enrichment." *Boston University Law Review* 84, no. 5 (2004): 1443–66.

Siegel, Reva B. "Home as Work: The First Woman's Rights Claims Concerning Wives' Household Labor, 1850–1880." *Yale Law Journal* 103 (1994): 1073–1217.

———. "Prochoicelife: Asking Who Protects Life and How—and Why It Matters in Law and Politics." *Indiana Law Journal* 93, no. 1 (2018): 207–32.

———. "'The Rule of Love': Wife Beating as Prerogative and Privacy." *Yale Law Journal* 105 (1996): 2117–2207.

Sklar, Kathryn Kish, Anja Schüler, and Susan Strasser. *Social Justice Feminists in the United States and Germany: A Dialogue in Documents*. Ithaca, NY: Cornell University Press, 1998.

Skocpol, Theda. *Protecting Soldiers and Mothers: The Political Origins of Social Policy in the United States*. Cambridge, MA: The Belknap Press of Harvard University Press, 1992.

Slaughter, Anne-Marie. *Unfinished Business: Women, Men, Work, Family*. New York: Random House, 2015.

Srinivasan, Amia. *The Right to Sex*. New York: Farrar, Straus and Giroux, 2021.

Stewart, Mother. *Memories of the Crusade: A Thrilling Account of the Great Uprising of the Women of Ohio in 1873, against the Liquor Crime*. Columbus, OH: Wm. G. Hubbard, 1888.

Suiter, Jane, Kirsty Park, Yvonne Galligan, and David M. Farrell. "Evaluation Report of the Irish Citizens' Assembly on Gender Equality." Independent Researchers Report, DCU Institute of Future Media, Democracy and Society, 2021. www.citizensassembly.ie/en/previous-assemblies/2020-2021-citizens-assembly-on-gender-equality/news-publications/publications/independent-researchers-report-on-the-process.pdf.

Suk, Julie C. "Are Gender Stereotypes Bad For Women? Rethinking Antidiscrimination Law and Work-Family Conflict." *Columbia Law Review* 110, no. 1 (2010): 1–69.

———. "An Equal Rights Amendment for the Twenty-First Century: Bringing Global Constitutionalism Home." *Yale Journal of Law and Feminism* 28, no. 2 (2017): 381–444.

———. "Gender Equality and the Protection of Motherhood in Global Constitutionalism." *Journal of Law and Ethics of Human Rights* 12, no. 1 (2018): 151–80.

———. "Gender Parity and State Legitimacy: From Public Office to Corporate Boards." *International Journal of Constitutional Law* 10, no. 2 (2012): 449–64.

———. *We the Women: The Unstoppable Mothers of the Equal Rights Amendment.* New York: Skyhorse, 2020.

Tambor, Molly. *The Lost Wave: Women and Democracy in Postwar Italy.* Oxford: Oxford University Press, 2014.

Teubner, Gunther. "Legal Irritants: Good Faith in British Law or How Unifying Law Ends Up in New Divergences." *Modern Law Review* 61, no. 1 (1998): 11–32.

Thomas, Tracy A. *Elizabeth Cady Stanton and the Feminist Foundations of Family Law.* New York: New York University Press, 2016.

Thomson, Judith Jarvis. "A Defense of Abortion." *Philosophy and Public Affairs* 1, no. 1 (1971): 47–66.

Thorarensen, Björg. "The Impact of the Financial Crisis on Icelandic Constitutional Law, Legislative Reforms, Judicial Review and Revision of the Constitution." In *Constitutions in the Global Financial Crisis: A Comparative Analysis,* edited by Xenophon Contiades, 263–83. Farnham, Surrey: Ashgate, 2013.

Thorsdottir, Thora Kristin. "Iceland: From Feminist Governance to Gender-Blind Austerity?" *Gender, Sexuality and Feminism* 1, no. 2 (2014): 24–41.

Tuerkheimer, Deborah. *Credible: Why We Doubt Accusers and Protect Abusers.* New York: HarperCollins, 2021.

Usborne, Cornelie. *Cultures of Abortion in Weimar Germany.* New York: Bergahn Books, 2011.

Vergara, Camila. "Chile Confounds." *New Left Review Sidecar,* June 2, 2021.

———. "Fear of Fascism, Hope for Popular Empowerment in Chile." *NACLA Report on the Americas* 54, no. 1 (2022): 7–10.

———. *Systemic Corruption: Constitutional Ideas for an Anti-oligarchic Republic.* Princeton, NJ: Princeton University Press, 2010.

Versteeg, Mila, and Adam Chilton. *How Constitutional Rights Matter.* Oxford: Oxford University Press, 2020.

Watson, Alan. *Legal Transplants: An Approach to Comparative Law.* Edinburgh: Scottish Academic Press, 1974.

Weinrib, Ernest. *Corrective Justice.* Oxford: Oxford University Press, 2012.

West, Robin. "From Choice to Reproductive Justice: De-constitutionalizing Abortion Rights." *Yale Law Journal* 118, no. 7 (2009): 1394–1433.

West, Robin, and Cynthia Grant Bowman. *Research Handbook on Feminist Jurisprudence*. Cheltenham: Edward Elgar, 2019.

Whitman, James Q. *The Legacy of Roman Law in the German Romantic Era: Historical Vision and Legal Change*. Princeton, NJ: Princeton University Press, 1990.

Willard, Frances Elizabeth. *Woman and Temperance, or, The Work and Workers of the Woman's Christian Temperance Union*. Chicago: J. S. Goodman, 1883.

Willard, Frances Elizabeth, and Mary A. Livermore. *American Women: Fifteen Hundred Biographies With Over 1,400 Portraits: A Comprehensive Encyclopedia of the Lives and Achievements of American Women During the Nineteenth Century*. New York: Mast, Crowell and Kirkpatrick, 1897.

Williams, Joan. *Unbending Gender: Why Family and Work Conflict and What to Do about It*. Oxford: Oxford University Press, 2000.

Wittenmyer, Annie. *History of the Woman's Temperance Crusade. A Complete Official History of the Wonderful Uprising of the Christian women of the United States against the Liquor Traffic, Which Culminated in the Gospel Temperance Movement*. Philadelphia: The Christian Woman, 1878.

Wolff, Hans Julius. *Roman Law: An Historical Introduction*. Norman: University of Oklahoma Press, 1951.

Zetkin, Clara. *Selected Writings*. Edited by Philip S. Foner. Chicago: Haymarket Books, 1984.

Ziegler, Mary. *Abortion and the Law in America: Roe v. Wade to the Present*. Cambridge: Cambridge University Press, 2020.

———. *After Roe: The Lost History of the Abortion Debate*. Cambridge, MA: Harvard University Press, 2015.

———. *Beyond Abortion: Roe v. Wade and the Battle for Privacy*. Cambridge, MA: Harvard Uniersity Press, 2018.

Index

Abbreviations used in this text, 241–43
Abortion
  access to, 47, 88–91, 96, 98, 107, 108,
    115–20, 201, 215, 227, 232
  bans on, as overentitlement, 21, 23–24, 88,
    93, 113–15, 118, 215–16
  funding restricted, US, 90
  German Constitutional Court decisions on,
    96–97, 99–103
  in Ireland, 105–13
  laws banning or restricting, 3, 21, 23–24,
    87–88, 92, 94, 95, 97, 104, 106, 109,
    115, 116, 117
  and misogyny, 113–14
  and reproductive justice, 91
  US Supreme Court decisions on, 87–88,
    92–93, 94–95
  See also *Dobbs v. Jackson Women's Health*
    (2022); *Roe v. Wade* (1973)
Abuse of power
  and #MeToo movement, 74–75
  as overempowerment, 74, 78
  in patriarchal legal regime (Roman law),
    83–84
  in public and administrative law (Germany),
    78–79
  sexual harassment as, 74
  See also Overempowerment

Abuse of right
  and duty of good faith, 78
  in French law, 75–78, 80–83, 260–61n82
  in German law, 78–80, 260n70
  as overempowerment, 11, 75, 84
  property disputes, 75–76, 77–78
  and purpose of right, 76–77, 85
  Roman law origins of, 83
  as a tort, 81
  withholding *guet* in Jewish divorce as,
    80–82, 260–61n82
  See also Overempowerment
ACLU (American Civil Liberties Union), 32,
  40, 52, 262n4
Adultery
  and divorce under Jewish law, 82
  Roman law asymmetric criminalization of, 6
  and Roman law power of life and death, 84
Affirmative action for women, 157, 167, 222–
  25, 290n45. *See also* Gender quotas;
  Men's rights advocates
Age of consent to sexual intercourse, 42, 46,
  145–46, 150
Alcohol consumption
  and campus sexual assaults, 40–41
  effects of Prohibition on, 150, 151, 154,
    273n94
  purchase age for near-beer, 38, 41

Alcohol consumption *(continued)*
  See also Liquor industry; Prohibition
    (Eighteenth Amendment); Temperance
    movement; Woman's Christian Temper-
    ance Union
Alito, Justice Samuel, 262n2
American Civil Liberties Union (ACLU), 32,
  40, 52, 262n4
American Rescue Plan (2021), 208
Anthony, Susan B., 185
Antidiscrimination law
  anti-stereotyping principle, 33, 36–37, 40,
    47–49, 50–51, 152–53
  formal equality, 14–15, 22–23, 31, 57–58
  and sex classifications, 8, 32–33
  tort-analogous remedies in, 23
  under US constitutional law, 8, 32, 37, 57
Argentina
  feminist protests in, 1
  legislation authorizing abortion, 115–16
  Supreme Court abortion decision (2012),
    116–17
Asian American women, 61–62, 256n9

Bachofen, Johann Jakob, 4, 5
Barrett, Justice Amy Coney, 220
Bartemeyer v. Iowa, 131–32
Basic Law, Germany, 78, 96, 99–101, 103–4,
  162, 164–65, 166, 186–87, 260n70
Bäumer, Gertrud, 185–86
Bebel, August, *Woman under Socialism*, 5
Belgium, corporate board minimum gender
  diversity law, 167
Bellinger v. Griffith, 131
Benediktsson, Bjarni, 177
Bergallo, Paola, 117
Bittenbender, Ada, 136, 137, 143–44, 147
Black feminism
  and domestic violence, 19–20
  and the Equal Rights Amendment, 19,
    291n59
  and families headed by women, 19, 20–21
  intersection of race, class, and gender, 12,
    18–21
  and juror exclusions, 19
  and motherhood, 19
  and poverty, 19
  See also Reproductive injustice; Reproduc-
    tive justice
Black Lives Matter, and structural racism, 21
Blackmun, Justice Harry, 43–45, 92, 93, 98,
  114–15, 118
Blackstone's *Commentaries*, on coverture, 6

Blair, Henry, 140
Bodily autonomy, 24, 112, 221, 262n8
Bradley, Justice Joseph P., 7, 73, 145
Bradwell, Myra, 140
Bradwell v. Illinois
  repudiated, 8
  and "separate spheres," 7, 73, 145
  and women lawyers, 7, 25, 128, 136, 137,
    140
Brennan, Justice William J., Jr., 38–39, 42,
  45–46
Breyer, Justice Stephen, 52
Bridges, Khiara, 20–21, 91, 247–48n76

Cady Stanton, Elizabeth, 7–8, 282n16
Califano v. Goldfarb, 35–37, 42
California
  corporate board minimum gender diversity
    law, 157, 167, 222–25, 290n45
  state disability leave and pregnancy, 91–92,
    263n19
  Unruh Civil Rights Act, 53, 54, 156–57,
    254n121
*California Federal S & L Ass'n v. Guerra (Cal
  Fed)*, 51, 252n103
Care, constitutionalism of, 15–26, 182–83,
  203–9
Care infrastructure, 25–26, 32, 56, 94, 181,
  199, 206–8, 216, 227–28, 229, 281n4
Cheng, Anne Anlin, 61
Childcare
  and COVID-19 policies (US), 208
  in German abortion jurisprudence,
    100–101
  Irish recommendations for public funding
    of, 204
  shared between men and women, 31
  Swedish policy, 31, 32, 56
  voter support for public provision of (US),
    208–9, 286n100
  See also Constitutional clauses protecting
    mothers; Maternity leave; Parental
    leave
Chile
  constituent assembly, 25, 178, 233
  gender parity, 25, 178, 233
  indigenous representation, 233
  military dictatorship in, 3
  proposed new constitution, 2, 25, 178, 233
  "A Rapist in Your Path" (protest anthem),
    1–2, 233, 234
Citizen participation in lawmaking, 207
  in Chile's constituent process, 178, 233

in Citizens' Assemblies in Ireland, 109–13, 202–7
in climate assemblies, 183, 207, 232–33, 286n96
in drafting of new constitution for Iceland, 172, 174–78
in the United States, 207, 231–33
Cleveland Board of Education v. Lafleur, 91
Climate change
citizens' assemblies on, 183, 207, 232–33
and US Constitution, 207
Colombia
Constitutional Court abortion decision (2006), 116
Constitutional Court abortion decision (2022), 115
decriminalization of abortion, 115
feminist protests, 1
Comparative constitutional law, 212–13
Comparative law
and cherry-picking, 212
John Dawson on unjust enrichment, 65
development of new paradigms, 213
empirical analysis, 212–13
engagement as approach to, 213
Ruth Bader Ginsburg's research on, 30
legal transplant, 55, 57, 213–14
prediction vs. persuasion as purpose of, 213
and restitution in US law, 64
as translation, 212
Concannon, Helena, 193–94, 201
Condictiones (Roman law of unjust enrichment), 64–65, 69
"The Conditional Emancipation of Woman" (Moberg), 30, 31
Constitution (US)
amendment process (Article V), 207–8, 215, 222, 229–33
Senate representation in, 229
See also Due Process Clause; Equal Protection Clause; Equal Rights Amendment (ERA); First Amendment; Nineteenth Amendment; Privacy, right to (US Constitution); Prohibition (Eighteenth Amendment); Takings Clause (Fifth Amendment); Thirteenth Amendment; Twenty-First Amendment
Constitutional clauses protecting mothers
in Chilean draft constitution, 178, 233
in French Constitution, 187–89, 231
in German Basic Law, 7, 99–100, 194–96
in Irish Constitution, 26, 191–94, 196–207, 231

in Italian Constitution, 187, 189–90
in Weimar Constitution (Germany), 182–86
Constitutional democracy, 10–11, 22, 25, 26, 178, 183, 211, 225, 233
Constitutional equality for women
debates about adoption of (Germany), 164–66
as eradicating existing disadvantages (Germany), 162–63, 167
and gender differentiation, 57–58, 59, 152, 158, 168–69, 181–82
and parity laws (France), 159–61
US litigation to prohibit sex discrimination, 32–37, 152–55
See also Equal Protection Clause; Equal Rights Amendment
Constitutionalism, 24, 88, 109, 120, 124, 140, 162, 180, 206, 207, 208, 214, 230, 234
Constitution making, women in, 9, 21–22
Contraceptive access
Eisenstadt v. Baird, 89
Griswold v. Connecticut, 89, 262n8
Ireland, 265–66n68
Corporate boards of directors
European Union legislation on gender balance on, 223
gender quotas in European countries, 159–60, 167, 173–74, 178, 205, 222, 223
minimum gender diversity law in California, 157, 167, 222–25, 290n45
Coverture, 6, 7, 73, 124–25, 144. *See also* Patriarchy, as legal system
COVID-19 pandemic
American Rescue Plan of 2021, 208
effects on children's education and care, 180, 181, 199
and Irish Citizens' Assembly, 202–3, 206
Marshall Plan for Moms, call for, 181, 199, 216, 281n4
and student tuition lawsuits, 63, 257n11
undervaluing of essential workers, 180–81, 203–4
women's sacrifices laid bare by, 25–26, 180–82, 208
Craig v. Boren, 38–41, 42
Crenshaw, Kimberlé, 19–20
Criminalization of abortion, 101, 103
Criminal law, rape, 12

Dahlström, Edmund, 31–32
Davis, Angela, 19

Dawson, John P., 64–65, 66, 258–59n42
De Beauvoir, Simone, *The Second Sex*, 4, 10, 49, 243n6
Declaration of Sentiments (1848, Elizabeth Cady Stanton), 7–8
Democracy
  entitlements in, 151, 212, 225
  as important governmental purpose, 224
  legitimacy of, 159, 173
  and power, 153, 158, 178–79, 207
  transition from patriarchy to, 8, 25, 73–74, 119, 123, 152, 212, 229, 233, 234
  See also Constitutional democracy; Parity between women and men
Denham, Judge Susan (Ireland), 197–98, 199
DeShaney v. Winnebago County Department of Social Services, 92
De Valera, Eamonn, 192–93, 194, 201
Dinner, Deborah, 263n19
Divorce
  frozen embryos as marital property in, 218
  and Irish motherhood protection, 197, 199–200, 231
  and men's rights litigation, 47
  and religion under French abuse of right doctrine, 80–82, 260–61n82
  and religion under New York legislation, 261n86
  and unjust enrichment, 70–71
Dobbs v. Jackson Women's Health (2022), 87, 88, 94, 207–8, 220, 227, 230, 232, 262nn2,4, 286n97
Domestic violence
  as allowed by patriarchy, 7, 8, 73, 228
  and intersectional feminism, 19–20
  shelters and men's rights litigation, 52–53, 253–54nn113,119
  and women's temperance movement, 40, 126, 127
Due Process Clause
  abortion rights in, 90
  and contraceptives, 89, 265–66nn68
  and mandatory unpaid maternity leave, 91
  and police power of the state, 143
  privacy rights in, 89
  and property rights of liquor sellers, 132, 270n37
  as protecting negative freedom of choice, 90, 92

Eighteenth Amendment. *See* Prohibition
Eisenstadt v. Baird, 89
Electoral college, 230

Ellis, Margaret Dye, 144
"The Emancipation of Man" (Olof Palme), 30–31, 32, 35, 55
Engels, Friedrich, 4, 5, 49
Equal pay, 53–54, 161, 189, 226
Equal Protection Clause
  and abortion bans, 93
  exclusion of pregnancy from disability benefits, 91–92
  gender-based peremptory strikes under, 47–49
  gender stereotypes scrutinized under, 34–38, 45, 48, 56, 58, 59, 93, 191, 224
  and integration of male spaces, 25, 51, 52, 153–54, 155–56
  intermediate scrutiny for sex distinctions, 37–38, 40, 42, 50, 58
  minimum gender diversity requirement, 157, 167, 222–25
  overempowerment as alternative approach to, 223–25
  as prohibiting arbitrary distinctions of sex, 33–34
  remedies for violation of, 57–58
  social security benefits, 34–35
  statistical data, 38–39
  statutory rape laws, 42–47
  strict scrutiny, 38
  as tool of legal feminism, 22
  traditional gender roles suspect under, 37
  women's exemption from jury duty, 155
  women's exemption from military draft, 50–52
Equal Rights Amendment (ERA)
  adoption and ratification history of, 229
  Black women's potential gains from, 19
  equal power under, 229, 291n59
  introduction of (1923), 8
  litigation to validate, 229
  Murray, Pauli, testimony on, 19, 291n59
  political question analysis of ratification validity, 230
  ratification deadline, 229–30
  special protections for motherhood under, 17
  stalling of, 178
  state ratifications after deadline, 230
European Convention on Human Rights, 108
European Court of Human Rights, 108, 109
European Court of Justice, 277n68
European Union, gender balance on corporate boards, 223

Farrell, Warren, 253n112
Federici, Maria, 189–90
Feminist legal theory
  critique of rape and sexual assault law,
    12–14
  and dependency, 18
  equal opportunities in the workplace, 14
  focus on motherhood outside the US,
    15–16
  intersection of race and class, 19, 20
  liberal equality under the law, 12
  origins in critique of patriarchal law, 4–5,
    7–8
  philosophical account of misogyny beyond
    hatred, 10
  "preservation through transformation," 13
  reproductive injustice, 20
  sexual harassment as sex discrimination, 13
  undervaluing of caregiving, 14–15
  work-family conflict, 15
Fineman, Martha, 18, 20–21
First Amendment, 156–57, 261n86
Folbre, Nancy, 244n8
Foster, J. Ellen, 136, 137, 141–43, 147
Fourteenth Amendment. See Due Process
  Clause; Equal Protection Clause
France
  abortion law, 265–66n68
  abuse of right (abus de droit), 75–78,
    80–82, 133, 260–61n82
  citizens' assembly on climate change, 207
  Civil Code, 68, 75–77, 81
  Constitution (1946), 187–89
  constitutional amendment process, 231
  constitutional amendments for equal access
    to power (1999 and 2008), 158–60, 161
  Constitutional Council, 158–60
  Cour de cassation, 68, 70–71, 77–78, 81,
    82, 260–61n82
  Declaration of Rights of Man, 80, 158, 159
  equal pay index legislation, 160, 161
  law on "real equality between women and
    men," 160–61
  motherhood protection in Constitution,
    183, 187–89
  parity between women and men, 157–61,
    179, 274n25, 275nn39,41
  unjust enrichment cases, 23, 67–68, 70–71
  women in constituent assembly, 158,
    274n25
  women's suffrage, 188
  in the World Economic Forum gender gap
    rankings, 190

Frankfurter, Justice Felix, 154
Franklin, Cary, 33
Frontiero v. Richardson, 33–34, 38

Gaspard, Françoise, To Power, Women Citi-
  zens! Liberty, Equality, and Parity (with
  Claude Servan-Schreiber and Anne Le
  Gall), 158–59
Geduldig v. Aiello, 91–92, 263n19
Gender budgeting, 174, 206
Gender gap measurement
  World Bank, 171, 213
  World Economic Forum, 171, 183, 190–
    91, 213
Gender parity laws, 25, 157–58, 159–61,
  167–70, 173–74. See also Parity between
  women and men
Gender pay gap reduction, 160, 161
Gender quotas, 25, 157, 159, 167, 170,
  174, 223
Germany
  abortion law, 95–105
  Basic Law, 78, 96, 99–101, 103–4, 162,
    164–65, 166, 186–87, 260n70
  children, parental authority over, 165
  Civil Code, 65, 78–80, 165
  constitutional amendment process, 231
  constitutional protection of mothers (Arti-
    cle 6.4), 17, 99–100, 182–87, 194–96
  early twentieth century women's movement,
    185–86
  equal rights for men and women (Article
    3.2), 163–65
  Federal Constitutional Court, 78–79,
    165–66, 168–71, 277nn62–63,
    278n78
  maternity leave (paid), 17, 195, 196
  Mutterschutz League, 16–17, 185–86
  parental leave (paid), 100, 101, 104
  parity laws, 162–71, 179,
    277–78nn62–63,68,78
  proportional representation system, 168
  reunification of, 99, 166–67, 196
  Roman law influence, 65, 69, 257n18
  Social Democratic Party, 164, 186,
    281–82n9
  unjust enrichment, 23, 65, 69, 257n18
  unmarried mothers, 16–17, 164,
    184–85
  Weimar Constitution (1919), 5, 17, 162–
    63, 182, 183, 184–86, 281n9
  in the World Economic Forum gender gap
    rankings, 190

Ginsburg, Ruth Bader
  ACLU Women's Rights Project, 52
  as advocate and litigator, 8, 32–35, 38
  on gender differentiated treatment, 152
  influence of Swedish sex role debate on, 22,
    29–32, 33, 35, 55, 57
  Pauli Murray's influence on, 19
  as Supreme Court Justice, 50–51, 57–58,
    165
  See also Legal feminism (United States)
Goesaert v. Cleary, 25, 38, 153–54
Gordon, Anna, 137–38
Griswold v. Connecticut, 265–66n68
Guillén, Vanessa, 60–61, 62

Halappanavar, Savita, 108–9, 200
Hale, Lord Matthew, entitlement of husbands
    to marital rape, 7, 244–45n22
Harlan, Justice John Marshall, 143
Harris v. McRae, 90, 91, 92, 94–95
Hartog, Hendrik, 244n19
Hodgers, Sheila, 105–6
Holmes, Justice Oliver Wendell, Jr., 288n18
Hong, Cathy Park, 256n9
Household work
  and feminist legal theory, 18
  gendered divisions of labor, 18
  men's role in, 18, 30
  motherhood protection under the law and
    sharing of, 160–61, 164
  as patriarchal entitlement of men in mar-
    riage, 7, 11, 73
  Swedish gender emancipation and sharing
    of, 30, 55, 56, 225
  and unjust enrichment, 69–70, 71–72
  wages for housework movement (1970s),
    216
Hoyt v. Florida, 155, 197
Hyde Amendment, 46–47, 90

Iceland
  abortion access, 265–66n68
  Bright Future Party, 177
  Constitutional Assembly, 175–76
  Constitutional Council, 176–77, 232
  constitutional gender equality guarantee, 176
  constitutional reform project, 172, 174–78
  financial collapse of 2008, 171–73, 175,
    176, 181
  gender budgeting, 174
  gender parity, 171–78, 179, 279n92
  Independence Party, 176, 177
  Left-Green Movement party, 173, 177

National Forum, 175–76
  Parliament (Althing), 172–74, 175, 176–
    77, 232
  Pots and Pans Revolution (2008–09), 172–
    73, 181
  Public Finance Act (2015), 174
  sexual abuse and abuse of power scandal
    (2017), 177
  sex work reforms, 174
  Social Democratic Alliance party, 173
  Special Investigation Commission, 173,
    279n92
  Supreme Court, 176
  Women's Alliance for a New Constitution, 177
  in the World Economic Forum gender gap
    rankings, 183, 190
Immigration and Nationality Act, 57–58
Iotti, Nilde, 189
Ireland
  A, B, and C v. Ireland (European Court of
    Human Rights), 108, 109
  abortion statute legalizing abortion (2018),
    111, 112
  Attorney General v. X, 107
  Citizens' Assembly on abortion reform,
    110–11, 200–201, 231, 232
  Citizens' Assembly on gender equality, 26,
    112–13, 202–7
  Constitution (1937), 191–94
  Constitutional amendment process, 231
  Constitution of the Irish Free State (1922),
    192
  Convention on the Constitution (2012),
    109–10, 200, 266–67n85
  deaths of women due to denial of abortion,
    105–6, 108–9, 112, 113–14, 200
  divorce, 197, 199, 231
  Eighth Amendment abortion ban, 105–7,
    266n69
  Eighth Amendment repealed, 110–12
  Fourteenth Amendment freedom of infor-
    mation about abortion, 107
  High Court, 197
  jury duty exemption for women, 196–97
  L. v. L., 197–98
  Protection of Life During Pregnancy Act
    (2013), 109
  publicly funded abortion, 112
  same-sex marriage equality, 110, 231
  Supreme Court, 107, 197–99, 265–66n68,
    284–85n70
  Thirteenth Amendment freedom of travel
    to obtain abortion, 107

T. v. T., 199
"woman in the home" clause, 26, 182–84,
    191–94, 196–207, 231, 284–85n70
women's suffrage, 193
in the World Economic Forum gender gap
    rankings, 191
Italy
constituent assembly, 189
Constitution (1945), 187, 189–90
corporate board minimum gender diversity
    law, 167
equal pay guarantee, 189
motherhood protection in constitution
    (Article 37), 189–90
nursing breaks for working mothers, 190
paid maternity leave, 190–91
unmarried mothers, support for, 189–90
in the World Economic Forum gender gap
    rankings, 190–91

Jackson, Vicki, 214
Jakobsdottir, Katrin, 177–78
"Jane Crow," 19
J.E.B v. Alabama, 47–49
Jewish law and divorce
abuse of right under, 80–82, 260–61n82
New York legislation and, 261n86
Josserand, Louis, 77
June Medical Services v. Russo (2018),
    118–19
Jury duty
Black juror exclusion, 19
female exemption from, 155, 196–97
female juror exclusion, 19, 48
preemptory strikes, gender-based, 47–49

Kagan, Robert, 214
Kahn v. Shevin, 34
Kavanaugh, Justice Brett, 41, 52
Kennedy, Justice Anthony, 92–93, 118
Kepley, Ada, 136, 137, 140–41, 147, 148
Key, Ellen, 15–16, 185, 282n17
Kollontai, Alexandra, 17
Koppelman, Andrew, 221

Ladies Get Paid, 54–55
Laffoy, Mary, 110
Lange, Helene, 185, 282n16
Latin America
decriminalization of abortion, 115–17
feminist protests of violence against
    women, 1–2, 233, 234
impunity for violence against women in, 3

Lawrence v. Texas, 212
Laycock, Douglas, 69
Legal feminism (United States), 22–23
and abortion rights, 90–92, 94, 263n14
Ruth Bader Ginsburg's approach to, 4, 8,
    9, 29
and needs of women in poverty, 91–92
and patriarchal norms, 22–23
and role of government in social and eco-
    nomic life, 57
and social reproduction, 14–15
Le Gall, Anne, *To Power, Women Citizens!
    Liberty, Equality, and Parity* (with
    Françoise Gaspard and Claude Servan-
    Schreiber), 158–59
Legislatures, dialogue with courts, 119
Lerner, Gerda, 5
Liquor industry
civil actions against temperance women,
    126, 127, 131, 132–34, 140
civil actions by women against, 127–31,
    269–70nn14,17
effects of Prohibition on, 124, 141–43,
    148, 149, 151
litigation challenging state prohibition laws,
    131–32, 134–35, 270n37, 272n68
See also Alcohol consumption; Prohibition
    (Eighteenth Amendment); Temperance
    movement; Woman's Christian Temper-
    ance Union
Lochner v. New York, 143

McCulloch, Catharine Waugh, 136, 137,
    144–47, 150, 244n18
McGuiness, Catherine, 197–98
MacKinnon, Catharine, 12–14, 15, 18–19,
    45
Manne, Kate, 10, 11
Mansfield, Lord, 66
Marriage
and constitutional privacy right, 89
constitutional protection of, 79, 184, 186
and coverture, 6, 7, 73, 124–25, 144
and definition of family, 164, 189
equality of spouses in, 31, 165, 189
freedom of, 80–81
same-sex marriage amendment (Ireland),
    110, 231
under Roman law, 6, 83
in unjust enrichment cases, 70–71
See also Adultery; Divorce
Marshall Plan for Moms, 181, 199, 216,
    281n4

Marvin v. Marvin, 71–72
Marx, Karl, 64
Maternal mortality rates
  American Rescue Plan efforts to reduce, 208
  Black women in the United States, 94, 217, 220
  in Ireland, 111
  and protection of unborn life, 114
  in states instituting abortion restrictions, 220, 289n36
  women in poverty in the United States, 220
Maternity leave
  in Germany, 17, 195, 196
  in Italy, 190–91
  paid vs. unpaid, 91
  in the Soviet Union, 17
  in Sweden, 56
  in the United States, 56, 91, 208
  See also Parental leave; Constitutional clauses protecting mothers
Men's rights advocates, 47, 49, 52–55, 59, 253nn112–113
Merlin, Lina, 189, 190
#MeToo movement, 1, 9, 10, 21, 40–41, 62, 74, 177
Mexico
  feminist protests of violence against women, 1
  Supreme Court abortion decision (2021), 115
Michael M. v. Superior Court, 42–47
Military
  sex-differentiated benefits for personnel (*Frontiero* case), 33–34, 38
  and Germany after World War I, 163
  male-only draft, 51–52, 58–59, 253n111
  and sexual assault, 59, 60–61, 62
  women's admission to Virginia Military Institute (VMI), 25, 50–51, 52, 58, 152–53, 252nn95,103
Misogyny
  as aftermath of patriarchy, 3
  conventional account of, 2, 10
  as enforcement of patriarchy, 10–11
  as hatred of women, 10, 22, 23, 60, 62
  and legal impunity, 2–3, 83
  and misogynists, 21, 23, 26, 29, 182, 207, 209
  redefined as overentitlement and overem-powerment, 4, 9, 11, 13, 18, 21–23, 60, 62, 63, 85–86
  and violence against women, 1, 2, 9, 10, 13, 23, 60, 62–63, 75, 85, 182, 228

  See also Abuse of right; Overempowerment; Overentitlement; Patriarchy, as legal system; Patriarchy, as social norms; Unjust enrichment
Mississippi University for Women v. Hogan, 37, 38
Moberg, Eva, 30, 31
Montana abortion ban, 87, 262n4
Morgan, Lewis, 4
Moritz v. Commissioner of Internal Revenue, 33
Motherhood protection. *See* Constitutional clauses protecting mothers
Mr. Lex or The Legal Status of Mother and Child (McCulloch), 144–47, 150, 244n18
Mugler v. Kansas, 270n37, 272n68
Murdock, Catherine Gilbert, 273n94
Murray, Judge (Ireland), 199–200
Murray, Pauli, 160, 171, 291n59
  "Jane Crow," 19
Myrdal, Alva, 30

Nadig, Frieda, 164
National Coalition for Men (NCFM), 47, 49, 51–55, 253n111
National Organization for Women (NOW), 155
National Women's Congress (1873), 137
Nebraska, Ada Bittenbender and reform of patriarchal laws in, 143–44
Nebraska Woman Suffrage Association, 143
Negotiorum gestio, 67
Neill, Reilly, 262n4
New York State Rifle & Pistol Association, Inc. v. Bruen, 207–8, 286n97
Nineteenth Amendment, 8, 150. *See also* Women's suffrage
Noce, Teresa, 189, 190
Norway, corporate board minimum gender diversity law, 167, 223

O'Connor, Justice Sandra Day, 92–93, 118, 165
O'Higgins, Chief Justice (Ireland), 197
Ohio
  constitutional convention, 133
  liquor licensing debates in, 133
  temperance crusades in, 129–31, 132–34
O'Sullivan, John Marcus, 193
Overempowerment
  abuse of right as, 75, 85

as a core engine of misogyny, 3–4, 8–11, 23, 60, 85, 207, 233–34
definition of, 11
and equal protection analysis, 223–25
exclusion of women from institutions as, 152–55
as perpetuated by law without patriarchal laws, 11, 13
sexual harassment as, 74–75, 85
of underpopulated states under US Constitution, 229
See also Abuse of power; Abuse of right; Misogyny; Overentitlement; Parity between women and men; Patriarchy, as legal system
Overentitlement
abortion bans as, 21, 23–24, 88, 93, 113–15, 118, 215–16
collective, to women's sacrifices, 11
as a core engine of misogyny, 3–4, 8–11, 22, 23, 60, 85, 207
COVID-19 pandemic as exposing, 25–26, 180–82, 208
definition of, 11
and lack of compensation for caregiving, 18
of men, to women's sacrifices, 8
and non-accommodation of pregnant workers, 228
and oversexualization of Asian American women, 61–62, 256n9
as perpetuated by law without patriarchal laws, 11, 13, 18
to sexual relations, 62
as unjust enrichment, 4
violence against women as enforcing, 14, 228
See also Constitutional clauses protecting mothers; Parity between women and men; Reproductive injustice; Takings Clause; Unjust enrichment

Palme, Olof, "The Emancipation of Man," 30–31, 32, 35, 55
Parental leave
in France, 160
gender-neutral, 18, 56
in Germany, 100, 101, 104
Irish recommendations for extension of, 204
paid leave for fathers, 56
in Sweden, 56, 255n137
and temporary provision in COVID-19 policy, 208

in the United States, 101, 182, 281n5
See also Maternity leave
Parity between women and men
in Chile, 25, 178, 233
constitutional amendments, 159, 160, 222, 230–31
constitutional equality guarantees, 176, 178
and democracy, 25, 152–53, 178–79
in France, 157–61, 179, 274n25, 275nn39,41
in French statute, 160–61
in Germany, 162–71, 179, 277–78nn62–63,68,78
in Iceland, 171–78, 179, 279n92
See also Constitutional democracy; Constitutional equality for women; Democracy, Gender parity laws; Gender quotas
Parke, Lord, 258n30
"Paternity fraud" (e.g. *J.E.B. v. Alabama*), 47–49, 252n90
Patriarchal gender relations, 10–11, 49, 59
Patriarchy, as legal system
abolished by legal gender equality, 8, 29
baseline entitlements in, 6, 10–11, 114–15
chastisement of wives, 7, 8, 73, 228
children, male legal authority over, 6, 144–46
control of women's sexual activity under, 5, 6, 7, 12–13, 49, 244n8
coverture as based in, 6, 7, 73, 124–25, 144
Equal Rights Amendment proposed to end, 8
husband's ownership of marital property, 6, 8, 126, 144–45, 146–47
male discretion under, 7
male drunkenness as exacerbating harms of, 124–25, 126–27, 146–47
male obligation to support wife, 7, 130
marital rape, male entitlement to, 6–7, 228, 244–45n22
nostalgia for, 49, 59
private property ownership in, 4
and temperance movement reforms, 136, 143–50, 151
transition from matrilineal kinship to, 4–5, 243n6
transition to democracy from, 8, 25, 73–74, 119, 123, 152, 212, 229, 233, 234
wives represented legally by husbands in, 7
See also Patriarchal gender relations; Patriarchy, as social norms; Roman law

Patriarchy, as social norms
  as enforced by postpatriarchal laws, 3, 11, 14, 18
  in gender relations, 3, 22
  and laws guaranteeing equality, 2, 3, 4, 10, 13
  as misogyny, 11
  as overempowerment, 82
  as overentitlement, 3, 59
  See also Misogyny
Paycheck Fairness Act (proposed), 226–27, 290–91n53
Pennsylvania Coal Co. v. Mahon, 288n18
Planned Parenthood v. Casey, 92–93, 98, 113, 114–15, 118
Poverty
  and lack of privacy right, 20–21, 90–91
  and race, 20
  and temperance movement, 125, 126–27, 128, 136, 146–48
  See also Reproductive injustice
Pregnancy
  coerced, 220
  and commercial surrogacy, 219
  consensual but unwanted, 14
  discrimination because of, 91
  economic hardships of continuing, 92, 93, 98, 102, 217, 219, 220, 227–28, 288n19
  job security during, legal protection of, 195–96
  right to terminate before viability, 87, 89, 93
  safe haven laws during, 220
  and statutory rape law, 42–43, 45, 46–47, 146
  teen, 43
  and temporary disability leave, 91
  working conditions and accommodations during, 190, 195, 217, 220, 227–28, 288n19
  See also Abortion; Constitutional clauses protecting mothers; Maternity leave; Parental leave; Reproductive justice
Pregnancy Discrimination Act, 288n19
Pregnant Workers Fairness Act (proposed), 208, 227–28
Privacy, right to (US Constitution)
  Dobbs case and rejection of, 88, 94
  and mandatory maternity leave, 89, 91, 92
  as negative freedom from state intrusion, 89–90, 92
  poverty and the lack of right to, 20–21, 90–91

Roe v. Wade privacy rationale, 88–90
  as shielding domestic violence, 245–46n43
  and substantive due process, 89, 262n8
Prohibition (Eighteenth Amendment)
  overview, 21–22, 24–25, 123–24
  and alcohol consumption patterns, 150, 151, 273n94
  as attacking unjust enrichment of liquor industry, 142
  bills proposing, 125, 137
  campaign of the WCTU for, 137–44, 147
  economic argument for, 139, 141
  as failure, 24, 123–24, 149, 269n1
  home production of alcohol, 150
  "home protection" rhetoric of, 142, 143, 151
  impoverishment of women and need for, 125, 126–27, 128, 136, 146–48
  and police powers of the state, 143
  and political power of the liquor industry, 124, 141–43, 148, 149, 151
  ratification of (1919), 136, 149
  repeal of (Twenty-First Amendment), 41, 149, 150–51
  as resetting entitlements of patriarchal law, 22, 24–25, 123, 124–25, 135, 139, 142, 147, 149, 151, 207
  and structural change, 123, 125, 143
  text of, 149
  as undermining property and business rights, 126, 127, 135–36, 137, 138–39, 140, 143
  violence against women as motivating, 40, 126, 127
  as weakening saloons as masculine space, 124, 125, 147–48, 149, 150, 273n94
  See also Liquor industry; Temperance movement; Woman's Christian Temperance Union
Prohibition Party, 140, 144
Proportional representation, as voting system, 56, 168, 225, 226
Prostitution, 144, 174
Protests
  in Chile, 2, 178, 233
  of the Dobbs decision overruling Roe v. Wade, 227, 232
  in Iceland, 172–73, 181
  by women, 1–2, 233, 234

Quasi ex contractu, 66
Quintus Fabius Maximus, 83–84
Quotas. See Gender parity laws; Gender quotas; Parity between women and men

Rape, 6–7, 12–13, 41, 42, 43–45, 46–47, 228, 244–45n22, 250–51n65,77
Reed v. Reed, 8, 32–33, 165, 248–49n17
Rehnquist, Justice William, 36, 42–43, 46
Religion, freedom of
abuse of right doctrine limiting, 80–82, 260–61n82
divorce under Jewish law, 81
First Amendment right to (US), 261n86
French constitutional right to, 80
New York divorce legislation, 261n86
Reparations for slavery, unjust enrichment argument for, 63, 256n10
Reproduction
of the nation, 182
as socially valuable, 99, 105
state interest in, 92, 99, 103
women's disproportionate role in, 105, 118, 183
Reproductive injustice
Black women deprived of right to motherhood, 19–20
forced sterilization of Black women, 20
and history of enslaved Black women, 19, 21, 247n70
maternal mortality rates, 94, 217
poverty of nonwhite families headed by women, 19
and privacy, absence of, 20–21, 90, 91
racially disparate charges of child neglect, 20
and structural racism, 21
and welfare reforms, 20
See also Reproductive justice
Reproductive justice
abortion rights and, 20, 91
Black feminist visions of, 24
and Black women's experience, 18–21
in pro-life abortion law in Germany and Ireland, 24
and right to have and parent children, 91
and Roe v. Wade privacy right, 24, 90–92, 94, 263n14
and state support for childbirth or maternity, 91
See also Constitutional clauses protecting mothers
Restatement of Restitution (1937), 64, 68–69
Restatement (Third) of Restitution (2008), 69, 70, 72
Restitution, 10, 64–65
Roberts, Dorothy, 20, 90–91, 247n70
Roberts, Justice John, 212

Roberts v. Jaycees, 156
Robilant, Anna, di, 259n56
Roca, Gilberte, 188–89
Roe v. Wade (1973), 23–24, 87, 88–92, 94–95, 98, 105, 118–19, 215, 227–229, 263n14, 265–66n68, 291nn55,58
Roman law
asymmetric criminalization of adultery, 6
consilium, 84
the family unit, 5
Justinian, 66, 85
Livy, 84
marriage under, 6, 83
paterfamilias (male head of the household), 5–6, 83
patria potestas, 5–6, 67, 83–84
as patriarchal legal order, 5, 83–84
Pomponius, 64, 65
power over life and death (vitae necisque potestas), 83–85
Savigny reclaiming, for German law, 65, 69, 257n18
status of slaves under, 67, 85
status of women under, 6
Ulpian, 83
unjust enrichment in, 64–69
and Western legal tradition, 5, 6
Rostker v. Goldberg, 51, 52
Rotary International v. Rotary Club of Duarte, 156–57

Sabin, Pauline, 150–51
Safe haven laws, 218, 219–20, 289n32
Salzman v. Bachrach, 72
Saujani, Reshma, 281n4
Savigny, Freidrich Carl von, 65, 69, 257n18
Scalia, Justice Antonin, 50, 212
Schneider v. Hosier, 129–30
Seidenburg v. McSorley's Old Ale House, Inc., 155–56
Selbert, Elisabeth, 163–64
Senate (US)
equal representation of the states in, 229
filibuster, 226–28
malapportionment protected by Article V, 229
Sessions v. Morales-Santana, 57–58
Sexual assault
criminal prosecution of, 13
and #MeToo movement, 9
in the military, 59, 61
See also Rape; Violence against women

Sexual harassment, 13–14, 62–63, 74–75, 85
Sex work, 144, 174
Siegel, Reva, 13, 95, 245–46n43, 252n103
Siggurdardottir, Johanna, 173–75
Slavery
  banned by the Thirteenth Amendment, 142
  and Black motherhood, 19, 21, 247n70
  and rape, 18
  reparations for, unjust enrichment as basis of, 63, 256n10
  and reproduction, 18
  in Roman law, 67, 85
Social reproduction, 3–4, 14–15, 182. *See also* Constitutional clauses protecting mothers; Feminist legal theory; Overentitlement; Unjust enrichment
Sombart, Werner, 17
Sotomayor, Justice Sonia, 52, 253n111
Souter, Justice David, 92–93, 118
South Korea, Constitutional Court decriminalization of abortion, 117–18
Soviet Union, paid maternity leave, 17
Statutory rape law, 42, 43–45, 46–47, 145–46, 250–51nn65,77
Sterilization, involuntary, 89, 262n8
Stevens, Justice John Paul, 46
Stewart, Justice Potter, 89, 92
Stewart, Mother Eliza, *Memories of the Crusade*, 127–29, 132, 269–70n14
Stöcker, Helene, 16, 185
Strip clubs, 174
Suicide risk, and Irish expansion of abortion access, 107–8, 109
Surrogacy, commercial, 218, 219
Sweden
  abortion access, 265–66n68
  antidiscrimination law, 57, 225, 255n145
  constitutional amendments on institutional reform, 56
  Dahlström, Edmund, "The Changing Roles of Men and Women," 31–32
  early twentieth-century feminism, 15–16
  emancipation of men, 22, 29–32, 33, 35, 55, 57
  gender emancipation legislative agenda adopted, 55–56, 57, 59, 225–26
  Ruth Bader Ginsburg's trip to, 30
  legislature (Riksdag) transformed to unicameral, 55–56, 225–26
  Moberg, Eva, "The Conditional Emancipation of Women," 30, 31

Myrdal, Alva, 30
paid maternity leave, 56
paid parental leave, 56, 255n137
proportional representation adopted, 56, 225, 226
public childcare and education, 56
sex-role debate, 31
Social Democratic Party, 30
tax reform, 55–56
UN Report, "The Status of Women in Sweden" (1968), 31–32, 55

Takings Clause
  as basis for challenging abortion bans, 216
  as obligating compensation for coerced pregnancy, 221
  property right in womb asserted under, 218
  public purpose under, 217
  and substantive due process, 216
Taxes
  expansion of the child tax credit (US), 208
  individualized income taxation (Sweden), 55–56
Temperance movement
  autobiographical memoirs by participants in, 125–26, 132, 133–34
  campaigns for legal reforms beyond alcohol, 136, 143–50, 151
  Christian morality of, 126
  constitutional arguments of, 141–44, 147–48
  crusades against saloons, 124, 125
  and husbands' abuse of patriarchal power, 124–25, 126–27, 146–47
  liquor industry civil actions against women, 126, 127, 131, 132–34, 140
  women lawyers in, 136, 137, 143–50, 151
  women's lawsuits against saloons, 127–31, 269–70nn14,17
  See also Prohibition (Eighteenth Amendment); Woman's Christian Temperance Union
Texas
  abortion law before *Roe v. Wade*, 89
  safe haven law, 289n32
  SB 8, 87, 217, 262n4
Thirteenth Amendment (ban on slavery and involuntary servitude), 142, 221
Thompson, Mother Eliza, *Hillsboro Crusade Sketches*, 133–34
Thomson, Judith Jarvis, "A Defense of Abortion," 221, 290n41

Torts, and unjust enrichment, 64
Toxic masculinity, 36–37, 40–41, 45, 47,
    124, 125, 126, 147–48, 149, 150,
    273n94
Trump, Donald, 209
Tuerkheimer, Deborah, 48–49
Twenty-First Amendment (repeal of Prohibi-
    tion), 41, 149, 150–51

Union Pac. Ry. Co. v. Botsford, 262n8
United Kingdom (UK)
    abortion access, 107, 265–66n68
    citizens' assembly on climate change, 207
United States Brewers' Association, 132
United States v. Virginia, 25, 50–51, 52, 58,
    152–53, 252nn95,103
Unjust enrichment
    cause of action, 64
    Dawson, John on, 64–66
    and divorce, 70–71
    in English law, 65–67, 258nn30–31
    as equitable principle, 66
    as forced transfers, 69, 71, 258–59n42
    French law, 23, 67–68, 70–71
    as gains "contrary to good morals," 65
    gender injustice as, 24, 68, 69–74, 114–15
    German law, 23, 65, 69, 257n18
    and gifts, 69, 71–72, 73–74
    Marxism and, 64
    in Roman law, 64–69
    in United States law, 63, 64, 68–74, 142,
        156, 256n10, 257nn11–12,
        258–59nn42–43
    and unmarried cohabiting partners, 69–70,
        71–72
    See also Overentitlement
Unmarried mothers
    legal protections for, 16–17, 164, 184–85,
        189–90, 204
    nonwhite families headed by (US), 19
    privacy of the family as diminished for
        (US), 20–21, 90, 91

Versteeg, Mila, 213
Violence against women, 1–3, 9–11, 14,
    40–41, 59, 61, 62, 126, 127, 160, 206,
    228, 233, 234. *See also* Domestic vio-
    lence; Rape; Sexual assault; Sexual
    harassment
Violence Against Women Act (VAWA) Reau-
    thorization Act (proposed), 228
Virginia Military Institute (VMI), 25, 50–51,
    152–53

Washington (state), Citizens' Assembly on
    Climate Change, 207, 232–33, 286n96
Weber, Max, 17
Weinberger v. Wiesenfeld, 34–35
Weinstein, Harvey, 1, 62, 209
Wessel, Helene, 164
West, Robin, 14–15, 45, 90, 263n14
*West Virginia v. Environmental Protection
    Agency*, 207–8, 286n97
Whole Woman's Health v. Hellerstedt (2016),
    118–19, 227
Whyte, Gerry, 284–85n70
Widows and widowers, 34–37
Willard, Frances, 135–40, 141, 142, 143–
    44, 148, 149, 185
Williams, Joan, *Unbending Gender: How
    Family and Work Conflict and What to
    Do about It*, 15
Wittenmyer, Annie, 132–33, 137
Woman's Christian Temperance Union
    (WCTU)
    campaign for Prohibition Amendment,
        135–44, 147
    establishment of (1874), 125
    feminist goals of, 136–39
    and labor rights, 137
    lobbying Congress, 144
    organizational structure of, 135, 137
    "The Temple" meetinghouse of, 140–41,
        148
    turn toward organizing, 134
    women lawyers campaigning for broad-
        based legal reforms, 136, 143–50,
        151
    women lawyers in Prohibition campaign,
        136, 137, 140–44, 147
    and women's suffrage advocacy, 125, 126,
        135–36, 137, 139, 143–44, 148, 150
    See also Prohibition (Eighteenth Amend-
        ment); Temperance movement
Woman's Rights Convention at Seneca Falls
    (1848), 7–8
Women lawyers, 118–19, 127–29, 136, 137,
    143–50, 151, 163
Women's Health Protection Act (proposed),
    227, 228, 229, 291nn55,58
Women's movements
    after financial crisis (Iceland), 173
    in Germany, 15–17, 162, 185–86
    for legal abortion (Ireland), 105, 112
    #MeToo, 1, 9, 10, 21, 40–41, 62, 74, 177
    motherhood, 15–17, 185–86
    parity (France), 158–59

Women's movements *(continued)*
  suffrage, 8, 125–26, 135, 137, 139, 143, 148, 150, 182
  temperance, 123–26, 136–39
  See also Equal Rights Amendment (ERA); Legal feminism (United States)
Women's Organization for National Prohibition Reform (WONPR), 149, 150–51
Women's suffrage
  in France, 188
  in Ireland, 193
  and Nineteenth Amendment in US (1920), 8, 150

and temperance movement, 125, 126, 135–36, 137, 139, 143–44, 148, 150
Woods v. Horton, 52–53
World Bank: Women, Business, and the Law index, 171, 213
World Economic Forum: gender gap studies, 171, 183, 190–91, 213
World War I, 182, 183, 184–85
World War II, 153, 182, 183, 188, 189–90
Wray, Christopher, 61

Yemen, 183

Founded in 1893,
UNIVERSITY OF CALIFORNIA PRESS
publishes bold, progressive books and journals
on topics in the arts, humanities, social sciences,
and natural sciences—with a focus on social
justice issues—that inspire thought and action
among readers worldwide.

The UC PRESS FOUNDATION
raises funds to uphold the press's vital role
as an independent, nonprofit publisher, and
receives philanthropic support from a wide
range of individuals and institutions—and from
committed readers like you. To learn more, visit
ucpress.edu/supportus.